Records of the Courts of Quarter Sessions and Common Pleas of Bucks County Pennsylvania

1684-1700

HERITAGE BOOKS
2011

HERITAGE BOOKS
AN IMPRINT OF HERITAGE BOOKS, INC.

Books, CDs, and more—Worldwide

For our listing of thousands of titles see our website
at
www.HeritageBooks.com

A Facsimile Reprint
Published 2011 by
HERITAGE BOOKS, INC.
Publishing Division
100 Railroad Ave. #104
Westminster, Maryland 21157

1943, 1998

— Publisher's Notice —
In reprints such as this, it is often not possible to remove blemishes from the original. We feel the contents of this book warrant its reissue despite these blemishes and hope you will agree and read it with pleasure.

International Standard Book Numbers
Paperbound: 978-1-58549-475-0
Clothbound: 978-0-7884-8674-6

AN HISTORICAL NOTE

Previous to the granting of the charter for the Province of Pennsylvania to William Penn there were few inhabitants in the region comprising what is now Bucks County, and they were located near the "Falls of the Deleware." All matters at law which they had came under the jurisdiction of the Court of New Sweden prior to 1655, and after that date under the jurisdiction of the Court at New York.

In 1667, Governor Lovelace organized three judicial districts, that of Upland extending up the Delaware to the "Falls", and embracing the country of Bucks County to that point. Until the time of William Penn, the inhabitants had to go to Upland, the present Chester, to transact their legal business. The earliest court there was held in 1672. Under Governor Sir Edmond Andross the English system of jurisprudence was introduced on the Delaware. His courts at Upland, Newcastle and Hoornkill had powers of courts of sessions and could decide all matters under £20 without appeal and under £5 without a jury. Previous to 1677, all wills had to be proved and letters of administration granted at New York. The Upland Court petitioned Governor Andross for this power on the ground that the estates were too small to bear the expense and inconvenience of going to New York. The Court was then given authority to grant letters on estates under £30, but for those of greater amount the Court in New York retained jurisdiction.

The first action to recover a debt, brought by an inhabitant of what became Bucks County, was on November 12, 1678, when James Sanderlins of Bensalem, entered suit against John Edmunds of Maryland, for the value of 1200 pounds of tobacco, and the case was decided in his favor.[1] In 1679, Edmund Draufton, also of Bensalem, brought suit against Dunck Williams to recover for his services in teaching the latter's children to read the Bible within a year for 200 guilders. At the expiration of that time he refused to pay. The Upland Court decided in favor of Draufton.[2] On June 14, 1681, Claes Jansen brought to the session of the Upland Court held at Kingsesse the ear marks of his cattle and hogs and asked to have them recorded, which was accordingly done.[3]

1 *Memoirs of the Historical Society of Pennsylvania*, Vol. II, p. 111.
2 *Ibid*, p. 131.
3 *Ibid*, p. 190.

The first court held in Bucks County of which there is record, was at "ye new seate towne" on the Delaware below the "Falls", not far from where Morrisville stands. The place was called Crewcorne and the court the "Court of Crewcorne (Creekhorne) at the Falls." This Court was functioning prior to 1680, but how much earlier appears to be unknown. On April 12, 1680, the Court sent to the Governor of New York the names of four persons for magistrates, according to order, but their names are not given.[4]

After the granting of the Charter to William Penn, on March 4, 1681, he formulated a preliminary constitution and set of laws for the government of the province, which were known under the title "The FRAME of the Government of the Province of Pennsylvania in America: Together with certain LAWS agreed upon in England, by the Governor and divers Freemen of the aforesaid Province. To be Further explained and confirmed there, by the first Provincial Council that shall be held, if they see meet." Under the "Frame", the Governor and Provincial Council were authorized to erect from time to time standing Courts of Justice in such places and numbers as they should judge convenient for the good government of the Province.[5]

All courts were to be open, and justice neither sold, nor delayed: all persons of all persuasions could freely appear in their own way and according to their own manner and there personally plead their own cause themselves, or if unable, by their friends; all pleadings, processes and records in courts were to be short and in *English,* and in an ordinary and plain character, that they could be understood and justice speedily administered. All trials were to be by twelve men, and, as near as might be, peers or equals, and of the neighborhood, and men without just exception.

In cases of life the Sheriff was required first to return twenty-four men for a Grand Inquest, of whom twelve at least should find the complaint to be true; and then the twelve men or peers, to be likewise returned by the Sheriff had the final judgment. Reasonable challenge was always to be admitted against the twelve men, or any of them.

All fees in all cases were to be moderate, and settled by

4 Davis, *History of Bucks County,* Vol. II, p. 228.
5 *The Frame* etc., Section XVII.

the Provincial Council and General Assembly, and be hung up in a table in every respective court, and any one who should be convicted of taking more was required to pay two-fold, and be dismissed from his employment, one moiety going to the party wronged. Before the complaint of any person could be received, he had to solemnly declare in court that "he believes in his conscience his cause is just."[6]

In 1683 an act was passed for the establishment of County Courts, and the first court for Bucks County organized under that act, was erected at Crewcorne on the old road leading from Tullytown to the landing at Bordentown Ferry.[7] In recording the minutes of the sessions of this Court, Phineas Pemberton stated that the meetings were held at the Court House of the County, but did not mention the place of its location. Frequently he mentioned that the Court adjourned to or met at Gilbert Wheelers. This public house, at the old Ferry, Gilbert Wheeler called "Crewcorne." This was the seat of justice until 1705, when it was moved to Bristol, where it remained until 1725, when it was again moved to Newtown, and finally located at Doylestown in 1813, where it has since remained.

The oldest records of the courts of Bucks County, Pennsylvania, are those of the Orphans' Court. This Court was held at Gilbert Wheelers, on the 4th day of the first month, 1683, "to inspect and take an account of the improvements and usages of the Estates of Orphans." Those present were "the Governor William Penn, Justices James Harrison, Jon Otter, Wm yardley, Wm. Beakes, Thomas Fitzwater and Phineas Pemberton Cl:." The first case for consideration of the court was that of the two sons of John Spencer who died on the 22nd day of the 10th month 1683.

The next oldest court records are those contained in a volume entitled "Records of the Courts of Quarter Sessions and Common Pleas of Bucks County, 1684-1730." The minutes of the first session therein recorded are those of a court held on the 11th of the 10th month, 1684. The date of the organization of this Court appears to be unknown, but that there was a court functioning before that time is shown in the minutes of a meeting of the Provincial Council, held at Phila-

6 *Laws agreed upon,* etc., sections V - IX.
7 MacReynolds, *Place Names in Bucks County,* p. 60.

delphia, the 20th of the fourth month, 1683, when the following appeal was brought before it:

"Richard Noble, Pl; on an apeal, Abra. Man, Def^t.

The Jugem^t of ye County Court against Richard Noble was reade, wth the reason of ye Apeale, and soe they proceeded to Tryall.

But for as much as ye apeal of Richd Noble before this board, is upon a Jugemt given by ye County Court of Philadelphia, concerning a Title of Land in ye County of Bucks, and that ye Law saith That all Causes shall be first Tryed where they arise, It is ye opinion of this board that ye apeal Lyes not Legally nor regularly before us and therefore doe refer ye Business to the proper County Court, and doe fine ye County Court of Philadelphia forty pounds for giving ye said Judgment against Law."[8]

A Provincial Circular Court was created by an act passed by the General Assembly on the 10th day of the third month, 1684, "to try all Criminalls & Titles of Land, and be a Court of Equity, to decide all Differences upon appeals from the County Courts."[9]

The Proprietor divided the Province into three counties but the lines of separation were not clearly defined. This soon led to confusion and uncertainty as to jurisdiction and the Provincial Council on the 8th of the second month, 1685, after considering the matter at two previous meetings, directed the following notice to be sent to the Sheriffs of the Counties concerned:—

"By the Presdt & Provil Councill of the Province of Pennsilvania & Territories thereunto belonging.

Whereas, there is a Necessity to ascertain the Bounds of ye severall Countyes of Pennsilvania, in Order to ye raising and Collecting of Taxes, publick Monys, and Otherways to adjust the Limitts of the respective Sheriffs for ye pforming of their Power and Duty: and also, that ye People might know unto what County they belong & appertaine to answer their dutys and places: and wheras the Govr. in presence of Tho. Janney & Phin. Pemberton, was pleased to say and Grant that

---

[8] *Colonial Records*, Vol I, p. 76.
[9] *Ibid*, p. 98; Pa. Archives, 8th Series, Vol. 1, p. 50.

yᵉ Bounds of yᵉ County of Bucks and Philadelphia should begin as followeth, Vizt.

To begin at yᵉ Mouth of Poctquesink Creek, on Delaware, and soe by yᵉ sd Creek, and to take in the Townships of Southampton and Warminster: in Obedience thereto and Confirmation thereof, The President and Councill have Seriously Weighed and Considered yᵉ same, have & doe hereby agree and Order that the bounds between the said Countys shall be thus: to begin at yᵉ Mouth of Poctquesink Creek on Delaware River, and to goe up thence a long yᵉ said Creek by yᵉ severall Courses thereof, to a S. W. & N. E. Line, which said Line devides the Land belonging to Jos. Growdon & Compa:, from yᵉ Southampton Township; from thence by a Lyne of Marked Trees along the said Line 120 Perches more or less, from thence N. W. by a Line of marked Trees, which said Line impart devided the Land belonging to Nich. Moor from Southampton & Warminster Townships, Contermeing the said Line as far as yᵉ said County shall Extend."[10]

The Courts having been organized and the jurisdictions defined, the administration of justice proceeded under the government of the Proprietor until the time of the revolution in England when King James II was succeeded by their Majesties King William III and Queen Mary. Penn had the misfortune to be suspected of treason and conspiracy and too great an attachment through correspondence with the late King. His failure to provide military assistance to the King went strongly against him with William, who was then engaged on the battlefields of Europe. An order in Council, dated March 10, 1692, was issued depriving Penn of his province and annexing it to the government of New York. By this the Province and Territories came under the authority and direction of Governor Benjamin Fletcher who took charge. A number of those whom the governor wished to continue in office declined to serve, among whom were Thomas Lloyd[11] and Phineas Pemberton. In the meantime Penn and his friends put forth their efforts to have the charges of treason and disloyalty disproved and having convinced the King and Queen of his innocence, finally on August 9th, 1694, thirty months after having been ousted, the government was restored to him by an order in Council. During the administration of Gover-

10 *Ibid*, p. 130.
11 *Ibid*, p. 364.

nor Fletcher the County Clerk was Robert Cole, who was present at a meeting of the Provincial Council on May 13, 1693, and "took the oath and test, and oath of Clark of the County of Bucks."[12]

Following the return of the Proprietor to his government, Phineas Pemberton was restored and confirmed as Clerk of the County Courts of Bucks, in full and ample manner, by William Markham, on September 20, 1695.[13]

Phineas Pemberton was born January 30, 1649-50, in Bolton-le-Moor, Lancashire, England, where he was engaged in the business of a grocer previous to his coming to America. He left Liverpool on June 6, 1682, and with his father, mother, wife, son and daughter, together with James Harrison and his family, arrived on the ship Submission, at Choptank, on the Patuxent River, in Maryland. Leaving their families there for the time being, they came by horseback to Philadelphia and then made the rest of the journey by water to the "Falls of the Delaware," where they stayed for a time to look over the region with a view of locating there. Harrison came as the agent and steward of the Proprietor, and Pemberton being well impressed with the country decided to settle in that locality. He purchased three hundred acres of land and later brought his family from Maryland and built a house which he called "Grove Place." While in England he married Phoebe, daughter of James Harrison, also of Bolton. Of their ten children, two married and left issue. In his new home he soon became prominent and active in the social and political affairs of the community, and the remainder of his life was devoted to public service which he performed with satisfaction to the Proprietor, and with distinction to himself.

Besides holding the office of Clerk of all the Courts of the county from their organization, he was commissioned the first Deputy Register of Wills, 1686, five months later becoming Register; appointed Receiver of the Proprietary Quit Rents for the county, 1689, and Master of the Rolls in 1695. He kept the records of the arrivals of settlers coming into the county and the marriages, births and deaths, as well as the Ear Marks for the owners of cattle and swine as required by law. At one time he was Surveyor General and was directed to survey and lay out roads. He served three terms in the Provincial Coun-

12 *Ibid*, p. 375.
13 Pemberton Papers, Hist. Society of Pennsylvania, Vol. 1, p. 57.

cil,[14] and for four terms in the General Assembly,[15] and was President[16] of that body during the latter half of the third term. These offices together with the great mass of writing which he left behind him are a testimonial of a very busy and useful life. In a letter dated at Pennsbury, 19th of June, 1686, John Saxby, writing to Patrick Robinson stated that the Council told him that P. Pemberton did all the writing for Bucks County.[17] In his minutes of the Court he wrote his name as Phinehas up to the time of the Court held on the 10th day of the fourth month, 1696, when he made an entry dropping the second h and thereafter wrote it Phineas. His useful career was terminated by a fatal illness on March 1st, 1701-02, in the 52nd year of his age, and he was buried in the old graveyard where also rest his wife and five of their children with members of the Harrison family. This graveyard four miles south of Morrisville, on the mainland near the Delaware River, opposite Biles' Island, is regarded as the oldest graveyard in Bucks County, if not the oldest in Pennsylvania.

Writing to James Logan on September 8, 1701, the Proprietor said "Poor Phineas Pemberton is a dying man, and was not at the election, though he crept (as I may Say) to meeting yesterday. I am grieved at it: for he has not his fellow, and without him this is a poor country indeed."[18] Samuel Carpenter wrote to Penn "Phineas Pemberton died the 1st mo last and will be greatly missed, having left few or none in these parts or adjacent like him for wisdom, integrity and general service, and he was a true friend to thee and the government. It is a matter of sorrow when I call to mind and consider that the best of our men are taken away, and how many are gone and how few to supply their places."[19] In a letter from the Proprietor to James Logan, dated at London, 21st, 4 mo., 1702, he wrote "I mourn for poor Phin. Pemberton the ablest as well as one of ye best men in the Province."[20]

The records which follow in this volume are those of the Courts of Quarter Sessions and Common Pleas of Bucks County, Pennsylvania, from 1684 to 1700. They are the minutes

14 *Colonial Records,* Vol. 1, p. 125.
15 *Ibid,* p. 570.
16 *Ibid,* pp. 547, 548.
17 Pemberton Papers, Vol. 1, p. 16.
18 *Memoirs of the Historical Society of Pennsylvania,* Vol. IX, p. 55; Logan Papers, Vol. I, p. 56, American Philosophical Society.
19 Jordan, *Colonial Families of Philadelphia,* Vol. 1, p. 281.
20 Logan Papers, Vol. I, p. 40, Historical Society of Pennsylvania.

complete, no omissions or eliminations have been made. By reason of its great age the volume has been subjected to the wear and tear of time. It was not begun as a book, but on loose sheets of folded paper the pages averaging 8 by 12. As the minutes of the sessions of the Court increased in number they were chronologically arranged, and at a later date all in *fasciculi* were bound into the present volume. Various makes of paper compose its pages, some thin and others of better quality and more durable. Because of this lack of uniformity some of the pages have been torn, with fragments missing along the margins as well as in the inner portions. Wherever such instances occur they have been indicated by * * * . The pages were not numbered originally but done by another hand at a later period. In the present volume this pagination has been maintained. Pages 50-54 are written in reverse in the original and have been so reproduced.

Because of time's habit, interlineations often requiring the use of the reading glass, and the peculiar script letters common to the period in which it was written, the book is a difficult one to read. Outstanding features of the handwriting are the use of the long letter s, indifferent spelling and use of capital letters, and frequent indications of a tired hand. In the reproduction every effort has been made to have a *vera copia, verbatim, literatim, et punctatim,* page for page and line for line transcript, as far as typography can make it, with the duplications and other peculiarities of the original maintained.

The transcription begun during the incumbency of the writer as President of the Colonial Society of Pennsylvania encountered so many unforseen obstacles that it has taken a long time for its completion. Notwithstanding, it has been of much personal interest and afforded great satisfaction in its accomplishment, and carries the hope that it may be of the same value to scholars as have been the previous publications of the Society.

J. E. Burnett Buckenham.

Somerhousen in the German Township
   and County of Philadelphia,
June 15th, 1943.

RECORDS
OF THE
Courts of Quarter Sessions and Common Pleas of Bucks County, Pennsylvania

The iith $\frac{io}{mo}$ 84

Robt Lucas declared in

this Court that   agt he did

   lieve in his contionce the Caufe
was Juft

Minuts of the Court (1)

in

Bucks County

The iith $\frac{io}{mo}$ 1684

Robt Lucas plt agt Thomas Bowman deft in an
   action of the Cafe for wth holding Seven pounds wch was
   due to the fd plt in the 3 month Laft paft
      Summonc granted for Tho Bowman —
    County of Bucks in the provinc of Pennfilvania
Thefe are to Require thee to Summonc Thomas Bowman
if he Shall be found in thy Balywick that he be and
appeare att the next Court to be held in Bucks County
afforefd on the 19th $\frac{ii}{mo}$ next enfueing then and there to
   Anfwer
to the Complt of Robt Lucas for wth holding of feven
pounds wch will be made appeare to be due to the faid
Robt Lucas in open Court & hereof Thou art not
to faile given undr my hand & Seale the iith day
of the $\frac{io^{th}}{mo}$ being the 36 yeare of the kings Raine
& the 4th of the propriatorys govrmt 1684
To the Sherrif of the fd   Willm Beakes
County or his Deputy Thefe
        The Sherrifs Returne
  This Summonce was executed according to direction
         The iith $\frac{io}{mo}$ 1684
    p Luke Brindley deputy Sherrife
  The declaration of the Said Robt Lucas plt

Robt Lucas plt agt   }   The iith io month 1684
Thomas Bowman defdt } Robt Lucas of the County of Bucks
in the Provinc of Pennfilvania makes Complt agt Tho:
Bowman of weft new Jarfey, that he the Said Thomas
Bowman detaines from him the Sum of Seven pounds w^{ch}
he the fd Robt Lucas will make appeare in open Court
to be due Sinc Spring laft therefore the fd plt prays

(3)

Judgmt of Court agt the Said deft for his faid * * *
yᵉ: damages he has Suftained for the want th * * *
was due, & Coft of Suite

iiᵗʰ $\frac{10}{mo}$ 1684   John Ackerman Conftable prfents Daniel
            Brinfon of Bucks
County for keeping unlawfull Cattle

[2]

The 16ᵗʰ day of $\frac{10}{mo}$ 1684

gilbert wheeler plt agt walter pomferet deft in
an acction of Cafe for with holding of five pounds 10ˢ
wᶜʰ was due to the Said plt

    An Arreft for the goods of the fd walter pomferet
County of Bucks in the Provinc of Pennfilvania
Thefe are by the kings Authority in the name of the
propriatory & govrnr to require thee that thou
Attach if found within thy Balywick of the goods & Chattles
   of walter pomferet
(of Burlington in weft new Jarfey) so much as thou in thy
difcretion Shall Judge by Reafonable Apprizement will amount
to & yeild as well the Sum of five pounds ========
as allfo Coft of Suite, & the Same So Attached in Cuftody
   keepe untill further ordr from the Comr of the Court
   except
the Said Walter pomferet Shall give Sufitient fecurity
for his Appearanc att the next Court to be holden in Bucks
County on the 14ᵗʰ day of the iiᵗʰ month next enfueing to
Anfwer unto gilbert Wheeler in an acction of Cafe —
or that he Render to him the full and Juft Sum of five
pounds ==== wᶜʰ to him he oweth & unjuftly detaineth
as its Said hereof faile not & have thou there this writ

given under my hand & Seale the 17ᵗʰ day of the $\frac{10}{mo}$ in
the 36 yeare of the kings Raigne & yᵉ: 4ᵗʰ of the ppria
=torys govrmt 1684

To the Sherrife of the County
of Bucks or his deputy Thefe

    The Sherrifs Return

The firft day of the iiᵗʰ month 1684

By vertue of this writ I have Attached of the goods of

Walter pomſeret one mare one horſe one yearling hors Colt
Luke Brindley deputy Sherrife

gilbert Wheeler plt –⎫
      agt   ⎬gilbert Wheeler makes Complt agt
walter pomſeret deft⎭ walter pomſeret how that the ſd deft under

tooke to work for him about 4 yeares Agoe for wᶜʰ the
* * * him his full due but the ſd deft after he had
* * * to his hands unjuſtly necglected Such A pte of
* * * is to the value of 5 £ to the great damage
* * * therefore the ſd plt prays Judgmt of Court * * *
for damage & Coſt of Suite

The firſt day of the iiᵗʰ month i684

3

The i6ᵗʰ day of the $\frac{\text{io}}{\text{mo}}$ 1684

Willm Biles plt agt Walter pomſeret deft in A plea
of Caſe ===== for wᵗʰ holding of five pounds ———
wᶜʰ was due to the Said plt

An Arreſt granted for the goods of the ſaid Walter
Pomſeret

County of Bucks in the Provinc of Pennſilvania

Theſe are by the kings Authority in the name of the propriatory
& govrnr to Require thee to Attach if found wthin thy
Balyweeke of the goods & Chattles of Walter pomſeret (of
Burlington in weſt new Jarſsey) So much as thou in thy
diſcretion Shall Judge by Reaſonable appriſement will amont
to & yeild as well the Sum of five pounds =============
as alſſo Coſt of ſuit & the Same So Attached in Cuſtody keepe
untill further ordr from the Commiſſioners of the Court
Except the Said Walter pomſeret Shall give Suffitiont ———
Security for his Appearanc att the next Court to be holden
in Bucks County on the 14ᵗʰ day $\frac{\text{ii}}{\text{mo}}$ next enſueing to Anſwer unto
Willm Biles in A plea of Caſe or yᵗ
he Render to him the full & Juſt Sum of five pounds
===== wᶜʰ to him he oweth & unjuſtly detaineth
as its Said hereof faile not & have thou there this writt
given under my hand & Seale the 17th day of the $\frac{\text{io}}{\text{mo}}$ in
the 36 yeare of the kings Raigne & the 4ᵗʰ of the propriatorys
govrmt i684

To the Sherrife of the County of
Bucks or his deputy Thefe
The Sherrifs Return
The firſt of the ii[th] mo 1684 by vertue of this writ I
have attached of the goods of walter pomſeret one
horſe one mare & one yearling hors Colt
Luke Brindly deputy Sherrif

Willm Biles plt ———
      agt
Walter pomſeret deft

} Willm Biles makes Complt agt Walter pomſeret of weſt new Jarſey for that

the ſaid walter pomſeret unjuſtly detaines from him the
Sum of five pounds w[ch] is due to the ſd plt upon acct
as the ſd plt will make appeare in Court there fore
the ſaid plt prays Judgmt of Court agt the ſd
deft for his ſd monys & Coſt of ſuite
The firſt day of the ii[th] month 1684

The 18th $\frac{io}{mo}$ 1684

(4)   Samuel Dark plt agt Walter Pomſeret deft in A
plea of Caſe ===== for with holding of three pounds ten
Shillings w[ch] was due to the Said plt

An Arreſt for the goods of the ſd Walter Pomſeret
County of Bucks in the Provinc of Pennſilvania

Theſe are by the kings Authority in the name of the
        Propriatory and
govrnr to Require thee that thou Attach if found wth in thy
balywicke the goods & Chattles (of Walter pomſeret (of
        Burling
=ton in weſt new Jarſey) So much as thou in thy diſcretion
Shall Judg by Reaſonable apprizement will amount to and
yeild as well the Sum of three pounds ten Shillings =====
as allſo Coſt of ſuite & the Same So Attached in Cuſtody
keepe untill further ordr from the Comrs of the Court Except
the Said Walter Pomſeret Shall give Suffitiont Se
=curity for his appearance att the next Court to be holden
in Bucks County the 9th of the $\frac{ii}{mo}$ next enſueing to Anſwer
unto Samuel Darke in A plea of Caſe or that he Render
to him the full & Juſt Sum of three pounds ten shillings
w[ch] to him he oweth & unjuſtly detaines (as its Said) hereof
faile not & have thou there this writ given under my
hand & Seale the 17th day of the io[th] month in the 36

yeare of the kings Raigne & the 4th of the propriatorys govrmt 1684

To the Sherrife of the County
of Bucks or his deputy Thefe
The Sherrifs Return

(5)
Ann milcome plt agt Edward Smith & Willm Smith deft in A plea of Cafe for wth holding of one pound Nine Shillings three penc wch was due to the Said plt above 3 months Agoe

A

Summonc granted for Edward & Willm Smith

Ann milcome plt
agt
Edward Smith—
&
Willm Smith—
deft————

The declaration of the fd Ann milcome plt Ann milcome of the County of Bucks In the Provinc of Pennfilvania makes Compt agt Edward Smith & Willm Smith of the County afforefd that they owe to her the Sum of one pound Nine Shillings three pence wch was due to her in y^e firft month laft as She will make appeare in Court & that they the faid defts unjuftly detaines her monys from her there fore the Said plt prays Judgmt of Court agt them for her fd monys & Coft of fuite

(6)   The 29th day of the $\frac{ii}{mo}$ i684

Samuel overton of the County of Bucks plt agt John Clows of the fd County deft in an acct of Cafe for wth holding of Seven pounds which is due to y^e Said plt

The declaration of Samuel overton

The 29th day of the $\frac{ii}{mo}$ i684

Samuel Overton plt
agt
John Clows deft—

Samuel overton makes Complt agt the Said John Clows how that the Said deft about 4 months ago Sent for the fd plt, to Come

to his houſe for that Joſeph Chorley ſervant to the Said deft
was Shot into the legg & that if the fd plt wold Come
& Cure the fd Servant the fd deft wold Content
him whereupon the fd plt wrought A Cure upon the fd –
Servant of the fd deft & that now the fd deft refuſes to
pay the fd plt, & unjuſtly detaines the Sum of Seven pounds
wch is due to the fd plt from the fd deft for working the
ſd Cure wherefore the ſd plt prays Judgmt of Court agt
the fd deft for his monys & Coſt of ſuite
      A Summonc granted for the fd John Clows
  County of Bucks in the provinc of Pennſilvania
Theſe are by the kings Authority in the name of the
    Propriatory & govr
to require thee to Summonce John Clows of
the ſaid County & Provinc that he be & appeare att the next
Court to be held in this County on the iith day of the $\frac{12^{th}}{mo}$
next Enſueing then & there to Anſwer the Complt of Sam:
overton for wth holding of Seven pounds wch is Said will
be made appeare in Court to be due to
the fd Sam: Overton & hereof thou art not to faile given
under my hand & ſeale the 29th day of the ii month being
the 36 yeare of the kings Raigne & the 4th of the propria
=torys govrmt 1684

To the Sherrife of the Said
County or his deputy Theſe
A writ granted for A Jury

(7)

      The 29th day of the $\frac{ii}{mo}$ 1684

Willm Biles of the County of Bucks plt agt Ralph =
Sidwell of the fd County deft in an acction of trover
& Converſion for with holding of goods he hath found
of the fd plts to the value of fifty Shillings, & refuſes to
deliver them upon demand

    The declaration of Willm Biles
      the 29th $\frac{ii}{mo}$ 1684

Willm Biles plt   ⎫
  agt   ⎬ Willm Biles plt makes Complt agt Ralph
Ralph Sidwell deft ⎭ Sidwell how that the Said Ralph

Sidwell hath found of his goods to the value of fifty
Shillings & refuses to deliver them to the fd plt tho
the Said plt demanded them upon the i9th Inftant & there
fore the Said plt prays Judgment of Court agt the Said
deft for his goods & damages & Coft of Suite

     A Summonce granted for the fd Ralph Sidwell
Cou: Bucks

    To the Sherif Thefe   By vertue of the kings Authority in
the name of the proprietary & govrnr Thefe are to Require thee
to Summonc Ralph Sidwell, Carpenter if wthin thy Balywick
to appeare att the next Court to be holden for this County the
iith day of the i2th month att the falls to Anfwer Such things as
Shall then & there be objected agt him & there have this
Summonce given undr my hand & feale the 26th ii month 1684
being the 36 yeare of the kings Raigne & the 4th of the propriatorys govrmt

A writ grantd for A Jury   The Sherrifs Return
The 29th $\frac{ii}{mo}$ 84   This Summonce was executed
         the 26th $\frac{ii}{mo}$ 1684

---

 8 County of Bucks in the provinc of Pennfilvania
At A monthly Seffions held by the kings Authority in the
name of Willm penn proprietary & govrnr of the Said
provinc & Territorys thereunto belonging att the
Court houfe of the faid County the iith day of the i2 mo
i684 in the 37 yeare of the kings Raigne & the 4th of
the propriatorys govrmt   This day was acknowlit
 The Juftices then prfent   in open Court one mortgage
James Harrifon Prfident   from Jon Acker
Tho Janney   Willm Biles   man to willm Beakes
willm Beakes wm yardley   This day willm Beakes
John otter   Signed and fealed one
John Brock Sherrife   letter of Attorney to A man
Luke Brindley his deputy   in London
Phinehas pemberton Clarke   wch was Certifyed under my
             hand & County
               feale

Willm Biles Appears to A rt of Trover & Converſion
   Ralph Sidwell Call'd appeareth not
   declaration read & proved
   The Courts Anſwer to Rich Hedleys pettition is that
Inas much the ſd Hedley has done his worke
well; & that he has not had A valuable Conciderration
for his worke he the ſd Hedley Shall have 5 £ more
then mentioned in his Contract, he the ſd Hedley doing
Some Smal matter of worke as the Revieuers ſhall
appoint; & remitting that worke wch he has done all
=ready above what is mentioned in the Contract & that
the ſd 5 £ is Intended to be payd in or before 10th month
   next
Juſtice otter Informes the Court that Derick Clawſon
is Atteſted Conſtable & that ffrancis walker is not
capable of serveing therefore the Court ordrs Claws
Jonſon Conſtable & that Jon otter, & Edmund Bennet
see that the Conſtable be Atteſted & make Returne there
of the next Court
the Collectors hath this day brought in theire accts of what
monys they have Collected, & pd in the ſd monys to the
   Treaſurors
according to ordr
It is ordered that in as much the Ptyes formerly ordered
   to Lay out the
Road to phinehas pembertons plantation have not done it
the Court doth ordr that Willm: Biles Lyonel Brittan

(9)

& Samuel Darke along wth Robt Lucas Lay out the
Said Road before the next Court & that it be layd
out to A landing below the Lower line of george Herrote
   Land
It is alſo ordered that the Road about the falls that is not
allready pfected be done afore next Court, & that Willm
   Beakes
along wth the ptyes for merly ordered to pfected it take
   Care
it be done
         The Court adjorns for one houre
Inas much as Ralph Sidwell hath not appeared to the
Suite the Court gives Judgmt that the ſd Sidwell ſhall
pay to the plt willm Biles fifty Shillings & Coſt of suite
Edward Smith haveing been cald into Court & aſked

for for the monys due to the wid milcome pleads
difapointments
by water and wether & prays one months time more w^{ch}
was
given him by Ann milcome daughter

walter pomferet hath defired the Court to ftay proceedings
agt: him for i0 days that in the meane time he
may make up his accts wth gilbert wheeler & willm
Biles wch the court grants him

The Court doth ordr that gilbert wheeler & Samuel
Dark do take Care to provide A place for na: Weft
that he may in al refpects Satisfye the Judgmt
of Court, & that phinehas pemberton returne
in to theire hands an acct of all the Courts ———
Sentenc upon him

Daniel Brinfon craves that he may have Na Weft to worke
for him, io days or untill the ptyes above can pvide
A place for him, & he will Engage for his Apperance
at the io days End or before if he be Calld for

It is ordered that willm Biles willm Beakes
Shall take care to buy io or i2 Ackers of Land to be Laid
to the
prifon for y^e: publique ufe of the County & that they do itt
if the Can before the next Court

The Court Adjorns till the 2nd 4th day of the
next month

Daniel Brinfon haveing been Calld into Court about
the prefentmt
of John Ackerman for keeping unlawfull Cattle and none
appearing agt him to pfecute the Court difcharges him
paying
his fees

10
The i8th day of the i2th month i684
Thomas Janney of the County of Bucks Truftee for John
neild his Servant plt agt
Jofeph Milner of the fd County deft in an acct of Cafe for
with holding, of Six pounds five Shillings due to the Said
Jon
neild Since the 5th month i683

The i8th day of the i2th month i684

Thomas Janney Truſtee } Thomas Janney makes Complt
to Jon neild plt   agt the
agt.   Said Joſeph milner how that
Joſeph Milner deft   the Said
                           deft in the 5ᵗʰ month 1683
                           borrowed
                           of him of the monys of Jon
                           neild his —

Servant To whom he the Said Thomas
Janney is Truſtee; The Sum of 6 £ 5ˢ & he the Said deft
    when he Borrowed the Said
monys promiſed to give Suffitiont Security for the
    payment there
of with Lawfull Intreſt for the Same dureing the
time he had it; but never Since wold the Said deft either
    pay
the monys Intreſt or give Security for they payment
    thereof where
fore the Said plt prays Judgment of Court agt the Said
    deft for
damages & Coſt of Suite
            A Summonc granted for the Said Joſeph milner
            County of Bucks in the Provinc of Pennſilvania
Theſe are by the kings Authority in the name of the
    propriatory &
govrnr to require thee to Summonce Joſeph milnor of the
Said County & Provinc that he be & appeare att the next
    Quartr

Seſſions to be held for this County on the 11ᵗʰ day of the $\frac{1}{mo}$

next then & there to Anſwer the Complt of Thomas
    Janney
Truſtee to Jon neild, for wᵗʰ holding of Six pounds five
    ſhillings
wᶜʰ is Said will be made to appeare in Court to be due to
    the Said Jon
Neild & hereof thou art not to faile given undr my hand
    & ſeale
The 19th day of 12 month 1684 being the 37 yeare of the
    kings Raign
& the 4ᵗʰ of the propriatorys govrmt

To the Sherrife of the Said County
or his deputy thefe

The i8th $\frac{i2}{mo}$ 1684 (11)

John Brock of the County of Bucks plt agt
Jofeph Englifh of the fd County deft in an acct
of Cafe for wth holding of ten fhillings due
to the Said plt

The declaration of John Brock agt Jofeph Englifh
The i8^th day of the i2 month i684

John Brock plt	John Brock makes Complt agt Jofeph
agt	Englifh how that the Said deft laft
Jofeph Englifh deft	Summer Came & defired to have his

horfes wch were then plowing to drive Cattell wth all (as farr
as gilbert wheelers) wch Cattell he an Indian had brought
out of the woods So wild they Cold not get them any
further without
affiftanc & the deft promifed ten Shillings reward for the
ufe of the
Said horfes wch fd horfes according to the fd plt he the fd
deft had but hath ever Since unjuftly
detained the fd monys from the fd plt wherefore the fd
plt prays Judgmt
of Court agt the fd deft for his fd monys & Coft of fuite
 A Summonc granted for Jofeph Englifh
 County of Bucks in the Province of Pennfilvania
Thefe are by the kings Authority in the name of the
Proprietory
& govrnr to Require thee to Summonc Jofeph Englifh of
the fd County & Province that he be & appeare att the
next Quartr
Seffions to be held for this County on the ii^th day $\frac{i}{mo}$
next then
& there to anfwer the Complt of John Brock Sherrife of
this County for wth holding of ten Shillings wch is Said
will be
made appeare in Court to be due to the fd John

Brock & hereof thou art not to faile given undr my
hand & feale the i9th day of the i2 month i684 being the
37 yeare of the kings Raigne & the 4th of the Propriato
rys govrmt

To the deputy Sherrife
of the fd County Thefe

The 2ist of $\dfrac{i2}{mo}$ 1684

(12)

Willm Sanford of
the County of Bucks plt agt David Davis of the Said
County Deft in an acct of Cafe for with holding of
nine pounds Elleven Shillings Eight penc wch was due
to be pd

to the Said plt the 30th $\dfrac{9}{mo}$ laft paft

The declaration of the fd plt

The 2ist $\dfrac{i2}{mo}$ i684

willm Sanford plt ⎫ willm Sanford makes Complt agt the
                              ⎪   fd David
      agt   ⎬ Davis how that the Said deft is
                              ⎪   Indebted
David Davis deft ⎭ to him the Sum of nine pounds
                                 Elleven —
                                 Shillings Eight pence wch Said Debt
the
Said Deft hath promifed to pay either by acceptable bills
     or monys
by the 30th of the 9th month laft paft as will be made to
     appeare
by bill under the hand of the Said deft bearing date the
     24th
of the Said ninth month laft paft but never Since hath the
     fd deft ever paid
him any monys nor given nor ordered him the fd plt
     any Bills except one
of two pounds five Shillings but unjuftly detaines his
     Said Debt

wherefore the Said plt brings his acction for his Said Debt & prays Judgment of Court agt the fd Deft for Damages & Coſt of Suite

   A Summonce granted for the Said David Davis
County of Bucks in the Provinc of Pennſilvania
Theſe are by the kings authority in the name of the propyatory
& govrnr to Require thee to Summonc David Davis of the Said County
& provinc that he be and appeare att the next Quarter ſeſſions
to be held for this County on the iith day of the firſt month next then & there to anſwer the Complt of Willm Sanford for with holding of nine pounds Elleven Shillings Eight pence w^{ch}
is Said will be made to appeare in Court to be due to the Said Willm Sanford & hereof thou art not to faile given under my hand & Seale the 2i day $\frac{i2}{mo}$ being the xxxvii yeare of the kings Raigne & the 4th of the propriatorys govrmt 1684

To the Sherrife of the Said County
  or his deputy Theſe

(13)
   County of Bucks in the Province of Pennſilvania
At A Quarter Seſſions held by the kings Authority in the name
of willm Penn propriatory & govrnr
of the fd provinc & territorys thereunto belonging att the Court houſe the iith day of the $\frac{1}{mo}$ 1684

   The Juſtices th prſent
   James Harriſon prsident
Tho Janney John otter willm Biles
Edmund Bennett willm yardley willm Beakes
John Brock Sherrif
Luck Brindley deputy
Phinehas Pemberton Clark

 Inas much as Rich Noble not knowing of the day of the orphants Court came this day to treat about the orphants of Clarkes this Court upon A full debate of the
matter do ordr that Rich Noble Shall have twenty pounds

pd him out of the lands of the orphants of the fd Clarkes
& that at
the next orphants Court an ordr Shall be Isued out to y^t
Intent & that he hath accepted of the Same
Samuel Dark & gilbert wheeler hath not given in an acct
to this Court of what they have done about Nathaniel
Weſt
therefore the Court doth ordr that the bring in an acct to
y^e
next Court
In as much as walter pomſeret hath not according to
requeſt
made up his accts wth willm Biles & gilbert wheeler nor
any
way made them Satiſfaction therefore this Court doth ordr
that the Sherriſ do take Care to Sell thoſe goods allready
attached by him & make returne thereof to the next Court
in order to Satisſye the Judgment of Court paſſed upon
them
Jane Lyon hath this day appeared in Court and deſired
to have
James Harriſon admitted guardian, & She being att
Lawfull
age to make Choyce, this Court haveing knowledg of the
ſd James Harriſons Suffitioncy hath Commiſſionated the
ſd James
Harriſon to act as guardian for her*

  The Court adjorns untill the 2nd 4th day of the
  next month

(14)

$$\text{The 18}^{\text{th}} \text{ day of the } \frac{\text{i}}{\text{mo}} 1684$$

Thomas wright of weſt new Jarſey plt agt Daniel Brinſon
of the County of Bucks in the provinc of pennſilvania
planter
deft in an acct of Covenant for wth holding of —— horſes

---

*The above entry crossed out in the minute book was evidently
intended for the records of the Orphan's Court.

to the value of 15 £ wch he the fd deft was obliged by
A bond of twenty pound to deliver upon demand

The 18th day of the $\frac{1}{mo}$ 1684

Thomas wright plt } Thomas wright makes Complt agt
                      Dan:
    agt   Brinfon how that the fd deft
                      entered
Daniel Brinfon deft } into A bond of twenty pounds to
                      the fd plt (bearing
                date the 19th day of the 10th month
                1682)

To deliver To the faid plt upon demand one
mare 2 horfes & 2 colts; & the fd deft contrary to
    Covenant keeps back & unjuftly detaines
pte of the fd beafts======= to the value of fiveteen pounds
& refufes to deliver them to the fd plt tho he hath
Severall times demanded them Therefore the faid
plt brings his acction agt the fd deft & prays Judgmt
of Court agt: him for Damages & Coft of Suite
        The Summonce granted agt Daniel Brinfon
        County of Bucks in the provinc of penfilyvania
Thefe are by the kings Authority in the name of the
    proprya
=tory and govrnr to require thee to Summonce
Daniel Brinfon of the fd County and provinc that he be &
appeare at the next Court to be held for this County on the
8th day of the 2nd month next then & there to anfwer the
    Complt
of Thomas wright for withholding of goods or Cattles to
    the value of
fiveteen pounds which is fd will be made appeare in Court
    ought to have beene delivered
upon demand to the fd Tho: wright & hereof thou
art not to faile given under my hand & feale the 18th
day of the firft month being the xxxvii yeare of the kings
Raigne & the 5th of the propriatorys govrmt 1684
To the Sherrife of the fd County
  or his deputy Thefe
                The fherrifs Return
A writ granted for A Jury
              Thomas wright prayd this action might
              be with drawn

(15)

The 25th day of the $\frac{3}{mo}$ 1684

Entry of } Ann milcome of the County of Bucks in the
the Action } provinc of penſil
vania wid plt agt gilbert wheeler & martha
his wife of the ſd County &
province deft in an action of Caſe for
ſlanderous words
Spoken by the ſd martha wheeler, agt the
ſd plt to
the defameination & diſcredit of the ſd plt
thereby
damnifying her to the value 200 £

The 25th 3 month 1685

The } Ann milcome makes Complt agt
Declaration —— } martha the
of } wife of gilbert wheeler how that the
Ann milcome plt — } ſd martha wheeler malitiouſly &
agt } Slandrou
gilbert wheeler & } =ſly; doth what in her lyes
martha his wife deft } endeavor to —
render the ſd plt unjuſt & odious
in the minds of
people, by making great
exclamations
agt her wth out any cauſe given
her
by the ſd plt at any time &
often Calld her Cheat
but pticulerly upon 3 day of the
$\frac{1}{mo}$ & upon
the 29th of the Said month She
the ſd martha
Cald the ſd Ann milcome Cheat &
ſaid ſhe
had Cheated her of 25 s thereby
wholely
deſtroying the Credit & reputation of the ſd plt who is
A wid

& hath beene of good Credit amongst the
neighbourhood &
the ſd plt hath uſed many endeavors to have re=
=claimed the ſd martha from thoſe Slanderous expreſſions
but Shee wold not be reclaymed but hath uſed them in her
publique diſcours above A yeare whereby the ſd plt is
disabled in her Credit & dampnifyed to the value of 200 £
wherefore the ſd plt brings her action agt the ſd defts & —
prays Judgment of Court agt them for damages & Coſt of
Suite

    25th 3 mo: 1685

A Summonce granted agt the ſd gilbert wheeler & martha
his wife
for theire Appearance at the next Court to be held for
this County the 10th of the $\frac{4}{mo}$ next to anſwer the Complt
of
the ſd Ann milcome

The ſherrifs return
  25 3 1685
    mo
A writ granted⎞
for A Jury — ⎠
 A 25 3mo 85

Subpeane for wittneſſ: Jane greaves John Ackerman &
Jon purslone

---

(16) County of Bucks in the provinc of Pennſilvania
At A Quarter Seſſions held att the Court houſe for the
County of Bucks by the kings Authority in the name of
Willm
Penn propriatory & govrnr of the ſd provinc & Terri
thereunto belonging the 10th day of the 4th month 1685

    The Juſtices then prſent

willm yardley		willm Biles
Willm Beakes	John otter	Edmund Bennet
John Swift		
Phinehas Pemberton Clark		
Luke Brindley deputy		The grand Inqueſt Calld
Sherrife		over & Atteſted

foreman
Hen: Baker
wm: Dark
Joſu: Boare
Rich: Ridgway
Law: Bannor
Hen: Marjorum
Joſep: milner
Lyonel Brittan
Jam: paxſon
wm paxſon
Jo: Engliſh ſr
Tho: Stakehous ſr
Tho: Adkinſon
Jam: Boyden
Hen Bircham
Tho: Dungan
wm: Dungan
Tho: Rowland
Ed: Lovet
Tho: Woolfe
Rand: Blackſhaw
wm Hycock

ffrancis Walker Atteſted doth Say that Joſeph Luinn upon the 3i day of the 3 month laſt paſt Swore Several oathes 3 times att leaſt John Hill Atteſted doth Say that the aboveſd Joſeph Luinn the day aboveſd ſwear many oathes the Court ordrs the ſd Joſeph Luinn Shall pay for the three oaths i5ˢ or Suffer i5 days Impriſonment in the houſe of Correction att hard labour & be fed with bread & water Derrick Clawſon for ſtriking his ſervant Joſeph Luinn unreaſonablely the Court ordrs him to be bound to his good behavior & to appeare att the next Court ffrancis walker & Claws Jonſon Stand ob= lidged in 20 £ to the propriatory & govrnr for the appearanc of the ſd Derrick Clawſon at the next Court & to be of good abearing in the meane time

The Court adjorns for one houre
Derrick Clawſon has engaged to pay the fine of Joſeph Luinn and his fees & Joſeph has engaged to ſerve the ſd Derrick for ten days after the Expiration of his Servitued for his ſo doing & what the fees Comes to grand Inqueſt prſentments brought in & read

(17) Katherin knight being examined concering A baſterd Child born upon her body who the father of it is & ſhe Says the father of it is Charles Thomas

Charles Thomas being aſked whether he own him Self to be the father of the ſd Child & he Says he be= lieves it is his Child

The Court orders that Charles Thomas Shall tomorrow morning be brought to this place and whipt 20 laſhes upon his bare back well layd on & is enjoyned to marry the ſd katherine & After he Shall make good the damage his mr has ſuſtained by this thing at the expiration of his time

The Court ordrs that katherin knight Shall be brought to this place & whiped to morrow ⸺ morning wth io Laſhes on her back
Whereas the ſd Charles Thomas after Sentenc of the Court did Sweare by the name of god & ſtampt & behave him ſelf rudely in the prſenc & hearing of the Court for wch the Court ordrs he ſhall pay 5^s or ſuffer 5 days Impriſonmt
Ann milcome plt & gilbert wheeler & martha his wife defts have
Joyntly deſired theire tryall may be deferred untill the next Court day to ſee if it Cann in the meane time be Ended & have both declared in Court that neither of them will take advantage by the ſd demurr but if the diferenc be not Ended betwixt them before the next Court that then they will joyne Iſue
  The diferenc being Ented the plt deſired to have the action
with drawn

The Sherrif makes return that the goods of walter pomſeret by him formerly attached were appriz'd by the apprizors as followeth

   The i4th $\frac{ii}{mo}$ 1684 one mare 2 Colts att
    9 £ : 10^s. 00^d

and further reports that the ſd   Henry Baker
wm Biles & g: wheeler wold   Henry margerum
accept them for theire debt   Lyonel Brittan
       Adjourned untill the 2nd 4th day of the 7th mo: next

       The 3 day of the 6th mo: 1685

(18)   James Boyden of the County of Bucks in the
Provinc of Pennſilvania makes Complt agt
Jon: Collins of the ſd province in an action of
Debt for wth holding of 19^s 2^d wch was due
to be pd to the ſd plt 10 month ago

declaration

James Boyden plt   ⎫   The 3 day of the 6 1685
      agt   ⎬   mo
John Collins deft ⎭   James Boyden makes Complt agt the
                               ſd John
                           Collins how that he the ſd deft is
                           Indebted
                   to him the Sum of 19^s 2^d
& the ſd deft unjuſtly detaines his ſd monys
tho due above 10 month ago & the ſd deft is about to
depart out of the provinc wherefore the ſd plt prays
Judgment of Court agt the ſd deft for damages & Coſt of
Suite

                   Attachment granted agt the goods of
                          the ſd Collins
Theſe are   wth drawn at the Same time Entered
                The 15th day of the 6th month 1685
       Joſeph Blowers of Burlington in weſt new Jarſey
       makes
The   ⎫ Complt agt gilbert wheeler of the County of Bucks
Action   ⎬   in the
entered   ⎭ Province of Pennſilvania in an acction of Debt for
       with
       holding of 18 £ 06^s 03^d Silver monys wch Sum was
       awarded to be payd to the ſd plt At or before the
       19th
       of the 3 month laſt paſt by Thomas mathews &
       martin Holt
       Arbitrators Indiferently Choſen by the ſd deft to
       heare & determin all
       difirences & accounts depending betwixt them —

Declaration   The 15th day of the 6th month 1685

Joseph Blowers plt ⎫ Joseph Blowers makes Complt agt
                    ⎪   gilbert wheeler
     agt   ⎬ how that the Said deft is Indebted to
gilbert wheeler deft⎪   him the
                    ⎪ Summ of 18 £ 06 s 03 d Silver monys
                    ⎪   wch Sum
                    ⎭ was awarded (to be pd to the ſd plt
in 10 days;) by martin Holt & Thomas mathews
   Arbitrators
Indiferently Choſen by the ſd plt and deft to heare
   & determin
all diferences & accounts depending betwixt them
   & yett
not with ſtanding the ſd deft Entered in to A bond
   of 20 £
to Stand to the award of the ſd Arbitrators So
   Indiferently
Choſen he refuſes to pay the ſd debt & Unjuſtly
   detaines his ſd
monys wherefore the ſd plt brings his action & prays
Judgment of Court agt the ſd deft for his ſaid
debt damages & Coſt of ſuite

Summonce granted the 15th 6 mo 1685
              for gil: wheeler to appeare At the next
              Quarter ſeſſions to be held the 9th 7mo next
              to anſwer the Complt of of ſd Blowers
The Sherrifs Return
A writt granted for Jury on tryall of Blowers plt agt wheeler
   deft

(20) At A Quarter Seſſions held for the County of Bucks
           by the kings Authority
        in the name of Willm Penn proprietary and
        Governor of the Province of Pennſilvania and
        Territorys thereunto belonging the 9th day of the
        7th month 1685

                    The Juſtices then prsent
              Thomas Janney   willm Biles
              John otter   willm yardley
                 Luke Brindley deputy Sherrife
                 Phinehas Pemberton Clarke

The petty Jury Joseph Blowers plt in an action
of debt agt gilbert Wheeler deft the sum
18 £ : 06ˢ 03ᵈ Silver monys wᶜʰ sum was awarded upon
the 8ᵗʰ $\frac{3}{mo}$ last past by Thomas mathews &
martin Holt arbitrators Indiferently Chosen
The Jury Attested
Joseph Blowers hath desired the action to be wᵗʰ drawn
gilbert Wheeler hath declared that he will pay the Charge
of Court
John Otter hath declared that upon the 3 day of the 6ᵗʰ
 mo 85
James Boyden Complained that Jon Collins
was Indebted to him the Sum of 19ˢ ; 2ᵈ where
upon the sd Collins was brought before the sd Jon otter &
Edmund Bennet Justices & yᵉ sd Collins acknowledged yᵉ
sd debt to be due to yᵉ : sd Boyden whereupon the sd
Justices gave theire Judgment the sd Collins
Shold pay the debt wᵗʰ Cost of suit wᶜʰ Judgment the sd
 Justices have
reported to this Court wᶜʰ Judgment by this Court is
 allowed
of, &
The sd Justic otter hath declared in Court the sd Jon
Collins did Sweare in his presenc wherefore this
Court ordr the sd Collins to pay 5ˢ wᶜʰ sd five shillings
the sd Collins hath desired to have time to pay it till
the next Court

Derrick Clawson has this day according bond appeared
nothing appearing agt him the Court
discharges him paying his fees

A prsentmt from Philadelphia County referred to the
 Court of this County Concerning a Child that was
 put to nurs to one Robt marsh of Southamton was
 this day read
ordrd that the sd march, be sent for and examined
 before
Some Justice of Peace

(21)

Gilbert Wheeler being last Court prsented for turning
of the high Road where it was layd out & fencing it
up hath this day beene Calld before this Court
& being examined about the sd prsentmt to wᶜʰ he

Submitted therefore this Court taking in to Con=
cideration the ſaid treſpaſſe of the ſd gilbert wheeler
hath ordered Thomas Janney & willm Beakes together
wth the overseers of the high way to veiue wher
the ſd Road Shall Lye & make it out & that gilbert
wheeler take down his fence that it may Run according
to
theire directions in 18 months time

This Court doth ordr that Henry marjorum do ſerve
as Conſtable for the falls for the Succeeding year
& that willm Hycock do ſerve Conſtable for the
middle Lotts for the ſucceeding yeare
for the further ſide of Neſhaminah & there about
Samuel Allen
& John purslone

This Court doth ordr that Joſuah Hoops Henry paxſon
& Jonathan Scaiſe to ſerve as peace makers
for this County the Succeeding yeare

This Court doth ordr that Henry Baker John Rowland
& Thomas Stake houſe & Edmund Cuttler do ſerve
over ſeers of the high ways
for this county for the ſucceeding yeare

The Court adjorns for one houre

The over ſeers of the high ways for the prſedent yeare
have brought in
an acc^t of the ſeverall psons that are in arreare in
doing theire duty according to ſummonce therefore
this Court doth ordr that the ſd overſeers Shall
Collect the ſd arrears

This day was dd & acknowledged in open Court A deed
of 200 Ackers of Land adjoyning to Rich Noble Land
in
this County by phinehas pemberton Conſtituted
attorney
on the behalf of Abraham man & Eliabeth his wife of
the County of Newcastell
unto Jacob pellexon of philadelphia

This day was deliv & acknowledged in open Court A
deed of 200 Ackers of Land Lying neare y^e: Cold
Spring
by Rich Lundy to willm Biles both of this County
for the uſe of Jacob Tellnor

The Court adjorns untill the 2nd 4th day of the $\frac{10}{mo}$ next

(22) 23 $\underline{9}$ 85
              mo

the ⎧ Sam overton of the County of Bucks in the provinc
action ⎨ of Pennſilvania plt agt Jacob Hall of the ſd County
entered ⎩ an pvinc in an act of Caſe for with holding of
4 £ 13 s due to the ſd plt

The Dlarat

The 23 9 85 County of Bucks in the province of
     mo   Pennsylvania

Sam Overton plt ⎫ Samuel overton makes Complt agt
   agt   ⎬ Jacob Hall how that the ſd Deft is
Jacob Hall deft ⎭ Indebted to the ſd plt the Sum of
in an act   foure pounds thirteen Shillings due
   of   for dyet & other ſervices &
  Caſe   things wch
                ſd Sum the ſd deft unjuſtly detaines
                and refuſes to pay
              wherefore the ſd plt brings his
                action of Caſe prays Judgmt
              of Court agt ye: ſd deft for the ſd
              Sum of 4 £ : 13 s damages & Coſt of
              Suite

23 $\underline{9}$ 85
    mo

Sumonce ⎧ Summonc granted agt Jacob Hall to Anſwer the
        ⎨ Compt of Sam overton at the next Quarter ſeſſions
        ⎩ to be held for this County the 9th of the 10 mo next

Return The ſherriſs Return The above mentioned Summonc
        was executed the 24th $\underline{9}$ p Luke Brindley
                              mo   deputy Sherriſ

Subpene A ſubpene for Jon Brock to give his evidence
         in A Caſe depending betwixt Sam overton plt
         agt Jacob Hall deſt

A writ for } the evidenc Summonced the 24th of 9th mo p
the Jury } Luke Brindley
deputy Sherrif
to trye the Caufe depending betwixt fd
overton plt agt Ja Hall deft
the 9th day of the 10th mo 1685 Samuel overton
defired to have the above action agt Jacob Hall
withdrawn

County of Bucks in the Province of Pennfilvania (23)

The 23 day of the 9th mo 1685

the
action } Nicholas moore Efqre of the County of Philadelphia
Entered } and
Province aforefd plt agt gilbert wheeler of ye:
County of Bucks & province aforefd in an action of
Debt for wth holding of forty foure pounds Sixteen
fhillings
and 10 d & Intreft for thirteen months

The
Declaration of
Nicholas moore Efqre plt
agt
gilbert wheeler deft

in an action of

Debt — —

} County of Bucks in the Province
of Pennfilva
nia the 23 day of the 9th month 1685
Nicholas moore Efquire of the
County
of Philadelphia & provinc aforefd
makes Complt agt gilbert whee
ler of the County of Bucks &
provinc aforefd how that the
fd deft is Indebted
the Sum of 44 £ : 16 s : 10 d
due to be payed to ye: fd plt upon
demand as will
appear by A bill under the hand
of the fd deft bearing date the 29th
of october 1684 & altho the fd plt
hath divers times made demand of his Said monys yet the
fd deft unjuftly detaines the Same wherefore the fd
plt brings his action of debt and prays Judgmt of Court
agt the fd deft for the fd fum of forty four pounds Six

teen Shillings & ten penc wth Intreſt for the ſame for 13 months damages & Coſt of ſuite
Summonc 23 9 85
                    ――
                    mo

Summonc granted agt gilbert Wheeler to anſwer the Compt of N moore att the next Quarter ſeſſions to be held for this County the 9th of the 10 mo: next

Sherriſs } The above written Summonc was executed the
Return   } 24th of the 9th moth 1685 p Luke Brindley deputy Sherriſ

A Writ   } ― to try the Cauſe depending betwixt N moore
for A Jury } plt & gilbert Wheeler deft ―

action wth drawn { The 9th of the 10th mo 1685 A note came to my Hand from Nicholas more deſireing me to with draw the action abovemention agt gilbert wheeler if the ſd wheeler wold pay the fees wheeler being demaned in open Court whether he wold pay the fees or no promiſed to pay them wherefore the action was accordingly with drawne

(24)   24 9 85
                      ――
                      mo

The action } Jacob Hall of the County of Bucks in the Provinc
Entered   } of Penn ſilvania plt agt Samuel overton of the ſd
             County and
             provinc in an action of Caſe for with holding of
             3 £ 6^s: 00^d due to be pd to the ſd plt

The   24th 9 1685
                             ――
                             mo
Declaration of   County of Bucks in the Province of
Jacob Hall plt   } Pennſilvania
   agt   }
Samuel overton deft } Jacob Hall makes Complt agt

Samuel overton both of the County, & provinc aforesd how
 that yᵉ:
Sd deft is Indebted to him sd plt the sum of three pounds Six
Shillings wᶜʰ sd Sum the deft unjustly detaines and
refuses to pay wherefore the sd pltf brings his action of
Case & prays Judgmt of Court agt the sd deft for the sd sum
 of 3 £ 6ˢ for damages & Cost of suite

$$24^{th} \quad 9 \quad 1685$$
$$mo$$

Summonc
{ Summonc granted agt Sam Overton to
answer the Complt of Jacob Hall att the
next Quarter Sessions to be held for this County
the 9ᵗʰ of the io mo next

Return
the above mentioned Summonc was executed
the 25ᵗʰ of the 9ᵗʰ mo: 1685

p Luke Brindley Deputy sherrif

The 9ᵗʰ of the io ᵗʰ month 1685 Jacob Hall desired to have
the above action agt Samuel Overton
with drawn

(25)

$$25 \quad 9 \quad 1685$$
$$mo$$

The action entered
{ ffrancis Hough of the County of Bucks in the
province of Pennsilvania plt agt Elenor
pownall of the sd County & provinc in an action
of Case for wᵗʰ holding of 5 £ : 13ˢ : 06ᵈ wᶜʰ is
due to be paid to the sd plt for work done

The Declaration of
ffrancis Hough plt
agt
Ellenor pownal deft

$$25^{th} \quad 9 \quad 1685$$
$$mo$$

County of Bucks in the Provinc of
Pennsilvania

ffrancis Hough plt makes Complt
agt Ellenor Pownal of the County &
Province aforesd how that the sd deft is
Indebted to the sd plt the Sum of

5 £ : 13ˢ : 06ᵈ for worke done for the ſd deft wᶜʰ ſd ſum
the ſd deft unjuſtly detaines & refuſes to pay wherefore the ſd
plt brings his action of Caſe and prays Judgment of Court
agt the ſd deft for the ſd ſum of 5 £ : 13ˢ : 06ᵈ damages
and Coſt of Suite

25ᵗʰ   9   1685
———
mo

Summonce { Summonce granted agt Ellenor Pownall to anſwer the Complt of ffrancis Hough att yᵉ: next Quarter ſeſſions to be held for this County the 9ᵗʰ of the 10 moᵗʰ next

Return { The above mentioned Summonc was executed the 25ᵗʰ of the 9ᵗʰ moᵗʰ 1685   p Luke Brindley Deputy Sherrif

A writ for A Jury granted to ſerve in the ſeveral action tryable the Quarter ſeſſions to be held the 9ᵗʰ of the 10ᵗʰ month next

A Supeane granted for John Brock John Brearley & willm morton to give in their Evidenc in A Caſe depending betwixt ffrancis Hough & Ellenor Pownal

Return   The above Subpene for wittneſſes was executed the 25ᵗʰ of the 9ᵗʰ moᵗʰ 1685
                         p Luke Brindley Deputy ſherrif
The 9ᵗʰ of the 10ᵗʰ mo: 1685 ffrancis Hough deſired
to have the above action agt Ellenor Pownall
                                     with drawn

(26)   2 day of the 10   1685
                               mo

The action } Samuel Burges of the county of Bucks in
Entered   the provinc of penſilvania plt agt Jon Wright
late of this County in an act of
Debt for wᵗʰ holding of 4 £ : 3ˢ : 00ᵈ
due to be pd to the ſd plt

2 io mo 1685

Attachment } an attachment granted agt the goods of Jon
granted } wright non Refident for his appearanc att y^e:
next Quarter feffions to be held for this County
the 9th of this Inftant ioth mo:

County of Bucks in the Province of
Pennfilvania the 2nd of ioth mo 85

Declaration of } Samuel Burges of the County & provinc
Sam Burges plt } afforefd makes Compt agt Jon wright late
agt } of this County how that the fd deffendent
John wright deft } in Aprill laft bought of the fd plt one pfell of
goods Come to foure pounds three fhillings
for wch fd fum y^e: fd deft gave A bill under his hand
but the fd deft unjuftly detaines the fd monys & never as
yet payd any pte thereof wherefore the fd plt brings his action
of
Debt & prays Judgmt agt y^e: fd deft for y^e: fd Sum of 4£: 3^s: 0:
damages & Coft of fuite
the 9th of the ioth mo: 1685

Samuel Burges defired to have the
above action agt wright with drawn

(27)

At A Quarter Seffions held by the kings authority in
the name of willm Penn Propryatory & govrnr of the
Provinc of Pennfilvania & territorys thereunto
belonging for the County of Bucks att the Court houfe
the 9th day of the io month being the firft yeare of the
king James the 2nd his Raigne & the 5th of the propry
atorys govrmt 1685

The Juftices then Prefent

James Harrifon Thomas Janney willm Biles wm yardley

Jon Otter Edmund Bennet The petty Jury returned by

Nicholas walnn Sherrif the Sherrif the day abovefd

Luke Brindley deputy   Robt Cartor   John White

Phinehas Pemberton Clark   James Boyden   george Brown
                            Lyonel Brittan   willm Sanford
                            Henry Burcham   Jonathan Scaife

Edmund Lovet   Thomas Adkinſon   Daniel Brinſon   Jon Clows

*Joſeph Hollinghed being Calld into Court there Comeing none
to proſecute him the Court diſcharges him paying his ffees

Edmund Bennet Complanig to this Court that Joſeph growden hath ffenced up the kings Road wherefore y^e Court orders y^t Na: Allen Conſtable do take Care to Speake to ſd Growden to open y^e: ſd Road or ſett gates ells furter courſe will be taken about it

Complt being made by willm Biles how that he had Rd Abuſe by Philip Conway
the ſd=Philip Conway being Calld into Court acknowledged his fault
& promiſed to be of better behavior
for time to come the ofence being paſſed by the ſd W B where
fore the Court diſcharges him paying his fees

Complt being made agt Jacob Hall for Selling Rum to the Indians
the ſd Jacob Hall was Calld into Court & the wittneſs examined

Andrew Heath aged about twenty years being Atteſted & examined
Saith that about 3 weeks afore micheal maſs laſt Saith he ſaw
Jacob Hall Sell 2 Single pints of Rum to an Indian wch he taſted and att another time neare the time afforeſd he ſaw an
Indian Carry away 3 bottles of Rum wch Contained i gallon &
1 pt: out of the ſaid Jacob Halls Houſe

---

*Scratched out in the original record.

Samuel Hough Aged about twenty being Attefted & examined
Saith that the fd Jacob Hall Sold An Indian i ga: i pt of Rum
being the day before philadelphia yearly meeting laft & that he
was the Interpreter betwixt the fd Indian & the fd Jacob Hall
the fd Jacob Hall being examined about it doth acknowledg
that he fold the above mentioned Rum to the Indians
wherefore the Court fines him the Said Jacob Hall in five pounds

Jofeph Hollinfhead having been Comitted to goale becaufe of
Several abufes done to Ellenor ffenbank of this County & for

(28) for not giveing Suertys for his good behavior the fd Hollinfhed
being calld & after proclamation made none appearing agt the fd Hollins head the Court difcharges him

    This day was deld & acknowledged in open Court by Jon
& Thomas Rowland unto Samuel Burges one deede of
A Certaine tract of Land being about 200 ackers lying
betwixt Randulph Black fhaw & the great timber Swamp

    This day was deld & acknowledged in open Court by gilbert
wheeler Conftitute Attorney for morgan Druet one bill of
Sale of ioo Ackers of land adjoyning unto the fferre houfe
land over agt Burlington unto Thomas Holm
    for the ufe of Hannah Salter

    This day was deld and acknowledged in open Court one
bill of Sale of 500 ackers of Land lying neare the
lands of Ar: Cook of this County by David powell Conftitute
attorney by grifith Jones unto Thomas Holme
for the ufe of Thomas LLoyd

    The Court adjorns till to morrow morning att 8 th Clock
    io[th] Inftant the Court being Calld

Robt Lucas & Robt Cartor were Ellected &
Attefted high Conftables for this County

The Court adjorns till the ioth of the i month next

4th   i2   85   County of Bucks & Province of Pennfilvania
      mo

The action ⎰ Phinehas Pemberton Clark of the fd County plt
entered— ⎱   agt Daniel
              Brinfon of the fd County planter deft in an action
              of Cafe for wth holding 7ˢ 6ᵈ due
              to the fd plt for fees
                  4th i2th mo 85

the Declaration ⎫ Phinehas Pemberton makes Complt
      of   ⎬   agt
Phinehas Pemberton plt ⎰ Daniel Brinfon of the County of
                       ⎱ Bucks and
      agt   Province of Pennfilvania Planter
Daniel Brinfon deft   how that
                       the fd deft is Indebted to him the
                       fd plt the
                       Sum of Seven Shillings Six pence due

to the sd plt for fees wᶜʰ the fd deft unjuftly detaines tho the
fd plt hath fent two feverall times on purpofe for
his pay wherefore the fd plt brings his action of Cafe agt the
fd deft & prays Judgmt of Court agt the fd deft for the fd fum
of Seven Shillings Six pence damages & Coft of fuite

This action is with drawn the plt being Satiffyed

             The 5th day of the i2th month 1685   (29)
The action ⎰ John Brock of the County of Bucks in the
entered   ⎱   Province of
             Pennfilvania yeoman plt agt Charles pickring late of the
             County of new Caftle in the fd Province
             yeoman deft in an

action of Cafe for wth holding of 5 £ : 12^s : 6^d
due to the
fd plt

the Declaration of ⎫ The 5th day of the i2th month 1685
John Brock plt   ⎬ John Brock of the County of Bucks &
agt   Province of Penn
Charles Pickring   Silvania makes Complt agt: Charles
deft —   Pickring late of
                      Crifteena Creeke in the County of new
                      Caftel and Provinc
                      afforefd how that the fd deft is Indebted
to the fd plt
the Summ of five pounds twelve Shillings
Six pence
wch fd Sum he hath divers times promifed
to pay to the
fd plt but doth not pay it; but hath
unjuftly detained the fame
above three yeares & never as yett payd
any pte thereof
wherefore the fd plt brings his action of
Cafe &
prays Judgment of Court agt the fd deft
for the fd fum
of five pounds twelve Shillings & Six
penc damages &
Coft of fuite

Summonce   5th 12th mo 85

A Summonce granted agt: Charles Pickring
to anfwer the
Complt of John Brock att the next Quarter
feffions to
be held for this County att the Court houfe
the 10th
of the firft month

Return   this Summonc was executed according to
direction the 18th $\frac{12}{mo}$
1685 by Luke Brindley Deputy Sherrif

Wittneffes* A Summonce for Epharm Jackfon to give
in evidence in yᵉ:
afforefd action

A Summonce for Joseph millner to give
in evidenc in the aforefd
action

executed 4ᵗʰ i 85
─────
mo

pr Luke Brindley

5ᵗʰ day of the 12ᵗʰ month 1685

The Declaration of ⎤ John Brock of the County of Bucks &
John Brock plt ⎟ Province
⎟ of Pennfilvania plt makes Complt agt
agt ⎬ Charles
⎟ Pickring late of Criftina Creeke in the
Charles Pickring ⎟ County
deft ⎦ of newcaftell & Province afforefd how
that the
fd plt agreed with the fd deft in
liverpoole in
old England in the yeare 1682 to bring
him

A paffenger for this provinc & pd him for the fame in Englifh
monys
to the value 5 £ : 12ˢ 6ᵈ in this Cuntry pay but the fd plt
was difpointed of the fd paffenger as he was not brought
as above wherefore the fd plt demanded back his —
monys but the fd deft refufed to pay the fame whereupon
whereupon the diferenc betwixt them depending was
Referred to willm yardley & Thomas Philips arbitrators In
diferently Chofen by the fd ptyes wᶜʰ fd arbitrators awarded
upon the 10ᵗʰ 3 mo 1683
that if the fd Charles went for England & returned back
the yeare following that then the fd deft fhold bring over
a paffenger att his owne charge if the fd plts Correfpon
dent in England put A paffenger Aboare wᵗʰ the fd deft
to wᶜʰ the fd deft agreed but he did not go
for England nor bring the fd paffengr according to the fd
award

───────────

* Crossed out in original record.

wherefore the ſd plt demanded his monys wᶜʰ the ſd deft promiſed
to pay but doth not pay it but hath unjuſtly detained the Same above three yeares & never as yet pay any pte thereof wherefore
the ſd plt brings his act of Caſe and prays
Jugmt of Court agt the ſd deft for the ſd
Sum of 5 £ : 12 ˢ: 6 ᵈ damages & Coſt of ſuite

(30) the 22 day of the i2ᵗʰ mo : 1685 an Execution was granted agt
Jacob Hall for the levying of A fine of five pounds Impoſed
upon him the 9ᵗʰ of the io mo laſt paſt (att A Quarter ſeſſions
then held) for ſelling Rum to the Indians Conterary to the laws of this Province
Jacob Hall gave Security for the above 5 £ to be pd to the
govrnr on demand wch ſd bond is in P Pembertons hands

<table>
<tr><td colspan="3">The 22 day of the</td><td>i2</td><td>1685</td></tr>
<tr><td colspan="3"></td><td>mo</td><td></td></tr>
</table>

The Action Entered } gilbert wheeler of the County of Bucks and Province
of Pennſilvania plt agt Daniel Brinſon of the ſd County and Province in an acction of Aſſault & Battery
to the damage of 5 £

The Declaration of gilbert wheeler plt agt: Daniel Brinſon deft } County of Bucks in the Province of Pennſilvania the 22 day of the i2ᵗʰ mo 85 gilbert wheeler of the County and Provinc aforeſd
makes Compt agt Daniel Brinſon of the ſd County
and Province how that the ſd deft upon the 9ᵗʰ
day of this Inſtant the i2 month Came into the houſe of the ſd plt

& did then and there aſſault beate and with his hands
violently Strike martha the wife of the ſd
plt & in A moſt outrageous manner as he hath heretofore
done did then greatly abuſe
the ſd martha wife of the ſd plt
by Calling her beast repeating the Same with proteſtations
that She was whore & often the Duch=
=man's whore which together wth the violence of to the great
affrighting hurting & terreſying of the ſd martha thereby
& Damnifying the ſd plt to y^e: value of 5 £
he the ſd plt being then not att home who had left the Con=
=cerns and management both of his publique & private
affaires
with his ſd wife and who through the violence of the ſd
deft was
made Incapable of managing the affaires and hath ever
sinc been in great pains through the violence of his
blows therefore
that the ſd deft may be brought to
an acknowlegment of the great wrong done & that the ſd
plt may not be Ruined in his family & Eſtate by such wicked
outrages in his abſence the ſd plt brings his action & prays
Judgment of Court agt the ſd deft for damages & Coſt of ſuit

Summonc   A Summonc granted agt Daniel Brinſon to
Anſwer
the Compt of gilbert wheeler at the next Quarter
Seſſions to be held for this County at the Court
houſe
the ioth day i mo next

Return   this was Executed the 23 day of the i2 1685
                                               ―――
                                               mo

ioth   i   p Luke Brindley Deputy Sherrif
―――――   witneſſes A Summonc granted for mary
 mo   Ackerman
 85
gilbert wheeler   Ellizabeth Ridgway & Ellizabeth Lucas to
prayed this   give in theire evidence in the action
action to be   depending betwixt gilbert wheeler plt
with drawn   and Daniel Brinſon deft

              this was execu ⎫
              ted the 2 1 85 ⎪
                       ―――   ⎬
                        mo   ⎪
              p L Brindley   ⎭

(31)

The Action Entered } The 24th day of 12 moth 1685
Roger Hawkins of the County of Bucks & Province of
Pennsilvania plt agt gilbert wheeler of the sd County
& Province in action of Case for with holding of
three pounds fiveteen Shillings due to the sd plt

The Declaration of Rogr Hawkins plt agt gilbert wheeler deft } County of Bucks in the Province of Pennsilvania the 24th day of the 12th mo 1685
Rogr Hawkins of the County and Province
afforesd makes Complt agt gilbert wheeler
of the sd County and Province how that the sd deft
is Indebted to the sd plt the Sum of five pounds
wch is due & owing for A psell of goods Sold to John wright late of the County afforesd in the 2nd month last past wch sd sum of five
pounds the sd gilbert wheeler promised to pay or Cause to be pd to the sd deft on acct of the sd wright att or before the latter end of the third month next ensueing but the sd plt hath only pd in pte
of the sd Sum 1 £ 5s 0d and the remameing pte being
three pounds fiveteen Shillings the sd deft unjustly detaines to the great damage of the sd plt wherefore the sd plt brings his action of Case
& prays Judgmt of Court agt the sd deft for
the sd Sum of three pounds fiveteen shillings damages & Cost
of suite

24th   12   84
mo

Summonce   A Summonce granted agt gilbert wheeler to Answer
the Complt of Rogr Hawkins att the next Quarter Sessions to be held for this County att the Court house the 10th day of the 1 month next

Return This was executed the 25th day of the 12th month
1685 p Luke Brindley Deputy Sherrif

wittneffes A fumm granted for Jofuah Boare to give in
evidenc in the action depending betwixt Rogr
Hawkins plt & g wheeler deft
this was executed the 2nd $\frac{i}{mo}$ 85 p L Brindley

$\frac{i0th \quad i}{mo}$ 1685 Rogr Hawkins declared that
he wold
have the above action with drawn &
accordingly
it is with drawn

The 12 day of the 11th month 1685

willm Hague appeared before James Harrifon one of
the Juftices
for this County & then oblidged him Self in the fum of
20 £
to the propryatory & govrnr for his appearance att the
next
Court to be held for this County the 10th $\frac{i}{mo}$ next & to
be of good
behavior in the meane time as allfo Robt Lucas & Jon
wood
have as fuertyes for the fd willm Hague in like manner
oblidged
them felves in 20 £ Apeice for the appearance of the fd
will and
for his good behavior in the meane time

(32)

At A Quarter feffions held by the kings authority in the name
of wm Penn Propryatory and govrnr of Pennfilvania and the
territorys thereunto belonging for the County of Bucks
att the Court houfe the 10th day of the 1ft month 168 $\frac{6}{5}$

being the 6th yeare of the propryatorys govrmt

The Juftices then prfent

James Harrifon	Thomas Janney	Edmund Bennet
william yardley	willm Biles	Jon Otter
willm Beakes		

Nicholas walm Sherrif
Luke Brindley his deputy
Phinehas Pemberton Clark

the Court being Called the Court adjorns untill
the ellection of the reprfentatives to serve in
Counfell and Affembly for this County
be Ended

poſt meridian

i deed of 100 Ackers of Land Conveyed by Jeffry
Hawkins to his brother Rogr was this day deld
& acknowledged in open Court by phinehas =
pemberton Conſtitute attorney by the ſd Jeffery
unto the ſd Rogr Hawkins

i deed of 130 Ackers of Land Conveyed
by Tho woolf unto Elizabeth gibbs was
this day dld & acknowledged in open Court
unto Edmund Lovet Conſtitute Attorney by the
ſd: Tho woolf

willm Hague having this day appeared in Court
the Court difcharges him & his baile none
Coming to pſecute him.

Jon Brock plt appeares to the action agt
Charles pickring,

    Charles pickring appeares not

In as much as y^e: ſd Charles pickring hath not this day
appeared according to Summonce this Court gives Jugmt
agt him by default & it is adjudged the ſd
Charles Shall pay the ſd fum of 5 £: 12^s: 6^d
& the Coſt of fuite

    The Court adjorns for 2 houres

(33)

In as much as Complt hath beene made this day to this
Court that the new road is not Layd out fo well as
it may be this Court orders that Robt Lucas Henry
Baker Sam Dark Rich Hough Thomas Stackhoufe
& Jon Brock with the Affiftance of John Swift &
Henry marjorum Henry pointer Robt Hall Nich
waln & Ifreal Taylor do lay out the ſd Road
to the ut moſt of Extent of the ſd County

In as much as the Conſtables of this County hath
this day prſented the want of men in the
Several diviſions of this County to veiue the
Sufitienty of al fences this Court doth ordr
that Rich Ridgway & Sam Dark ſerve in ye:
office for that pte of the river below the falls
as far as the govrnrs plantation
Henry marjerum & Andrew Ellot above the falls
Jon palmer & Jonathan Scaiſe for the middle
p pte Neſhaminah Robt Heaton Ezra Croſdale
Lower pte of Neſhamina James Boyden & Robt Hall
that pte the river below the govrnrs

David Davis hath this day appeared in Court & hath
deſired that his appearance may be Recorded
wch is accordingly Recorded in as much as he
Reports that he was bound by the laſt aſſizes
here to appeare here

David Davis haveing been Cald into Court this day
to give Security for the Eſtate of H Comley orphan Son of
H. C. deceased according to A former ordr of the
laſt orphants Court & to give in his accts & he
hath promiſed to give Sufitiont Secury for the
ſd Eſtate in one months time or for ſo much of
the Eſtate as is realy in his hands & will ſurrendr
up all the Specialtys that he hath taken on the
ſd Eſtate and the accountſ of what is due
by the ſeveral pſons Concerned in the ſd
Eſtate

The Court adjorns untill the 9th 4th month next

(34) At a private Seſſions held by the kings
Authority in the name of willm Penn proprya
tory & govrnr of this Provinc and Territorys
there unto belonging this i3 day of the 2 86
                                           ──
                                           mo

The Juſtices then prſent

James Harriſon   willm yardley
willm Biles   willm Beakes
          P P Cl:

Inas much as David Davis laſt Court of Quarter

Seſſions promiſed to give ſecurity for the Eſtate
of Henry Comeley orphan to Henry Comeley
& that the ſd David Davis is Since dead
therefore the Juſtices Saw there was A neceſſity
to meete together this day to Concider of Away
how to ſecure the Eſtate of the ſd orphan where
=fore it being ppoſed wch way it Shall be ſecured
David powel on the behalf of the ſd David Davis
hath offered that if this Court will ordr any pſons
to Rc what goods there is in David Davis Cuſtody
or on the plantation he did occupy he will
deliver them or So much of them
as Can be ſpared & will give ſecurity for
the remaneing pte of what is due So that
he may be Suſitiontly diſcharged for what he
pays on the orphans acct: wherefore
this Court orders that willm Biles and
willm Paxſon do go on 5th
day next & then Rc ſuch goods & specialtys as ſhall be
delivered by David powell for the uſe of the
ſd orpant, & give him diſcharges for ſo much
as they Rc from him either in ſpecialtys
or goods at the prices as they ſhall be valued
by 2 Juditious pſons or more as may be
Choſen by the ſd wm Biles willm paxſon &
David powel

  This Court adjorns

                (35)

<u>Ejectione ffirme</u> Bucks in Pennſilvania The 22 day of the
           3 month <u>1686</u>

<u>The action
Entered</u> Abraham Cocks of the ſd County plt agt
     micheal Huff
     of the ſd County Deft in an action Ejectione
      firme
     for with holding the fferry houſe over gainst
     Burlington & lands wth the appurtenances
      thereunto belonging

The Declaration of Abraham Cocks plt agt micheal Huff deft } Bucks in Pennsilvania the 22 day of the 3 month 1686

Abraham Cocks of the County & provinc afforesd
planter makes Complt how that he had Confirmed
to him by leafe (bearing date the eight day of the 3 mo
1686 & to be Expired the 30 day of the 2 month
next enfuing from Joseph English Junior of the sd
County planter) one houfe Called the fferry houfe over
agt Burlington & 32 Ackers of land with the appur–
=tenances thereunto belonging late in the poffeffion of
Samuel Clif of the afforesd County deceased and
father in law to the sd Joseph and that after poffeffion
of the sd houfe & lands was delivered
to the sd Abraham Cocks micheal Huff of the sd County
ordinary keep entered the sd houfe and —
forceably keeps poffeffion thereof & of the lands
thereunto appertaining to the damage of
the sd Abraham Cocks and Conterary to the kings
peace wherefore that the sd plt may have the sd
houfe and lands with the appurtenances thereunto
belonging according to Contract he the sd plt brings
his action Ejectione ffirme and prays Judment
of Court that the sd micheal Huff may be removed

The Endorsmt } 24th 3 mo 1686

micheal Huff thou may pceive that Abraham
Cocks hath brought his action agt thee for the houfeing
and lands in thy poffeffion tryable at the next
Court to be held for this County the 9th 4 mo
next Thefe are therefore

    to defire thee to defend thy tittle or they undr whom
    thou Claims to appeare to this declaration and make him or them felves defts there unto
    and by rule of Court Confefs the leafe Entry & Ejectmt & Infift only upon the tittle Ells Judgt will be Entered by default & poffeffion will be delivered accordingly to the plt.
            Phinehas Pemberton
     22 3 86   Cl p Bucks
       mo

Summonc granted agt micheal Huff to anfwer the Complt of Abra:
    Cocks att the next Court to be held for this County att y^e :
    Court houfe the 9th of the 4th month next

Return this was Executed the 25th of the 3 month 1686
   p Luke Brindley deputy fherrif

(36)
     County of Bucks in Pennfil: the 22 day of
The action Entered   the 3 mo 1686

    Nicholas moore Efquire of the County of Philadelphia plt agt gilbert wheeler of the County of Bucks deft in an action of debt for with holding of i2 £ : 04^s: io^d due to be pd upon demand

The declaration of
Nicholas moore plt Bucks in pennfilvania the 22 3 86
               mo
  agt   Nicholas moore Efquire of the County
gilbert wheeler deft of
    Philadelphia and province afforefd makes
    Complt agt gilbert Wheeler of the County of Bucks afforefd
    how that the fd deft is Indebted the Sum of
    34:£ : 16^s: 10^d Currant monys of Pennfilvania due to be

payd upon demand as will appear by A
bill undr the hand of the ſd deft bearing date
the 27th of 8ber 1684 and all tho the ſd plt
hath divers times made demand of his ſd monys yet
the ſd deft unjuſtly detaines the ſum of
12 £ 04 s : 10 d being pte of the ſd Debt
wherefore the ſd plt brings his action of Debt
and prays Judgmt of Court agt the ſd deft for
the ſd Sum of twelve pounds Sixteen ſhillings
and tenpence damages & Coſt of ſuite

Summonce granted 22 3 mo 1686 agt gilbert Wheeler to anſwer the
Complt of Nicholas moore att the next Court
to be held for this County att the Court houſe the 9th of the 4th mo next

Return this was Executed the 23 day of the 3 month
1686 p Luke Brindley Deputy Sherrif

with drawing The 9th of the 4th month 1686
Nicholas moore deſired to have the action with drawn

(37)

At A Court of Quarter Seſſions held by the kings
Authority in the name of Wm penn propryatory
and govrnr of Pennſilvania and the territorys
thereunto belonging for the County of Bucks
at : the Court houſe the 9th day of the 4 mo
1686 being the 6th yeare of the propryatorys govrmt

The Juſtices then prſent
Thomas Janney   Willm Biles
willm yardley   John otter

Sherrif
Nicholas waln
Luke Brindley deputy
phinehas pemberton Clark

Abraham Cocks plt being called to profecute his fuite agt micheal
Huff deft appeared
  micheal Huff being calld appeared
The Jury Attefted John Clows foreman John Brock Rich Hough
Lyonel Brittan Jon wood Tho: Tunneclif H: Baker
Samuel overton Tho: woolfe Robt Heaton wm: Paxfon
    Tho: Stakehouf fen^r
    the declaration of Abraham Cocks being
Read & proved by the teste mony of ffrancis Roffell & phinehas pemberton who fay the faw the leafe fealed & delivered on
the premises & after faw the fd micheal Huff to Enter the fd houfe
& Land

after micheal Huff being Calld to Anfwer fd he had no tittle to the fd houfe or Land & therefore Shold yeild it up the Jury returned & Calld over do fay they find for the plt

Therefore the Court gives Judgment & it is adjudged that
the fd Abraham Cocks Shall have poffeffion accordingly delivered to him

this day was delivered and acknowledged in open Court one deed of 50 ackers of land fold by Jon Bainbridge of this County to James Clay poole of Philadelphia
by Rich Hough Conftitute attorney to Thomas Woolfe
  Conftitute attorney to the fd James Clay poole of
    Philadelphia bearing
date 7th 3 month 1686

this day was returned and acknowledged in open Court by Shadrach walley Conftitute attorney by Robt Holgat one deed of 250 ackers of Land bearing date i9th of the 3 month 1686 unto Robt Heaton of this County

this day was delivered and acknowledged in open Court by phinehas pemberton Conftitute attorney
to Thomas Holmes of Philadelphia one deed
of one hundred and i8 ackers of land bearing

date the 18 day of the 3 mo^th 86 unto Nicholas
Waln of this County

(38) whereas there was Judgment of Court formerly paſt
agt Charles pickring by default in an action depending
betwixt the ſd Charles deft & John Brock plt and
the the ſd Charles hath this day appeared in Court
and there alledged that he Cold not poſſible appeare
att the Court when the ſd Judgment was obtained
being farr diſtant wherefore he the ſd Charles offered
that if the ſd Jon Brock wold be pleased to lett fall
the ſd Judgmnt & take no advantage thereof he
the ſd Charles wold referr the ſd matter w^ch
was the grownd of the ſd action to Such pſons
as ſhould be by them Indiferently Choſen where
upon the ſd John Brock hath deſired the ſd Judgment
of Court may be made voyd & they have both this
day in open Court declared that they have wholey
referred the ſd matter to James Harriſon
Nicholas Waln Thomas Janney & william yardley
psons Indeferently Choſen by them to whom they
leave the Same and all matters relateing there to to
be wholey defided & determined by the ſd partyes
& for theire true pformance and obſervance
of the ſd award the ſd partyes Shall make the ſd
Charles pickring & John Brock have oblidged themſelves
theire heires Executors & adminiſtrators Each to other
in
in the penal Sum of ten pounds for Confirmation
whereof the ſd Charles pickring & Jon Brock the ſd
day have put here to theire hands

         Charles pickring
         John Brock

the Court adjorns for one houre

Robt Doue & Ellizabeth Andrews hath this day
 appeared
in Court and there acknowledged A bond bearing date
the 3 day of the 12th month 1685 wherein they are
oblidged to Richard Bagnel of Burlington in Sixty
pounds to Confeſs or Cauſe to be Confeſſed Judgment in
the County of Bucks of all & ſingular there reſpective
Shares of all theire lands good cattles & Chattles that
they are then poſſeſſed of or with in the space of 4

yeares Shall be poſſeſt of & they the ſaid Robt
Doue & ffrancis Andrews have this day appeared
in this Court & have accordingly Confeſt Judgmt
of all theire eſtate they have or ſhall have as above
ſd

whereas there was A diferenc depending betwixt (39)
    Ellenor
pownall and ffrancis Hough wch diference so depending
was heard and determined by willm yardley & Thomas
Janney wch Judgmt was this day Read & by this
Court approved of
where as Severall pſons upon Ne ſhaminah
creeke have complained of the want of A road to
the ferry houſe over agt Burlington this Court doth
therefore ordr that Edmund Bennet Nicholas waln
Robt Heaton Jon otter Iſrael Taylor & Robt
Hall & Shadrach walley do lay out A Road from
wrights town to the ſd fferry houſ being a convenient
    Landing and give an
acct thereof to the next Court
whereas there was formerly ordered ſome pſons
to lay out A road to the Extent of this County
from the ferry houſe att the falls & thereupon
the ſd Road was accordingly layd out but Richard
Thacher makes Complt that the ſd road runs through
his land to his great damage wherefore this Court
ordrs N waln and Henry paxton to veiue the
ſd road in that place & endeavor to regulate
it as well as may be for the Eaſe of the ſd
thacher
this day was delivered and acknowledged in open Court
    by
Nicholas Waln of this County one deed of 200 ackers of
lands bearing date 6th 4 month
1686 to James Dilworth* Conſtitute attorney to Edmund
    Cuttler
of this County
This day was delivered and acknowledged in open Court
by the ſd Nicholas Waln one deed of 50 ackers of land
    bearing

---

* Name crossed out in record book.

date the 5th 4th month i686 unto Thomas Stackhoufe
Junior of this County.
This day was delivered and acknowledged in open Court
by
Richard Ridgway of this County one deed of A Small
piece of land being in Eftimation about 4 ackers of
Land bearing date the firft 4 mo: i686 unto philip
Conway of the fd County
This day was delivered and acknowledged in open Court
by philip Conway abovefd one deed of 2 peices or
parfells of land the one being the above mentioned
of about 4 ackers and the other of 50 ackers
bearing date the 6th 4 month 1686 unto
Thomas Dickenfon of this County
*This day was delivered and acknowledged in open
Court by phinehas pemberton Conftitute
attroney to James Harrifon of this County one deed of
iio ackers
of land bearing date the firft of the 4th month 1686
unto Edward Stanton of the Said County

(40) This day was deld and acknowledged in open Court
one deed of four hundred Eighty ackers of Land
bearing date the 5th 4 mo: i686 by James Dillworth
of this County to, Jon Hornor of weft new Jarfey
This day was delivered and acknowledged in open Court
by Jeffery Hawkins of this County one deed of iio
ackers of land
bearing date the i 10th mo i685 to Jon Collins of
the fd County
This day was delivered and acknowledged in open
Court by Phinehas Pemberton Conftitute attorney
by James Harrifon of this County one Conveyance
of iio ackers of land bearing date the firft of
this Inftant the 4th month unto Edward ftanton
of this County
The Court adjourns to the 8th of 7th month next
          Willm Beakes plt agt: Lawrenc Bannor
          deft:
The   The 28th day of the   5 i686
                                    mo

---

*This paragraph has four scratch marks in ink over it in the original
record.

action Entered	Willm Beakes of the County of Bucks and Provinc of Pennſilvania plt agt: Lawrenc Bannor of the ſd County & provinc deft. in an action of debt for with holding of 4 £ 10 ˢ 00 ᵈ
28 5 86 mo	
Summonce	granted agt Lawrence Bannor to anſwer the Complt of Willm Beakes at the next Court to be held the 8 day of the 7 next mo
	Return this was executed the 28: 5 86 mo by me Luke Brindley Deputy Sherrif
the Declaration of Willm Beakes plt agt Lawrenc Bannor deft	Bucks in Pennſilvania the 25ᵗʰ day of the 5 1686 mo Willm Beakes of the County afforeſd yeoman makes Compt agt Laurence Bannor of the ſd County Huſbandman how that the ſd deft is Indebted the Sum of foure pounds ten ſhillings Currant Silver monys of Pennſilvania due to be payd to the ſd Willm Beakes the 29ᵗʰ day of the 7ᵗʰ month laſt paſt as will appeare by A bill under the hand & ſeale of the ſd Lawrenc Bannor bearing date the 20ᵗʰ day of the 2 month 1685 & altho the ſd plt hath divers times made demand of the

ſd debt yet the ſd deft unjuſtly detaines the
Same wherefore the ſd plt brings his action
& prays Judgmt of Court agt the ſd deft for
the ſd Sum of 4 £ : 10ˢ 00ᵈ damages & Coſt of Suite

County Court of Bucks — — action entered } The 28 $\frac{5}{mo}$ i686 (41)
Willm Beakes plt agt Lawrenc Bannor deft in An action upon A Replevin for 2 oxen Impounded by ſd Deft

The 28ᵗʰ $\frac{5}{mo}$ 86

County Court of Bucks

A Replevin granted
 for the twoo oxen of Will Beakes Impounded by
  Laurenc Bannor

The Sherrifs Return
 This was executed the 28ᵗʰ $\frac{5}{mo}$
 i686 by mᵉ Luke Brindley
  deputy Sherrife

The Declaration of Willm Beakes plt agt Lawrenc Bannor deft } willm: Beakes of the County of Bucks & Provinc of Pennſilvania Complaines of Lawrence Bannor of the ſd County in A plea for that

$=\overline{18}$. $\frac{.\ \ 6}{mo}$ where as the afforeſd Lawrence Bannor did on the 28 day of the $\frac{5}{mo}$ Laſt paſt take of the
goods of the ſd plt that is to Say 2 oxen
of the price of 12 £ : and tha Same did un=
=juſtly detaine againſt the ſuertyes & Safe pledges

of the Said Willm Beakes whereupon the íd
Willm Beakes Saith he is worſe & hath damage
to the value of forty Shillings & therefore he
hath brought this Suite & Craves Judgmt of
this Court agt. the afforeſd Lawrenc Bannor
for the Said damage & Coſt of Suite

23 6 86
   ––
   mo

Summonce granted agt Laurence Bannor to anſwer
the Complt of W: Beakes (in A plea for takeing
of 2 oxen of the ſd Wm: Beakes & unjuſtly
detaineing the ſame) att the next Court to be held
for this County the 8th day of the 7th month next

Return The 24th 6 1686 the within Summonce was
                 ––
                 mo

executed according to direction by Luke Brindley
deputy ſherriſ

(42) Pennſilvania   16th 6   86
                                                  ––
                                                  mo

County Court ⎫
     of   ⎬ Joſeph knight plt
   Bucks   ⎭   agt
                Ralph milner deft in A plea of Debt
                for with holding of twenty pounds

Declaration
County Court of ⎫ Joſeph knight plantife ⎫   16th 6   86
    Bucks   ⎭   agt   ⎬   ––
                    Ralph milner deft   ⎭   mo

Joſeph knight of the towne & County of
  Philadelphia
Cuttler Complaines agt Ralph milner of the
  County of Bucks
wheelwright in A plea of Debt for that
  whereasthe
Said deft by his penal bond under his hand &
  Seale dated
the 17th day of the 10th month 1685 bound and
  oblidged
him ſelf to have pd to the ſd plt his heires or
  aſſigneſs therein

mentioned the fum of twenty pounds Currant Silver

monys of the Said provinc Conditioned for the Saveing harmles

from al action or Caufes of action or charges that may come or accrew for or by reason of a bond of tenn pounds ═══

bearing date the 19th day of the 10th month 1685 ═══

wch the fd plt: at the requeft of fd deft Entered into

& Stands bound thereby wth the fd deft to Jon Crapp of Philadelphia Senior for the pformance

of the Condition therein expreffed as the fd obligation of

twenty pounds herew^th in Court to be produced will

teftefye all wch the fd plt doth averr, and altho the fd plt hath divers times requefted & defired the

fd deft to pforme his Covenats & Contracts wth the fd

Crapp that he the fd plt might not be any ways Indemnifyd

by the fd penal bond of 10 £ yet never the lefs the fd

deft hath hitherto neglected & not pformed the Same

where fore the fd John Crapp hath brought his action

of debt agt the fd Jofeph knight herein plantife and

at A Court held at philadelphia the 7th of the 5 month

laft paft the Said John Crapp obtained Judgmt agt the

Said Jofeph knight herein plantif for the fd Sum of

ten pounds & the Cofts of Suite whereupon Execution was

accordingly granted as will be made appeare in Court

by the records of the ſd Court of Philadelphia whereby
the ſd plt Joſeph knight is there by demnifyed to
the value of ten pounds wth the Coſt of ſuite allowed &
adjudged by the ſd Court where upon the plt brings his
Suite & craves Judgmt of this Court agt the ſd deft for
the ſd Sum of twenty pounds Currant ſilver monys as
afforeſd wth Coſt of ſuite

$$\frac{16^{th} \quad 6 \quad 86}{mo}$$

Summonce A Summonce was granted agt Ralph milner
to anſwer the above Complt of of Joſeph
knight att the next Court of Quarter
Seſſions to be held for this County att
the Court houſe the 8th day of the 7th month

Return This was executed the 25 of the 6th month
1686 by me Luke Brindley deputy Sherrif

Jon pidcock plt agt g wheeler deft in plea
of debt for wth holding 25 £

$$\text{iſt} \quad \frac{7}{mo} \quad 86$$ Joſeph knight prayed the ſd
action agt
Ralph milner might be wth drawn
wch is accordingly   (43)

(44)

John gray agt gilbert wheeler of A plea of debt:
gilbert wheeler plt agt Jon pidcock in a plea of
covenant

gilbert wheeler plt agt Jon pidcock deft
in A plea of treſpaſs on the Caſe

(46)

Att A Court of Quarter Seffions held by the
kings authority
in the name of Willm Penn Propryatory and
govrnr
of the Province of Pennfilvania and the
Territorys there
unto belonging for the County of Bucks att the
Court houfe of the fd County the 8th day of the
7th month
being the 2nd yeare of the raigne of James the
2nd
over England &c king & the 6th of the
Propryatorys
govrmt 1686

The Juftices then prfent
Arthur Cooke   Thomas Janney   Willm Biles
and Willm yardley
Sherrif Abraham Whearley
deputy Sherrif Luke Brindley

Phinehas Pemberton Cl:
John gray agt gilbert Wheeler in A plea
of Cafe
Jon gray appears   gilbert wheeler appears
Jury attefted   the dec
The declaration being read the deft
acknowledged the Complt: & Confeffed the
debt & promifed to pay the Same in Rye
att 3^س the bufhell & wheat att 4^س the
bufhell the one half thereof in twoo days
time and the other half in ten weeks time
to be pd in Rye two thrds & wheat one
thrd & delivered att the prices above att
the houfe of the fd Jon gray
This day was delivered and acknowledged in
open
Court one patten of 500 ackers of land wth
an affignment on the back thereof from
Willm Cartr to Robt Cartor bearing date
the 23 5 mo 86 by Ifral Taylor Conftitute
attorney to fd Wm Cartor

whereupon the Court ordrs that if the
Said gilbert wheeler faile in payment according

to promife that then Execution be granted
for Leying the fd debt on the eftate of the
fd g wheeler upon requeft of the fd Jon gray

(47)

John pidcock plt agt g wheeler deft in an
action of debt for 25 £
John pidcock appeares: gilbert wheeler deft apprs
the declaration being read & the bill of debt for 25 £
being
produced the fd deft Confeffed the bill
willm yardley Conftitute attorney to Jon Alfop
delivered i Conveyance of 1000 ackers of
land date the i9th day of the 5th month 1684
unto Tho: Tunneclif
Jeffery Hawkins acknowledged & delivered one
deed of iio ackers of land to Jon Collins
bearing date the firft day 7 mo
gilbert wheeler agt Jon pidcock in A
plea of Covenant
The declaration being read
the deft craves A hours time to put in his plea

The Court adjorns for one houre

The Anfwer Read defends the force & puts him
Self on the Cuntry
grand Jury Attefted Jon Brock Charles Biles Rich
Ridgway Richard Lundy micheal Huff Ifrael Taylor
Robt Heaton Jofeph Englifh fr John
Coates John Cuff ffrancis Hough Tho Stackhoufe Ser
Jon Collins
Jeffery Hawkins Jofhua Boare Jofeph wood
bill found   RandulphSmalwood
being Convicted of abufeing and endeavoring
to force Ellizabeth Wilfon by the teftemony
of the fd Ellizabeth & by the teftemony of Ifaac
partington & Willm ffowler puts him felf on god &
the Cuntry
his Cuntry hath found him guilty
The Court adjorns till 7 tomorrow morning

petty J:
Attefted   John Clows one of the Jury for not attending
the

Wm Beakes
Jo milner
Jo: Brock
Sa overton
Tho Tunneclif
La: Bannor
Lio: Brittan
Jo: purſlone
wm Dungan
wm paxſon
wm Dark ⎱ atteſted
Jon Hough ⎰

Court according to the houre appointed the
Court fines him in ten ſhillings
This fine was remitted by ordr of Court

(48)

Wm Beakes
J: milner
J Brock
S overton
T Tuneclif
L Bannor
L Brittan
J purſlone
W Dungan
w paxſon
w: Dark
J Hough

John Pidcock being Indicted & arraignd for
makeing an aſſault on his maſter g wheeler
hath pleaded gilty to the ſd Indictmt
and the Court awards Judgmt on his ſd
   Confeſſion
Randulph Smalwood being Indicted &
   arraigned
for Scandelizeing & defameing Rachel milner
wife of Ralph milner & ſd Smalwood hath
pleaded not gilty & for his tryal hath put him
Self on god and the Cuntry
wᶜʰ Cuntry hath found him gilty
atteſted
whereupon the Court awards Judgmt
george glave being Indicted & arraigned for
   aſſaulting
Edmund Bennet hath pleaded gilty & refers
him ſelf to the mercy of king propryatory
& the bench
whereupon the Court awards Judgmt
The Court give Judgmt & it is adjudged
that george gleave Shall for his offence pay
to the govrnr A fine of 10ˢ & his fees &
that he be bound to the good behavior & to
appeare att the next Court

The Court gives Judgmt that Jon pidcock
for his offence Shall pay to the govrnr A
fine of 3 £ & be bound to his good behavior
& to appeare at next Court
The Court adjudges that Randulph
   Smalwood

for his firſt offence be whipped on his bare back 20 Laſhes & pay fees
The Court adjudges that the ſd Randulph for
his defameing Rachel milner Shall pay A fine of 10 £ to the governr & 10 £ damages to to Ralph
milner & fees & be bound to his good behavior and
to appeare att the next Court
The Court ordrs the ſd priſoners to be taken into
Cuſtody and Secured untill the ſd fines & fees be
pd or ſecured to be payd.

(49)

the Court nominates & appoints Conſtables
for the falls Jon wood
James Dilworth for the uper pte of neſhaminah
for the lower pte of neſhaminah
John Bowen
for the midle lotts Rogr Hawkins atteſted
wch Conſtables Shall Serve for the Succeding yeare
willm Dungeon for the lower pte of the river
The Court appoints Henry Baker Jon Rowland Thomas Stakehouſe & Edmund Cuttler do ſerve overſeers of the high ways for the succeeding yeare
The Court appoints the ſame peace makers y^t: were the laſt yeare
This day was delivered and acknowledged by one conveyance of 102½ ackers of land bearing date the firſt day 3 moth 86 by Rich Ridgway Conſtitute attorney to Daniel Brinſon to Jon Nicholls & Ellias Nicholls
This Court ordrs that Phinehas Pemberton & Jo Nicholls Shall heare & examine the County Treaſurers accounts & bring them into the next Court & that in the meane time the Collectors bring in theire arreares of the monys due & theire accounts forthwith

  The Court adjorns for one houre

This day was deld & Acknowledged one deed
of 150 ackers dated the 1 day of 7 mo: 86
by Henry pawlin to willm paxson
grand Jury prsented gilbert wheeler upon the
Information of Jon pidcock for selling Rum
Contrary to the law
to wch prsentmt he has pleaded not gilty & traverses
the sd prsentmt
A petition dated the 8th day 7 mo: 1686 from Tho Cartor of
Philadelphia Concering A boy of sd Cartors then in Custody of
wm Beakes was read in Court to wch the Court answered haveing
heard the alegations on both sides that the boy mentioned in the sd
petition Shold be delivered by the sd wm Beakes to the Said
tho Cartor the sd Cartor first paying sd Beakes 4 ga: Rum and

(50) wm Beakes to pay charges of Court
wee Jon pidcock and gilbert wheeler both of
the County of Bucks do acknowledge our selves
to be bound to the propryatory and govrnr
in the sum of Six pounds for
the true payment of A fine of three pounds
to the propryatory & govrnr Imposed on the
sd pidcock by this Court & for fees to be paid
upon the said Conviction to be levyed on the
lands goods & Chattles of the Said pidcock & wheeler
theire heires Executors & administrators
wee george glave & Jon: Hough both of this
County do acknowledge our selves to be bound
to the propryatory and govrnr in the sum of
three pounds for payment of A fine of 10^{s}
& fees upon the sd Conviction to be levyed as above
george glave in like mannor stands obliged to
the govrnr in 40 £ to be of good behavior &
appeare at the next Court
John pidcock in like mannor stands oblidge to the
govr in 40 £ to be of good behavior to ward
all people & to appeare at the next Court

The Court adjourns untill the 20th $\underline{8}$ next
$\phantom{The Court adjourns untill the 20^{th} \underline{8}}$ mo

This day Rich Noble hath appeared in Court & defired to
have the monys that hath been made appeare formerly
to the orphans Court to be due wch was 20 £ owing
to him out of the Eftate of willm Clark pte thereof being
Con-
= tracted by the fd Clark & his wife in theire life time
& for the fuftenance of the orphans of the fd
Clark Sinc there parents deceafe therefore this Court
doth ordr that i00 Ackers being pte of the tract of
land belonging to the fd orphans Shall be layd out to the
fd R Noble in full
Satiffaction for his debt; if it appeare that
the whole tract of the fd orphans Land do amount to
300 Ackers or upwards

              adjourned 5th   8   next
                               mo

      County of Bucks in the Province of Pennfilvania
At an orphans Court held by the kings Authority in
    the name
of Willm Penn propryatory and govrnr of the fd
    Province
and Territorys thereunto belonging att the Court
    houfe
the 2 day of i month being the firft third day of the
weeke in the fd month 1685
        The Juftices then prfent
  James Harrifon   Willm Biles   Willm Beakes
  Jo'n otter   Edmund Bennet Willm yardley
      The Sherrif N waln
         his   Deputy L Brindley
              phinehas pemberton Clark
John Otter & Edmund Bennet have brought in an
    acct of the
Age of James Spencer
the age of Samuel Spencer
& the death of theire father as will apeare upon
    record
before
and the acct of the Eftate they Say they have not
    as yett
brought in therefore this Court orders that A true &
pfect acct of the fd Eftate of the fd Spencer be
    brought
in to the next Court

the Indentures of Peter Hall were drawn & fealed
before 2 Juſtices according to order

according to order Lawrenc Bannor hath brought in an
acct of the orpans of Willm Venables & it doth appeare
by the ſd accts that of Heycocks & venables
Eſtate there remains 400 ackers of Land wth the Improvements thereon to the ſd orphans of venables
Except two pounds Nineteen Shillings five pence w^{ch}
ſd ſum is Chargeable upon the ſd Eſtate of Land w^{ch}
ſd acct is by this Court allowed & accepted
David Davis hath pleaded that he was not Legally Summonced
to this Court & therefore had not time to Anſwer the Said Summonce
this Court orders that David Davis Shall bring in his acct.
in twelve days time to willm Biles & wm Beakes in wch ſd time
the ſd Davis has promiſed to bring in his accts.
this Court orders that there be no monys
or debts that are pte of the Eſtate of H Comley orphan drawn out of any Suffitient pſons hands by the ſd Da Davis untill Such
time as the ſd Da Davis has brought in his accts & Sattiſfy
the ptyes ordered to take the accts & that the ſd Eſtate is
Secured for the uſe of the ſd orphan by the ſd David

(51)

This Court doth ordr that the Indtures for peter Hall be
drawn & ſigned before Some 2 Juſtices of peace
willm Biles being aſked about the placeing of the 2 orphants
of James Hall unplaced do Say they made Enquiry for A place but
before they heare of A place the mother of the Said Childrn removed them out of this County
Lawrence Bannor hath brought in an Impfect acct of the
Eſtate of the orphants of willm venables therefore this
Court doth ordr that Lawrence Bannor bring in A

true & pfect acct unto phinehas pemberton
before the firſt day of the iith mo
next

this day was deld A deed of 5000 Ackers of Land
ſold by Tho Rudyard unto Andrew Robinſon by
Robt
Lucas & Luke Brindley Conſtitute attorney by
Thomas
Rudyard unto Lyonel Brittan Conſtitute attorney by
Andrew Robinſon

this day was deld & acknowledged in open Court A
deed of 200 Ackers of Land ſold by
Ann milcome to willm Biles

this day was deld & acknowledged in open Court A
deed of 50 Ackers of Land Sold
by Ann milcome to philip Conway

this Court adjorns untill the firſt third of the
firſt month next

A Summonce for David Davis to appeare att the
orphants
Court to be held the 2 $\frac{i}{mo}$ next then & there to give
an acct of the Eſtate of Henry Comley orphant &
to give Secury for the ſd Eſtate

Whereas Complt hath beene made to me by Joane the
wife of Joſeph
Engliſh Senior of the County of Bucks & Province of
Pennſilvania how that David Davis
of this County was nominated Executor to the laſt will
& teſtament of Henry Comley late
of this County deceaſed & former Husband to the ſd Joan
& that the ſd
David hath adminiſtered on the ſd Eſtate & taken
the Same into his poſſeſſion
& that Shee is afraid that if Some Speedy Courſe be not
taken for the ſecuring of the ſd Eſtate now in the hands
of the ſd
David, that Henry Comley orphant & Son to Henry
Comley
aforeſd will Suſtain loſſe in his Eſtate by the ſd David
Theſe are therefore by the kings Authority in the name
of the
Propryatory & govrnr to require thee to Summonce the ſd
David Davis that he be & appeare att the next orphants
Court
to be held for this County the 2nd day of the firſt month

(52)
next then & there to give A true acct of the ſd Eſtate as allſo to give
Suffitient Securty for the ſame to the ſd Court & hereof faile not given undr
my hand & Seale the 8th day of the 12 being the 5th yeare of   mo
the propryatorys govrmt   1685

him the Art miſtery & faculty of Skinner & glover
for the placeing of 2 more more of the Childrn the Court doth ordr yt:
willm Biles & willm Dark take Care to Enquire of places that
may be Convenient for them & that they do it wth what Expedition may be
Lawrenc Bannor haveing beene Calld into Court to give an
acct of the Eſtate of the orphants of willm venables & he ſaith
he hath them not ready therefore the Court doth ordr that he make Ready his accts before the next orphants Court & bring them to the Clarke

The Court adjorns untill the firſt 3 day of the weeke in the 8th month next

County of Bucks in the Province of Pennſilvania
At an Orphants Court held by the kings authority in the name of willm Penn propryatory & govrnr of the provinc & territorys thereunto belonging: for this County att the Court houſe the 7th day of the 8 1685
                                                                    mo

(53) The Juſtices then prſent

Thomas Janney   willm yardley   willm Biles
     Edmund Bennet   Willm Beakes

Edmund Bennet &c being Cald to an acct about the Eſtate
of the Childrn of John Spencer & do ſay that there is as yett matters depending that the aCount Cannot as yet be brought in therefore this Court ordrs that they bring in theire accounts to the next Court & the time of the Childrs freedome & of theire fathers death

County of Bucks in the
Province of Pennſilvania
The 3d day of the $\frac{i}{mo}$
1684

At an orphants Court held for this County the day above ſaid
att the Court houſe by the kings authority in the name of
willm Penn Propriatory & govrnr of the Said
Province & Territory

  The Juſtices then preſent
  James Harriſon prident
  Willm Biles willm Beakes
  John Otter Edmund Bennet
   willm yardley

Jon Oter & Edmund Bennet do Say that they have not as yet
pſected the accts relateing to Jon Spencers orphants therefore
the Court ordrs that they be pſected & brought in to next Court
James Harriſon doth Say that he hath Spoke wth the orphants Con=
=cering theire willingneſs to be bound to the ſd Executors &
they have declared theire willingneſs to be bound untill the
age of 21 yeares & they are bound James Spencer to
to Jon Otter for 7 yeares & Samuel Spencer to Edmund Bennet
for 9 yeares but the days of theire freedome they know not
therefore they are ordered to give an acct thereof att or be
fore the next Court
Hannah the widow of James Hall hath this day prſented to the
Court her Neceſſity of releiuf her Huſband being dead
haveing left 4 Smal childrn the Eldeſt peter Hall 5
yeares of Age the 7th of the 2nd month next wch Child the Court
together wth the Conſent of the Said wid hath placed him wth
willm Dark as an apprentice until the age of 2i yeares
& the ſd willm hath promiſed to find him meat drink waſhing
Lodging & Apparell during the Said terme, & to teach him

$\dfrac{20^{th} \quad 8 \quad 86}{mo}$ (55)

At A Court of Quarter Seſſions held by adjornmt
The Juſtices then prſent
James Harriſon   Thomas Janney
willm yardley   willm Biles
Jon Otter
Abraham Whorley Sherrif
P P Cl Com

This day was deld and acknowledged in
open Court one Conveyance of the moyety of
of land bearing date 14th 7 mo 1686 — — — by Abr
whorley attorney Conſtitute to Antony Tomkins unto
willm yardley
by ordr of Cha: pickring attorney conſtitute by george
martin

This day was deld and acknowledged in open
Court one Conveyance of 230 ackers bearing
date the 18th day of 8 month 85 by N waln
to Robt Heaton attorney Conſtitute by
Jedidiah Allen

This day was deld and acknowledged in open
Court one deed of Sale & mortgage
of 500 ackers of land bearing date the 8th day of 7th mo
1686 by Abraham whearley Attorney Conſtitute to Dan=
=iel Jones unto Rogr Hawkins attorney Conſtitute to
Andrew Robeſon

The Court adjorned to the 8th 10th month
next

(56) At A Court of Quarter Seſſions held by the kings
authority in the name of wm Pen Propryatory
and govrnr of the Provinc of Pennſilvania
& Territory thereunto belonging at the
Court houſe for the County of Bucks the 8th
day of the 10th month being the 2nd yeare of
the Raigne of James the 2nd ovr England &c
King & the 6th of the Propryatorys govrmt
1686

The Juſtices then Preſent
James Harriſon   Arthur Cook   Thomas Janney
wm yardley
Abraham whearley Sherrif
Phinehas Pemberton Clark

Simon Roufe plt ⎫ Simon Roufe appears by
      agt   ⎬   his attorney wm Looker
wm Biles ⎭ wm Biles deft appears
Robt Dow Summonced to be on
the Jury the Court fines him in 5 ^{s} for
his non appearance he after appearing the Court
tooke of the above fine
The Jury being attefted for tryal of the
Caufe betwixt Roufe and biles wch Jury is
as followeth
Jon: Cuff: Richard Thacher James paxfon
Samuel Burges Richard Ridgway Ed: Stanton Jr
Lawrenc Bannor Jon Cuttler Steven Sands
Richard Lundy Jon Croffdale Thomas Stakehoufe
The Declaration Read
   wm Biles anfwer read
the atteftation of Joseph frezey taken before
Samuel Dennis Juftice in Eaft Jarsey read
Joiuah Bradley attefted doth Say about the time
of the laft orphans Court here Roufe was here & wm
Biles Said that he had bought of Simon Roufe
one Negro; & was to give him for him 30 £
and that he paid him in hand 4 £ & that he had

pd more in pte i2 £ but the fd Roufe had Cheated   (57)
him & that he wold
give him 20 Skins or 20 Shillings but whether he doth not
well know & fd he wold give no more & further fth not
the plt attorney acknowledged to have Re in pte 17 £ as
   allfo 30 ^{s}
A lettr from wm biles to fd Roufe dated the 6th $\frac{2}{mo}$ 85
   read
  plt being Calld appeares   deft Calld appears
          after adjornmt
verdict the Jury being Calld over do Say thet they are
   agreed
& find for the plt that the declaration is true according
according to Evidence
Tho: Holme on behalf of the govrnr ⎫ plt appeares
      agt   ⎬
  Ifrael Taylor deft ══════ ⎭ deft appeares
george glave being bound to appear at this Court &
to be of good behavior in the meane time hath

been this day Calld & none appearing agt: him the Court
difcharges him paying his fees
John Smith being bound to appeare at this Court according
to recognizance appeared & the Court difcharges him paying
his fees.
   adjourned for one houre
i deed dated the 22 ii[th] mo: 1685 of one moyety of A tract of Land
formerly
in poffeffion of Daniel Brinfon was
deld and acknowledged in open Court by Rich
Ridgway attorney Conftituted by Daniel Brinfon
unto jon wood of fd County
John Pidcock being bound to appeare at this Court
& to be of good behavior in the meane time has
been this day Calld & none appeareing agt him the
Court difcharges him paying his fees

(58) James grayham plt being Calld Henry waddy appeares
  on his behalf
gilbert wheeler deft being Calld appeares
John Cuff one of the Jury for abfenting him felf
with out the Courts leave & afore bufinefs was
ended the Court fines him in io [s]
The Jury attefted Edward Stanton Robt Doue Rich
  Thatcher
James paxfon Samuel Burges Rich Ridgway Lawrenc
  Bannor
Jon Cuttler Steven Sands Rich Lundy Jon Croffdale
Thomas Stakehoufe
declaration read
Anfwer read
& g w after acknowledged the debt & that he wold pay
  the monys
in any goods he had
verdict The Jury returned & Calld over bring in theire
verdict & fines for the plt wth 15 [s] damages
& Coft of fuite
   the Court adjorns till 9 tomorrow morning
Tho Holmes plt apeares
  agt
Ifrael Taylor apeares

The Jury Attefted & Calld over
Declaration Read
Anfwer Read
Ifrael Taylor promifes to pfect al his Surveys
& make returns thereof in three months time
& that he will make Returns of wrights towne
in twoo weeks time: & that he will give an account
in ten days time of all the lands that he has furveyed or begun
to Survey Since he Came into office & the time when
it was furveyed

Tho Holme plt   apeares   (59)
      agt
Ifrael Taylor deft   apeares
The Jury attefted
Declarat read
Anfwer read
Tho Holmes Commiffion read dated i8th 2 mo: 1682
proved the right of Survey mony to him
Ifrael Taylors Commiffion read dated the ioth $\frac{7}{mo}$ 1683

proved he ought to be accountable to y^e: plt for his
furveys
looke back
        The Court adjorned for one houre
Jon: Brock having made Complt: to this Court
that he is out of purfs Conciderably on the
Countys account & therefore defires to know
wch way he Shall have his monys pd him
& this Court ordrs that y^e: tax be collected wth
Expedition & he pd out of it
verdict   the Jury Calld we find that the deft hath
Surveyed land & received mony for the fame w^{ch}
doth belong to the plt:
            in the Cafe Roufe plt
                    biles deft
Judgmt *it is adjudged that the debt be pd that wch
remains unpd with 20^s damages & Coft of fuit
        *James graham plt
            wheeler deft
Judgmt—*it is adjudged that the deft pay
the debt wth 15^s damages & Coft of fuite

*Tho: Holme plt
Ifrael Taylor deft

(60) A petition read from Randulph Smalwood
It is ordrd by this Court That Randulph Smalwood be releafed from Imprifonmt & that he firft make Satisfaction for the time he has been abfent from from his mr & that he Imediately give
bond to fatis fye the fine damage & Coft of fuit by Servitude after the Expiration of his time wth Jacob Hall and that he give Such Security in 3 days time & it is further ordrd that he give bond to ferve the govern 6 months after he hath ferved out his time wth fatiffaction of his fine with Jacob Hall & to Serve 6 months after that wth Ralph milner & to give his own bond for the fee

The Court fines gilbert wheeler for his difturbing the Court & Stoping the Juftices in the pformance of there duty in 15^s

Jugmt The Court gave Judgmt y^t: Ifrael Taylor Shold bring in his accounts & y^t:
the monys due from the fd I: Taylor to fd Tho Holme Shold be repayd him
by the fd Ifrael Taylor

Judgmt The Court gave Judgmt that wm Biles Shold pay Simon Roufe ii £: io^s: 0 &
20^s damages as alfo Coft of fuite

Judgmt The Court gave Judgmt that gilbert wheeler Shold pay 5 £: 16^s: 0^d to James grayham
and 15^s damages as allfo Coft of fuite

The Court adjorns till the 2nd 4th day of the firft month next

Henry paxfon plt ————— ————— ————— —————⎤
     agt   ⎬
Robt Cartor & Jon Cartor fon of the fd Robt Defts⎦
in an action of treffpafs
The Complt Entered the 23 ii mo.: 1686
Summonc granted for fd Robt & Jon Cartor y^e: 9th 1   86
                                                                              mo

---

* Crossed out in original record.

(61)
At A Court of Quarter Seſſions held by the kings authority
in the name of wm Penn Propryatory and govrnr
of the Provinc of Pennſilvania and Territorys there
unto belonging at the Court houſe for the County of
Bucks the 9th day of the firſt month being the 3d yeare
of King James the 2nd his Raigne & the 7th of the
Propryatorys govrmt 1686

  The Juſtices then preſent
  James Harriſon
  Thomas Janney Willm: yardley
  Arthur Cooke Willm: Biles
   A whearley Sherrif
   P P Cl: Com c:
  ffrancis Hough plt appeares
  Henry paxſon plt — — appeares
   agt
  Rob Cartor & Jon Cartor defts appeares
   The deft Craves time for want of his
    wittneſſes
   wch is allowed untill afternoone
1 deed of 125 acker of Land deld in Court bearing date the
  4th day of the
1 mo: 1686 by Robt preſmall unto Jon Baldwin
  adjorned for one hour
Henry paxſon appeares
Robt Cartor appeares
 The Jury Atteſted
The declaration Read
The anſwer Read
 wm plumley atteſted doth Say Seeing the ſmoak &
  ſmelling
the fire went to the meadow & there found the
hay rick on fire there was Robt Cartor & his ſon
Jon & Henry paxſon ſd Robt What had thou done
to wch he Sayd I have done fooliſhly & Sayd
his Son had fired it

(62) Henry pawlin & wm peas atteſted
H p doth Say that he was prſent when the land was
 layd out for Henry paxſon & the meadow was pte of the
  land layd
 out to Henry paxſon

w peas doth Say that he was one that was At Laying
out of Henry paxſons land & that the pt of yᵉ:
meadow owned by Henry paxſon to be his was
layd out to Henry paxſon at the firſt ſurveying
of the ſd land

Iſrael Taylor atteſted doth Say that when the ſd land
was firſt layed out the meadow
was wthin the ſd Survey

James plumley atteſted doth Say when Iſrael Taylor
had ſhewed the breadth of the land to Henry
paxſon that Henry paxſon was not willing
that Iſrael Shold make any further
Survey but Iſrael Said he wold do it to
full fill his vmore (sic) and Henry paxſon was pſwaded
to go along wᵗʰ them Some way but at laſt
the Said Henry bid him be gone & Said he diſcharged
them of his land

wm plumley Says he Cannot well tell what quantity of loads the
hay was

Henry pawlin Said he thought it was about 5 or 6
tun & ſd he heare Robt Cartor ſay
he thought it was about as much

Rich Lundry atteſted doth Say he thinks it was about
4 tun of hay

Samuel Burges atteſted doth Say that he heard Henry
paxſon Say that Robt Cartor had offered him
Such Satiſfaction for the burning of his hay that he
thought he Shold not
put him in Suit
the Jury Returnd

verdict we find for the plt damages 5 £ wᵗʰ
Coſt of Suite

Judgmt   the Court gave Judgmt & it was adjudged
the ſd Robt Cartor Shold pay the ſd Sum
of 5 £ wth Coſt of ſuite

(63)

Joſeph Hall being calld into Court for Slandering &
abuſeing
arthur Cook, Juſtice of peace Confeſſed the Same &
ſubmitted
to the benc
wherefore the Court fines him in 40 ˢ

The Court adjourns thill tomorrow morning at 9 A Clock

deld and acknowledged in open Court one Conveyance of 160 = ackers of land dated the 27th day of 5 mo 1686 by wm Biles attorney Conſtitute by Hannah Salter to P Pem:

attorney Conſtitute by Tho LLoyd

Abra: wearley Requeſt to this Court that his owne Bond for 20 £ orpanage monys belonging to Spencers Childrn & now in the hands of Jon Otter might be accepted

To wch the Court Anſwers they will accept it and ordrs the Clark to take the ſd Bond from the ſd A whearley

Thomas Holm pap agt Iſrael Taylor read
The Court there upon ordrs that Iſrael Taylor Shall pforme the Judgmt of the laſt Court

The Court adjourns till after the Ellection

Joseph Hall being Calld & the fine demanded he refuſed to pay the Same or Secure it to be payd therefore this Court ordrs that he remaine A priſoner till the Said fine & fees be payd

the fine & fees diſcharged by wm Biles

one releaſe of 150 ackers of land dated the 10th day 1 mo 1686

this day was Sealed and delivered by nicholas waln unto the Juſtices of this Court for the uſe of Henry walmsley

orphan of Tho: walmſley deceaſed

in like mannor he Sealed & deld A releaſe of the ſame date of 100 ackers for the uſe of Tho walmſley brother to the ſd Henry

The Court ordrs that theſe releaſes be kept by Ezra Croſſdale for the uſe of the ſd orphans till further ordr from this Court

The Court adjourns untill the 27 of the 2 nth mo

[Here begins a half page insert between pages 62 & 63 of the original records]

deld and acknowledged in open Court by wm Biles unto Charles Biles brother of wm one Indenture of ptition for one moiety

of A Certaine pfell of land Layd out for
472 ackers granted to the ſd wm Biles
& Charles Biles wm: bearing
date the 14th day of the 8 mo 1686
in like mannor deld & acknowledged one Indenture
of partition for the other moiety of the ſd land
dated as above by Charles Biles unto wm
Biles Brother of the ſaid Charles
one Conveyance of ye ſd wm Biles moiety of the
before mentioned tract of land bearing date
the 18th day of the 8 month 1686 was by the
ſd wm Biles deld & acknowledged in open Court
to Jon Cuſf of the ſd County

(64) At A Court held at the Court houſe
by adjournmt the 27th 2 1687
$\overline{\text{mo}}$

The Juſtices present
A Cook   Ja: Harriſon
wm yardley   N waln
A whearley Sherrif
P P Cl:
Commiſſion Read

Acknowledged and delivered in open Court one
conveyance of 60 ackers of land bearing date
the 27th of the 2 mo: 87 by Nicholas waln
unto Jon Auſtin

The Court adjourned untill the
8th day of the 4th month next

County ff: Bucks
Richard Thather plt
    agt:
Samuel Abbot deft:

County ff: Bucks   65
At A Court of Quarter Seſſions held by the
kings authority in the name of wm Penn
Propryatory and govrnr of the Said Provinc
and Territorys thereunto belonging held
at the Court houſe the 8th day of the
4th month 1687.

          The Juſtices present
      A Cook   J Harriſon   wm yardley
      Tho Langhorn   Jo: growdon   Nich Waln
      A whearley Sherrif
          P P Cl:
The Juſtices Commiſion Read
& the declaration by them ſubſcribed
Rich Thather plt ⎫
     agt   ⎬ appears
Sam Abbot   ⎭ apears
Henry paxſon Summonced to appeare on the grand
Jury who appeared not wherefore the Court
fines him in 5 ^{s} This againe taken of
The grand Jury atteſted
John Rowland Robt: Heaton Jacob Hall
John white Jonathan Scaiſe Tho: adkinſon
Tho: Stakehouſe Senr: Jon: Nicholls Henry Pointr
Jon: Cuff Shadrach walley Seemercy Adams
Sam: Allen Jon: Purſley Tho: green
  The Complt of Jane Coverdale agt Philip Conway
Jane Coverdall atteſted doth Say that Philip
Conway about 3 months ago: came to her bed ſide & did
    Say he had ſworn
he wold fuck her either by night or by day
& about A month after that he Came to the houſe
& ſd he had Sworn about 4 yeares he wold fuck
her & ſhe Said ſhe was ſo afraid leſt hee Shold lay

(66) violent hands on her that Shee was forced
to Calld back A youth that was newly gone out of the
houſe to Stay untill ſaid Conway was gone
Elliza Hickman Atteſted doth say that about
the going away of the laſt froſt philip Conway
Came in to the houſe of Rich Ridgway
drunk & was very abuſive & threw Severall things
into the fire & Swore ſeverall oaths 4 at
leaſt by the name of god & once Curſed the Quakers
  Elliza: Ridgway atteſted doth Say to the Same
effect

          Court adjourns for one houre

    one Conveyance of one hundred ackers of land in fee
        dated
    the 8th day i2 moth i684 was delivered and acknowledged

in open Court by Jon: Swift unto : Henry pointer
for the tryall of Cafe between Rich Thather plt agt
Abott deft

The Jury Attefted   John Brock   Tho Rowland
walter Bridgman   Jacob Janney   wm Dark
Ed Lovet   wm Buckman   Tho woolf
Abra Cox   Samuel Overton   James Moone
Tho: Tunneclif

The declaration read

The Anfwer read

prfentmts brought in by the grand Jury

The plt declareing for 16 £ & upon the
examination of the accounts the debt appearing
undr: 5 £ the fd thatcher not having his accts
ready the deft Craved Anon fuite
according to the law in that Cafe wch was
accordingly granted by the Court

one conveyance of three hundred ackers of land in fee
dated the firft day of the 4th month i687 was delivered &
acknowledged in open Court by
John Rowland & Tho: Rowland unto gilbert wheeler

2

one Conveyance of twoo hundered ackers of land in
fee dated the 7th day of the 4th month i687 was dld
& acknowledged in open Court by Jon green to his fon
Tho green

Jon Rowland acknowledged in Court that on the ift day
of the 7 month
laft paft he Rd of g wheeler 5 £ being in full of A bill
he had
under the hand of fd wheeler & one Jon wright for the
payment of fo much dated
the 8th of the 2 mo 1685

The Court adjourns till tomorrow moring at 6
A Clock

67

philip Conway for his oaths & Curfe in the houfe of
Rich Ridgway the
Court fines him in 25^s
the fd Conway behaved him felf contemptuoufly toward
y^e: Court

        & for his Contempt the Court
fines him in five pounds
for his attempting to lye wth Cloverdales
wife the Court ordrs him to give fecurity
for his good behavior & appearanc at next Court
& that he Shall pay fees of Court in all the fd
Cafes
     whereupon he was commited to the Sherrifs Cuftody
untill the Said fines & fees be pd or Secured to be
payd & Security given for his Good behavior
gilbert wheeler being Calld upon his Recognizance for his
  appearance this day in Court accordingly apeared
      gilbert wheeler being Indicted for felling
Rum to the Indians & upon his Indictemt
he was arraigned there upon
he pleaded not gilty & for his tryall put
him felf upon the Cuntry
The Jury Attefted   John Brock   Tho: Rowland
walter Bridgman   Jacob Janney   wm Dark   Edmund
Lovet   wm Buckman   Tho woolf   Abra: Cox   Samuel
overton   James moone   Tho Tunneclif

firft Indict   The Jury returned bring in theire verdict do fay
that gilbert wheeler is guilty of felling
Rum to the Indians on the iith day of the
2 month laft paft & fo they fay all
whereupon the Court awards Judgmt

2nd   The bill agt g: wheeler for felling Rum to ye.
Indians the 2nd day of 2 mo returd by y^e
Jury that they find for g wheeler & fo they Say all

(68)   Philip Conway being Indicted for felling Rum to
the Indians upon his Indictemnt was araynged
& upon his arraignent pleaded not guilty &
for his tryal put him Self upon the Cuntry
the Jury Attefted John Brock   Tho: Rowland   walter
Bridgman   Jacob Janney   wm Dark   Edmund Lovet
wm Buckman   Tho woolf   Abraham Cox   Sam overton
James moone   Tho Tunneclif
returned do find for p: Conway & fo they fay all upon w^{ch}
fd Indictmt the Court difcharges paying his fees:
martha the wife of g wheeler being prsented
for fchoulding & Currying Shee being Calld g wheeler
her hufband appeared on her behalf & fubmitted to the
Court for wch the Court fines her in 5^s

Joseph Hollinſhead being prsented for Common
Swearer being calld he Submitted to the Court for wch the
Court fines him 5 {s}
upon the prſentmt of the upper and Lower Road of
this County from the falls towards philadelphia the
Court ordrs the Said Roads be repaired before
the latter End of the 7th month next

Judgmt
The Court gave Judgmt & it was adjudged that
gilbert wheeler Shold pay 5 £ to the govrnr
according to the law in that Caſe made and
provided agt the Sale of ſtrong liquors to ye: Indians
Be it Remembered that Philip Conway doth here in open
Court acknowledg him ſelf to ſtand indebted to the govrnrs
uſe in 40 £ to be Levyed on his lands goods & Chattells
Conditioned that the ſd Philip Conway Shall appear at the
next Court of Quarter Seſſions to be held for the County
of Bucks & to ſtand to and abide the Judgmt of the ſd Court
& thence not to depart without Lycenc & in the meane
time to be of his good behavior towards all the kings
Subjects

The Court adjourns untill the 29th day of this month

County ſſ Bucks.   (69)
At A Court of Quarter Seſſions held by the kings
authority in the name of wm Penn Propryatory and
govrnr of the Province of Pennſilvania and Territorys
thereunto belonging (at the Court houſe) for the afforeſd
County the 14th day of the 7th month being the 3d yeare
of king James the SecOnd his Raigne over England &
the 7th of the Propryatoryatorys govrmt 1687

The Juſtices then prſent

Arthur Cooke   william yardley
Thomas Langhorn   Nicholas waln
     A: whearley Sherrif

     Da LLoyd the kings attorney
     P P Cl.

Jon Auſtin plt appears agt Jon Clawſon appears not	The Jury Atteſted between Jon Auſtin plt & Jon Clawſon deſt
wm Beakes Junr plt appears agt Tho: wood deft appears not	Joſuah Hoops Jon: White Henry marjorum Joſ: milnor
Jon Brearley plt appeares agt Tho wood deft appears not	Henry Pawlin ffrancis Roſſel John Palmer Sam Dark wm Dark Tho: Stakhouſe
Auſtin agt Clawſon — —	Jeffery Hawkins Rich Ridgway

witttneſeſs   Samuel wilton atteſted doth Say that Jon Clawſon
his servant & Son did enter upon the land of his
mr Jon Auſtin & did mow & Carry away graſs from
thenc about 3 weeks after corn harveſt
James Spencer atteſted doth Say that he being the
Servant of the Said Jon Clawſon was ordrd by his
ſd maſter to Cut graſs & when they had Cut it
& weare making of his Son Derrick Clawſon Came
to them in that time & Shewed them the tree
Jon Auſtin ſd was his marked tree & that they Cut ſd hay
     within the ſame & ſays that
ſd hay was cut about 3 weekes after they had
* * * * *

(70)   Jon Auſtin plt appeares
verdict   The 14th of the 7th mo 1687 we of the Jury do find for
the plt 40 s wth Coſt of Suite

Jury   The Jury Between wm Beakes Junior plt & Tho wood deft
Joſuah Hoops   Jon white   Henry Margerum   Joſeph milner
    Henry Pawlin
ffrancis Roſſill   Jon palmer   Sam Dark   wm: Dark   Tho
    Stakehouſe Jnr
Jeffery Hawkins   Richard Ridgway
Beakes agt wood   Jury atteſted
A whearley Atteſted doth Say that upon the 4th day
of this month Tho wood acknowledged
to him he owed the ſd Beakes 9 £
Jo: Hull Atteſted doth Say that upon the 3 day
of this month Tho: wood ſd if he Cold get 6 £ wm
Beakes wold take it inſtead of 9 £
wm Morton Atteſted doth Say that laſt weeke
he ſpoke wth Tho: wood & ſd he heard he denyed
to pay wm Beakes the 9 £ he owed him wood ſd no

	I never denyed it but intend to pay it but if he sue me he shall get nothing by it
verdict	The Jury Say they find for the plt wth Cost of Suit
Jury	The Jury attested Betweene Jon Brearely plt & Tho: wood Josuah Hoops Jon white Henry Marjorum Joseph milner Henry pawlin ffrancis Rossill Jon palmer Sam Dark wm Dark Thomas stackhouse Junr Jeffery Hawkins Rich: Ridgway
	Brearley agt wood
	The bill being produced in Court wm: yardley one of the Justices doth Say that he drew the sd bill & is A wittness to it
verdict	the Jury Say they find for the plt wth Cost of suite
Judgment	in the Case Between J: Austin plt & Jon: Clawson deft
by default	The Court gave Judgmt that Jon Clawson Shall pay 40^s damages & Cost of Suite to Jon Austin
Judgment	in the Case Between wm Beakes Junr plt & Tho: wood Deft the Court gave Judgmt that Tho wood Shall pay 9 £ to sd Beakes Junr & cost of Suite

(71)

whereas Hannah overton attested before wm yardley that
Tho: Tunneclif was abusive to her that she
was afraid of her Life & of her Childrns lifes whereupon
sd Tunneclif was ordered to appeare at this Court to give
Security for his good behavior
Be it Remembered that Thomas Tunneclif doth
here in open Court acknowledg him self to stand
Indebted to the govrnrs use in 20 £ to be leviyed on
his lands goods & Chattles
   Condition   Joseph miller Likewise in io £
                & ffrancis Rossill Likewise io
Conditioned that the sd Tho: Tunneclif Shall
appeare att the next Court of Quarter sessions
to be held for the County of Bucks
& to be in the mean time of good behavior towards all the kings
Subjects
Tho: Tunneclif Imediately as he was bond abused
the bench & Said I Care not A pin for none of
you you have abused me & wronged me

Execution	& bid them do theire worſt wherefore the Court adjudges that ye aboveſd ſum be pticulerly levyed on the lands goods & Chattels of the pticular pſons & Charge of Court The overſeers of the high way laſt yeare are ſtill Continued becauſe they have not appeared this day in Court
The Several plantives before memtioned Craved the Court that they might have Execution granted them upon the Severall Judgmts by them obtained wch was accordingly ordered by the Court that Execution ſhould be granted them when they pleaſed to take it out Philip Conway being bound laſt Court in 40 £ for his appearance at this Court & for his good behavior in the meane time the ſd Conway being in Cuſtody for other miſdemeanors & being in the priſon below the Court was very unruly in words & actions to the great diſturba==nce of the kings peace & to the Court in the Exerciſe of theire dutys Curſing the Juſtices & other officers kicking his legs againſt the door & Endeavoring to make a disturbance
(72)	wherefore the Court ordrs that the Said 40 £ So forfeited by him be Levyed according to his Said Recognizance on his Lands goods & Chattles
The Court adjourns untill the i4th day of the ioth month next
(73)	County ſſ. Bucks At A Court of Quartr Seſſions held by the kings authority in the name of wm Penn Propryatory & govrnr of the Said Provinc and Territorys thereunto belonging held the i4th day of the ioth month i687 att the Court houſe of the ſd County being the 3 yeare of King James the 2nd his raigne & 7th yeare of the propryatorys govrmt
The Juſtices then prſent
Arthur Cook   Thomas Janney   Joſeph growden
wm: yardley & nicholas waln
A: Whearley Sherrif
P. Pemberton Cl. Com:
one conveyance of 500 ackers of land in fee acknowledged and delivered in open Court by Abra: whearley Conſtitute attorney to Anthony

Thompkins unto Rich Ridgway attorney to grifith
Jones dated the 22 day 6 87
  ────
  mo

wm Smith }
  agt   } appeares   }
Tho millard } appeares not — } The Jury attefted

Anthony Burges }   } declaration read & the bills
  agt   } this with   } therein mentioned and one
Luke Brindley } drawn —   } letter & pettition from T milla

Richard Thatcher } appeares } declaration read referred as
  agt   }   } on the other fide
Sam: Abott   } appeares }

Joseph Chorley }
  agt   } with drawn
mathew pugsley }

Henry grub }
  agt   } with drawn ——
David Lilly} Charge 5^s:9^d —

one conveyance of 500 ackers of land in fee acknowledged
and delivered in open Court by Robt Doue attorney
to Tho: Adkinfon, unto Jofeph kirkbride dated the
i2 day 8 mo 87

(74)

delivered and acknowledged one releafe of lands
by Richard Lundy to his father in law Thomas williams
of 200 ackers of land dated i2th day of 9 mo 1685
Richard Thatcher and Samuel Abbot have refted
theire action to be Ended and arbitrated by Jofeph
growdon & nicholas Waln provided they give in
theire award within twenty days after
this day for pformance whereof the fd Rich Thatcher
& Samuel Abbot do oblidge themfelves
theire Executors miniftrators & affignefs Each
to other in the Sum of 20 £ to be pd upon defa
to y^t: part pforming
       adjourned for one houre
The Court gives Judgmt by default and it is adjudged that
Thomas millard Shall pay to willm Smith 3 £ : 14^s: 0^d and
damage wth Coft of Suite
A petition of wm black Read
ordered that J growdon to Speake wth the magiftrates of
philadelphia to know what they have done about fd black
& what they Expected

one Conveyance of A Small tract of land from Jeffery
Hawkins in fee delivered & acknowledged by ſd Jeffery
Hawkins unto his ſon Daniel Hawkins dated the
firſt day of this Inſtant y\ :io month

ordered that Abraham wherley & Phinehas Pemberton
do examin the accounts of wm Biles as they ſtand
between him and the County

adjourned untill the i4th $\frac{\text{i}}{\text{mo}}$ next

County ff: Bucks 75

At A Court of Quarter Seſſions held by
the kings authority in the name of wm
Penn Propryatory and govrnr of the Provinc of
Pennſilvania and territorys thereunto belonging
(at the Court houſe) for the afforeſd County the i1th
day ot the 1 month being the 4th yeare of king James
the 2nd over England &c and 7th of the propryatorys
govrmt $\frac{1687}{8}$

The Juſtices then Preſent
Arthur Cook wm yardley Joſ: growdon N: waln
Abraham wharley Sherrif
P: P Cl: Com:

The grand Jury Atteſted ⎫
Iſrael Taylor bound in io £ ⎪
to the propryatory for ⎬ appeares
his appearance here this ⎪
day for abuſe done to ⎪
nicho: walln Juſtice of peace ⎭

mary fckeane bound ⎫
to appeare at this Court ⎬ appeares
on the penalty of 20 £ ⎭
& Examined

Richard Thatcher plt appears ⎫ the Jury Atteſted between
agt   ⎬
Sam Abbot deft appeares   ⎭

Joan Huff ⎫
agt   ⎬ this action
James Sutton deft ⎭ withdrawn

Jacob Hall plt } appeares not }
   agt   } this action withdrawn
Tho Tunneclif deft } appeares not }

Joan Huff plt ——— } this action
   agt   } defired to
Jofeph growdon deft } be forborn
                      by both plt &
                      deft ———

gilbert wheeler plt } appeares
   agt   } this action withdrawn
Jofeph Chorley deft } appeares

Jofuah Ely plt } this to be
   agt   } Entered
John Brock deft } for the   } at the requeft of the p[lt]
                  next
                  Court

Declarat—Thatchers Declaration red } one Conveyance of 20
Anfwer—Abbots Anfwer Read   } ackers of land in fee from
                                     wm Pickring to Jon peng
                                     =oit was delivered an[d]
                                     acknowledged in open
                                     Court

The grand Jury Return brought in no prfentmts   (77)
The Court adjourns for on houre

Abraham Wharley Complaines to this Court agt:
Randulph Smalwood for that there is due to him for fees
2£ : io^s : 06^d upon wch the Court ordrs Execution fo be granted
agt: fd Randulph Smalwood for the fd Sum
wm: Looker petition read for requefting the monys obtained
in Roufe Cafe agt wm Biles
mary Beakes acknowledged one letter of Attorney to her
brother in law Edmund Beakes of Porif head in the County o[f]
Summerfte in England date the i4th day of the i mo 1688
Randulph Blackfhaw Complaines that he wants mony due
to him for repaireing the high ways to wch the Court anfwer
they will return anfwer next Court
mary fckeane examined and Attefted hath declared
as written on A loofe pap
Ann oxley the midwife Examined and attefted doth fay
as declared on A loofe pap

verdict the Jurys verdict in Thatchers Cafe agt About
the find for the plt 5£ : i3ˢ: 0ᵈ: and io⁸ damage wᵗʰ Coſt
of ſuite to be payd in goods Equivalent to ſilver mony
or in ſilver
this day was deld and acknowledged in open Court one
Conveyance of 50 ackers of land in fee dated the i3
day of the $\frac{i}{mo}$ 1688

the Sherrif Returns the Execution the goods diſtraining
are overprized and therefore Cannot ſell for want of buyers
In as much as the apprizers formerly Choſen have overprized
the goods taken on Execution therefore this Court appoints
and Chooes John Brock wm Paxſon & Robt Heaton to
be apprizers until further ordr Atteſted
    wm Beakes acknowledged one letter of attorney
made to Thomas Cotterill of Almſberry in
the County of gloſter dated i4ᵗʰ $\frac{iſt}{mo}$ being this day

ſteeven Beakes acknowledged one
letter of Attorney Edmund Beakes
of portiſ head in the County of Sum=
=merſet dated i4ᵗʰ $\frac{iˢᵗ}{mo}$ being this day

78 ordered that whereas the Sherrif has Returned the laſt
Execution in Rouſes Caſe this Court ordrs that
another Execution be granted to the Sherrif for
the Anſwering the debt to ſimon Rouſe
The Court gave Judgmt: and it is adjudged that Samuel
Abbot Shall pay to Rich Thatcher the Sum of 5£ : 13ˢ: 00ᵈ
and io⁸ damage wᵗʰ Coſt of ſuit
ordered that an Execution be granted
for the Levying the aboveſd
Sum
ordered that Richard Thather allow
Samuel Abbot 10ˢ for damages on the non ſuite
formerly granted
    adjourned to the 13 day of the 4ᵗʰ mo next
acctt of all fines and forſeituers from the
firſt holding Courts in this County untill the
i2ᵗʰ day of the 4ᵗʰ month i688 given in to
wm markham Secratary

County ff: Bucks
At A Court of Quarter Seffions held by the kings authority
in the Name of wm Penn Propryatory and govrnr
of the afforefd Province and Territorys thereunto
belonging at the Court houfe of the fd County the
i3th day of the 4th month being the 4th yeare of
the kings Reigne & 8th of the Propryatorys govmt
 The Juftices then prfent
 Arthur Cook wm yardley
 Nicholas Waln Henry Baker
 Abraham Wharley Sherrif
 wm: Croffdale his deputy
 Phinehas Pemberton Cl: Com:

Actions Entered

Jofuah Ely ⎫
 agt ⎬ in A plea of Cafe { both ——— ⎫
Jon Brock ⎭   { Appeared ⎭

   declaration filed   The Jury Attefted
   plea Read   John Swift Henry Marjerum

Evidences ⎧ mahlon Stacy ⎫ walter Bridgman Tho: Stakehoufe, fr.
    | John Redman ⎬ Attefted
    | mary Staniland ⎭ Robt Heaton Henry paxfton
   ⎨ Proved the declaration Tho: Stakehoufe Jr: Jof: Clows
    | Jofeph milner Attefted James paxftone Rich: Lundy
    ⎩ for the deft   wm Dark James moon

adjournmt The Court adjourned for one houre

verdict we find for the plt Seven pounds Eleven Shillings to be
   pd by the deft with Coft of fuite the plt firft makes
   the deft an affurance of the boy

Judgmt The Court awards Judgmt according to verdict
   and that Execution Iffue accordingly

deed of three ackers of Land in fee dated the ioth day
   of the 9th month 1688 deld & ackd
   by Jofeph Englifh grantor to ffrancis Roffell

(80) Action David Evan plt ⎫ { appeares ⎫
      agt ⎬ A plea ⎨   ⎬ The Jury attefted
   Jofeph wood deft ⎭ { appeares ⎭

declaration plea Read Anfwer Read

Evidences	John Brearley ⎫ wm Beakes— ⎭	attested proved the mare when dead had Shot in her flank & green Corn in her mouth &: the marks of sd mare
	Ellias Nicholls	attested that Jon Wood father of sd Jos: Said a mare lay on his Corn & he must or wold shoote her.
attested	Jon Owen	proved the marks of the bell about the mare that was killed
	Hugh Williams	proved the marks of the mare
	Josuah Elly & mary Eire	attested proved that Joseph wood shot at the flank of A horse or mare in the beginning of the 2nd month
	Josuah Elly Senr	proved yt: at after the report of the gun he saw he saw Joseph with the gun on his neck
	mary wood— ⎫ Sarah wood ⎭	attested proved yt: Jos: wood shot Salt at A horse about 9 days afore the killing of the sd mare

verdict the Jury return find for the plt 5 £ for the mare and 40 s damages wth Costs of suite

Judgmt the Court thereupon awards Judgmt according to law

Execution ⎧ Joseph wood being required by the Court to satisfye:
the sd Judgmt he refused the Same whereupon ye:
Court Comitts him in Execution to the Sherrifs
Custody untill the sd Judgmt be satisfyed ⎭

Indictmt Israel Taylor being Indicted last Court for defameing ffrancis the wife of John Swift upon his Indictment

Arainemt he was arraigned
pleading upon his arraignment pleaded not gilty and for his tryal put him self on the Cuntry

		(81)

The Jury attefted
Richard Ridgway Henry Marjerum Walter Bridgman
Tho Stakehoufe fenr Robert Heaton fAndrew Ellet
Tho Stakehoufe Junr Jofeph Clows wm Dark
James Paxftone Rich Lundy James moone

Evidentes
    John naylor Attefted doth Say that Ifrael Taylor Said he veryly believed that nich meaning the man of John Swift did lye wth John Swift wife and that he believed in his Contience he did god good fervice in telling of it John Towne attefted teftefyes as above the laft Claws Excepted
    Andrew Dunk Attefted doth Say that he heard Ifrael Taylor tell micheal Bucher that gabriel Shallow fd nicholas Randulph wold lay his head upon his mrs lap until i2 a Clock at night and then they wold go together into the barn
    mark Betrice teftifys the fame
    Benjemame Jons Attefted doth Say that gabriel Shallow Said nicholas Randulph wold fleepe with his head in his mrs lap & Shee fleep wth her head in his lap & that he Called John Swift Cuckoldy Rogue & that his muftard pot wold work when he was from home and that they wold go into the barn together in the night

deed   of 250 ackers of land in fee dated the ift day 4th month 1684 delivered and acknowledged by Rich Hough grantor to Henry marjorum grantee

Jury Returned do Say they find him guilty
    in mannor and form as he ftands Indicted

Judgmt   The Court awards Judgmt that Ifrael Taylor Shall give Security for his appearance at next Court and to keepe the peace in the meanetime and to pay al charge of Court and y^t Execution

Execution   Iffue accordingly

Recognizance   memorand that Ifrael Taylor oblidges him felf in io and Benjemame Jons in 5 £ to the propryatory and govrnr to be levyed on theire lands goods and Chattles

* * * * *

82 The accts of wm Biles the Receiver of the County tax was examined according to An ordr of A former Court by Phinehas Pemberton & Abraham wharley and were againe this day examined and made up in open Court and it appears by the books of affeffmt ⎱   £   s   d

that the whole Tax amounted to — — ⎱ 128: 04: 05½
of wᶜʰ the ſd wm Biles ⎰ £ s d
acknowledged he had Red — ⎱ 56: 19: 09
out of wᶜʰ he has diſburſt
as it made appeare in
open Court by the Courts
order and otherwiſe wᶜʰ } 59. 06: 07
the Court allowed of
the ſum of —— ——

So that this Court doth
allow of the aboveſd acctt
and acknowledg that the } 02: 06: 10
County is debtr to ſd wm
Biles the Sum of —— ——

and further that it doth appeare by the
acctt now brought in by the ſd wm Biles
As may be ſeene in pticulars on } 07i: 04: 08½
the file that there remains unpayd
of the ſd aſſeſſmt — the ſum of —— ——

and whereas it doth appeare that the County is ſtill debtr
to John Brock Randulph Blackſhaw gilbert wheeler
and others this Court doth ordr yᵗ: the ſd wm Biles do
take the moſt expeditious way for getting of the arrears
of the ſd aſſeſſmt and paymt of the ſd debts or that if
the ptyes to whom the County is debtr will take upon them
to Collect So much as is due to them that then the ſd
wm Biles do give A Cattalogue of the names of ſo
many as are in arreare as may anſwer the ſd debt
and that A warrant be
Iſſued out from anyone Juſtice of Peace or more
to Impower the ſd pty to levy the Same by
diſtreſs and ſale on the pſons goods refuſeing to pay theire
aſſeſſmt unpd
and further the Court ordrs Henry pointer Samuel Allen
Collect the arreares of the tax betweene Neſhaminah
* * * * *

83   13ᵗʰ   4   88
         ——
         mo

A deed of 1000 ackers of land in ffee dated the 12ᵗʰ day 2 mo 1688
acknowledged and delivered

by P. Pemberton attorney to Jacob Tellner grantor unto
Rich Lundy grantee
A deed of 50 ackers in fee dated the 6th day $\frac{1}{mo}$ 88 ack &
deld by Joſ: Engliſh grantor to arthur Cook attorney to Rich
willſon grantee
upon David LLoyd the Attorney generalls motion in relation to levying
the fines and forfeitures the Court thinks fitt to take time to deliberate
upon it and to Speake with the Commiſſioners of propryety afore
they return anſwer what Courſe muſt be taken for levying of the ſame
and do ordr that in the meane time the ſd Eſtreats above writ be
taken out of the Records of the ſd County may be Certefyed under the
Clarks
hand
This was done at the Same Inſtant
The Court adjourned to the i2th $\frac{7}{mo}$ next

County Court ff Bucks 84

At A Court of Quartr Seſſions held by the kings authority
in the name of wm Penn Propryatory and govrnr
of the afforeſd Province and Territorys thereunto be=
longing at the Court houſe of ſd County the i2th day of
the 7th month being the 4th yeare of the kings reigne
and 8th of the Propryatorys govrmt i688

The Juſtices then Preſent
wm yardley   Joſeph growdon
Nicho: Waln   Henry Baker
A wharley   Sherrif
wm Croſſdale   deputy Sherrif
P. P Clark

ffrancis Hough ⎫
    agt   ⎬ debt
Iſrael Taylor ⎭

deed ⎧ 1 deed in fee from wm Biles
⎪ grantor delivered by Rich
⎪ Ridgway his attorney to
⎨ Jo: Engliſh grantee for
⎪ 200 ackers dated the 5th $\frac{5}{mo}$
⎩ Ellected and appointed

Conſtables for the upper pte of the river

Conſtable
- wm Beakes atteſted
- for the lower Tho wms
- for the midle Lotts Je: Hawkins
- for yᵉ: upper pte of neſhaminah Tho ſtakehouſe Atteſted
- for the other pte of Neſhaminah & thereaway neamiah Allen

overſeers of the highway
- over ſeers of high way Ellected for the upper pte of neſhaminah
- Robt Heaton Henry Poynter
- for yᵉ: lower pte thereof Samuel Allen Junʳ
- for the lower pte of the rivere wm Dungan
- for the middle lotts Joſeph Kirkbride
- for the upper pte of the river Joſeph milner

(85)

Recognizance Iſrael Taylor being bound by Recognizance none appearing agt: him the Court diſcharges him paying his fees

ſſra Hough agt Iſrael Taylor } Att: Jon Brock app another attorney being Appeares Joyned wᵗʰ Jon Brock and not appearing

non ſuit — Iſrael Taylor Craved A non ſuite wᶜʰ was granted and the Court ordrd the plt to pay the Coſts

deed — A deed in fee of one acker of land dated 10ᵗʰ $\frac{7}{mo}$ 88 from ſſra: Roſſill grantor acknowledged & delivered to Tho Brock attorney to Joan Huff grantee

Corronors return — A return of the ſudden death of Rogr Scott was this day made to this Court under the Jurys hands

Recognizance Daniel Hawkins & Robt Benſon appeared according to Recognizance Court diſcharges them paying fees

Eſtreat. John oldfeild appeared not but forfeted his Recognizance being 5 £

Eſtreat John Ruſh being Calld according to Recognizance appeared not therefore forfeited the ſame being 20 £

	⎧ Jacob Hall not being well defired the Court to allow
petition	⎨ to the next adjournmt for bringing in his Complt
	⎩ agt Jon Rufh fd Rufh being Calld and not appearing
anfwer	the Court allowed of it

              The Sherrif Returned his execution levyed on the
              goods of Jon Brock i gray mare & i7 grofs buttons

Execution   at 7 £ 11^s wch the Court declared was not
              Suitable & over priced & therefore y^e: Court orderd that another
              Execution be granted & layd on such goods as
              will anfwer mony

adjournmt   adjourned to the 2 $\frac{8}{mo}$ 88

            Pennfilvania County Court ff Bucks   (86)
           At A Court of Quarter Seffions held by adjourn mt by
           the kings Authority in the name of wm Penn propryatory
           and govrnr of the afforefd Province and territorys
           thereunto belonging at the Court houfe of the faid
           County the 2nd day of the 8th month being the 4th
           yeare of James the 2nd his Reigne over England &c—king
           and the 8th of the propryatorys govrmt 1688
                    The Juftices then prfent
                      willm yardley   Henry Baker
                      wm Crofdale   deputy Sherrif
                          P P Clark
           i deed of 50 ackers in fee dated the ift $\frac{8}{mo}$ 88
           delivered and acknowledged in Court by Jon
           Naylor grantor to Jon Smith grantee
           whereas John oldfeild was Calld laft Court being bound
           to appeare there and appeared not Came this day
           and appeared & alleadged that he was Sick and unable
           to Come Sooner
           * Whereas there Shold have been A tryall this day
           between Jon Swift plt & Tho millard deft & y^e:
           Court Cold not be held for want of Juftices they
           Submitted the Same to Reference & oblidged them
           felves in prfence of the Juftices then prfent
           Jon Swift & Tho millard for them theire heires Executrs
           & adminiftrators do oblidg them felves Each to other in y^e:
           penall fum of fifty pounds to Stand to & abide the award

*[This paragraph is crossed out in the original records.]

& Judgmt of Jon: Jones Nicholas Waln wm gabitas &
& Thomas marle Indiferently Chofen between them
provided they give in theire award before the 20th day of y^e :
9th month next In witnefs whereof they have openly declared
the Same & hereto put theire hands   John fwift
                    Tho: millard

adjourned to the 12th $\frac{10}{mo}$ next

       Pennfilvania County Court ff: Bucks   (87)
(1) At A Court of Quarter Seffions held by the kings authority
in the name of Wm Penn Propryatory and govrnr
of the afforefaid Province and Territorys thereunto be=
=longing att the Court houfe of the Said County the
12th day of the 10th month being the 4th yeare of y^e :
Reigne of James the 2nd of England &c king and 8th
of the propryatorys govrmt 1688
     The Juftices prfent
   wm: yardley   Jofeph growdon   Henry Baker
    Jon: Brock   Nicholas Waln
     Abraham Wharley Sherrif
      wm Corfdale   deputy Sherrif
       Phinehas Pemberton   Cl: Com:

Comiffion: The Commiffion of Peace Read
Laws: The laws laft made Read
       The grand Jury

grand Jury { Richard Ridgway fforeman
Henry Paxton   Jofeph miller   John wood   Andrew Ellet
Jon: Palmer   Samuel Dark   Jon Crofdale   Henry Bircham
Jofeph Englifh   Jon: Hough   Shadrach walley   wm: Buckman
ffrancis Roffill   attefted

adjournmt   adjourned for one houre

adjournmt: { The Court Calld and adjourned untill 8 in the
morning

deed — { i deed in fee of 2 ackers of land dated the 6th day
acknowledged { of the 7th month 1688 delivered and acknowledged by wm
Croffdale (attorney to James Swafer grantor) unto
James Croffley for the ufe and upon the requeft made
of Richard willfon grantee

88

deed ack : } one deed in fee of 125 ackers dated the i3: $\frac{\text{io}}{\text{mo}}$ i688 acknow
:nowledged } ledged and delivered by James Hill grantor to James Moone for the ufe of him Self and his fon James moone grantees

Inditmt   Bucks ff: i2th $\frac{\text{io}}{\text{mo}}$ i688

(1) The Jurrors for the propryatory and govrnr by y^e: kings authority do prfent A Run away negro who Says he Coms from verginia and Calls him Self by the name of george for that he upon the i7th day of the 9th month laft paft did Steale and fraudelently take and Carry away twoo turkeys worth 6^s being the goods of Tho: Janney Senr Conterary to the kings peace and agt the law in that Cafe made and provided

profecutr   peter worral pfecutr
witneffes   { Tho Janney Junior }
                     { Jofeph Hollinfhead }   wittneffes Attefted
A true bill   This bill found by the grand Jury
arrignmt   upon wch Bill the fd negro was Arraigned
pleading   And he pleaded guilty

Inditmt   Bucks ff: i2th $\frac{\text{io}}{\text{mo}}$ i688

(2) The Jurrors for the propryatory and govrnr by the kings Authority do prfent A Run away negro who Says he Come from verginia and Calls him Self by the name of george for that he about the beginning of the 8th month laft paft did fteale and fraudulent =ly take and Carry away 1 ax 1 Skellet Corn peafe — Stockings and other goods to the value of twenty five Shillings being the goods of Thomas Rogers Conterery to y^e: kings peace and agt the law in y^t: Cafe made & provided

profecutr   Tho Rowland profecutr
witneffes   { Tho Rogers — }
                     { Samuel Hough }   wittneffes Attefted
A true bill   This bill found by the grand Jury

arrinmtt	upon wch Bill the ſd negro was arraigned
pleading	and upon his arraignemt pleaded guilty of takeing all the afforeſd goods Save half A buſhell of peaſe

Bucks ſſ   The i2th io / mo   i688

Indictmt (3)	The Jurrors for the propryatory and govrnr by the kings authority prſent A Runn a way negro who says he Comes from virginia and Calls him ſelf by y^e: name of George for y^t he upon or about y^e: beginning of the 8th month laſt paſt did Steale and fraudelently take and Carry away one Cloath Coate one leather Coate twoe Shirts; one ſuſtian waſt Coate one hat one Silk neckcloth to the value of five pounds being the goods of Rogr Hawkins Conterary to the Publique Peace & agt the law in y^{t.} Caſe made & Provided
Proſecutr	Roger Hawkins Proſecutor
witneſſes	{ Joſeph Hollinshead } { Samuel Hough } wittnesses atteſted
A true bill arrignemt pleading	This bill found by the grand Jury upon wch Bill the Said negro was arraigned And upon his Arraignemt pleaded guilty
Indictmt (4)	Bucks ſſ: The Jurors for ye Propryatory & governor by ye Kings authority doe present y^t John Collins of the County affore Said Huſbandman on the twenty Seventh day of the eighth month laſt paſt did by Violent aſſault & fforce Robb and take away from the perſon of gilbert wheeler upon the Kings high way & Road within the ſd County one mare and other goods to the value of tenn pounds being the prop goods of gilbert Wheeler afforeſd Conterary to the publique peace and agt the law in Such Caſe made and Provided
Proſecutr	Joſeph Wood Proſecutor
witneſſes	{ gilbert wheeler John martin Jacob Hall Edward Cartor Joan Huff Daniel Beakes Ellenor Beakes } witneſſes atteſted

A true Bill	this bill return found
arrainemt	upon wch Bill the Said Collins was arrained
pleading	and upon his arrainemt pleaded not guilty
requeſt	but craved A few houres time of the Court to give in what he had
Anſwer	further to Say in anſwer wch was granted by the Court

90

grand Jurys } The i2th ioth mo: i688
  prſentmt   we the grand Jury do Preſent it needfull that A Suffitiont Cart Roade Shall be layd out from the upper plantations above the falls unto the fferry houſe where the Common landing is over agt Burlington

                  Richard Ridgway fforeman

Action	⎫ gilbert Wheeler agt Luk Brindley in A plea of debt
wheeler	⎬
agt	⎪
Brindley	⎭ gilbert Wheeler appeared
non appearance	Luke Brindley appeared not
Sherrifs	⎱ wm Croſdale deputy Sherrif made Return that he had given him lawfull
Return	⎰ Summonce
Declarat	Pennſilvania County Court ſſ: Bucks

        gilbert wheeler ⎫
            agt   ⎬ &c: Read
        Luk Brindley ⎭

Bond	and the bond therein mentioned proved by the Evidence
Evidences	of wm Biles atteſted the other wittneſs to the ſd bond being Robt Jeffs deceaſed proved by the writeing
	The penal Sum of the bond and the Sum declared for
Queſtion	being 31 £ & the real debt being but i5 £ i2^s the Juſtices on the bench aſked of ſd gilbert wheeler whether he Expected Judgment for any more yⁿ: the reale debt
Anſwer	To wch ſd g wheeler made Anſwer he Expected Judgmt for no more then i5 £ i2^s with Coſt of ſuite
Judgmt by default	Whereupon the Court gave Judgment by default & it was adjudged that Luke Brindley Shold pay to gilbert wheeler the Sum of i5 £ : i2^s with Coſt of ſuite and that

Execution	Execution Shold Iffue accordingly
Compt about ye tax	wm Biles Receiver of the County tax made Complt to this Court that there was A greate deale of the County tax yet unpd & in Arreare and yt: he Cold not levy the Same without a warrant
Courts ordr	Chattles of the party refufeing to pay his Share of fd tax unpd to the afforefd wm Biles by twoo Juftices of Peace for Levying the fd tax in Arreare & unpd on the goods & Whereupon this Court ordrs that A warrant be granted

91

County Court ff Bucks

(2) A pattent & Affignmt thereon acknowld & delivered	A pattent of 296 ackers of land to Edward Luff dated the 30th 3mo 1688 with an affignment of the fd pattent & grant of the fd Land therein mentioned on the back fide of the fd patent in fee dated the 4th day of the 4th month 1688 was delivered and acknowledged by Tho: Lambert Attorney to Edward Luff grantor unto Henry marjorum granted
deed acknowledged	A deed in ffee dated the tenth day of the 10th month 1688 delivered & acknowledged by Jofeph Englifh grantor to wm Biles grantee being for 162 acres of land
action	Edward Hancock agt Tho Revel in A plea of debt both upon Call appeared and the deft declaring yt: he was but yt day arrefted to appear to the fd action wch appeared to be true by the Sherrifs return ye: action was deferred by Confent of both partyes untill the next Court the fd Tho Revel giveing bond
deffered to next Court uppon baile	with Suffitiont Suertyes to appeare at the next Court
Action	Tho: millard agt S: Burdon in A plea of Debt
appearance	both calld appeared
Declaration	Tho millard agt Samuel Burdon read

Anſwer	The deft Saith he hath pformed the award & ows nothing and of this he puts him Self upon the Cuntry for A tryal
Iſſue Joyned	& the ſd plt in like mannor
Jury return	Therefore the Sherrif is Commanded to return A Jury of twelve more &c :
The Jury	The Jury Atteſted Tho Rowland fforeman Ezra Croſdale Henry marjorum James Paxſtone Steephen Sands Peter Worral Wm Clows James moone John Towne John Penquoit Richard Lundy wm Dark

92

declarat articles	The articles Read & acknowledged by the deft
bond	The bond Read & acknowledged by the deft
award	The award Read & acknowledged by the deft
Jon ffleckney evidenc	The Atteſtation of John ffleckney of Burlington taken before James marſhall Juſtice for yᵉ ſd place read
Ant: Burtoɪ	Anthony Burton Atteſted Saith he was with John ffleckne on Burdons Iſland when he went to veiue the work and yᵗ: he Saw Tho millard had not ſtuff to work on for the firſt mill being the mill Contracted for and mentioned in the afforeſd articles and award & further faith not
Tho: Terry	Thomas Terry Atteſted Saith he wrought at the mill and to his knowledge Thomas millard wanted plank to work on and further Saith not
ffra: Roſſil	ffrancis Roſſill Atteſted Saith that he veiued the work when ffleckney and Burton aforeſd did & he Saw no timber to work upon for the firſt mill as aforeſaid
Jon ffurnas	John ffurnas Atteſted for the defet Saith that he wrought for Samuel Burdon att the ſame time and Some time before and he never heard Tho millard aſk for or Complaine for want of ſtuff to work on and ffurther Saith that ffrancis Roſſill when he Came to veiue the work was Drunk So that he reeled too and fro in the path and fell down to the grownd

Edward Lancaſter	Edward Lancaſter atteſted for the deft Saith he wrought with Samuel Burdon from the 4th month laſt paſt and was often in work with Thomas millard and that he knew not that Tho millard did want Stuff to work on but for the moſt part found him ſelf work about the mill agreed on according to the articles Except it was at the latter End of the work

                        The Jury went forth

adjournment   The Court adjourned for one houre

93

deed acknowled	one deed in ffee of two hundred and three ackers of land dated the 10th day of the 8th month 1688 was acknowledged and delivered by Samuel Dark attorney of Lyonel Brittan grantor unto Stephen Beakes grantee
Judmt on the (1) Indictmt	The Court gave Judgmt upon the firſt Indict agt george the negro for Stealeing the turkes they not being reſtored it was adjudged that he Shold pay by Servitude as the Court hereafter Shold order unto Thomas — Janney ſenr aforeſd to the value of 18s and Charge of Court and be whipt for the Said offence Elleven Stripes on his bare back
on Indictmt (2)	The Court gave Judgmt upon the Second Indictmt agt george the negro for Stealing og goods from Thomas Rogrs pte of the goods being reſtored it was adjudged that he Shold pay by Servitude as the Court hereafter — Shold order unto Thomas Rogers afforeſd to the value of 48s and Charge of Court and be whipt ii Stripes on his bare back
on Indictmt (3)	The Court gave Judgmt upon the third Indictmt agt george the Negro for Stealing the goods of Roger Hawkins the goods being reſtored it was adjudged that he Shold pay by Servitude as the Court hereafter Shold order unto Roger Hawkins afforeſd to the value of 50s and Charge of Court the ſd Hawkins deſiring from the Court no further Satiſfaction Save that he be whipt on his bare back i9 Stripes
ordr Commitmt:	ordered that he be once whipt in the Sight of the Court untill A Conveniant place of ſervitude be found for him the Court Committs him to the Sherrifs Cuſtody

Recognizance difcharge	paterick kelly being Called according to recognizance none appearing agt him the Court difcharged him payi[ng] his fees
Commitmt	Richard Thatcher Junior for abufeing the Juftices on [the] bench the Court Committed into Cuftody untill the next morning
adjournmt	The Court adjourned untill 8 A Clock next morning

(94)

Attion	Tho millard agt Sa Burden
Jury	The Jury Returned
verdict	we find for the plantif according to evidence
requeft	The deft Samuel Burden Craved an appeale to the provincial Court in Equity
Judgmt	The Court gave Judgmt and it was adjudged that Samuel Burden Shold pay to Thomas millard the Sum of twoo hundered pounds
requeft for an appeale Bond offered	The deft Samuel Burden Craved an apeale to y^e: next provin =cial Court in Equity and tendered his own bond for 400 £ to pay all Cofts of the fd Court & of this Court occationed by the afforefd action and to pfecute the fd — appeale with effort
bond accepted appeale granted	wch fd bond was accepted by the Court & Liberty of an appeale granted to the fd Sa: Burden deft to the next provincial Court in Equity
Indictmt (4) requeft	John Collins upon the Indictmt affrefd returned into Cou[rt] and Confeft he had affaulted gilbert wheeler on the high Road but not with any Intent to Robb him gilbert Wheeler Craved the Court to forbeare any further proceedure agft: the Sd Jon Collins for that the Said Collins had made him full Satiffaction for any wrong or Injury he had done to him
fees promifed	and fd Wheeler promifed to pay all fees due on the fd Indictm^t:
order on the prfentmt of the want of A Road	upon the grand Jurys prfentmt of the Want of A Roade from the upper plantations above the falls of Delaware to the landing agt Burlington the Court orders —— Henry Baker John Brock wm yardley Jof: miller Richard Hough John Rowland Jofeph Englifh and

fine Commitmt	Abraham Cocks to lay out the Said Road and give an acctt there of to the next Court: Richard Thatcher Junior afforefaid for Infulting the Juftices upon the bench and giving them abufive words the Court fines him 50 ˢ and Committs him to the Sherrifs Cuftody untill he Shall find Suertyes for his good behavior & his appearance at the next Court
adjournmt	adjourned untill the 3 day of the firft month next

County ff: Bucks
At a Court of Quarter Seffions held the
i3 day 4ᵗʰ mo 88
           9   Juftices Wm Biles
Commiffion Read   Henry Baker Jon Brock
Conftables ellected
Jofeph Chorley for below the falls to the govrnrs
peter worrall for above the falls
adjourned untill the 27ᵗʰ Inftant

    Pennsylvania
County Court Bucks ff:
At A Court of Quarter Seffions held by the kings autho=
=rity in the name of Wm Penn Propryatory &
govrnr of the afforefd Province & territorys
thereunto belonging held by adjournmt the
27 day of the firft month being the 5ᵗʰ yeare
of the kings Reigne & 9ᵗʰ of the proprya=
=torys govrmt 1689
The Juftices prfent
Jofeph growdon Wm Biles Henry Baker
Nicholas Waln John Brock
Wm: Beakes Sherrif
Phinehas Pembeton Cl:

Commiffion	Read
engagemt	Signed Wm Biles Henry Baker John Brock the reft haveing Signed it formerly
action	Randulph Blackfhaw agt Charles Pickring in a plea of Cafe Blackfhaw defired the Court that the action might at prfent be ftayed untill another Court becaufe he had

	not his Wittneſſes in Readineſs one of them being gone out of the province
A deed	in fee from Jo: growdon grantor to ſte newel grantee of 202 acres dated the i2ᵗʰ day i2ᵗʰ mo 1688
A deed	in fee dated the i2ᵗʰ $\frac{i2}{mo}$ 1688 for 102 ackers acknowledged & delivered by Jo: growdon grantor to Abel Hinkſton grantee
A deed	in fee for 102 acres dated the i2ᵗʰ $\frac{i2}{mo}$ 1688 ack by Jo: growdon grantor to Abel Hinkſonte attorney to Wm Reale grantee
A deed	in fee for 102 acres dated ioᵗʰ $\frac{i2}{mo}$ 1688 ack & dld by Jo: growdon grantor to Stephen newel Attorney wm Reale grantee
A deed	in fee for 40 acres dated ioᵗʰ $\frac{i2}{mo}$ 1688 ack & dld by Joſeph growdon grantor to Abel Hinkſtone attorney to Tho ffox & Joſeph willſford grantees
(97)	
A deed	of 100 acres of land in fee dated the 23 day $\frac{i2}{mo}$ 1688 de & ack by Wm Hayhurſt grantr to Henry Hudleſton grantee
Recognizanc	Richard Thatcher being Calld appeared the Court diſcharged him paying his fees
ye negro	george being brought into this Court to anſwer the Several Judgmts of the laſt Court that was then adjudged to be payd by Servitude
Recognizance	Richard Ridgway engaging by bond for the appearance of george the negro hath accordingly brought him into this Court
diſcharge Commitmt	Whereupon this Court Commits the ſd george negro in execution to the Sherrifs Cuſtody untill further order .

non fuite	Action Randulph Blackſhaw agt: Charles Pickring pickring deft appeared according to Summonce & Craved a non ſuite the ſd Blackſhaw haveing declared that he was not in readines to pſecute his action the Court granted him A non ſuite on the ſd action
Recognizance	Hugh march being bond in 20 £ for the appearance of Job Houle the ſd Houle being Calld appeard Jon Swift & philip Conway being Calld declared they had no thing at prſent to object wherefore the Court
difcharge	difcharged the ſd Houle
Recognizance	Tho millard being bound in 30 £ & ffarncis Roſſill in 15 £ for the appearance of Tho: millard at this Court the ſd millard being Calld appeared & Samuel Burden declared he had nothing at this time to object
difcharge	Wherefore the Court difcharged him
Recognizance	Charles Brigham being bound as by the Information of Joſ: growdon & Arthur Cook Juſtices being Calld appeared & more Complaints Coming agt: him the Court ordered him to give Security to
Commitmt	appeare at the next Court Wch he the ſd Charles — refuſed whereupon this Court Commits him to ye: Sherrifs Cuſtody untill he give Security as above

(98)

A deed	of Sale & mortgage of of 2 Iſlands in this County agt Burlington Called kips Iſland & A little Iſland northward of the ſame dated the 6th day i mo: 1688/9 acknowledged & ded by nicholas Waln attorney to Samuel Burdon grantor to Arthur Cooke Subſtitute attorney of Sam: Carpentr to Joſe Burden grantee
A deed	of 100 acres of land in fee dated the 10th day of the i mo: 1688 ack & ded by Tho: Rowland grantor to philip conway grantee
A deed	of 100 acres of land in fee dated the iſt 4/mo 88 ack & ded by wm Dungan grantor to Arthur Cook grantee

Recognizance	Edward Cartor & Tho: Brock oblidged themselves in 40 £ to the propryatory for the appearance of John Allen at this Court who appeared accordingly & nothing objected agt: him whereupon the Court
disfcharge	difcharges him

ordered by this Court that george the negro be deliverd
from his Imprifonmt to Stephen Newel w^{ch}
Said negro is by this Court adjudged to ferve
the fd Stephen Newel or his affignes fiveteen yeares and at
the end of fiveteen yeares to be returned
to the mafter of the fd negro or affignes if he the fd
mafter or affignes make demand of him in Concd
eration whereof the Said Stephen
Newel is to pay il £ 4^s to anfwer
the feveral Judgmts of Court

Stephen Newel & Jofeph growdon both
declared & promifed that they wold pay the Said ii £ : 4^s
to anfwer the Judgements of Court in Cuntry
produce at Currant price the pay
to be delivered at philadelphia at or
before the latter end of the third month

99

next to Such perfon or perfons as Shall be appointed
by this Court to Receive the Same for payment of
wch Said mony the Said Stephen Newel & Jofeph
growdon in open Court oblidged them felves theire
executors & adminiftrators

arbitration not Concluded }	Thomas millard & Sam Burden appeared in Court declared that they had agreed to put y^e: matters of difference between them to arbitration but the fd partyes not agreeing on the pfons to arbitrate it Entered into no engagemt before this Court
adjourned	to the i2th day of the 4 i689 mo

Penfilvania
  County Court Bucks fs:
 At A Court of Quarter Seffions held by the kings authority

COMMON PLEAS OF BUCKS COUNTY, PENNSYLVANIA 105

in the name of Wm: Penn Propryatory
& govrnr of the afforefd province & territorys
thereunto belonging the ii[th] day of the 7th
month 1689 being the 9th yeare of the
propryatorys govrmt

The Juſtices prſent

wm: Biles   Henry Baker
John Brock   Nicholas Waln
Wm Beakes Sherrif
Phinehas Pemberton   Cl: Com:

Actions

Mary Beakes —
   agt: } in a plea of debt— —
Tho: Coverdale   } with drawn by ordr
                        of wm Beakes

John Swift
   agt: } in a plea of Caſe —
Philip Conway

Tho: Revel
   agt:
     Junr   } in a plea of affault
Richard Thatcher   } & trefpafs —
   &
Ifrael Taylor —

Richard Ridgway
   agt: } in a plea of Caſe
John Heefem —   } with drawn by
                        ordr of
                        Richard Ridgway

Recognizances

Philip Conway Come forth & Save
thee & thy balle elſe thou forf thiy
recognizance

wm Roles bring forth p: C: Ells
thou
for feiteſt thy recognizance

H: march bring forth p C:
John Swift Come forth & pſecute
the peace agt: p: C: or ells he
Shall be difcharged

Jon: Swift Come forth & Save thee
wm Roles bring forth J: S:

101

A deed   of 125 acres in fee dated the io[th] day of the i2[th] mo
              1688 was acknowledged & delivered by Henry
              paxſon grantor to wm plumley grantee

A deed   of ioo acres of land in fee dated the io[th] day of
              the i2[th] month 1688 was acknowledged & deld
              by wm plumley grantor to Henry paxſon grantee

A deed	of 310 acres of land in fee dated the 8 day of the 7th month 1689 was acknowledged & delivered by Richard Noble grantor to moſes maſley grantee
A deed	of mortgage for 310 acres in fee dated the 9th day of the 7th month 1689 was acknowledged & delivered by moſes maſley grantor to Richard Noble grantee
A deed	of a tract of land about one hundred acres in fee dated the tenth day of the 7th month 1689 was acknowledged & deld by Tho: Coverdale grantor to Henry Siddall grantee
Conſtables	Conſtables appointed for the Succeeding yeare for the upper part of the River peter worrall for the Lower part near the falls of the River Joſeph Chorley atteſted for the Lower part of the river Tho: greene for the middle Lotts John Rowland atteſted for the upper pte of Neſhaminah James Paxſon atteſted for the Lower pte of Neſhaminah John white
action	The action between Jon Swift plt & philip Conway deft declaration & anſwer read the plt was pleaſed to deſire the Court that ye: ſd Conway might purg him ſelf by his atteſtation wch was Condecended to the deft
	philip Conway atteſted declared that he had Said he knew who killed the Colt of John Swift but upon his atteſtation declared that he knew nothing neither directly nor Indirectly of of the kiling of the ſd Colt neither did he ever of his owne knowledge know that Jon Swift had any Colt killd
action	Jon Swift plt appeared philip Conway deft appeared
Jury	atteſted
	declaration read
	Anſwer Read

COMMON PLEAS OF BUCKS COUNTY, PENNSYLVANIA 107

evidence
    Edmund more attefted doth Say that about Chrismas laft paft
    ph: Conway Said
    to Jon Swift that he wold have the man y^t the killd his Colt to
    come & work out the price of the Colt with him but if he
    pleafe to accept of 50^s in recompence for the Colt
    the fd Conway wold give him a bill undr his
    hand for the paymt of fo much if there was a
    pen & ink in his houfe & further Saith that he
    the fd Conway Said he was prent at the killing of the fd Colt

evidence
    Job Houle attefted doth Say that that philip Conway told
    him he was prfent by when the Colt was Shot & y^t:
    when Jon Swift was at his houfe he had offered
    40 or 50^s for the fd Colt if he y^e: fd Jon Swift wold Say no
    more
    of it & that young mark Betrice killd the fd Colt

evidence
    philip parker attefted doth Say that philip Conway fd he
    was prfent when young mark Betrice killed Jon fwift
    Colt & y^t: the fd Colt gave 2 or 3 Jumps & then
    feldown dead

Tho Coverdale defire an witnes Concering a will
made by Daniel Hawkins to be examined it haveing
Relation to a trect of land left to fd Coverdale by fd
Hawkins & the fd land by fd Coverdale this day
conveyed to Henry Siddall to wch the Court heard the fd
evidence being Jon Clement Attefted doth Say that
Saw the fd will bearing dated the 30th of the

103   ioth month 1688

Sealed & delivered by fd Hawkins & further Saith that the
fd Hawkins did give his land to fd Coverdale
& his heires forever

    The Court adjourns forone houre

negro   The Court ordrs that Richard Rigway or
his affignefs do Re the money due from
Jos: growdon & Stephen Newel upon y^e:
acctt of the negro & that y^e: fd Richard Ridg
have an ordr Signed by Some one Juftice
for to Impower him to rece the Same Richard Ridgway
    haveing this
day in open Court promifed to Anfwer all

	the Charges that has beene out upon him the negro & allowed by the Court
ordered	that a requeſt be drawn to the govrnr that Regiſter may be appointed in this County for the probat of wills that people be not put to yᵉ: Extrordinary Charge of going to philadelphia
A deed	of 50 acres of land in fee dated the firſt day of the 7ᵗʰ mo: 1689 by Rich Willſon grantor to Jon gibbs grantee
A deed	of about 90 acres in fee dated the 8ᵗʰ day of the 4ᵗʰ month 1688 by Luke Brindley grantor to peter worral grantee
	Iſaac Burges being Calld & none appeareing agt: him yᵉ: Court difcharges him paying his fees
Jury	returned Calld over do Say they are not agreed were returned back againe
petit Jury	The grand Jury atteſted return againe not agreed whereupon the Court return them back
Recognizance	John Swift being Calld upon his recognizance appeared & the Court difcharged him none appeareing agt him
Recognizance	philip Conway being bound to good behavior & appearance at this Court accordingly & none appeareing agt him the Court difcharged him paying his fees

Jon Swift agt: Philip Conway

Jury Returned to find for the deft & so they Say all

The Court adjourns untill 8 a Clock to morrow morning

| action | Tho: Revel agt Rich Thatcher junir & Iſrael Taylor } trefpaſs & aſſault | plt appeared & Iſrael Taylor appd |

	declarat read
	Anſwer read
	Iſſue Joyned
	Jury return
Jury	Calld over & declaration & Anſwer againe read
evidenc	grace Langhorn Thomas preiſtcorin Richard Thatcher Senior } atteſted Benjemaine Jons Ezra Croaſdell

105

grand Jury return brought in the bill agt Rich Thatcher Ignoramus
& at Same time prſented ſd Thatcher for bringing a dead hogg to the houſe of Iſrael Taylor on the firſt day of the weeke

overſees of ye: high ways	over ſeeres of the high ways for the ſucceding yeare for the upper pte of Neſhaminah Henry paxſon and for the Lower pte of Neſhaminah Henry Bircham for the other ſide of Neſhaminah Tho: Hardin for the Lower pte of the river John Cooke middle Lotts Randulph Black ſhaw for the upper pte of the River wm: Clows
action	Jon Swift agt philip Conway
Judgmt	The Court gave Judgment and it was adjudged that John Swift Shall pay Coſt of Court
Judgmt Eſtreat	the Court gives Judgmt & it is adjudged y^t: philip Conway for the lye he told in Jon Swifts Caſe whereof he was Convicted by his owne Confeſſion before this Court that he Shall pay 2^s 6^d

grand Jury againe brought in prſentmts about the roads in this County

ordered	that the overſeers of the high Roads do take Care to repair the ways & bridges by the grand Jury prſented
action	Tho: Revel ⎫ agt: ⎬ Richard Thacher Junr ⎬ & Iſrael Talor ⎭
Jury	return & Calld over
verdict	=find for the plt 30 ˢ damages with Coſt of ſuit Iſrael Taylor abuſed the Jury but upon his Submiſſion & acknowledgmt of his fault the Jury deſired the Court to paſſe it by
Recognizance	Richard Thatcher Junior being Calld appeared according Recognizance Richard Thatcher Junior for his Contempt to yᵉ: Court and abuſes done to yᵉ Tho: Revel. & for ſuſpition of takeing a hogg that was none of his owne the Court Commits him into the Sherriffs Cuſtody untill he find Suffitient Suertyes for his appearance at the next Court & for his good behavior in the meane time
Commitmt	Charles Brigham being Calld & none appeareing agt him the Court diſcharges him paying fees
A deed	of fifty acres of land in fee dated the 10 day of yᵉ: 7ᵗʰ month 1689 acknowledged & delivered by Nicholas Waln grantor to wm Hayhurſt grantee
Judgmt	The Court gave Judgmt in Revells Caſe agt ⎧Rich Thatcher Junr & Iſrael Taylor & it is adjudged ⎩that the ſd Thatcher & Taylor Shall pay 30 ˢ — damage wᵗʰ Coſt of Suite according to verdict & that execution Iſſue accordingly adjourned to the 11ᵗʰ 10 mo 89 next

Bucks ſs: 107

At a Court of Quarter Seſsions held by the authority of king William & Queen mary in the name of William Penn propryatory &

govrnr of the afforefaid Province and —
Territorys thereunto belonging At the
Court houfe for the Said County the ii[th] day
of the io[th] month being the 9th yeare of
the propryatorys govrmt 1689

The Juftices then prfent
Jofeph Growdon
William Biles   Henry Baker
John Brock   Nicholas Walln
William Beakes Sherrif
Phinehas Pemberton   Cl: Com:

The Juftices being met for Several reafons thought
it not Convenient to Sit there being no actions to
try therefore the Court was not opened

Bucks ff: 108

At a Court of Quarter Seffions held by the
kings and Queens authority in the name of
Willm Penn propryatory & govrnr of the
afforefaid province & territorys thereunto
belonging at the Court houfe for the faid
County the 12 day of the firft month being
the io[th] yeare of the propryatorys govrmt
1689

Juftices prfent
Jofeph growdon   wm Biles
wm yardley   Henry Baker
Nicholas Waln   John Brock
wm Beakes Sherrif

P Pemberton   Cl: Com:
grand Jury Attefted

John Shippey }
    agt   } plea of Cafe
Ifrael Taylor }

Jofeph growdon }
    agt   } plea of Cafe }
Tho Hutchins— } demurred   }

Tho: Revel }
    agt: } plea of debt
Ifreal Taylor }

Arthur Cooke }
    agt   } plea of Cafe }
Jofeph Crofs } with drawn— }

Tho: Coverdale for Comeing
in Court before the bench
drunk the Court fines him in
five Shillings

paterick Conway & philip Conway
being Calld into Court & fecurity
being required of them to anfwer

gilbert wheeler agt Luke Brindley	plea of Cafe with drawn	the feveral Compts objected agt: them & wch they refufeing the Court Commits them into the fherrifs Cuftody till further order
gilbert wheeler agt John pidcock	plea of Cafe demurred	

A deed of 200 acres of land in fee dated the 24 day of the $\frac{3\ 89}{mo}$

was acknowledged & deld by Sam Burges & Rud: Black fhaw grantors to Rich
Lundy grantee

A deed of ioo acres of land in fee dated the io day of the 12 mo: 1688 ack & dld by Jofeph growdon grantor to Claws Jonfon grantee

109

Complt made by Derick Clawfon that formerly he delivered to Arthur Cook & James Harrifon 3 wolves two of them bitches & one dog & that he hath but Red in part of the fame 7^s the Court being Satiffyed of the truth thereof by Arthur Cooke orders that He be pd what remaines due to him out of the firft mony that Comes to the receivors of the publique ftock

notice from John Blackwell not to pay Quit rents to any but Robt Turner or his fubftitutes Read

adjourned for one houre

A deed of Some land for a mill pond in fee dated the 20 day of the 9th mo 89 ack & dd by Wm Beakes attorney to Jon otter grantor to ffra Roffill grantee

Conftables nominated & appointed for the lower pte of the fettlemts between nefhaminah & poquefin Samuel Allen Junior for the upper pte John purflone attefted

Eftreat wm Clows & Tho kirl being fummonced to appeare on the Jury & not appearing the Sherrif being attefted they had lawfull Summonc the Court fines them in three fhillings apeice

prſentmts brought in by the grand Jury
the death of Ann Hawkins prſent to the Court to be
Caſual by
faling from a mare

adjourned to 8 a Clock tomorrow morning

1 Inditmt philip Conway & patrick Conway for breaking
open the houſe of wm: ffisher read
pleaded not giuilty for
tryal put them ſelves on the Cuntry

2 Inditmt philip Conway for ſealing amare read
pleaded not giuilty for
tryal put him ſelf on the Cuntry & deſired time till the next
Court for tryal

3 Indictmt paterick Conway for ſtealing half a hide of
leather read
pleaded not guilty & for tryal put him Self on the Cuntry

4 Indictmt agt paterick Conway & philip Conway for
Robing of wm ffiſher of one Colt read
plead not guilty for
tryal put them ſelves on the Cuntry

motion being made by wm Biles the Rec^{or} of the publique
Stock of the County that there was Several neceſſary
Charges of the County to be defrayed as the fees
of the Councel & aſſembley men killing of woolfs &c
& that he had
no effects in his hands
whereupon the grand Jury prſented the the neceſity of haveing
a new tax raiſed

paterick & philip Conway brought to y^e: barr

Jury Called over & atteſted
no Chalenges made agt them

wm ffiſher Atteſted aged about 35 years Saith that about y^e:
latter end of January being at the houſe of philip Conway
in order to Seeke a mare of his that was loſt
after he had found her he returned
home againe

at wch time he found his houſe broken op & his Cheſt unlocked
the key ſtuck in his Cheſt wch key at his going away
he hid under his beds tead & none knew of the having
of it there Save paterick Conway was prſent when
the key was hid that upon Serch of his goods he found
pte of his goods in philip Conways houſe viz: an Inke
horn

Sam: roſe aged about 19 yeares Atteſted Saith that on the 6th
of the weeke at night being laſt day of January
being to haul the hay of wm ffiſher went there for
Some hay where they found al well on the next
morning went againe where they found a man

111

& horſe had been and tracked the ſd man & horſe in the
Snow between 3 & 4 miles & as they
did apprehend the track did lead towards the houſe of
philip Conway & further Saith not

Janes paxſon aged about 40 years atteſted Saith that he being Conſtab
Serced the houſe of philip Conway where was found an
Inkhorn wch wm ffiſher owned to be his & not any
thing Ells & further Saith not

prſentmts brought in by the grand Jury

3 Indictmt agt: paterick Conway for ſtealing ½ hide of leather
read

adjourned the Court for one houre

grand Jury prſent the neceſſity of a Tax to defray the
requiſit Charge of the Councill & aſſembleymen
wch the County is in arreare to them

petit Jury Return on the firſt Indictmt of brakeing wm ffiſhers hou
do Say y^t: paterick
Conway & philip Conway are not guilty

3 Indictmt agt pa: Conway
Charles Thomas aged about 41 yeares atteſted doth
Say in Dec laſt pat y^t he Came to w: fforſt mill with
lether at wch time he ſold ſd pa 1 ſide of lether
where his lether lay out of doore 2 or 3 days & he
then telling over his lether he miſt i ſide there of and after
Some time wm ffiſher; told him he ſaw 2 ſides of lether

in pt: Conway houſe & yᵗ: paterick Conway told ſd ffiſher yᵗ: Charles Thomas ſold him one & gave him — another

wm ffiſher atteſted doth Say Seeing 2 ps of ſides of lether in phi: Conways houſe pa: Conway told him he bought one of Charles Tho: & yᵗ: he gave him yᵉ other

Jury returned Say Pa Conway is guilty of ſtealing the ſide of lether from Charles Thomas

Jon Shippey agt Iſrael Taylor	Jury Atteſted decl Read Anſwer Read

wm: Biles atteſted doth Say that Iſrael Taylor laſt fall was 12 months did Come to him & promiſe to pay him on John Shippeys acctt: two ponds ten Shillings

Joſeph Croſs atteſted doth Say that Iſrael Taylor about the beforementioned time told him he had Anſwered to wm Biles two pounds ten Shillings for worke done for ſd Iſrael Taylor

Rich: Thather Junr atteſted doth Say that he heard Jon Shippey Say to Iſrael Taylor if he wold pay to wm Biles 50 ˢ he wold ſaw him 1500 foot of Sawing

Jon purſlone atteſted doth Say yᵉ day Andrew Jenks dyed he heard Iſrael Taylor Say have been at wm Biles to paſs my word to him for 50 ˢ for work: thou haſt done & will thou now leave my work

adjourned this Court to morrow morning at 7 a Clock & the orphans Court tomorrow

ᵏJudgmt given agt: paterick Conway for ſtealing of Charles Thomas Thomas & it is adjudged that the ſd paterick Shall make 3 fold

grand Jury Returnd bring in three prſentmts

ᶦThis paragraph is crossed out in the record.

Israel Taylor being Calld into Court upon the prsentmt for the
   abuse done to Thomas Tunneclif he Confest the fact
   whereupon the Court orders he give bond for his
   peace & appearance at the next Court

Recognizance Israel Taylor oblidges him self in 8 £
   to be pd to the propry
   & govrnr his heirs & successors to be levied on his
   lands tenemts goods & Chattles Conditionaly for the
   appearance of Israel Taylor at the next Court of
   Quarter sessions & to keep the peace in the meane time to all

113

James Shippey ⎱ Jury returned & Calld over
   agt   ⎰ do say they find for the plt wth 4 ^d
Israel Taylor   damages & Cost of suite

A deed for 150 acres of land in fee
   Dated the ioth day of february 1689 by Robt
                                          ——
                                          90
   Heaton Attorney to Henry fflower
   grantor to Tho: Harding grantee

Henry marjorum Calld for selling Liquors upon the
   grand Jurys prsent mt he desired to have what
   was done past by & he wold for the future he wold forbear

Henry marjorum upon the prsentmt of his swearing by
   god submitted to the Court for wch the Court fines
Estreat him 5^s

   philip Conway Indicted for stealing i mare
         Indictm read
         pleaded not guilty for tryal puts him self
         upon the Cuntry

   Chaleng agt g wheeler

         Jury attested

   Indictmt read

   John Swift aged about 43 yeares saith that he tooke up a
   mare Supposed to be about 3 yeares of age un marked of Colou
      bl mealy mouthed about
   4 yeares past in the 2nd month next of wch mare he gave

notice to the raingers but they refufed to take her & y*:
he fpoke to James Harrifon to buy her to w*ch
J Harrifon gave way but put no price upon her
upon w*ch he Eare marked her
w*th a half peny Cut on the
under fide of the nearror eare & w*ch mare he
Saw feveral times Since in philip Conways Cuftody but more
 pticulry
about 3 weeks ago / & about the i3 day of the 1 1688
                                                ―――――
                                                mo 9
& that Since then he Saw the mare with her eare mark Changed

114

Nicholas Randle aged about 23 yeares attefted doth Say that
about the latter end of the 2 next will be 4 yeares paft John
                             ―――
                             mo
Swift & others took up a mare about 3 yeares of
age un Eare marked of Colour bl mealy mouthed a —
broad forehead a wid noftrill whereupon notice was given
to Luke Brindley & Robt Heaton y*e: Rangers to take
her away for the govrnr but they refufed & about
6 weeks after y*e: fd mare broke away but afore fhee
broke away Shee was Eare marked by Jon Swift
with a half penny Cut on the under fide of the nearror
Eare about a yeare after (She broke loofe) philip Conway
told him he wold have the fd mare & feveral times
after that he faw the fd mare in fd Conways Cuftody
& pticulerly about 2 or 3 weekes ago in harnes at p: C: houfe being
 about y*e:
latter end of the i2th month laft paft
& farther Said y*: when he fpoke with Conway
about the fd mare he told him he beleived y*: Jon Swift
had bought the mare of James Harrifon to w*ch Conway
Said that the govrnr was not here to fell the mare
& that James Cold not & y y* he the fd Conway wold have her
 attefted the i3 day of ift month 1689 in open Court
                                  ――――
                                   90
 for the County of Bucks p Nicholas Randal
micheal Bucher aged about 23 years attefted doth Say y*:
 he was prfent when the mare above mentioned was
 taken up of the aforefd marks & Colour & that
 he Saw the fd mare Severall times in the

Cuſtody of philip Conway & that he ſaw him ſeveral
times Rid on her about 2 yeares ago he Chalenged
the mare under him & he thereupon Rid away from
him / that he knew of a half penny Cut on the under
ſide of the nearror Eare put there by Jon Swift

Atteſted the i3 day of 1 month 1689 in open Court
$$\overline{90}$$
for the County of Bucks p the marke of
X
micheal Bucher

4th Indictmt

 wm ffiſher atteſted doth Say he had ordr to take up a Colt by
  Capt markham belonging to y^e: govrnr wch according
  ly he did & when he had y^e: Colt in his yard
  the 2nd day of this Inſtant pat & ph. Conway
  came to his houſe demanded the Colt the ſd ffiſher
  refuſeing to deliver it pa: Conway knockt him over
  & philip Con: in the meane time tooke away the ſd
  Colt

3 Indtmt Jury Cald over to the ſd Indict ſay Philip Conway
  is guilty of ſtealing the mare whereof he ſtands Ind^t

4 Ind Jury ſay paterick Conway & philip Conway are
  guilty of forceably takeing a Colt from wm ffiſher
  whereof he ſtands Indictd

5 Indt Jury atteſted

Witneſ atteſted John purſlone aged about 60 years ſaith y^t: he
  loſt a hog of Colour neare white about
  2 yeares ago with a ſlit in the further eare & y^t
  he doth ſuſpect Ric Thather the younger ſtole the
  ſd hogg & about the ſame time he loſt the ſd hog
  another hogg of his Came home cut Croſs the noſe

 Tho Revel aged about 35 yeares of age atteſted doth
  Say that about the beginning of harveſt laſt Richard
  Thather Jnr brought a hogg to the houſe of Iſreal
  Taylor a hog of Colour neare white Some what red
  on the Sholders but whether it was Sanded or blood he
  knows not & one of the eares had a ſlit in it but
  whether he knew not wch hog ſd Rich Thather told him was

2 yeares old or upwards
attefted

116

Ifrael Taylor aged 30 doth Say that Rich Thather Junr did bring to his houfe a Hog of red Colour with one or both Sholders Sanded about 80^{lb} weight when he was killd as he Suppofed wch hog was brought to his houfe Some time afore harveft & y^t: he told fd Thather he wifht he had not brought the fd Hog for he doubted it was his fathers hog

A deed   of 250 acres of land in fee dated the i3 day of the firft month 89 ack & ded by Ifral Taylor grantor to wm Biles for the ufe of Jon Coates grantee

Jury   Calld over
do Say they find Rich Thather guilty of ftealing a Hogg

Tho Revel ⎫
  agt   ⎬ Jury Attefted
Ifrael Taylor ⎭

dect Read: Anfwer Read:
Jof growdon attefted to the bill
Ezra Croafdel / fd he heard Ifrael Taylor deney he owed him any thing
ffra: Roffill attefted Saith he knows nothing of the bill
Jury Returned do fay they find for the plt with 6^d damages & Coft of fuite

117*

paterick Conway   paterick Conway
philip Conway   for ftealing One halfe
Rich Thather   hide of lether the prop
                 goods of Charles Thomas
                 Shall make three fold
                 Satiffaction being 30^s
                 to be levied on his
                 goods & Chattles or for

---

*Pages 117 and 118 are on the sides of a small sheet about one quarter the size of the other pages.

want of goods & Chattles
to be & to remaine bond
man to Charles Thomas
untill he be satiffyed
& to be whipt on his
bare back 15 stripes
in the fight of the Court & people
paterick Conway & philip
Conway ――――― for takeing
away by force & violent
assault from the pson of
wm ffisher one Colt the prop goods
of wm pen propryatory
& govrnr Shall make
4 sould Satisfaction
being 4 £ : to be levyed
on your goods & Chattles
Lands & tenements or
for want of
Lands
&
whipt on your bare back each
in the fight of the
people

paterick 15 & philip one stripe

118

philip Conway for fraudelently
takeing & stealeing being the 3 ofences
one
being the prop goods of
wm pen propryatory &
govrnr Shall make 3 sould
Satisfaction being 12 £ to be
levyed on his lands & tenemts
& be whipt on his bare back 39 stripes
goods & Chattles & Banished
out of the govrmt never to
return againe upon the
penalty of one hundered pounds
Richard Thather Junr for
fraudelently takeing & stealing
one hogg shall make
3 sould Satisfaction to y^{e}:

owner & be whipt on his
bare back twenty one ſtripes

119

At a Court held by adjournmt the
26th day of the 1 mo: 1690
 prſent
   Arthur Cook
   wm Biles   wm yardley
   nicholas waln   John Brock
   Henery Baker
   wm Beakes Sherriſ
   Steven Beakes deputy Sherriſ
     P P Clark

Severall accts & requeſts this day brought in from
them yt: have Served In Councill & aſſembly that
they may be Satiſſyed what the law alows
them for theire attendance
this Court with the approbation of the grand Jury
have thought good to order that a tax be raiſed
for defraying the neceſſary Charge of the
County & it is therefore ordered that a tax be
forth with raiſed of 300 £ ――――― on the
males & land according as the law directs
& that the Collectors after named do Collect the ſame
with in theire ſeveral diviſſions as may be rated
on them for theire Shares
& give an acctt of the lands and males with in the Several
   diviſions
viz: for above the falls to Jon wood &
Joſeph milner
from thence to the govrnrs
plantation Steven Beakes from thence to
neſhaminah Creeke & up the Creeke to Robt Hall plantation
   James Boyden Junior
thence up the Creek to the uppermoſt
land taken up on Neſhaminah Tho Rowland
for the midle lotts wm Dark for between
Neſhaminah & poqueſſing to the upper moſt part of
Jo: growdons land Samuel Allen the younger
from thence to the upper moſt lands taken up

Henry pointer & that acctt of the lands & males be
returned to the Juſtices the 23 day of the 2nd mo
next At the Court houſe
>adjourned to the 23 day of the 2 mo next

* * *   adjournment   * * *

*Henry pointer atteſted doth Say that about the time aforeſd

120

he was prſent at the takeing up of an unmarked mare of
the Colours & property aforeſd wch he Saw in the
Cuſtody of philip Conway about a yeare ago w^{ch}
he doth believe was the ſame mare taken up by
Jon Swift but Cannot ſay poſſitively its the mare

Jury returned Calld over ſay they find
Philip Conway guilty of ſtealing a mare of
the govrnrs

adjourned for one houre

Court Calld

>adjourned till tomorrow morning at 8 a Clock

>adjourned the orphans Court till tomorrow

Judgmt paſſed upon the 4 ſeveral Inditms

Judgmt awarded by the Court in the Caſe of J Shippey agt I
Taylor that ſd Taylor Shall pay Shippey 2 £ 10^{s} wth
4^{d} damages & Coſt of ſuite & that execution Iſſue
accordingly

Tho Revell declared Iſrael Taylor had Satiſfyed him what was
awarded by the verdict & deſired Judgmt to be ſuſpended

ordered that execution Iſſue agt the goods of Rich Thatcher
for fees due to the ſeveral officers if he does not
take Speedy Courſe to Satiſfye the Same

---

*Crossed out in the record.

Recognizance Rich Thather Junior obliges him felf in 20 £
to be pd to the propryatory & govrnr his heires
& fucceffors Conditional for His appearanc at y^e:
next Court of Quarter feffions & to be of good
abearing in the meane time

adjourned to y^e: 26 Inftant

orphans Court to ye fame time

County Bucks fs:

At a Court of Quarter Seffions held by the king
& Queens authority in the name of willm Penn
propryatory & govrnr of fd province & territorys
annexed at the Court houfe
for the fd County the ii^th day of the 4th month
i690

Juftices prfent
willm Biles   Nicholas waln
Henry Baker   Jon Brock
wm yardley   Sherrif
P P Clark

Ifrael Taylor calld appeared nothing appearing agt him the Court
difcharges him

A deed of 6 acers of land in fee dated the 4th day of the 4th month
i690 acknowledged by wm yardley attorney to Sa: Burges
grantor to wm Biles & Jofuah Hoops grantees for the ufe of
them felves &
Tho: Janney & Rich Hough

a deed in fee dated the i8^th i2 89
                             mo
ack & dld by wm Beakes grantor to Tho: Tunneclife
attorney to Jon worrilow & walter worrilow in truft for
the ufes therein expreffed

meffage from the affembley delivered by Edmund Bennet that
there is due from this County to the Clarks of the affembley
1 £ : 7^s : 0^d & defired that Care be taken to anfwer the fame

	ordered thereupon that the fame be payd out of the the County Stock when it Comes in
Tax	whereas Tho Rowland, laſt Court was ordered to bring an acct of all the lands & males between 16 & 60 from Robt Halls to the uppermoſt lands taken up in order to be Taxed for the uſes then expreſſed & y^t Tho Rowland Since is dead & y^t: diviſion is now thought too large for one man therefore its
ordered	that wm Hayhurſt from ſd Robt Halls pltation & new Town & y^t: Shadrach walley from thence to the uppermoſt land taken up give an acctt of all the lands & males between 16 & 60
agreed	with Iſrael Taylor to bring in an acctt of all lands Surveyed & Seated or unſeated with in the
122	limits of this County for wch the ſd Iſrael is to have 20^s diſcounte out of the County tax to be raiſed & if ſd Iſrael gives a juſt & true acct faire drawn out at or before the next Court
whereas	it appeares that there is occation for a Corroner a boy being lately drowned & none being Commiſſionated it is
ordered	that wm: Biles & Arthur Cook & wm yardley take Care to Endeavor that a Cornor & Regiſter be appointed in this County
ordered	that the ſd perſons requeſt the Council that the upper Road for the upper moſt plantations in this County be layd through Philadelphia County
Complt	being made by John Cartor that his brother Edward Cartor doth not allow him meate and apparrel
ordered	that A: Cook & wm Biles forth with take Care about it & see for what time time y^e: ſd Jon was placed to him by the orphans Court & to Endeavor to redreſs the Complt

adjourned to the 10th day of the 7th mo next

30th $\frac{4}{mo}$ 1690 execution granted agt: Philip Conway
for Damages and Coſt in Jon Swifts Caſe 16 £ : 3ˢ : 3ᵈ
return executed the Same day p wm yardley
                                                         Sherriſe
in the hands of mark Bettrice by a bond
taken of ſd mark for payment of ſaid mony

18th $\frac{4}{mo}$ 1690 execution granted agt Paterick Conway
& Philip Conway in wm: ffiſhers Caſe for
damages & Coſts is 6 £ 16ˢ 1ᵈ
returnd executed the 30th $\frac{3}{mo}$ 1690 p wm yardley
                                                         Sherriſe
in the hands of mark Bettrice by a bond taken of
ſd mark for paymt of ſd mony

Action Entered } Peter Jenings }
the 16th $\frac{7}{mo}$ 1690 }   agt: } plea of Caſe   123
                                    Thomas ffox }

Summonce granted the   day of the   month 1690

Return made by wm: yardley Sherriſe that the ſd ſummonc
was executed the   day of the   month 1690

Action Entered } John Teſt   }
the 20th $\frac{7}{mo}$ 1690 } agt   } plea of Caſe
                                       Thomas ffox }

Summonce granted the   day of the   month 1690

Return made by wm yardley Sherrif that the ſd
Summonce was executed the   day of the   mo: 90

Action Entered } Joſeph ffarington }
the 20th $\frac{9}{mo}$ 1690 } agt   } plea of debt
                                       John Tatham }

Summonce granted the 27 day of the 9 month 1690

Return made by wm yardley Sherrif that the ſd ſum
was executed the   day of the   month 1690

Action Entered | John Brock
the 27th 9 1690 / mo | agt | in a plea of debt
 | gilbert wheeler |

Summonce granted the   day of the   month 1690

return made by wm yardley Sherrif that the ſd Sum
was executed the   day of the   month 1690

Action Entered | Tho Tunneclif
the 27th 9 1690 / mo | agt | plea of Caſe
 | John Lee |

Summonce granted the   day of the   month 1690

return made by wm yardley Sherrif that the ſd Sum
was executed the   day of the   month 1690

Penſylvania
County Court Bucks ſſ: 124

At A Court of Quarter Seſſions held by the king & Queen
authority in the name of william Penn Propryatory
& govrnr of the afforeſaid Province & territorys
thereunto belonging at the Court houſe for the
Said County the 10th day of the 10th month being
the 2nd yeare of the king & Queens reigne & 10th
yeare of the propryatorys govrmt 1690

The Juſtices then prſent

Tho Janney   Willm Biles
Nicholas waln   Henry Baker   Jon Brock
John Cook Corronor
willm yardley Sherrif
P Pemberton Cl:

grand Jury   atteſted

Action | peter Jenings
 | agt | Calld but neither partie appeared
 | Tho ffox |

Action | John Teſt
 | agt | Calld neither partie appeared
 | Tho: ffox |

Action   Joſeph ffarington ⎫
              agt   ⎬ ffarrington appeared
            John Tatham   ⎭   Jon Tatham appeared not

Requeſt   being made by Jon Tatham to reſpite the action
            makeing it appeare that he was ſick & Indiſpoſed
            & not able to Come, Edward Hunlock & Richard
            Bagnet Engaged for his appearance at the next Court
            to anſwer to the action with out further
            Summonce or proceſs
            _____

            accidental death of John ſtolon returned & read
            adjourned the Court for one houre

Action   Tho: Tunneclif ⎫ both appeared
                  agt   ⎬
     125   John Lee ——   ⎭ The action with drawn
            & Tho Tunneclif agreed to pay half the
            Charge
            _____

            Iſrael Taylor Calld appeared pleaded not guilty & for
            tryal puts him ſelf on the Cuntry

            Jury atteſted

            Indictmt Read

            Richard Thather atteſted doth Say that being at work at Iſrael
                Taylors in the fall
                la laſt was 12th month he ſaw Iſrael Taylor give the
                heifer of John Naylor bread ſeveral times &
                he the ſd Taylor ſd to ſd Thather come let us kill
                the heifer, but at that time
                he left the ſd Taylors houſe for want of proviſions
                & in a few days after Iſrael aſked the ſd Thather to
                Come againe for he had proviſions enough & he
                came there & ſaw in the ſeller of ſd Taylor in
                a brrl Several pieces of ſmall meate & he
                then ſaw the hinder part of a hide of
                Colour red & the end of the taile white & he
                Saw the ſd Taylor bury the ſd piece of hide
                & that about 10 or 12 weeks ago the ſd Thatcher
                went to the houſe of Iſrael Taylor the ſd Thather then
                underſtanding that he was under ſuſpition of
                being guilty of aſſiſting in the killing of the ſd heifer
                he aſked the ſd Taylor's wife what heifer it was
                that was killed & who killd it & ſhee ſaid Ben Jons

& Ifrael kill her & that fhee beleived it was
naylors heifer

Bartholemew Thather attefted doth Say laft fall was 12 months
ago he was at Ifrael Taylors where he ftayed alnight
& faw Ifrael Taylors wife drefs fome meate w^{ch}
he thought was young heifer beefe & before that
time the heifer of John naylor was wanting #

\# The will of Richard Thather being delivered into
Court it was ordered that Phinehas Pemberton
Clark shold keep it untill further order

126

adjourned for one houre

verdict jury returned do fay Ifrael Taylor is not
guilty of the felony whereof he ftands Indicted

A deed in fee of 200 acres dated the 3 day of the 9th
month 1690 acknowledged by Jofuah Hoops attorney
to Jof Englifh grantor to Sa Dark grantee

The executions before mentioned both returned Satiffyed

wm Biles acknowledged in open Court that
he had Red full satiffaction from Derick Jonfon 1 bl mare
with a long taile & dule back with Some white haires
in her fore head & a half peny Cut on the further eare
wch fd mare the fd Derrick is allowed to take up when
he can find her & her encreafe that Shall lawfully
appeare to belong to her & that he the fd wm Biles
will warrnt the fd mare & her Increafe to the fd Jonfon &
defend
from all perfons

Reported to this Court by John Brock that Richard
Thatcher did confefs he owed to Derrick Jonfon the
Sum of one pound eight Shillings & that
it was to be payd in good wheate

Judgmt given & its adjudged by the fd Jon Brock that
the fd Sum Shall be accordingly payd wth Cofts wch Judgm
is aproved of by this Court & thereupon
ordered that execution Iffue accordingly

Judgmt given & its adjudged that John naylor Shall pay
Cofts of fuite & that execution Iffue accordingly

Israel Taylor promised to pay the fees in both actions wherein
Revel was Concerned agt him to the officers

adjourned the Court to the 20th day of this month to the house
of Tho Janney

8th io 1690 ececution granted agt Rich Thatcher for 3 £ : 9ˢ : 4ᵈ
mo   for fees

returnd 13 io 1690 executed p wm yardley Sherrife
mo

12 io 1690 execution dated agt Rich Thatcher & Israel Taylor
for 4 £ 14ˢ 6ᵈ in Revels Cafe

16 io 1690 returnd executed on the effects Israel Taylor in Tho
mo   Brocks
hands 2 £ 7ˢ 0ᵈ & of the good of Rich Thatcher 1 hors
apprized at 5 £

12 io 1690 execution agt sd Thatcher in Derick Jonsons Cafe
mo   was dated 1 : 16 : 0

127

Att a Court held by adjournmt the 20th day
of the 10th month 1690 at the house of Tho:
Janney

Tho Janney   wm Biles
Nicholas waln   John Brock
wm yardley Sherrif
P: P: Cl:

Richard Thather being bound in 20 £ : to appeare at
this Court none appearing agt: him the Court
discharges him

Action
decl read ⎫ John Brock   ⎫
bill read — ⎬   agt   ⎬ action debt gilbert wheeler appeared not
           ⎭ gilbert wheeler ⎭   John Brock appeared

wm: Biles appeared on sd wheelers acctt & sd
that g: wheeler was before him this day
& Confest the bill mentioned in the declarᵗ

John Brock Confeſt he had Red in pte of the ſd
bill the ſum of 1 £ : 10ˢ 09ᵈ

Judgmt given by default that in as much
as the ſd gilbert wheeler did not appeare here
according to ſummonce but Confeſt the bill
before wm: Biles one of the Juſtices of peace
it is adjudged that gilbert wheeler ſhall
pay to John Brock 4 £ : 05ˢ: 03ᵈ & 5ˢ dama
═ges with Coſts of Suite / & that execution Iſſue
accordingly

*Ordered that in as much as yᵉ Severalˡ orders of
Court about the Collecting of the arrears of
the firſt Tax is not observed that wm:
yardley the Sherriſe do Collect the arrears
of the Tax & that a warrant be Iſſued
accordingly to Impower him

whereas it is the Sherriſe hath made return of
the executions out agt: the goods & Chattles of Joſeph
Holden for the ſeveral Sums obtained by

128

John Duplovis philip Richards & Cornelius empſon
that there is no goods nor Chattles to Satiſfye the ſd debts
& that the ſd pſons have requeſted to have execution
agt the ſd Holdens land it is ordered by this Court
that execution Iſſue agt the lands of the
ſd Holden to Satiſfye the Severall Judgmts
obtained by the aforeſd perſons

whereas the grand Jury did prſent the neceſſity
of haveing the County devided into townſhips it is order
that Henry Baker Thomas Janney wm Biles
Phinehas Pemberton Arthur Cook Edmund
Bennet James Boyden Nicholas waln
Joſuah Hoops Jon Rowland
Joſeph growdon Saml Allen & that they
meete together the day before the next
Court at the Court houſe & then
& there devide this County into Townſhips that
the Same may be prented to the next Court

---

* Crossed out in the record.

to have the approbation thereof
whereas the grand Inquefts prfented the
neceffity of having weights & meafures equall
according to law its referred to be further
confidered of

adjourned to the ii day of the firft month
next

The 3 Executions aforefd granted agt the land of Jofeph Holden
in Duplovie Richards & Empfons Cafe dated the 20th day
of the iith month i690
i3 1 1690 execut in Is: Taylors Cafe for i7^s 6^d
mo 1
returned agt Rich Thather ———

Bucks fs

129
County Court y^e: iith 1 90
mo 1

(1)
Action Entered } Jofeph ffarington agt John Tatham plea Debt
the 20th 9 i690 } ffor tryal at the ioth Court but the —
mo tryal Refpited to this Court becaufe of
the fd Jon Tathams Sicknef or Indifpofednefs

(2)
Action Entered } John Smith plt agt Thomas peirce deft in a plea
the i i2 i690 } of
mo

(3)
Action Entered } Zachariah whitpaine plt agt gilbert wheeler
the 16th i2 i690 } deft in a plea of Debt
mo

Summonce granted the i6th i2th month i690 for fd wheelers appearanc
the iith of the firft month next Enfueing

return made executed the i6th of the i2th mo: i690 on fd wheeler
by willm yardley Sherrif

withdrawn by wm Biles order

(4)

Action Entered the 23 day of 12th mo 1690 } Thomas Revel plt agt Ifrael Taylor deft in plea of Cafe

Summonce granted for fd Taylor in fd Revells Cafe dated the 23 12 mo 169

Return —

Summonce granted for Thomas Brock & John Jones wittnefes in the Cafe Revel agt Taylor

Return

(5)

Action Entered 24th 12 mo 1690 — } Andrew Heath agt wm Beakes in a plea of trefpa

Summonce granted for fd Beakes appearance in fd Heaths Cafe the 24 12 mo 90

return

Summonce granted for James Sutton & John Richardfon witneffes in fa Cafe Heath agt Beakes the 4th of the ift month 1690/1

return — &

130

(6)

Action Entered the 25th 12 mo 1690 } willm: yardley plt agt Hugh marfh & Robt mar in an action of Debt

Summonce granted the 25th of the 12th mo 1690 for fd marfh appearance in fd Cafe

Return

(7)

Action Entered the 25th 12 mo 1690 } Thomas Janney by his attorney John Neild plt agt John Lees & Jofeph milner defts in plea of de

Summonce granted for ſd Lees & milners appearance date the
25th i2 1690
        mo

Return

   with drawn by order of Thomas Janney

(8)

Action Entered } Thomas peirce plt agt: John pidcock in a plea of
the 25th i2 i690 } Caſe
     mo

Attachment granted agt ſd pidcocks goods & Chattles for his appearance in ſd peirces Caſe dated the 22 day of the iith mo i690 ——

Return the 23 of the iith mo i690 by vertue of this warrant attached of the goods of John pidcock i buck ſkin 3 doe ſkins 2 guns a parcel of Red Lead about 30 lb weight

  Bucks ſſ

131

      At a Court of Quarter Seſſions held by the
      king & queens authority in the name of
      willm Penn propryatory & govrnr of
      the ſd province & territorys thereunto
      belonging at the Court houſe the iith day of
      the i i690 being the iith yeare of the
         mo 1
      propryatorys govrmt

               The Juſtices then prſent
        Arthur Cook   Joſeph growdon
        Henry Baker   Nicho waln &
            wm yardley Sherriff
             P P Clark

action Jos farrington }
               agt } both appeared & deſired one
          Jon Tatham} hours time before the
                           matter was brought
                           to tryal wch was allowed

action Tho Revel }
            agt } neither appeared
       Iſrael Taylor }

action Andrew Heath ⎫
              agt ⎬ both appeared
      wm Beakes ⎭

      declarat read

      Anſwer

      Iſſue Joyned

action wm yardley   ⎫ plt appeared the
              agt   ⎬
      Hugh marſh & Rob marſh ⎭ deft appeared not
      whereupon the Court Suspended the action
      untill tomorrow

    Jury atteſted

Andrew Heath ⎫ Declra & anſwer read   132
        agt ⎬
wm Beakes ⎭

wittneſſes wm Thomas James Sutton Joſeph Henry atteſted
               Tho kirl atteſted george Cockram Joſeph ſteward
                  atteſted
               Tho Tunneclif atteſted Ann Ellot Sarah biles
               atteſted John wood Andrew Ellot atteſted

      Adjourned for one houre
      adjourned untill tomorrow morning at 9 a Clock

Jury returnd Say they find for the plt wᵗʰ 3ˢ
   damages & Coſts of Suit

Joſeph ffarington ⎫
            agt ⎬ both Calld appeared
    John Tatham ⎭

      declarat read
        Anſwer read
      obligation Read & Conſeſt to by yᵉ: deft
      award read — & Confest

*Upon Complt of Daniel garner how that he was
abuſed beaten & aſſaulted by Richard Thatcher
Tho Coleman & Tho Coverdale: the ſd Thather
being Calld in Court for the ſd abuſe & other

---

* Crossed out in the records.

misdemeanors & Suerties demaned of him
for his appearance at next Court & keeping
the peace in the meane time but for want
thereof the Court Commits him Into Cuſtody untill
he Shall find fuerties and appeare at ſd Court
and as for the abuſe done by ſd Coverdale
& Coleman its referred to wm Biles to Inſpect &
take Care of

Jury returnd do Say they find for the plt w[th]
Coſts

John Thatham deſired the Court to allow him
an appeale

adjourned the Court for one houre

A deed of morgage of 400 acres of land by John pidcock
grantor to Edward Hunlock grantee dated the 12th of
10 mo: 1690 with a ſcedule thereunto annexed was
tendered by Ed: Hunlock to ſd pidcock to back
nowledged

133   acknowledged according to law w[ch] ſd pidcock refuſed to
do with ſheweing
any Cauſe for his ſo refuſeing

John Smith agt ⎱ appeared — ⎱
Tho peirce — ⎰ appeared   ⎰
declaration read & both partes
referd the matter to the bench

Tho peirce agt ⎱ both appeared
Jon pidcock agt ⎰ declarat read
Anſwer read
Jury atteſted
declarat proved by the atteſtation
of Tho peirce gilbert wheeler &
policarpus roſe

Jury returned find for the plt 20[s]
with coſt of Suite
the
Adjourned the Court to 9 tomorrow morning

Adjourned the orphans Court untill 2 a Clock
tomorrow

wm yardley
    agt } both appeared read
Hugh marſh & Robt marſh

declaration being read
bill obligate read
deft Anſwer he owned the bill to be his
  act & deed
Tho peirce produced a diſcharge undr John
  Smiths hand in full & the ſd peirce pro=
  =miſed in open Court to pay & diſcharge all
  Coſts & fees

adjudged by the Court that the action agt peirce be with drawr

Judgmt Entered in thathr Caſe agt Beakes According
  to verdict & that execution Iſſue accordingly

134

Judgment given & it is adjudged that John Tatham
  pay to Joſeph ffarington 50 £ with Coſt of Suite

Diference
  after Judgment given both parties referred to y^e:
    Juſtices on the bench what Shall be abated
    of the penalty

Judgment
  given that John pidcock Shall pay to Tho peirce
  20^s with Coſt of ſuite & that execution Shall Iſſue
  accordingly

Tho Revel agt } both Calld & neither of the appeared
Iſrael Taylor

adjourned for one houre

13th i / mo / 1690 / 1

whereas Joſeph ffarington & John Tatham
referred to the Juſtices on the bench what
they Juge in equity the ſd John Tatham
Shall pay to the ſd ffarrington in full Satiſfaction of the
  afforeſd Judgement whereupon the
ſd Juſtices do Judg award & determine that

the ſd John Tatham Shall pay to ſd —
ffarrington, 28 £ in Silver mony or in
good merchantable wheate at Silver mony
price in one months time after the day of the date hereof
& further that the ſd John Tatham
Shall pay to the reſpective officers the fees due
to them by reaſon of the afforeſd Judgmt & —
upon paymt of the Said mony that the ſd parties
Shall ſeale Each other general releaſes & that
if the ſd John Tatham Shall faile payment
of the ſd mony as above expreſſed that then
execution Iſſue according to the Judgment
firſt obtained & further it is expreſſed that
the ſd John Tatham Shall make payment to the
ſd Joſeph ffarrington or his attorney at the
ferry houſe over agt Burlington

<u>135</u> george Brown being Calld upon his recognizance
being bound for aſſaulting & abuſeing <u>wm.</u>
Biles one of the Juſtices of the peace of this
County; & upon his examination Confeſt that he
twice he puſht him with his hand whereupon
the Court gave Judgmt & it was adjudged
that the ſd george Browne, Shall give his own
bond for his appearance at th next Court & be of
good abeareing in the meane time & Shall pay
a fine of 20^s to be diſpoſ of as the Juſtices here
after Shall think fit
geo: Brown acknowledged him ſelf Indebted to y^e:
propryatory & govrnr in io £ to be levyed on his
lands & tenements goods & Chattles
conditioned for his appearance at the next
Court & to be of good abearing in the meane <u>time</u>

adjourned till tomorrow morning
at 9 a Clock

adjourned the orpans Court to 10

whereas the pſons appointed to devide the County have
not done it is ordered that the ſd pſons meete
to gether on the 20 day of the 2 month next to
devide it into townſhips

adjourned the Court unto the 20 day of the 2 month next

County Court Bucks ff 136

At a Court of Quarter Seffions held by the king & Queens authority in the name of wm Penn propryatory & govrnr of the province of Penfilvania & territorys thereunto belonging at the Court houfe of the aforefd County the 10th day of the 7th month 1690

Juftices prfent
Jofe: growdon   wm Biles   Tho: Janney
Nicholas Waln   Henry Baker
John Brock
wm yardley   Sherrif
P P Cl: Com:

Commitmt   wm Evans for Sufpition of Confederacy of fellony with Jofeph Trevithan is Commited to Cuftody untill further order

adjourned untill 9 a Clock tomorrow moring

Action   Jon Jones & attorneys ⎱ a
                    agt ⎰ plea of debt
Jofeph Holden deft
patterick Robinfon Jon Swift his attorneys appeared
Jofe: Holden appeared not

declara Read

A Coppy of the letter of attorney & Certificate on the back bond   read & proved

bill   read & proved by the atteftation of Jon: Swift & Henry pointer

Judgmt given & it is adjudged that Jofeph Holden Shall pay to Jon Jones, or attorneys the Sum of thirty pounds Silver mony as allfo the Sum of Six pounds eight Shillings & Six pence with Intereft for the thirty pounds from the firft day of the 3 month 1690 with Coft of Suite to wch marfh the fd Holdens attorney affented

ordered   by the Court that Paterick Robinfon becom bound upon record in Court in 100 £ that John Jones Shall ratefye what he & other attorneys has done in relati -on to the afforefd action

137   Paterick Robinſon oblidges him Self his heires executrs
& adminiſtrators to the Juſtices
now prſent on the bench being Joſeph growdon
wm: Biles Thomas Janney nicholas waln Henry
Baker & John Brock theire executrs & adminiſtr
the Sum of one hundered pounds to be levyed
on his goods & Chattles Lands & tenements —
Conditioned for the procureing of an authentick
power from John Jones or that ſd Jon Jones or heires executrs
adminiſtrators in 12 month time do Ratefye
what ſd paterick Robinſon & the rest of the attorneys
of John Jones has done or Shall do in relation
to an action of debt for 36 £ 8ˢ 6ᵈ now
brought agt Joſeph Holden
         Pat: Robinson

Action John Duplovies⎫
    agt   ⎬ plea of debt
   Joſe Holden⎭

paterick Robinſon appeared

letter of attorney to Impower him produced &
 Hugh marſh attorney appears

letter of attorney to prove the Same was produced
 debt acknowledged by the attorney

Judgmt given & it is adjudged that Joſeph Holden Shall
 pay to John Duplovie the Sum of 13 £ : 18ˢ 7½ᵈ
 The ſd plt attorney haveing promiſed to allow what
 Shall be further made appeare upon acctt if any
 be

Action philip Richards plt⎫
    agt   ⎬ in a plea of debt
   Joſeph Holden deft⎭

paterick Robinſon attorney appeares

letter of attorney produced to prove the ſame

Hugh march attorney appeares

Declaration read

Anſwer he ownes the debt

Judgmt given & it is adjudged that Joſeph Holden Shall
    pay to philip Richards the ſum of 10 £ : 2ˢ 3ᵈ
    The ſd plts attorney haveing promiſed to allow what Shall
    be further made appeare to pd on acctt

action   Jon wood plt ⎫
               agt   ⎬ in a plea of Caſe
          John Swift deft ⎭

        plt appeares

        deft appeares

decl   read

Anſwer he doth owne the takeing up the negroes

  The matter referred to the bench

Judgment given that John Swift Shall pay to John wood
    25ˢ & yᵗ : John Swift Shall pay Coſt of ſuite

Action   Samuel Beakes plt ⎫
                 agt   ⎬ in a plea of debt both appeared
           Jonathan Eldridge deft ⎭

declaration read — — —

Anſwer he Confeſſes the debt

  Judgmt given & it is adjudged that Jonathan Eldridg
    Shall pay to the plt the Sum of two
    pounds three ſhillings Seven pence with Coſt
    of Siute wᶜʰ Sum of 2 £ : 3ˢ 7ᵈ willm Embley
    in open Court declared he wold pay to the plt or
    attorney in 3 months time
    & willm Biles likewiſe in Court promiſed to pay
    the fees

Deed   of 72 Square Rods of land in fee dated the 4 day
    of 7ᵗʰ mo 1690 by Tho Janney grantor Joſuah Hoops
    & wm yardley for the uſe of themſelves & the reſt of the
    grantees

adjourned for one hour

A deed   in fee of 200 acres of land dated the ioᵗʰ day
    of the i2ᵗʰ month i689 by P Pemberton grantr
    to mary Radclif the widow of the grantee

A deed	in fee of 250 acres of land dated the 8th day of the 7th month 1690 by wm Clows & margery clows grantors to Joseph Clows grantee
A deed	in fee of 250 acres of land dated the 8th of the 7th month 1690 by Joseph Clows grantor to wm Clows grantee
grand Jury attested	
Indictmt	agt Tho Brock for extortion in his ferriage pleaded guilty
A deed	of 500 acres of land in fee dated the 9th day of the 7th month 1690 by John Rowland grantor to gilbert wheeler grantee
A deed	of 236 acres in fee dated the 15th of the 9th mo: first yeare of the reigne of wm & mary by wm Diles attorney to Jon Cuft grantor to Sam Beakes grantee
A deed	of 60 acres of land in fee dated the 20th of the 6th mo: 1690 by Joseph growdon grantor to Tho: scot grantee
Action	Israel Taylor agt Tho Brock Jo stedon Ra Boome ffra Rosill & mathew miller deft plea of Case Israel Taylor appeared Tho Brock ffra Rossill & John stedon appeare on the behalf of them selves & the rest
declarat	Read
Answer	they Confest to the declaration & Sayd that they wold pay Israel Taylor 5 £ : 10s & Cost of Suite
reply	Israel Taylor, that he was Content with it & Craved Judgmt for the same
Judgmt	given & it is adjudged that the sd defts Shall pay to sd plt 5 £ : 15s with Cost of suite & that execution Issue accordingly

142   RECORDS OF THE COURTS OF QUARTER SESSIONS AND

Penſylvania   (140)

County Court Bucks ſs:

(1)
action = Entered ⎫ John Jones by his attorney Samll Carpenter——
the 2i 6   ⎬
    ―――― mo   ⎪ Paterick Robinson John ſſuller & John Swift plt
    1690   ⎭
                                agt
                                                        £
          ⎧ Joſeph Holden deft in an act of Debt 66: 8ˢ::6ᵈ
          ⎨ granted the i9ᵗʰ day of the 6 month i690 p A Cook
Attachmt— made by the Sherrif executed the 2i 6 90
Return   ――――
                                                      mo
                                wm yardley ſherrif

---

(2)
Action Entered ⎫ John Duplovie plt ⎫
the 23 day of ⎬   ⎬   £ ˢ ᵈ
  6 1690   ⎪   agt   ⎪ in action of Debt 15: 16: 7
  ――――   ⎭   ⎭
   mo   Joſeph Holden deft
Attachmt for ſd Holdens appearance agt his goods granted
        the 2i day of the 6ᵗʰ month i690 p A Cook
Return made the 30ᵗʰ of the 6ᵗʰ month 1690 Executed p
    wm yardley Sherrife ――――――――――――――   ―――――

---

(3)
action Entered ⎫ Philip Richards plt ⎫
the 23 day 6 ⎬   ⎬ in an action of debt
        ―――― ⎪   agt   ⎪
         mo   ⎭   ⎭
       i690   Joſeph Holden deft
Attachment for the ſd Holdens appearance agt his goods granted

Return	the 2¹ day of the 6ᵗʰ month i690 p A Cook made the 30ᵗʰ 6/mo 1690 executed p wm yardley Sherrif

(141)

(4) Action Entered the 24ᵗʰ of the 6ᵗʰ month — i690 ————	⎫ ⎬ Ifrael Taylor plt ⎪ agt: ⎨ Thomas Brock ⎪ Ralph Boome ⎪ John ftedon ⎪ ffrancis Roffill ⎭ mathew miller	plea of Cafe Sum: 8 L — —
Summonce	granted the 26ᵗʰ 6/mo 1690 p Jon Brock	
Returne	made executed the 30ᵗʰ day of the 6ᵗʰ month 1690 p wm yardley Sherrif	

---

(5) Action Entered the 26ᵗʰ 6ᵗʰ/mo 1690	⎫ ⎬ Pilocarpus Rofe plt ⎨ agt ⎭ John Pidcock deft	plea of trefpafs & affault
Summonc	granted the 26ᵗʰ 6/mo 90 p Jon Brock	
Return	made the 29ᵗʰ day of the 6 month i690 Executed p wm yardley fherrif	
Summonce	for wittneffes in fd Cafe granted the 26 day of 6ᵗʰ mo: 90 for Jon Lee & his wife Rachel Lee martha Lee & Robt Benfon	
Return	made the 28ᵗʰ & 29ᵗʰ of the 6/mo. 1690 executed p wm yardley Sherrif	

(6)

Action Entered the 26ᵗʰ 6ᵗʰ / mo } gilbert Wheeler plt / agt / John Pidcock deft } in a plea of Caſe

Summonce — granted the 26ᵗʰ 6/mo i690 p Jon Brock

Return — made the 29 day of the 6ᵗʰ month 1690 Executed p wm yardley ſherrif

(7)

Action Entered the 26ᵗʰ 6/mo 1690 } Iſrael Taylor plt / agt / John Shippey deft } in a plea of Caſe   (142)

Summonce — granted the 26ᵗʰ day of the 6ᵗʰ/mo i690 p Jon Brock

Returne — made the 29 day of the 6ᵗʰ month i690 p w yard Sherrif

Summonce — granted for appeareranc of witneſs wm Roles the 26ᵗʰ
6 mo 90

Return made — the 29ᵗʰ 6/mo 90 executed p wm yardley Sherrif

(8)

Action Entered the 28ᵗʰ 6/mo 1690 } John wood plt / agt / John Buttler deft } in a plea of Caſe

Attachmt — granted the 28ᵗʰ day of the 6 month 1690 p Jon Brock

Return,— made the 29ᵗʰ & 30 days of the 6ᵗʰ month i690 p wm yardley Sherrif

COMMON PLEAS OF BUCKS COUNTY, PENNSYLVANIA 145

(9)
Action Entered ⎫ John wood plt ⎫
the 28th 6   ⎬   agt ⎬ in a plea of Cafe
      mo   ⎭ John Swift deft ⎭
     1690

Summonce   granted the 28 day of the 6 i690 p Jon: Brock
                                       mo

return   made the 29th day of the 6th month i690 executed
                           p wm yardley Sherrif

Action Entered ⎫ mary Beakes adminiſtratrix to her late huſband
the 28th 6   ⎬ willm Beakes by her attorney Samuel Beakes plt
      mo   ⎭
     1690   agt
               Jonathan Eldridg def ————————

Arreſt granted   the iith 4th mo i690 p wm Biles
return made   the iith 4 90 taken into Cuſtody
                          mo

143

Cornelius Empſon Craved in open Court that wm Embley
might be his attorney to profecute an action of
debt agt Joſeph Holden for 8 £ ſilver mony
wch was allowed by the Court

wm Evans being examined about a horſe found in the Cuſtody
of Joſeph Trevitham Said that he lent the ſd Trevithan
the horſe

adjourned the Court untill 8 a Clock tomorrow
morning
                                              £   s   d
Execution Signed for Jon Jones for the Levying of 36: 8.: 6
& 2 £ : 3s 1d, Coſts on the goods of Joſeph Holden

Action Cornelius Empſon plt ⎫
              agt   ⎬ Caſe of debt
       Joſeph Holden ———   ⎭

appeares by his attorney willm Embley

Jo Holden appeares by his attorney Hugh marſh

decla: read

Anſwer Confeſt the debt

Judgmt given & it is adjudged that Joſeph Holden Shall pay to Cornelius Empſon the Sum of 8 £ : Silver — mony with Coſts of ſuite & that execution Iſſue accordingly

Iſrael Taylor
        agt } plea of Caſe
Action John Shippey

    plt appeares

    deft appeares

decla read

Anſwer that he owes the plt 33^s & will pay Coſts of ſuite

the plt: declared that the Same pd to him will Satiſſye him

Judgmt given & it is adjudged that John Shippey Shall pay thirty three ſhillings with Coſt of Suite & that Execution Iſſue accordingly

144

Joſeph Trivithan to his Indictm pleaded not guilty for tryal puts him Self on the Cuntry

Tho ffox atteſted Saith that upon the 8th day of this Inſtant he came to the houſe of Jos: growdon & ſaid Jos: growdon had ſent him for Cloths for he & his wife ha fallen in the river & wanted them & thereby obtaned from the negro woman i Cloth Coate i p pluſh breeſhes i womans cloak

John Hawkins atteſted Saith that upon munday laſt being the 8th Inſtant he ſaw the ſaid Trevithan at the houſe of J gro: where he ſaid he Saw the ſd Trevithan have upon his horſe i Cloth Coate one

paire plufh breaches & womans Cloake wch under —
pretenc of Jofeph growdons being wet in the
river he had obtained from the negro —
woman

Action withdrawn rofe agt pidcock

Conftables for above the falls Jofuah Hoops
  for below to penfberry Jofeph Chorley
  for the middle lotts — wm Duncan
  for the upper part of Nefhaminah John White
  for the other fide of the upper pt of Nefhaminah Jon purflone
  for the lower pt on the other fide Sam Allen Junr:
  for the lower pte of the river Tho green

Jury returned do fay they find Jofe Trevithan as he is
Charged in the Indictment

Tho king to his Indict pleaded not guilty
puts him felf on y^e: Cuntry for tryal
Hugh marfh attefted Says in or about the 3 month laft paft
 Says that Tho King fd
there was a witch neare
by being asked who it was fd he Sufpected ffra: Searls wife
for Shee was an ugly Ile favored woman & he did
believe her to be one

Robt marfh attefted Says he heard Tho king Say that there
 was
a witch hard by

Action Jon wood } plea of debt
―――   agt
145 Jon Butler

plt appeares

deft appeares not

declarat read

Ric Ridgway attefted Saith that he knows that Jon
wood did deliver a conciderable quantyty
of wheat & that he beleives Buttler owed Jon wood
at his going away above 20 £ to be the beft of knowledg
21 or 22 £ as he heard Jon Butler fay & further
Saith that Jon Butler promifed Cattle for the fd Corn

Joſeph wood atteſted proves Every article of the acctt

Judgmt given by default & it is adjudged that John Buttler Shall pay to John wood the ſum of 5 £ ii^s wth 3 £ damages & coſt of ſuite that execution Iſſue accordingly

Jury returned finds Tho king guilty of defameing Joan the wife of ffrancis Searle in Saying he believed She was witch

gilbert wheeler promiſed to pay the fees of polls act

Action g wheeler ⎱
         agt ⎰ Caſe

J pidcock

plt appeare

deft appeares

decl read

Anſwer read

acctt brought in & read & atteſted

Jo Hollinſhed atteſted proves pt of the debt

verdict find for the plt wth Coſts of ſuite

adjudged that John pidcock Shall pay 2 £ : 14^s : 00^d wth Coſts of ſuite & that execution Iſſue accordingly

A deed in fee of 296 of land dated the i2th day of the firſt m($_c$
$\frac{1689}{90}$ ack & dd by Hen: marg: grantor
to John Clark grantee

146

Judgmt given & it is adjudged that Tho king Shall pay Coſt of ſuite & be bound to keep the peace & appeare at next Court of Quarter ſeſſions

regcognizance Tho king acknowledgs him ſelf Indebted to the pro prya & govrnr in the ſum of 10 £ to be levyed on his lands & tenemts goods & Chattles upon

Condition that he Shall appeare at the
next Court of Quarter Seſſions & to keep
the king & queens peace in the meane
time

    Adjourned to 8 in the morning

Judgmt given & it is adjudged that wm Evans none appearing
agt him Shall be diſcharged paying fees & Coſts

Judgmts given & it is adjudged that Joſeph Trevithan upon
his Indictm Shall make double Satiſfaction wch is he ſhall
pay to Joſeph growdon ten pounds & that Joſeph
growdon Shall pay the Coſts & fees the goalers fees excepted
& whereas
the ſd Trevithan hath not eſtate to anſwer the ſd
Satisfaction it is adjudged that the ſd Trevithan
for the Same Shall Serve the ſd Joſeph growdon
one yeare & a Quarter except he doth ſerve
very well & ſathfully one yeare then to be free at the
yeares End to wch Judgment both Joſeph growdon &
Trevithan declared theire Satiſfaction

Jon: pidcock being Calld appeared & declared polcarpus Roſe
had made him Satiſfaction

polcarpus Roſe appeared & nothing appearing agt him the Court
diſcharges him paying his fees

    overſeeres of the high way

* 148 for above the falls Ruben pownal
for below to y^e: govrnrs Joſeph Chorley
for y^e: lower pte of the river Rich wilſon
for y^e: lower pte of Neſha minah Derick Clawſon
for the upper pte of Neſha minah wm Hayhurſt
the middle lotts John webſter
for the lower End of Neſhaminah on the further
ſide walter fforeſt & Sam Allen
for a bove Tho: Harding

Ajourned to the 7th of the 8th mo next

execution agt the goods & Chattles of Joſeph
Holden in Jon Duplovies Caſe in Philip —

---

* There is no page numbered 147 in the record; 148 follows 146.

RECORDS OF THE COURTS OF QUARTER SESSIONS AND

Richards Cafe & in Cornelius Empfons Cafe were dated the 19^(th) 7/mo 1690 & returned by the fherrife the 29 7/mo 1690 no Goods or Chattles to be found   wm yardley

County Court Bucks fs
149

Entered the 20 day 1 month
1691
2
(1)   { Daniel Cox by   his attorney John Tatham
        agt   plea of Debt
       Gilbert wheeler }   Sum dated 26^(th) 3/mo 90/1

Entered   Gilbert wheeler
the 21 day   agt   } in a plea of Slander
i month   John Tatham —   Sum granted the 26 day of 3 mo 90/1

(2)
14^(th) 3/mo i69i an arreſt granted agt Henry Boucher to anfwer the Complt of Jofeph knight 29 3/mo 1691 return made by wm yardley fherrif not to be found

Zacharia whitpaine
        agt   } in a plea of Debt
gilbert wheeler —   not carryed on —

Entered
23 3   Jofeph England
mo   agt   } in a plea of Debt ———— } with drawn
1691   Lawrence Parker   Arreft dated 25^(th) 3/mo 9i } by ordr of
(3)   philip England

John Bud
    agt   } plea of debt not pfecuted
Daniel gardner

(4)
Entered } Tho Hudſon agt Jacob Hall action of debt } with drawn
25th 3   ſum dated 26 3 9i } by ordr of
—— mo   —— mo   Wm Biles

(5)
Entered } John otter agt: ffrancis Roſfill
25th 3   Sum dated 26 3 91
—— mo   —— mo
1691

(6)
Entered
25: 3 9i Joſeph Chorley }
—— mo   agt } in a plea of
        margery Clows } Caſe   Sum dated 26 3 i69i
                                                                                     —— mo
                                          with drawn by ordr of ſd Chorley

(7)
Entered John Tatham }
the 25 3   agt } plea of Caſe
—— mo
169i   Joſeph Growdon }   ſum dated 25th 3 169i
                                                                  —— mo
                          John Tatham not appearing a non ſuite
                        granted thereupon

Entered Tho Revel ——— }
the 25 3   agt
—— mo
(8)   ffrancis Roſfill } action
                           of debt   ſum dated 25th 3 i69i
                                                                    —— mo

The 26th 3 1691
      —— mo

150	Thomas Brock }	
	agt } of a plea of Cafe ím dated 26ᵗʰ	3 9i
	ffrancis Roſſill }	mo

        9ᵗʰ 3 i69i execution granted agt Jon Pidcocks
           mo
        goods for 3 £ : iiˢ 7ᵈ in Tho peirce Cafe

debt 1 : 0 : 0   iiᵗʰ 3 9i returnd taken in execution i raw
                       mo
Cl :—1 : 2 : 1½   buck ſkin 3 raw doeſkinſ i8 boards
Jury—0 : 8 : 0   about 350 foot 2 smal guns with one Lock 31 lb red lead
Sherrif 0 : 9 : 6   18ᵗʰ 6 9i appriſed by the apprizors
                       mo
witnes 0 : 12 : 0   wm Paxſon Robt Heaton the boards 6ˢ pc
   3 : 11 : 7½   the Skins 4ˢ 6ᵈ the guns ioˢ the lead i5ˢ 6ᵈ

        the guns Lead & Skins were ordr to me by Tho peirce
        for mony he owed me
about the latter end of the firſt month Jon pidcock deſired
me to let him have the goods as apprized & he wold pay
what they were valued at & gave me a Cannoe in pte
at 20ˢ & the reſt promiſed to pay on demand if ſd peirce
did not

County Court Bucks ſs   151

        At a Court of Quarter Seſſions held by the
        authority of william & mary king & Queen
        of England &c : & in the name of william
        Penn propryatory & govrnr the ioᵗʰ day
        of the 4ᵗʰ monᵗʰ being the 3 yeare of the king
        & Queens Reigne & iiᵗʰ yeare of the propry
        atorys govrmt 169i

          The Juſtices then prſent
       Arthur Cook   Joſeph Growdon   wm Biles
       Nicholas waln   Henry Baker   John Brock
       John Cook   Corronor
         wm yardley   Sherrif
          Phinehas Pemberton   Clark

     george Brown continued on recognizance untill next Court

COMMON PLEAS OF BUCKS COUNTY, PENNSYLVANIA 153

        Judgment given by willm Biles in Cafe for thirty apple trees &
three fhillings & nine pence between Ifrael Taylor
plt & Rich Thatcher defend whereupon it was adjudged
that Rich Thatcher Shold pay Ifrael Taylor 3^s: 9^d & thirty
apple trees or for want of the apple trees the fd Thacher to pay
ten Shillings Inftead thereof wch Judgment is by this Court
allowed and adjudged that execution Iffue accordingly

	John otter agt ffrancis Rofill	act debt both appeared

        Declara read

        bond Red read

Anfwer   deft owned the bond

plant   declared that he defired nothing but ten pounds with the
        Intreft fince it was due

    A proclamation agt vice from the govrnr read

        Tho Revel agt: ffrancis Rofill in an action of debt
        both appeared declarat read bill read

Anfwer   ffrancis Rofill owned the debt but not the damages

reply   Tho Revell declared that the debt without damages
        wold Satiffye him

    152 Tho: Brock agt: ffrancis Roffill in a plea of Cafe

        both appeared

        declara read

Anfwer   ffrancis Roffill owned the debt & the plant declared he

reply   defired not the damages

Judgment   given & it is adjudged that ffrancis Roffill pay to
        John otter ten pounds with Intreft fince it was due
        & coft of fuite & that execution Iffue accordingly

Judgmt   it is adjudged that ffrancis Roffill pay to Tho
        Revell 7 £: 01^s: 3^d with Coft of fuit & that execution
        Iffue accordingly

Judgmt   it is adjudged that ffrancis Roffill pay to
               Tho Brock 10 £ : 19ˢ 5ᵈ with Cofts of fuite & that execution
                  Iffue accordingly

*Action   Daniel Cox   ⎫   gilbert wheeler appeared
                    agt   ⎬
               gilbert wheeler ⎭   Daniel Cox appeared by attorney

               Edward Hunlock & george Hutchinfon & Thomas Revel
               Edward Hunlock & Thomas Revel both of Burlington
               in weft Jarfey do acknowledg them felves to ftand
               Indebted to gilbert wheeler in the fum of two
               hundred pounds Currant mony of this province
               to be levied on theire goods & Chattles lands and
               tenements Conditioned for that whereas an
               action being brought this Court by Daniel Cox
               agt Gilbert wheeler on a bond of 100 £ dated
               the 3 day of Aprill 1690 & that they appearing on
               behalf as attorneys to the faid Cox & theire power
               not appearing to be Sufitiont from the fd Cox to pfecute
               the fd action if therefore the fd Hunlock & Revell
               Shall hereafter
               upon demand from fd Wheeler procure a legal authority from
               fd Cox, to Ratefye what Shall be done by the fd
               Hunlock & Revell in Relation to the faid tryal &
               make good al damages that Shall be adjudged to be payd
               by fd Cox then the above Recognizance
               to be voyd Ells to remain in force

Cox   letter of Attorney read
agt   declara read   ⎫
wheeler   Anfwer read   ⎪   geo: Hutchinfon   153
          Iffue Joyned   ⎬   James Hill
          Jury attefted   ⎪   Barnard Devonifh
          bond read   ⎭

James Hill fays that Gilbert wheeler was arrefted by him over night & that
    geo Hutchinfon engaged to bring him forth next morning
    & accordingly next morning he thinks

---
* This paragraph crossed out in record.

geo: Hutchinſon ſent for him where he found ſd wheeler in ſd
Hutchinſon houſe & the bond was ſealed & delivered
before the ſd wheeler was acquited from the arreſt he was
under

Bernard Devoniſh Saith that he arreſted ſd wheeler late over night
& geo: Hutchinſon engaged that ſd wheeler ſhold be forth Coming
next morning & next morning he tooke Charge of him &
delivered him to the high Sherrif

geo: Hutchinſon Saith what is before expreſſed & further ſaith yᵗ:
next morning the Sherrife tooke Charge of him

action John Tatham ⎫
agt ⎬
Joſ: Growdon ⎭
John Tatham appeared by his attorneys aforeſd who Say they are not Informed anything concerning the ſd action & therefore deſired a continuation untill in an action of Caſe ⎰ next Court ⎱ Joſ: Growdon appeares & Craves a non ſuite with Coſts

non ſuits ⎰ whereupon it is adjudged that John Tatham not appearing
⎱ he ſhall ſuffer a non ſuite, & pay the Coſts

Jury return

action Jon Tatham ⎫
agt ⎬ Jury fines for the deft with Coſts of ſuite
gilbert wheeler ⎭

Judgmt it is adjudged that Daniel Cox pay Coſts of ſuite

action gilbert wheeler ⎫
agt ⎬
John Tatham— ⎭

ordered that the ſherrif ſum the witneſ in the aforeſd Caſe
wheeler agt <u>Tatham</u>

adjourned for 1 houre

gilbert wheeler & John Tatham, by his attorneys deſired the action
to be Continued untill next Court whereupon it is
continued

adjourned to the 16ᵗʰ of the 7ᵗʰ mo next

(1)   Bucks ſs: Actions Entered for the Quarter Seſſions
Action   to be held the 16ᵗʰ <u>7</u> 1691
                                              mo

154 Gilbert Wheeler ⎫
           agt   ⎬ in an action of Slander ⎫
       John Tatham ⎭   ⎬ with drawn
                Entered for Tryal laſt Court but — ⎪
                the tryal of its ſuſpended by Conſent to this ⎭

2 Action   Stephen Beakes ⎫
  Entered   agt : ⎬ in an action of Caſe
  the 29 6 George Brown ⎭
        mo
     i691

3) Action   Stephen Beakes ⎫
   Entered   agt : ⎬ in an action of Cafe
   29ᵗʰ 6   Joſeph Steward ⎭
         mo

   169i   Summonce dated the i 7 91
                                     ――
                                     mo

4 Action   John Tatham   ⎫
  Entered   agt   ⎬ in an action of Caſe
  3i 6 169i Gilbert wheeler ⎭
     mo
              Summonce dated the i 7 9i
                                      ――
                                      mo

5 Action   John Tatham   ⎫
  Entered   agt   ⎬ in an action of Caſe
  the 3i 6 Joſeph Growdon ⎭
         mo
   169i   Summonce dated the 1 7 9i
                                     ――
                                     mo

                                              155

7 Action ⎫   James Bleake by his Attorney ⎫
  Entered ⎪   Christopher Snodon   ⎪
  3i 6   ⎬   agt   ⎬ in a plea of Caſe
     mo   ⎪   John Clawſon —————   ⎪
  1691   ⎭   ⎭

         Summonce dated the i 7 9i
                                  ――
                                  mo

Bucks ff:

At a Court of Quarter Seffions held by the king
& Queens authority in the name of William
Pen propryatory & govrnr at the Court
houfe for the afforefd County the i6th day of the
7th month being the 3 yeare of the king & Queens
reigne & iith yeare of the propryatory govrmt
169i   The Juftices then prfent

Arthur Cook   Jofeph Growdon   Thomas Janney
Henry Baker
  wm yardley   Sherrif
  P   P   Clark

A deed of a peice of meadow land about 5 ackers in fee
dated i4th day of the 7th month i69i delivered and
acknowledged by James moone fenior & James moone
Junior grantors to Sam Dark grantee

grand Jury attefted

Action gilbert wheeler ⎫ both appeared
              agt   ⎬
        John Tatham   ⎭ & defired the action to be fufpended

for one houre wch was granted by the Court

Action Stephen Beakes ⎫ plt appeared the deft appeared not
              agt   ⎬ but it was alledged by R Hough
        Jofeph Steward ⎭ that there was Caufe for his

abfenc by reafon of a referrence difcourfed between
the parties therefore it is by Confent referred to an
other Court

           Stephen Beakes ⎫ attorney to Jon Jonfon
156   agt   ⎬ both appeared
           Geo Brown   ⎭

The declaration read

Anfwer read

Judgmt, given and it is adjudged that Stephen Beakes
Shall fuffer a non fuite & pay Coft of Court

george Brown acknowledged what was due to Jonſon
& promiſed to pay the ſame to Stephen Beakes before
the next Court of Quarter ſeſſions wch he acknow
=ledges to be due 26 buſhels of wheate with Intreſt

*but Stephen Beakes refuſed to Rec it ſo & diſcharges the ſd
geo: Brown from his promiſe

Adjourned for one houre

grand Jurys prſentmts brought in

overſeeres of the High ways

for above the falls Reuben pownal
from thence to the govrnrs Edward Lucas
from thence below to neſhaminah Richard wilſon
for the Lower part of neſhaminah James paxſon
for newtown
for middle Lots James moone
for the lower part between neſhamina & poqueſin
John Gilbert & Sam Allen Junior
for ſouthhampton Tho Hardin

Tho Brock atteſted faith that Christopher Snodon deſired
the action agt John Clawſon to be ſtayed this Court

Aprizers appointed untill furter ordr
Sam Dark Joſeph kirkbride & John Rowland

george Brown being bound to appeare laſt Court
was continued & therefore deſired this
Court to diſcharge him who as accordingly diſcharged

157

action   gilbert wheeler agt John Tatham againe Calld
withdrawn   gilbert wheeler deſired the action to be with drawn

Daniel Cox by his attorneys

Action   John Tatham agt G Wheeler
withdrawn   by ordr of John Tatham in open Court

---

*Crossed out in record.

The Conſtables for this County already Choſen are ſtill Continued till further ordr

Action John Tatham } both appeared & Joſeph Growdon
    agt   } made Claim of the benefit of
Joſeph Growdon } the law for magiſtrates &
Councill men becauſe the time was but Short &
therefore was not prepared for tryal & therefore
the Court, gave him time untill the next Court

adjourned untill 8 a Clock tomorrow morning

    Juſtices prſent   A Cook Joſeph Growdon
     Tho Janney   Henry Baker   Jo: Brock
     wm yardley   ſherriſe
     P   P   Cl

ordered   whereas the grand Jury prſented at a Court
       held the 12th 1 89 the
by the Court $\overline{mo}$
      neceſſity of haveing a tax raiſed to pay the Councell
that a   & ſſembley men
      for theire attendance already & other publique Charges of
tax of   the County
      it was accordingly ordered by a Court held the 26th 1 90 that
300 £ ſhall $\overline{mo}$
      a Tax of 300 £ be raiſed according to on the lands & males
be raiſed   of this
      County for the uſes aforeſd & that returns be pfected
for the ſd   according
      to former ordr of lands & males & now ordered that &
uſes   duplicates made thereof to every
      Collector for raiſeing the ſd mony

158   george philips being taken up for a runaway by
    Thomas Brock & brought before this Court being
    ſearſhed was found in his pocket 1 purs in
    which was foure pounds 9^d ſilver mony & one braſs
    9^d bit who upon his examination Confeſt that he
    had taken the Said monys in the night time out
    of the Cloſet of Denis Linſtone with whom he had
    lived about 3 months as alſoe one paire of gloves
    wch ſaid gloves he the ſd philips Confeſt he tooke out of
    the ſaid Cloſet

Judgment given and it is adjudged that the ſaid George
philips Shall make ſatiſfaction to the partie greived
as the law requires by ſervitude & that he the ſd
george philips have 15 ſtripes on his bare back
well Layd on now in the ſight of the Court
& that he be Confined in the Sherrifs Cuſtody (untill
his maſter have notice hereof) & that he be not ———
delivered to his ſaid maſter witout order
from Joſeph Growdon to whom this Court
referrs the ſd Denis Linſtone to treate about the
ſd george philips freedome or ſervitude being obte
ined as is ſd Conterary to law

ordered y^t: the Said monys be kept by Phinehas
Pemberton as allſo the Gloves
& that after alcharges fees & Coſts are deducted
that the remameing part be delivered to the
owner thereof

adjourned to the 10th month next

County Court Bucks ſſ 9th $\underline{\text{10}}$ 1691   159
mo

Action Suſpended laſt Court untill this Court —			
John Tatham a agt Joſeph growdon	in a plea of Caſe		
Action Entered the 23 9th mo: 1691	Joſeph Growdon agt John Gray als Tatham	in a plea for treſpaſs done	Sum Granted the 23 $\underline{9}$ 1691 mo
Action Entered the 23 9th mo: 1691	Joſeph Growdon agt John White	in a plea of treſpaſs ——	Sum Granted the 23 $\underline{9}$ 1691 mo
Action Entered the 23 9 mo 1691	Joſeph Growdon agt Edward Cartor	in a plea of treſpaſs	Sum Granted the 23 $\underline{9}$ 1691 mo

| Action Entered the 23 9th mo 1691 | Joseph Growdon agt Henry Hudlestone | in a plea of trespass | Sum Granted the 23 9 1691 mo |

| Action Entered the 23 9 mo 1691 | Joseph Growdon agt Tho : Stakehouse Junr | in a plea of trespass | Sum Granted the 23 9 1691 mo |

County Court Bucks ss:

At

A Court of Quarter Sessions held by the authority of Willm & mary king & Queen of England &c: & in the name of Willm Penn propryatory & govrnr of the province of Pensylvania & Territorys annexed att the Court house for the aforesd County of Bucks the 9th day of the 10th month being the 3 yeare of the king & Queens reigne & iith yeare of the propryatorys govrmt 1691

The Justices then prsent

Tho Janney willm Biles Henry Baker John Brock
wm yardley Sherrife
P P Cl: Com

the mony found upon Geo: philips viz 2 £ : 10^s : 9^d & one bad 9^d bitt wch was delivered to phinehas pemberton to be kept, for the owner thereof untill the owner was known being what remained Charges being deducted out of the whole for takeing of him up & other fees then Contracted, was delivered to Arthur Cook; by the sd phinehas pemberton wch this Court doth allow of & discharges the sd phinehas Pemberton of the sd mony the remaneing part thereof wch was kept back for fees & Charges was 30^s the whole being 4 £ & 9^d & one 9^d bitt

whereas there has none Comen to Complaine agt Geo philips for any misdemeanor Committed by him the Court by Consent of the boy has put him to H Baker for 6th months to see what may in the meane time be alledged agt him

adjourned to the 9th 1 mo next

28 day of the ii^th 169i Joſeph Holdens Land was taken in execution by willm yardley Sherrife to ſatiſfye the debt and Coſt of Jon Duplovies Philip Richards & Cornelius Empſon

Bucks ſs: (161)

At A Court of Quarter Seſſions held by the king & Queens authority in the name of wm Penn propryatory & govrn A the Court houſe for the afforeſd County the 9th day of the firſt month 169i/2

Juſtices prſent
Joſeph Growdon   wm Biles
Nicholas waln   Henry Baker
willm yardley   Sherrif
P Pemberton   Clark

Atteſtation Samuel overton atteſted doth Say that he lent two Chaines to John Clows
that he never Rd the ſd Chaines either from ſd Clows or any other pſon directly or indirectly Since that time

Dunckin Williams & his ſon william williams, being bound over to this Court upon Complaint of Joſeph Growdon & his baile deſireing to be diſcharged declareing they will not ſtand bound any longer & the ſd Dunckin
williams Craveing untill an other Court to prepare him ſelf

Comitmt for tryal, wch is allowed & the Court Commits them into Cuſtody untill they Shall give
Suffitient Security for his appearance at next Court & keeping the peace in the meane time
*& Hannah williams the ſd Dunckin williams daughter being Committed
upon the ſd Complt: She is likewiſe Committed untill the next Court or untill ſecurity be given for her appearance at next Court
But at the requeſt of Joſeph Growden Shee is ſet at liberty upon her promiſe to appear at next Court

John Bowen & Ralph Boome being Calld upon Complaint of Geo: Philips

---

*Crossed out in original record.

It appearing that the fd Geo Philips was Ilegaly fold by John Bowen
& Ralph Boome unto Denis Linck who lives out of the province
it is ordered that John Bowen Shall Difcharge Ralph Boome
& Reimburfe what Denis Linck has payd towards the price he
was to give for him & that Ralph Boome Difcharge the
faid Linck: & that the faid Geo Philips Shall ferve the
Said John Bowen in Confideration of the damage done to him by fd
    Philips 2 yeares from this day & that he the fd John
Bowen Shall pay to Henry Baker for what Cloths he hath bought for
him what they may be Judged to be reafonably worth & y^t: all parties
declared theire Satiffaction herein

         adjourned the 4th month 8th day

162

The Second day of the $\frac{3}{mo}$ i692 the Land of Jofeph
Holden formerly taken in execution was
apprifed to eighty pounds
  by Jofuah Hoops James Dilworth Robt Heaton
    Tho: Stakehouse Jon Purflone Peter Chamberlaine
    Ifrael Taylor Hugh marfh Robt marfh
    Jonathan fcaife Henry Hudleftone Jofias Hill

163 At a Court of Quarter Seffions held by the king &
Queens authority in the name of wm Penn propry
atory and govrnr at the Court houfe of the fd County
the 8th of the 4th month 1692

      Juftices prfent

      Jofeph Growdon   wm Biles
      Nich waln   Henry Baker
      John Cook   Corronor
      P: P: Cl Com:

—A deed of 27 acres of land in fee dated 6th $\frac{2}{mo}$ 92 from Jofeph Englifh
grantor to Tho Brock Grantee was dld & ack by P. P. attorney
to y^e: fd grantor

—A deed of 500 acres of land in fee 8th io mo 169i acknowledged and
delivered by John Rowland Grantor to Henry Baker
grantee

—A deed of 200 acres of land in fee 4th 4 mo 92 acknow

ledged & delivered by John Cooke attorney to Sam Allen Grantor
John
Baldwin Grantee

—A deed in fee of 500 acres of land in fee dated 16ᵗʰ day $\frac{7}{mo}$ 169i
acknowledged
and delivered by Joſeph Chorley attorney to Jacob
Hall grantor unto wm Biles attorney to Thomas
Hudſon grantee

—A deed in fee of 200 acres of land acknowledged and
delivered by Samuel Allen grantor to Samuel
allen his ſon grantee dated the 8ᵗʰ day of the
4ᵗʰ month 1692

—A deed in fee for 200 acres of land acknowledged and
delivered unto Jon Baldwin by
Sam Allen grantor for the uſe of his grand
daughter Elizabeth Pegg dated the 7ᵗʰ day of the
4ᵗʰ mo : i692

Complaint being made agt Boome for Some extavigant
ſpeeches he Submitting to the Court it was ordered
that Ralph Boome ſhold pay to the wittneſſ 4 ˢ &
other Coſts of Court

wm Duncan wm being bound to this Court to appeare to anſwer
the Complt of Joſeph Growdon deſired the ſd Court to
ſuſpend the tryal untill another Court for that his
wittneſes were not in readyneſs

2 Rods through the Land added in breath to the breath mentione
A deed of one hundred & 20 acres in fee dated the 8ᵗʰ $\frac{4}{mo}$ 169i
acknowledged and dd by R: Ridgway grantor to
Sam Beakes grantee

Corronors Inqueſt Concerning the death of Ellizabeth Chappel
taken before John Cooke Corronor the i5ᵗʰ of the
3 month i692 was this day returned into this
Court that the death was Caſual by falling of
her horſe into the water

Corronors Inqueſt Concerning the death of an unknown pſon
found neare the mouth of Neſhaminah Creeke
the 8th day of the 3 month 1692 taken before
John Cooke Corronor the 12th day of the ſd 3
month was this day returned into this Court
that he was wilfully murthered

upon due examination of things it appeared that a Conſiderable
Quantyty of blood on the wall and on the bed of one
Derick Jonſon or Clawſon about the ſuppoſed time
that the above murthered pſon loſt his life
was diſcovered & the ſd Derick
refuſed to give any acctt how the
ſd blood Come there whereupon this Court Commits
him the ſaid Derick claws ali Jonſon into
Safe Cuſtody of the Sherrſf untill he ſhall be delivered by due
Courſe
of Law

ordered that the ſaid Dearricks houſe be ſearched forthwith
for ſuſpitious goods or other things that may make
any further diſcovery by John Purſlone James
Paxſon & Tho Stakehouſe with what further aſſiſtance
they may ſee Cauſe for the doing thereof

adjourned to the 7th mo next

Entered   Seſſions held the 14th 7. 92
                                  ——
                                  mo

29th ⎫ wm Biles   ⎫
 6   ⎬   agt: ⎬ in a plea of Caſe
——   ⎪   ⎪
mo   ⎪   ⎪
1692 ⎭ gilbert wheeler ⎭

29th   ⎫ Stephen Beakes ⎫
6th mo ⎬   agt   ⎬ in a plea of Caſe
1692   ⎭ gilbert wheeler ⎭

30th	John whitpaine	
6 mo	by his attorney	
92	willm Nichols	in a plea Ejectione firme
—	agt	
	John Teft	

Examina^t of Derrick Jonſon Saith he Showed the blood on the wall to Edward Lane & his Brother Claws Jonſon & to mary Boyden

he also Saith there was no blood on the bed but whas by a man that Came to thraſh for him 3 yeares ago & that he had Spoke of the blood fully as much as it was

Corronor Saith that when he went to veiue the blood on the wall he perceived that it had run in Several ſtreames down the boords on the wall wch ſtreames Continued untill they went behind the planks that lay on the grown floore

Examina^t of Brighta the wife of ſd Derrick Saith that the blood ſeene on the wall was diſcovered between day & ſun riſeing & that there was a Sheet hanged on the out ſide of the bed in ſtead or manner of a Curtaine & that there was no blood on the bed
being aſked when they put freſh Straw in the bed ſhee Said Shee was not Certaine but ſhee thought about the latter end of march or beginning of Aprill

adjourned the Court to the i4^th of the 7th mo next

Penſylvania

Bucks County Court

166

At a Court of Quarter Seſſions held by the king & Queens authority in the name of willm Penn propryatory & govrnr of the afore Said Province & Territorys thereunto belonging
at the Court houſe for the Said County the i4^th day of
the 7th month being the 4th yeare of the reigne of willm & mary king & Queen of England &c: & i2^th yeare of the propryatorys govrmt Anno dm: 1692

The Juſtices prſent

Arthur Cook   Joſeph Growdon   willm Biles
Nicholas Waln   Henry Baker
John Cook   Corronor
Samuel Beakes   Sherrif
Phinehas Pemberton   Cl: Com:

Entered the 29th $\frac{6}{mo}$ 92

Willm Biles plt
    agt
Gilbert wheeler deft } action of the Caſe
Summonce dated the 3i $\frac{6}{mo}$
declaration & Summonce ſerved
by Sa Beakes Sherrife the 2nd $\frac{7}{mo}$ 92

this action withdrawn by order of willm Biles

entered 29th 6mo 92

Stephen Beakes plt
    agt
Gilbert wheeler deft } action of the Caſe
declaration & Summonce ſerved
by Sa Beakes Sherrife the 2nd $\frac{7}{mo}$ 92

this action withdrawn by ordr of the plt

Entered the 30th $\frac{6}{mo}$ 92 wm Nichols letter of attorney from Ed Antil Leaſor

John whitpaine plt:
by his attorney wm Nichols
    agt:
John Teft deft } proved in action of Ejectmt
declaration with the notice endorſed
Served & read upon the premiſes the 2nd 7th mo 92

It appearing to this Court that this action was not brought according to — former method the Court was not willing to admit the tryal but Gilbert — wheeler then poſſeſſt of the premiſes prayed that he might be admitted defent & that the action might be — brought on notwithſtanding they had varyed from the former method & So did the plant attorney whereupon the Court gave way & ordered the tryal accordingly Shold be pmitted to paſs and thereupon Iſſue was Joyned

deft   pleaded not Guilty as to terme with force & armes
Anſwer

> but as to the treſpaſs defends the force for that the ſd Ed Antill
> Leaſor did enter upon the premiſes as a diſeizor   (167)

reply   And the Sd Edward Antil by his ſd attorney replyes that he did
not enter as a diſſeizor & this he deſires may be enquired of by
the Cuntry & So doth the deft in like mannor wherefore

venire the Sherrife is Commanded to return a Jury

Jury returned }
Richard Hough
Robt Heaton
James paxſon
John Rowland
Edmund Lovet
Joſeph kirkbride
John white
Samuel Dark
Stephen Beakes
Joſeph milner
Job Bunting
Thomas Brock
} atteſted

declara read

Anſwer read

deed from gilbert wheeler unto Ed Antill of the premiſes read &
owned by Gilbert wheeler

two letters read Said to be from Gilbert wheeler to Ed Antill owing
mony due to be pd to Ed Antill but the ſd letters were not owned
nor diſowned by ſd wheeler the one dated December the 18th 1686
the other dated auguſt the 10th 1689

A deed in fee for 200 acres of land dated the 20th of the 9th month 1690
acknowledged & delivered
by Hugh marſh & Anthony morgan grantors
unto Joſias Hill grantee

A mortgage dated the 20th of the 9th month 1690 for 200 acres of Land
acknowledged
& delivered by Josias Hill grantor to Anthony morgan grantee

Adjourned the Court untill tomorrow morning at 8 a Clock

petition of Evan Prothera read Concerning george Philips Servitude
petitioner referred to treat with John Bowen for the said Philips time of servi=tude & if done to Content of all parties the Justices will ratefye the agreem

ordered that it be assented to that if the Said Evan prothera do make reasonable
Satisfaction to John Bowen his prsent master & that the sd Jon Bowen
and geo: Philips be agreeing to the same that then the sd Evan Prothera
the remainder of the time he is to serve the sd John Bowen by order of Court for what loss time the sd geo Philips & Evan Prothera Can agree for

Thomas Bowman attested doth Say that to his knowledg after that Ed Antill

168 had attached the goods of gilbert wheeler to his knowledg Gilbert wheeler Stood in So much feare of Ed Antill that he durst not Come to York for a time except privately untill that he had given him a mortgage of his land

Constables & overseerers of the High way — appointed —

Constables for

above the falls Ruben Pownal—
thenc to the govrnrs Ed Lucas—
thence below to neshaminah Ricd Wilson ————
Neshaminah — Tho: Stakehouse sr ————
middle lotts—Edmund Lovet—
the other side of Neshaminah Jon: Gilbert ————

over Seers of the High way for the sd places

Peter Worral
Stephen Beakes
willm Dungan
Henry Pawlin
Abraham Cox
Saml Allen

Jury returned Brought in theire verdict for the plt ————

An Appeale presently thereupon Requested by the defent to the next provincial
Court in Equity wch was then by the Court allowed of & adjudged that he the sd deft
giveing Security to prosecute the sd appeale & pay Costs ought to
have an appeale

By Consent
& on
requeſt to the Court } of both plt & deft that the ſd appeale might be deferred to the provincial Court in Equity wch Shold happen in Spring next wch was allowed of by the Court & ordered that ſecurity be taken accordingly

Recognizance morand that Gilbert wheeler and Robt Cole both of the affreſd County
Came before this Court & acknowledged them ſelves to be Indebted to
Edward Antill of new York Gente: in the Sum of fifty pounds Currant
mony of this Province to be pd to the ſd Ed Antill for true paymt
whereof they grant for them ſelves theire heires executors & adminiſtrators
that the Said Sum be levied & recovered from their lands and tenemts goods Chattles & hereditaments of them the ſd Gilbert Wheeler
& Robt Cole theire heires executors & adminiſtrators & aſſigns where
ever they be found

Condition — And this upon Condition that the ſd Gilbert Wheeler Shall appeare
at the provintial Court which Shall be held for this County in the Spring next and then & there Shall proſecute his appeale
wch is taken in Equity with effect and if he be Caſt in the ſd Court Shall not only
pay all the Coſts and damages he ſhall be Caſt in al
the ſaid Court but alſo all the Coſts & damages of this prſent Court

A deed in fee of 248 acres of land dated the 8th day of the 4th month 1692
was acknowledged & delivered by Henry Baker grantor to Job Bunting grantee

A deed in fee of 60 acres of land dated the 7th day of the 4th month 1692
was acknowledged & delivered by Robt Heaton attorney to John Auſtin grantor unto Nicholas waln grantee

169

road — whereas the order formerly for laying out the road from the
upper plantations upon Delaware to the Landing at the ferry
houſe agt: Burlington was not obſerved & that Some of the pſons

ordered are removed its therefore now

ordered that Henry Baker Ruben Pownal Joſeph milner Enoch yardley Jacob Janney Richard Hough Abraham Cox & Edmund Lovet or any 6 of them do lay out the Said Road & give an acctt thereof to the next Court

townſhips whereas there was Encouragemt formerly for the deviding of this County into Town ſhips from the Council & that there upon there was an ordr from the Court to pticulers for the deviding the Same & that it was not pformed accordingly its therefore now

ordered That Arthur Cook Joſeph Growdon John Cook Tho: Janney Richard Hough Henry Baker Phinehas Pemberton Joſuah Hoops wm Biles Nicholas waln Edmund Lovet & Abraham Cox James Boyden or the greater number of them meet together at the meeting houſe at neſhaminah the 27th of this Inſtant & devide this County in to Town ſhips

adjourned this Court to the meeting houſe at Neſhaminah to the 27 day of this Inſtant month

At a Court held by adjournmt the 27th day of the 7 mo: 1692

The Juſtices then prſent

Arthur Cook   Joſeph Growdon

Tho: Janney   Nicholas waln   Henry Baker

Sam Beakes   Sherrif

P Pemberton   Cl: Com:

whereas there was a tax formerly
ordered it is now ordered that the Same be forthwith raiſed that warrants be iſſued to the
Conſtables of every deviſion for the doing thereof yt when
Rd it be pd to Joſeph growdon
Arthur Cook, Nicholas waln & Sam Beakes
that the publique Charges of the County
may be defrayed

ordered that the receivers be accountable to every Court of Quarter ſeſſions from time

to time as they receive any of the
ſd mony
adjourned to next third day at Court houſe

i4 8/mo 1692 the lands of Joſeph Holden taken in Execution
to ſatiſſye the debts & Coſt of Duplovies Richards & Empſon
were Sold to Joſeph Growdon at ſeventy ſeven
pounds by Sam^ll Beakes Sherriſe

170

Entered the 23 9 mo 1692

John Nichols   by his attorneys Phinehas Pemberton & Henry Baker

witneſſes   agt
  Bartholomew Joſeph & Amos Thatcher
Joſeph Henbery   Executors of   } plea of debt
  John Brearley
        Richard Thatcher

Summonce dated the 26 9/mo 92

Entered the 23 9/mo 1692   Sum for witneſes date 29 9/mo 92

Tho: Brock
        agt
Roger Litgraine
Anthony Banks   } plea of debt
    Rich Thatcher Bartholomew Thatcher
      & Joſeph Thatcher

Sum dat: 26 9/mo 92

Entered the 23 9 month 1692   Sum for witneſes dated 29th 9/mo

wm Biles
wm Yardley   agt
P Pemberton   } plea of Debt
     Ralph Boome   Sum dat 28   9   92
                                                mo

                          with drawn by order of wm Biles

Entered 26 9 mo 1692   Sum for witneſes dat 29   9   92
                                                     mo

Joſeph Chorley
         agt   } plea of Caſe
Edward Lucas   Sum dat 28   9   92
                                           mo

John Nichols
        agt   } plea of Caſe
John Smith   withdrawn

John Nichols
        agt: } plea of debt
Thomas Stakehouſe Junr   withdrawn

Ric Thatcher
        agt   } plea of Caſe
Henry Greenland
                Arreſt granted dated 4th day   9   92
                                              mo
                return executed 4 day   9   92 & baile
                                      mo
                Taken for him

Bucks ſſ   (171)

    At a Court of Quarter Seſſions held by the king &
Queens authority in the name of wm: Penn propry
ator & govrnr of the Province & Territorys there
unto belonging at the Court houſe for the afore
ſaid County the 14th day of the   10   1692
                                        mo

Juſtices preſent

wm: Biles   Nicholas waln   Henry Baker
Sam: Beakes   Sherriſe
P Pemberton Cl: Com

adjourned to Joſeph Chorleys houſe

The prſentments of the over ſeeres of the high way for Buckingham brought in

A deed in fee for 340 acres of land dated the 2nd day of the ninth month 1692 acknowledged and deliv by wm Biles attorney to Elliz Bennet grantor to n waln grantee

action Jos Chorley
          agt } both appeared
Ed Lucas

declar read

Anſwer not guilty put them ſelves upon tryal

Jury Atteſted

witneſſes examined

adjourned for one houre

verdict   find for the deft

A deed in fee of 500 acres of land dated the 12th day of the 7 mo 92 was ack & dd by Rich Lundy grantor to ffrancis Roſſill grantee

An Appeale requeſted by Joſeph Chorley
but the pretended damages not being 10 £ Sterling & the Jury declareing they had reviued the ox & that he was So little harmed by the Shot that the ſd Chorley needed not to have loſt 2 days work for any harme the ox had Rd by the Same as alſo the deft: Craveing the benefit of the law that where the debt or damages is pretended to be above 5 £ & it prove under that in ſuch Caſe the plt Shall loſe his action whereupon the Court ſaw no Cauſe to grant him an

appeale ——

Judgment Granted and it is adjudged that Joſeph Chorley pay Coſts & that Execution Iſſue accordingly

Richard Thatcher ⎱ both Called but ⎱
      agt   ⎰
Henry Greenland ⎰ neither appeared ⎰ adjourned to the
                                                                   8th of the firſt month

J: Whitpaine a ⎱
172   agt   ⎬ ejectione firme
J   Teſt ────── ⎰   s   d

	s	d
filing dec. & Coppy ──	2 :	3
Sum: & return ──────	2 :	6
Sum: for the Jury ──	1 :	0
entering the action ──	0 :	7½
Anſwer & Coppy ────	2 :	0
Judgmt & Coppy ────	2 :	7½
verdict	.1 :	3
recording letter attor	3 :	0
Juſtices fees ───────	3 :	6
appeale ───────────	7 :	0
recognizance ───────	1 :	0
amo & coppy ───────	1 :	0

                        1 : 7 : 9

3 evidences   3 : 0
Holdens good apprized at

but Sold att

Execution agt Thatcher & Taylor
in revell Caſe ── ── 4 : 19 : 6
agt Thatcher in ──⎱ 1 : 16 : 0
Derrick Jonſons Caſe⎰
fees ─────────────── 3 : 09 : 4
Taylors Caſe ─────── 0 : 17½: 6
pd grace Langhorn 1 : 05½: 0
apprizers ───────   0 : 01 : 5
Sherriſs fees ─────── 1 : 16 : 0
                          ────────────
                          13 : 19   9

taken in execution   ⎱
to ſatiſfye the above ⎬ 2 : 07 : 6
in Tho Brocks hand ⎰
for Iſrael Taylor ſhare

i red Cow ─────── 3 : 10 : 0
i horſe ─────────── 5 : 0 : 0

Rich Thatcher pd him⎱
ſelf in Iron ware to ⎬ i : 8 : 2
wm Beakes ──────⎰

Ste Newel—ferving the warrant is : 0
rideing Charges — 0 : 6
Summonce — 0 : 7½
order of Court — 0 : 7½
Coppy thereof — 0 : 7½
= 3 : 4½

pd in Tho ſtackhous ⎱ 1 : 8 : 0
to Derrick ⎰ .
Holden Caſe ══════ 13 : i3 : 8

Jon Jones execut   38 : 11   7

Sherrifs fees
    Jon Duplovie —— i5 : 08 : 06

Sherrifs fees — —
    Philip Richards— ii : 10 : 03

Sherrifs fees
    Cornelius Empſon 8 : 15 : 04

Jon Swift for the pp.^{tr}
  agt Philip Conway Execution is 16£ 3^s : 3^d
    pat & Philip Conway is   6 : 16 : 1

                         22 : 19 : 4

*[173]

Pennſylvania

Bucks ſs: At a Court of Quarter Seſſions held by the authority in the name of wm Penn Propryatory of the aforeſaid Province & Territorys thereunto belonging at the houſe of Sam^1: Beakes the 8th day of the 1^{ſt} month 1693

                Juſtices prſent
        Joſeph Growdon   wm Biles
        Nicholas Waln   Henry Baker
        John Cook —— Corronor
        Sam Beakes Sherrife
        P P Cl Com:

    Adjourned the Court for one houre

---

*Number lost with the portion of page torn off and missing.

Recogniz: wm Duncan being Calld on his recognizance none appearing agt him the Court
difcharges him paying his fees

Recognz: Derick Clawfon als Jonfon being bound by recognizance in 100 £ & Claws J
& Peter Rambo in 50 £ apeice for the appearance of fd Derick Clawson
als Jonfon at this Court & for his good abearing in the meane time
were all them Calld but none of them appeared

Recogniz: Robt Benfon being Calld on his Recognizance appeared none appearing agt
him the Court difcharges him paying his ffees

Sum: Stephen Newel being Summonced to Court for Selling a Servant out of
y^e: Province he alleadged htat he had not fold him but lent him for Some time & that he wold bring him back in 3 months time

A deed of 5 acres of land in ffee dated the 8th day of march acknowledged & delivered in open Court by Thomas * * *
his wife grantors to Tho: Brock Grantee

A deed in fee of 5½ acres of land was acknow * * *
by Tho green & Rachel his wife grantors * * *
Burton grantee
Richard Thatcher being bound Commited into * * *

requeft — of ffellony being Calld requefted his Tryal might be deferred time & that in the meane time he might * * *
until his Tryal wch is left to the difcretion * * *
the fd Thatcher Shall apply him Self * * *

Recogn: Job Houle being bound to this Court * * *
Complaint Coming agt him by Tho Brock * * *

174

* * * n als Jonfon & Jon Clawfon & Peter Rambo againe
* * * appeared not
reas Prudence the negro of An fforeft was oblidged * * *
appeare at this Court & hath departed the fame without examination
ordered that warrant do Iffue to apprehend the Said Negro for
the apprehending & for the Safe keeping of the Said negro, that She may

Anſwer
all ſuch Complaints as Shall be layd agt her at the time this
Court Shall be adjourned unto & that Wm Biles Take Care about it

Adjourned this Court untill the day the aſſizes Shall be
the 14th day of 2nd month next

At a Court of Quarter Seſſions held by adjournmt a
the Court
houſe for the afforeſd County the 14th day of the
month 1693

The Juſtices prſent

Joſeph Growdon wm Biles

Nicholas waln Henry Baker

Saml Beakes Sherrife

P: P: Cl: Com

Addington plt⎫
 agt   ⎬ in a plea of Caſe this action with drawn by orde
Hewit deft —⎭ of ye: plt:

* * * & Rich Burges, atteſted to Dericks Indictm Iſrae
Taylor
Atteſted
* * * for 250 acres of land dated this day acknowledged & dd
* * * Taylor grantor to James yates grantee

Tho Lacy being bound by recognizance to appeare her
being
* * * to get mary Roles with Child appeared accordingly
* * * being examined about the Same declared that Tho: Lac
had
* * * with child & Sayd he lay with her Several times on
* * * time was the firſt
day afore Isaac page dyed wch is Said to b
about the
the 9th month & lay with her but once afterwards & tha
was about 13 or 14
* * * from this time

Tho Lacy give bond to anſwer the ſd Complt at the next Cour

* * * Tho: Lacy acknowledged him felf Indevted to
the propryetor

* * * Ifrael Taylor in 5 £ to be levyed on their lands &
Tenemts

* * * les & this is upon Condition for the appearance of
the fd

  * * * next Court to the aforefd Compt of mary
Roles

  * * * el Taylor had arrefted him & that he defired
* * * granted him he being about to depart the * * *

the goods mentioned in the acct owned by the deft but not
were delivered upon the acctt of the finifhing of a barn

wm Plumley attefted for the plt   175

Robt marfh attefted for the deft

A Contract for Hugh Marfh his finifhing Ifrael Taylors barn read &
parties

 Job Houle appeared according to recognizance & none appearing agt him.
difcharges him paying the fees

adjourned for one houre

 Robt Benfon Jon Clark Jon Crofdell Jon penquoit Jof Chorley Witneffes
agt: R Thather for ftealing amare attefted

 grand Jury Impaneled & attefted

 Richard Thather being Calld appeared according to recognizance
ordered that he be taken into the Sherrifs Cuftody untill further order

adjourned for one houre

 one deed of 300 acres of land in fee dated the i4th $\frac{2}{mo}$ ack &

  H marfh & Sa: marfh grantors to Jo Eaftbourn grantee

Jury returned to find for Hugh Marfh deft with Cofts

def^t came into Court & acquainted that Ifrael Taylor had Satiffyed h
                to be fufpended
 Rich Thatcher Calld & arraigned upon his Indictmt.
pleaded not guilty put him felf for tryal puts him felf on the Cuntry
    x x x el Taylor had arrefted him & that he de^hired
    x x x granted him he being about to depart the

Robt Benſon Atteſted doth Say that he never Saw the mare but Said he bought the mare & Colt of John Clark

Joſeph Chorley atteſted doth Say that on a firſt day John Clarke * * * on a black mare wch ſd Ric Thatcher ſd was his mare * * * in her foreh head wch Thather now Confeſes was the mare that Croſdells paſture

Robt Cole atteſted doth Say that he ſaw Rich Thather when he brought mare over the river wth a mare Colt with her of a bla * * * with a large Star in her face & a Snip on her noſe & a Croſs on one Ear
& he aſked ſd Thather where he had the ſd mare he ſd b * * * an eaſt Jarſey man & that he bought her on the road be * * * Brinſon, & doctor greenlands & that Jon Richards * * * Houghtons was prient when he bought her wch mare Thather Confeſſes that it was the fame wch he ſold to Jon * * *

Jon Croſdell atteſted doth Say that Thater Came to ſee the mare brothers paſture & that ſd Thather Confeſt it was the mare he Clark & that he knows that ffrancis white or his mother * * * the Same mare of Tho ſtakehouse Junior

jon penquoit Saith as above

Derick Clawſon appearing this Court according to recognizance the Court diſcharged him of the ſd recognizance & his * * *

Jon Gilbert being accused with begeting a bastard Child on a negro on the window fforeſt.   & it appeare on * * *

Judgmt given & it is adjudged that Rich Thatcher Shall pay to ffrancis white 40^s & Coſt it being all that ffra white deſired to have awarded him & that he be whipt i5 Laſhes on his bare back adjourned to the 4th month next

176

Pennſylvania

Bucks ſs: 177   (176)*

At a provincial Cercular Court held by the king & Queens authority
in the name of William Penn propryeter & govrnr of the Said province & territorys thereunto belonging at the Court
houſe for the Said County the i4^th day of the 2nd month 1693 being the 4th yeare of the king & Queens reigne

* This page is numbered as above.

The Judges prſent

Samuel Jenings   Joſeph Growdon

Samuel Beakes Sherriſe

P P: Cl: Com

Commiſſion Read

grand Jury atteſted

Edward Lane Jon: purley & Tho: ſtakehouſe ſenr atteſted

Court adjourned for 2 houres

Adjourned untill tomorrow moring at 10 a Clock

    grand Jury returned do prſent Derick Clawſon als Jonſon for murthering an unknown perſon found neare the mouth of Neſhaminah Creek the 8th of the 3 month 1692 being Suppoſed to be murthered about the beginning month 1692

Derrick Jonſon als Clawſon being brought into Court & the grand Jurys prſentmt
read to him he pleaded not guilty & he Craved to have further time for his Tryal he not being
prepared for it wch was allowed him by the Court untill the next provincial Circular Court to be held for this County being the kings not So full as hereafter is expected & y^t: the kings attorney here to proſecute

Recognizance Edward Lane John Purſley Thomas Stakehouſe Senr
& Richard Burges acknowledges them Selfs to be Indebted to the govrnr: each of them in the Sum of forty - pounds
to be levied on theire lands & tenements goods & Chattles
Condition that the appeare at the next Circular provincial this County to give in Evidence the truth of theire
the prſentm^t agt Derick Clawſon als Jonſon for the muther of an unknown peron found nere the mouth of neſhaminah

adjourned for 2 houres

    grand Jury returned do prſnt Brighta the wife of Derick Jonſon Elliza: Jonſon ſiſter of the ſd Derrick for aideing & aſſiſting the to murther the aforeſd the aforeſd unknow pſon

    preſented alſ a young man his name Suppoſed to be John He * * * Derrick Clawſons ſiſter ordered that Brighta the wife of Derick Jonſon & Elliza * * * ſd Derick Clawſon als Jonſon be Committed into the * * * ther order * * * ta Jonſon & Elliza; Jonſon be adjourned for 2 houres

* * * they were Charged with * * *
* * * pleaded not guilty * * *
* * * that Derick Jonſon * * *

178   grand Jury i4ᵗʰ 2 1693
                          mo

Provincial Court
   for Bucks
i4ᵗʰ day 2 month
     i693

Jon Swift   Tho Hardin   Joſuah Hoops
geo Brown   Jos milner   Jo: Bunting
Abra Cox   Samll Dark   Henry paxſon
Jona: ſcaife Jos: kirkbride ffra Roſſill
Janes Paxſon   wm Beakes   Jon palmer

*178a

* * * held by the kings
* * * wm Penn Propry-
* * * Said province &
* * * nging att the Court
* * * County the i4ᵗʰ day
* * * ——i693 being the 4ᵗʰ
* * * gs Reigne & 8ᵗʰ of the
* * * vrmt

* * *   Arthur Cooke

* * *   Joſeph Growdon

* * *   rley Sherif

* * *   Pemberton Cl:

grand ⎱   The grand   atteſted
Jury ⎰

Recognizance Iſrael Taylor being bound in io £ to the propryatory for his appearance here this day for abuſe done to Nicholas appearanc waln Juſtice of peace appeared accordingly & was diſcharged

---

*This page is not numbered in the Record Book

Recognizance Mary Skeane being bound to appeare att this
    Court to the propryatory in 20 £

appeared accordingly

Examinat ſd mary Skeane being Examined Concerning a baſtard
Child brought forth by her Said She was fforced by
one walter pomſeret who is father of it the Said
pomſeret liveing in weſt Jarſey being according to her
atteſtation & Examination formerly taken before A Cook

midwife An oxley atteſted & Examined Said Shee Confeſt y^e:
Same to her about 24 hours after the ſd Child was
born

A deed of 200 acres of land in fee dated the i3 day of $\frac{\text{i}}{\text{mo}}$ i688
was acknowledged & delivered in open Court by
Wm Pickring grantor to Jon penquoit grantee

*178b

action whereas * * *
        plt & * * *
        to Joſeph * * *
        willing * * *
        not being * * *
        Joyntly * * *
        Court * * *

decl Declaration * * *
plea Anſer aſo * * *

  Jury——Called over and
  atteſted

Evidences { Rich Th * * *
           { & Barthol * * *

adjourned the Co * * *

complaint was made * * *   that
        Randulph * * *   for fees the
        Sum of 2 £ 10^s: 0 * * *   and before the
        ioth month laſt paſt * * *
            thereupon was a * * *   agt the ſd Randulph

*This page not numbered in the Record Book.

	Smalwood for the ſd Sum & that Execution Iſſue accordingly
petition	of Wm L Read Requeſting the Court for the monys obtained by Judgmt in Rouſe Caſe agt Wm Biles
A letter of	attorney acknowledged by mary Beakes to her brother in law Edmund Beakes of portiſhead in the County of Summerſet in England dated the i4th $\frac{i}{mo}$ i688 & Certefyed undr the County ſeale
Complt	was made by Randulph Black ſhaw that he wants mony due to him for repaireing the highway to wch the Court Says they will give him an anſwer next Court
verdict	the Jury return & Calld over do Say they find for y^{e}: plt five pounds thirteen Shillings & io^{s} damages with Coſt of ſuite to be pd in goods Equivalent to ſilver mony or in Silver

179

A deed of fivety achers of land in fee dated the i3 day of the firſt month i688 Was acknowledged & delivered in open Court by Henry pawlin grantor to John Taylor grantee

Return made by the Sherrif that the goods taken in Execution in Rouſe Caſe agt Biles are overprized & Cannot Sel for want of buyers

apprizers	In as much as the former apprizers overprized goods taken in Execution this Court nominates & appoints Jon Brock Wm paxſon & Robt Heaton to be apprizers untill further ordr & were atteſted accordingly
ordered	that whereas the Execution granted Simon Rouſe agt the goods of wm Biles was returned not Satiſfyed for want of buyers that another Execution be granted the Sherrif to Satiſfye the ſd Rouſe the Judgmt of Court formerly obtained

A lettr of attorney dated the 14th 1ft/mo 1688 was acknowledged
by wm Beakes of this County to the uſe of Thomas
Cotterill of Amſberry in the County of gloſter England
& Certefyed in Court undr the County ſeale

A letter of attorney dated the 14 day of the 1ft month
1688 was acknowledged by Stephen Beakes
of this County to the uſe of Edmund Beakes
aforeſd & Certefyed in open Court under the
County Seale

Judgmt given & it is adjudged by this Court that Sam
Abbott pay to Richard Thatcher the Sum of five
pounds thirteen Shillings & Coſt of Suit & that Execution Iſſue
accordingly & that the 10^s damages be allowed to
Sam — Abbott on the non Suit formerly obtained

prſentmts brought in by the grand Jury

ordered by the Court that the overſeeres of the high way
do take Care to repair the high ways prſented

prſentmt agt Iſrael Taylor deferred for Tryal at the next Quarter Seſſions

adjourned this Court untill the 13 day of the 4th month
next Enſueing

Bucks ſs: Penſylvania
180 At a Court of Quarter Seſſions held by the
Kings authority in the name of William Penn
Propryetory and Govrnr of the affore Said Provinc
and Territorys thereunto belonging at the
Court houſe for the afforeſaid County the 13 day
of the 4th month being the 4th yeare of the
kings Reigne & 8th yeare of the proproprya
torys Govrmt 1688

The Juſtices Preſent
Arthur Cook   William yardley
Nicholas Waln   Henry Baker
Abraham Wharley   Sherrife
wm Croſdel Deputy Sherrife
Phinehas Pemberton Cl: Com:

Action	Joſuah Ely plt	
	agt	in a plea of Caſe both appeared
	John Brock deft	

declarc read
Anſwer that the deft owed not the mony & for Tryal put him Self upon
Iſſue Joyned the Cuntry & ſo did the plt whereupon the Sherriſe was —
venire Commanded to return the Jury
Jury returned & atteſted

> John Swift Henry Marjerum walter Bridgman
> Thomas Stakehouſe Robt Heaton Henry paxſon
> Tho: Stakehouſe Junr Joſeph Clows James paxſon
> Richard Lundy willm Dark James Moone

witneſes mahlon Stacy John Redman mary Staniland all Atteſted
Proved the declarc:
wittneſſes Joſeph milner atteſted for the deft
adjourned the Court for one houre

verdict we find for the plt Seven pounds Elleven Shillings to be payd by the deft with Coſt of ſuite the plt firſt makeing the deft: an aſſurance of the boy

Judgmt The Court awards Judgmt according to verdict & that
Execution Iſſue accordingly

A deed of Three hundred acres of land in fee dated the i0th day of the 9th month 1683 delivered and acknowledged by Joſeph — Engliſh Grantor to ffrancis Roſſill grantee

Action	David Evans plt		181
	agt	in a plea both appeared	
	Joſeph wood deft		

declarcon: read
Anſwer deneys the fact & for Tryal puts him Self upon the Cuntry
Iſſue Joyned —

venire wherefore the Sherriſe is Commanded to return the Jury
Jury returned & Atteſted being the Same Jury before mentioned
witneſſes John Brearley william Beakes Ellias Nichols John owen
Hugh williams Joſuah Ely mary Eire Joſuah Ely Junior
all atted proved the declar:

witneſſes for the deft mary wood Sarah wood atteſted proved y^t:
Joſeph wood Shot Salt at a horſe about 9 days afore the
killing of the Said mare

verdict we find for the plt 5 £ for the mare & 40^s damages with
Coſts of Suite

Judgmt   The Court thereupon awards Judgmt according to law

execution ⎧ Joſeph wood being required by the Court to Satiſſye the
        ⎨ Said Judgement he refuſed the Same whereupon
        ⎩ the Court Commits him in Execution to the Sherrifs Cuſtody

Comitment untill the ſd Judgmt be Satiſfyed

action mary Jeffs plt ⎫
          agt   ⎬ with drawn
     Joſeph Chorley ⎭

action John Nichols plt ⎫
           agt   ⎬ with drawn
    Juſeph Chorley deft ⎭

action Stephen Beakes plt ⎫
           agt   ⎬ with drawn
    John Pidcock deft ⎭

⎧ Indictmt ⎫ of Iſrael Taylor being defferred for Tryal untill this
⎨ or   ⎬
⎩ prſentmt— ⎭ Court for defameing ffrancis the wife of John Swift

Bucks ſs: The Jurrors for the propryetory & govrnr by the kings authority
do prſent that Iſrael Taylor of the County of Bucks aforeſaid
Chyrurgeon about the i4th day of the iith month laſt paſt did
Scandelouſly and malitiouſly defame ffrancis the wife of
John Swift of the aforeſaid County yeoman agt the ——
Kings peace and agt the Statute law in Such Caſe made
& provided   The i4th $\frac{i}{mo}$ 1688

verdict of the grand Jury we of the grand Inqueſt do find this

bill

pleaded to the Said Indictmt not guilty & for Tryal put him Self upon
183* the Cunty

---

*There is no page numbered 182 in the Record.

venire   whereupon the Sherrife was Commanded to Cauſe to Come before the Juſtices i2 honeſt & Lawfull men

Jury returned and Atteſted
          Richard Ridgway Henry Marjorum walter Bridgman
          Tho: Stakehouſe Senr: Robt Heaton Andrew Allott
          Tho: Stakehouſe Junr Joſeph Clows wm: Dark
          James Paxſon Richard Lundy James Moone

witneſſes John naylor Atteſted doth Say that Iſrael Taylor Sayd he veryly beleived that nick meaneing Nicholas Randolph the Servant of John Swift did lye with John Swifts Wife and that he believed in his Conſcience he did god good ſervice in Telling of it

          John Town Atteſted doth Say that ſd Taylor Sayd he verily beleived nick meaning the ſd Nicholas Randle did lyewith John Swifts wife

Evidences
          Andrew Dunk atteſted doth Say that he heard Iſrael Taylor tell micheal Butcher that Gabriel Shallow Sayd nicholas – Randel wold lay his head upon his Mrs lap until i2 a Clock at night & then they wold go together into the barn

          mark Betrice atteſted Teſtefyes in like manner

          Benjemame Jones Atteſted doth Say that Gabriel Shallow Said nicholas Randel wold Sleep with his head in his Mrs lap & Shee Sleep with her head in his lapp & that he Calld John Swift Cucoldy Rogue & that his muſtard pot wold work when he was from home & that they wold go into
deed   the barn together in the night

deed   of 250 acres of land in fee dated the iſt day of the 4th month i684 delivered and acknowledged by Richard Hough grantor to Henry margerum grantee

  verdict in Swifts Caſe Jury Say they find Taylor guilty in — manner & form as he Stands Indicted

    Judgment The Court award Judgment that Iſrael Taylor Shall Shall give Security for his appearance at the next Court & to keepe the peace in the meane time & pay all Charge

Execut: of Court & that execution Iſſue accordingly

Recognizance memorand That Iſrael Taylor oblidges him Self in

15 £ & Benjemame Jones in 5 £ to be pd to the proprietor
to be levied on theire lands & Tenemts goods & Chattles & upon
this
Condition that Ifrael Taylor appeare at the next Court of
Quarter Seffions & to keepe the kings peace in the meane
time

184

The accts of William Biles the Receivor of the County Tax
were examined according to an ordr of a former Court
by Phinehas Pemberton & Abraham Wharley & were
againe This day examined & made up in open Court & it

	£	s	d
appears by the books of Affeffment that the whole Tax amounted to	128:	04:	05½
of which the Said William Biles acknowlcd -ged that he had Red	056:	19:	09
& he hath disburft as is made appeare in open Court By the Courts order & otherwife which this Court allows of	059:	06:	07
So that this Court doth allow of this abovefd acctt & acknowledges that the County is debtor to Said willm Biles the Sum of	02:	06:	10
And further that it doth appeare by the acctt now brought in by the fd william Biles — That there remaines unpayd of the fd affeff ment the Sum of	7i:	04:	08½

And whereas it doth appeare that the County is Still
debtor to John Brock Randle Black fhaw gilbert
wheeler & others this Court doth order that the Said
william Biles do take the moft expeditious way for
getting of the arreares of the fd affeffment & payment
of the fd debts or that if the parties to whom the
county is debtor will take upon them to Collect fo
much as is due to them that then the fd willm Biles
do give a Catalogue of the names of So many as are in-
arreare as may anfwer the faid debt & that a warrant
be Iffued out from any one Juftice of peace or more
to Impower the faid partie to levy the Same by diftrefs &
& Sale on the parties goods refufeing to pay theire affeff
- ment unpaid

And further the Court orders Henry pointer & Samuel Allen to Collect the arreares of the Tax between neſha-mina & poqueſſin with what expedition may be & that Nicholas waln be aſſiſtant to them therein

A deed of 1000 acres of land in fee dated the i3 day of the i2th month 1688 acknowledged & delivered by Phinehas Pemberton attorney to Jacob Telner grantor unto — Richard Lundy grantee

A deed of 50 acres of land in fee dated the 6th day of the i^{ſt} month 1688 acknowledged & delivered by Joſeph Engliſh grantor to Arthur Cook attorney to Richard Wilſon grantee

185

motion being made by David Lloyd the Attorney Generall in relation to Levying the fines and forfetures the Court thinks fit to take time to adviſe upon it & to - Speake with the Commiſſioners of propryety afore they return anſwer what Courſe muſt be Taken for levying

ordered that in the meane time the Said Eſtreats above writen be taken out of the records & be Certefyed under the Clarks hand

wch Said Eſtreats were Imediately extracted out of the records according to ordr

Adjourned this Court to the i2th 7/mo next

Bucks fs: Penſylvania

At a Court of Quarter Seſſions held by the kings authority in the name of william Penn Propryetor and govrnr of the afore Said Province & Terri- torys thereunto belonging at the Court houſe for the Said County the i2th day of the 7th month being the 4th yeare of the kings Reigne & —— 8th yeare of the propryatorys govrmt 1688

The Juſtices prſent

Joſeph Growdon	william yardley
Nicholas Waln	Henry Baker
Abraham wharley	Sherrife
willm Crosdel	Deputy Sherrife
Phinehas Pemberton Cl: Com:	

A deed of 200 acres of land in fee dated the 5th day of the 5th month 1688 acknowledged & delivered in open Court by william Biles grantor unto Richard Ridgway attorney to attorney to Joſeph Engliſh Grantee

Conſtables Ellected & appointed for the upper part of River wm: Beakes Att:
for the Lower pte _____ Tho williams
for yᵉ middle lotts _____ Jeffery Hawkins
for the upper pte of Neſhaminah Tho: Stakehouſe Atteſt
for the other ſide of Neſhaminah Neamiah Allen

overſeers of the High way appointed for the upper pte of Neſhaminah Robt Heaton Henry Pointer
for the Lower pte thereof Samuel Allen Junior
for the Lower pte of the river willm Dungan

186

over Seers of the High way for the middle lotts Joſeph kirkbride
for the upper pte of the River Joſeph Milner

Recognizance   Iſrael Taylor being bound by Recognizance for his appearance at this Court & none appearing agt him this Court diſcharges him paying his fees

Action   ffrancis Hough by his attorneys

John Brock & Tho: wood plt ⎫
    agt   ⎬ in a plea of debt
Iſrael Taylor deft   ⎭

appearance John Brock   ⎫
               &   ⎬ appeared but wood & Brock being
          Iſrael Taylor   ⎭ Joynt attorneys & wood not appearing

Taylor Craved a non Suite wᶜʰ was granted him & the Court non ſuite awarded the plt to pay the Coſts

A deed   of one acre of land in fee dated the 10th 7/mo 1688 was acknowledged & delivered by ffrancis Roſſill Grantor to Thomas Brock attorney to Joane Huff grantee

action   wm Brian agt Jon Pidcock withdrawn

Inqueſt ⎱ of the Suden death of Roger Scot was that it was accidentall
return ⎰ Through is owne Carleſnes

Recognizance Daniel Hawkins & Robt Benſon appeared according to
to Recognizance & none appearing agt them the Court diſcharges them paying theire fees

Eſtreat John oldfield not appearing according to Recognizance forfeited the Same being 5 £

Eſtreat John Ruſh being bound by Recognizance appeared not — accordingly but forfeited the Same being 20 £ :

requeſt being made by Jacob Hall he not being well deſired that in as much as the ſd Ruſh appeared not that the Court wold give him time to the next adjournmt for bringing in of his complt agt the Said Ruſh

Anſwer the Court allowed of

return of an execution made by wm Croſdel deputy Sherrife for the Satiſfying of Judgmt obteined in Joſuah Elys Caſe of the goods of John Brock i gray mare and i7 groſs of buttons att 7 £ : ii^s wch goods being brought to this Court & the ſd Ely Complt of the wrong done by the Sherrife in that caſe the Court Juding them to be unſuitable goods to raiſe the mony & over prized awarded that another execution be granted & layd on Such goods as will anſwer the Judgmt obtained

Adjourned to the 2nd $\frac{8}{mo}$ 1688

187

Bucks ſs :   Penſylvania

At a Court of Quarter Seſſions held by adjournment by the kings authority in the name of william Penn Propryatory & govrnr of the afforeſaid Province & ——— Territorys thereunto belonging at the Court houſe of the Said County the 2nd day of the 8th month being the 4th yeare of the kings reigne over England &c : & 8th of the propryetors govrmt 1688

The Juſtices prſent

william yardley   Henry Baker

wm Croſdel   Deputy Sherrife

Phinehas Pemberton Cl : Com :

a deed of 50 acres of land in fee dated the i^{ft} of the 8th month i688
acknowledged & Delivered in open Court by John Taylor
grantor to John Smith grantee

whereas John oldfeild was called laſt Court according to his
recognizance & appeared not he Came this day and
appeared before the Juſtices & alleadged that he was
Sick & unable to Come Sooner

adjourned to the i2th ioth month next

  Jon Swift & Tho: millard Submitted theire action to arbitra
- tion & with drew the Same

Bucks ſs: Penſylvania

  At a Court of Quarter Seſſions held by the
kings authority in the name of william Penn
Propryetor & govrnr of the afforeſaid Province
& Territorys thereunto belonging at the Court
houſe for the Said County the i2th day of the
ioth month i688

  The Juſtices prſent

  William yardley Joſeph Growdon Henry Baker
  Nicholas Waln John Brock
  Abraham wharley Sherrife
  wm Croſdel deputy Sherrife
  Phinehas Pemberton Cl: Com:

Commiſſion of Peace read

Laws read

grand Jury Impaneled & atteſted Richard Ridgway foreman
 Henry Paxſon Joſeph Milner John wood Andrew Ellot Jon Palmer
 Sam Dark Jon Croſdel Henry Bircham Joſeph Engliſh Jon Hough

188

 Shadrach walley wm: Buckman ffrancis Roſſill

adjourned the Court for one houre

adjourned the Court untill 8 a Clock in the morning

a deed in fee of 2 acres of land dated the 6th day of the 7th month
i688 acknowledged and delivered (william Croſdel attorney
to James Swafer grantor) unto James Croſdel attorney
upon the requeſt made of Richard Wilſon grantee

a deed of 125 acres of land in fee dated the 13 day of the 10ᵗʰ month 1688 acknowledged & delivered & open Court by James Hill grantor to James Moone for the uſe of him ſelf and his Son James Moone grantees

Indictmt

Bucks ſs: 12ᵗʰ 10 1688
           ———
            mo

(1) The Jurrors for the propryeter & Govrnr by the kings authority do prſent a run away negro who Says he Coms from virginia and Calls him Self by the name of george for that he upon the 17ᵗʰ day of the 9ᵗʰ month laſt paſt did Steale & fraudulently take and Carry away 2 Turkeys being the goods of Tho: Janney Senior Conterary to the kings peace and agt the law in that Caſe made & provided

peter worral Pſecuter

wittneſſes Thomas Janney Junior⎱
            Joſeph Hollinshead —⎰ Atteſted in Court

bill found ———

arraigmt   pleaded guilty

Indictmt Bucks ſs

(2) The Jurrors for the propryetor & govrnr by the kings authority do prſent a runaway negro who Says he Coms from verginia and Calls him Self by the name of george george for that he about the beginning of the 8ᵗʰ month laſt paſt did Steale & fraudulently Take & Carry away 1 ax 1 Skellet Corn peaſe Stockings & other goods to the value of Twenty five Shillings being the goods of Thomas Rogers — Conterary to the kings peace and agt the law in that Caſe made & provided

Proſecuter Thomas Rowland

witneſſes Thomas Rogers ⎱
           Samuel Hough ⎰ atteſted in Court

bill found

arrainemt pleaded guilty of Takeing all the aforeſaid goods Save ½ buſhel of peaſe

189
Bucks fs　　　　　　　　The 12th 10th moth 1688

Indictmt
(3)

　　　The Jurrors for the propryetory & govrnr by the kings authority prfent a run away who Says he Coms from virginia & Calls him felf by the name of george for that he upon or about the beginning of the 8th month laſt paſt did Steale and fraudulently take and Carry away one cloth Coate one lether Coate Two Shirts one fuſtian waſt Coate one hat one Silke neck cloth to the value of five pounds being the goods of Roger Hawkins Conterary to the kings peace and agt the law in that Cafe made and Provided

Profecutor　　Roger Hawkins

witneffes　Jofeph Hollinshead ⎱
　　　　　　Samuel Hough ⎰　atteſted in Court

bill found

arrainemt　he pleaded guilty

Indictmt
(4)

Bucks fs: The Jurrors for the propryetor & governr by the kings authority do prfent that John Collins of the County aforefd Hufbandman on the 27 day of the 8th month last did by violent affault Robb & Take away from the perfon of gilbert wheeler upon the kings high way & Roade within the Said County one mare and other goods to the value of Ten pounds being the proper goods of Gilbert wheeler afforefaid Contera-ry to the kings peace and agt the law in Such Cafe made & Provided

Profecutor　　Jofeph wood

witneffes ⎧ Gilbert wheeler ⎫
　　　　　　⎪ John Martin ⎪
　　　　　　⎪ Jacob Hall ⎪
　　　　　　⎨ Edward Cartor ⎬ atteſted in Court
　　　　　　⎪ Joan Huff ⎪
　　　　　　⎪ Daniel Beakes ⎪
　　　　　　⎩ Ellenor Beakes ⎭

the bill found

arrigmt　pleaded not guilty but Craved a few houres time of
requeſt　the Court to give in what he had further to Say wch was granted
Anfwer　the Court

Roades grand Jurys prſentmt   i2ᵗʰ i̶o̶ 1688
                                                        mo

    we the grand Jury do prſent it need full that a Suffitiont Cart Roade Shall be layd out from the upper plantations about the falls unto the fferry houſe where the Common landing is over agt Burlington   Richard Ridgway foreman

190

action	Gilbert Wheeler plt	plt appeared
	agt	
	Luke Brindley deft	deft appeared not

a plea of debt

non appearance

Sherrifs return   willm Croſdel deputy Sherrife made Returne upon his — atteſtation that he had given him lawfull Summonce

Declarat read

Bond therein mentioned proved by the Evidence of william Biles atteſted the other witnes being Robt Jeffs deceaſed proved by the writeing

Queſtion { The penal Sum of the bond & the Sum declared for being 3i £ and the real debt being but i5 £ : 12ˢ the Juſtices on the bench asked of Said gilbert wheeler whether he expected Judgmt for any more then the real debt

anſwer { To which Said wheeler made anſwer he expected Judgmt for no more then 15 £ i2ˢ with Coſts of Suite

Judgmt by default { whereupon the Court gave Judgmt by default & it was adjudged that Luke Brindley Shold pay to Gilbert wheeler the Sum of i5 £ : i2ˢ with Coſt of Suite & that Execution shold Iſsue accordingly

Complt about ye Tax { William Biles Receivor of the County Tax made Complt to this Court that there was a great deale of the County Tax yet unpaid and in arreare & that he Cold not levy the Same without a warrant

order   { whereupon this Court orders that a warrant be granted to the aforeſaid william Biles by Two Juſtices of peace for Levying the Said Tax in arreare & unpayd on the goods and Chattles of Such refuſeing to pay his Share of the Said Tax

A patent and affignemt thereon of 269 acres of land in fee dated the 30th day of the 3 month 1688 and the affignemt thereupon dated the 4th day of the 4th month of the Said yeare was delivered and acknowledged by Thomas Lambert Attorney to Edward Luff grantor to Henry Marjerum grantee

A deed of i62 acres of land in fee delivered and acknowledged by Jofeph Englifh Grantor to william Biles Grantee

action Edward Hancock agt Thomas Revel in a plea of debt both upon Call appeared and the deft: declareing that he was but that day arrefted to appear to the Said action which appeared to be True by the Sherrifs return the action was deferred by Confent of both parties untill the next Court the Said — Revel giveing bond with Suffitient fuerties to appeare at the next Court

action Thomas Millard agt Sam Burden in a plea of debt

appearance both upon Calld appeared

191

declarat Read

Anfwer the defendt Saith he hath performed the award & owes nothing

Iffue Joyned } and of this he put him Self upon the Cuntry for Tryal & the plt in like manner   Sam Burden

venire { wherefore the Sherrife is Commanded to Caufe to Come i2 honeft & lawfull men &c:

Jury Attefted   Tho: Rowland Ezra Crofdel Henry Marjerum James Paxfon Stephen Sands Peter worrall willm Clowes James Moone John Towne John Penquoit — — Richard Lundy willm Dark

articles read & acknowledged

award read and acknowledged

bond read and acknowledged

wittneffes for the plt } { John ffleckney
Anthony Burton
Thomas Tery —
ffrancis Roffill } all attefted

witneſſes for the deft } { John ffurnas / Edward Lancaſter } atteſted

adjourned the Court for one houre

one deed in ffee of Two hundred acres of land in ffee dated the 10th day of the 8th month 1688 acknowledged and delivered in open Court by Samuel Dark Attorney to Lyonel Brittan grantor unto Stephen Beakes grantee

Judgmt on the firſt Indictmt agt George the negro for Stealing the Turkeys they not being restored it was adjudged that he Shold pay by Servitude as the Court hereafter Shold ordr unto Thomas Janney 18ˢ & Charge of Court and be whipt for his Said offence Elleven Stripes on his bare back

Judgmt on the 2nd Indictmt agt George the negro for Stealing of goods from Thomas Rogers parte of the goods being reſtored it was adjudged that he Shold pay by Servitude as the Court hereafter Shold order unto Thomas Rogers afforeſaid to the value of 48ˢ & Charge of Court & be whipt eleven Stripes on his bare back

Judgmt on the 3 Indictment agt George the negro for Stealing the goods of Roger Hawkins the Goods being reſtored it was adjudged that he Shold pay by Servitude as the Court here after Shold order unto Roger Hawkins aforeſaid to the value of 50ˢ and Charge of Court the ſd Hawkins deſire =ing from the Court no further Satisfaction Save that he be whipt on his bare back 19 ſtripes

ordered that he be once whipt in the Sight of the Court

192

Commitment untill a Convenient place of Servitude be found for him the Court Committs him the ſd George negro into the Sherrifs Cuſtody

Recognizance Paterick kelly being Called according to recognizance none appearing agt him the Court diſcharges him paying his diſcharge ffees

Commitment Richard Thatcher Junior for abuſeing the Juſtices on the bench the Court Commits him into Cuſtody untill the next morning

adjourned the Court untill 8 a Clock tomorrow morning

action Tho: millard agt Sa: Burden

verdict we find for the plt according to evidence

*requeſt the deft Samuel Burden Craved an appeale to the provincial Court in Equity

Judgmt the Court Gave Judgmt & it was adjudged that Samuel Burden Shold pay to Thomas Millard the Sum of Two hundered pounds

requeſt ⎱ the deft Sam: Burden Craved an appeale to the next provin-
for an ⎰ cial Court in Equity & tendered his owne bond for 400 £ to pay
appeale ⎱ all Coſt of the ſd Court and of this Court occationed by the aforeſd action & to proſecute the ſd appeale with Effert
wch ſd bond was accepted by the Court & liberty of an appeale granted to the Said Samuel Burden deft to the next Provincial Court in Equity

Indictmt Jon: Collins returned into Court & Confeſt he had aſſaulted 4th Gilbert wheeler on the high road but not with any intent to Rob him

requeſt made by Gilbert wheeler & Craved the Court to forbeare any further proceedure agt the Said Collins for that the Said Collins had made him full Satisfaction for any wrong or Injury he had done to him & Said wheeler promiſed to pay all fees due on the said Indictment

order on the ⎱ upon the grand Jurys prſentmts of the want of a
prſentmt of the ⎰ roade from the upper plantations above the falls of Delaware
want of a Road ⎰ to the landing agt Burlington the Court ordrs Henry Baker John Brock wm yardley Jos: milner Richard — Hough John Rowland Joſeph Engliſh and Abraham Cox to lay out the Said Road & give an Acctt thereof to the next Court

Eſtreat Richard Thatcher Junior aforeſd for his abuſe done to the Juſtices on
Juſtices on the bench the Court fines him in 50s & Commits — him to the Sherrifs Cuſtody untill he Shall find Suertyes for his good behavior & his appearance at next Court

adjourned the Court untill the i3 day of the firſt month next

---

*Crossed out in Record Book.

193

Bucks ſs: Penſylvania

At a Court of Quarter Seſſions held by the kings authority in the name of william Penn propryetory & govrnr of the aforeſaid Province & Territorys thereunto belonging at the Court houſe for the ſd County the i3 day of the firſt month 1688

Juſtices Preſent
William Biles   Henry Baker   John Brock
Phinehas Pemberton Cl: Com:

Commiſſion Read

Conſtable Ellected Joſeph Chorley for the falls

peter worrall for above the falls

action
Edward Hancock
    agt:
Tho Revell
with drawn
by the plt ordr

adjourned the Court untill the 27ᵗʰ Inſtant

Bucks ſs: Penſylvania

At a Court of Quarter Seſſions held by the kings authority in the name of william Penn propry-etor & govrnr of the afforeſd Province & Territorys thereunto belonging held by adjournmt at the Court houſe for the afforeſaid County the 27ᵗʰ day of the firſt month 1689

The Juſtices Present
Joſeph Growdon   william Biles   Henry Baker
Nicholas Waln   John Brock
william Beakes Sherrife
Phinehas Pemberton Cl: Com:

Commiſſion of Peace Read

action   Randle Black Shaw plt
    agt
Charles Pickring deft

in a plea of Caſe

requeſt was made by Said Black ſhaw & declared that he was not in readineſs to bring his action on to Tryal & deſired to have it deferred untill another Court

A deed of 202 acres of land in ffee dated the 12th day of the 12th month
1688 acknowledged & delivered by Jof: Growdon grantr
unto Stephen Newel Grantee

A deed of 102 acres of land in fee dated the 12th day of the 12th month
1688 was acknowledged & delivered by Jofeph Growdon Grantr
to Abel Hinkstone Grantee

A deed of 102 acres of land in fee dated the 12th day of the 12th month
1688 was acknowledged & delivered by Jofeph Growdon
grantor to Abel Hinkstone attorney to william Reale grantee

194

A deed of 102 acres of land in fee dated the 10th day of the 12th month 1688
was acknowledged & delivered by Jofeph Growdon Grantor to
Stephen Newel Attorney to william Beal Grantee

A deed of 40 acres of land in fee dated the 10th day of the 12th month
1688

A deed was acknowledged & delivered by Jofeph Growdon
grantor to Abel Hinkftone Attorney to Thomas ffox and —
Jofeph wilsford grantees

A deed of 100 acresof land in fee dated the 23d day of the 12th month
1688 acknowledged & delivered by william Hearft Grantor
to Henry Hudlefton Grantee

Recognizance   Richard Thatcher being Calld according to recognizance
appeared the Court difcharges him paying his ffees

negro George being Calld for into this Court to anfwer the several
Judgmts of laft Court that was then adjudged to be payd by
Servitude

Recognizance Richard Ridgway according to recognizance —
brought the fd Negro into Court whereupon the Court difcharged
the fd Ridgway from the fd Recognizance

Commitment whereupon this Court Commits the fd George the negro in
Execution into the Sherrifs Cuftody until further order

non Suite Charles Pickring deft in Randle Blackshaws Cafe
appeared according to Summonce & Craved a non fuite
agt fd Blackshaw the Said Blackfhaw haveing declared

he was not in readynes for Tryal a non ſuite thereupon
was granted

recognizance Hugh Marſh being bound in 20 £ for appearance
of Job Hole the ſaid Hole being Calld appeared John Swift
& Philip Conway being Calld appeared & declared they had
nothing agt Hole whereupon the Court diſcharged him

recognizance Charles Brigham being bound as by the Information
of Joſeph Growdon & Arthur Cook Juſtices being Calld appeared
& more Complts Comeing agt him the Court ordered him to
give Security to appeare at the next Court which he the
Said Charles refuſed whereupon the Court Commits him
in to the Sherrifts Cuſtody untill he give Security

recognizance Tho: millard being to appeare at this Court according
-ly appeared none appeareing agt him the Court diſcharged
him

A deed of Sale & mortgage of 2 Iſlands in fee lying in this
County the one Calld kips Iſland & the other a little Iſland
northward of the other & both lying agt Burlington
dated the Sixth day of the firſt month 168 8 was —
$\overline{9}$
acknowledged & delivered by by Nicholas waln attorney to
Samuel Burden grantor to Arthur Cooke Subſtitute —
attorney to Samuel Carpenter attorney to Joſeph Burden grantee

195

a deed of ioo acres of land in fee dated the Tenth day of the
first month i688 was acknowledged and delivered in
open Court by Thomas Rowland grantor to
Philip Conway grantee.

a deed of 100 acres of land in fee dated the firſt day of the
fourth month i688 was acknowledged and delivered
by william Dungan grantor Arthur Cooke Grantee

Recognizance Edward Cartor & Tho: Brock being bound in 40 £ for
the appearance of John Allen at this Court who appeared
accordingly & nothing being objected agt him the Court
discharged him

ordered by this Court that George the Negro be delivered
from his Impriſonment to Stephen Newel w[ch] Said
negro is by this Court adjudged to ſerve the Said Stephen

Newel or his affigns fiveteen yeares and at the
End of fiveteen yeares to be returned to the mafter
of the fd negro or affignes if he the fd mafter or affignes
make demand of him in Confideration whereof the faid
Stephen Newel is to pay Elleven pounds foure Shillings to
anfwer the Several Judgments of Court formerly Impofed upon him
Stephen Newell and Jofeph Growdon both obliged them
Selves theire Executors and adminiftrators to
pay the Said Sum of Elleven pounds foure Shillings to
anfwer the Sevearl Judgments of Court aforementioned
in Cuntry produce at Currat price & to deliver the
Said pay at Philadelphia at or before the latter End
of the third month next enfueing to Such perfon or perfons
as Shall be appointed by the Court to receive the fame

action John Brock plt   ⎫ withdrew his action by the plts ordr
             agt   ⎬
       Job Houle John Butler   ⎬ withdrew his action by the plts ordr
             &   ⎬
       Ellizabeth venables   ⎭

action Stephen Beakes plt   ⎫
             agt   ⎬ withdrawn by the plts ordr —
       John Pidcock deft   ⎭

adjourned to the 12th day of the 4th month next

no bufnes prfenting in the 4th month no Court was held

Penfylvania

County Court Bucks fs: 196

At a Court of Quarter Seffions held by the kings author
-ity in the name of william Penn Proprietory & govrnr
of the aforesaid Province & Counties annexed the
11th day of the Seventh month 1689 at the Court
houfe for the fd County being the 9th yeare of the
propryetorys govrmt

The Juftices Present

William Biles   Henry Baker
Nicholas waln,   John Brock
wm: Beakes   Sherrife
Phinehas Pemberton   Cl: Com:

actions

mary Beakes plt
    agt } by the plts ordr withdrawn
Thomas Coverdale deft

Richard Ridgway plt
    agt } withdrawn by the plts ordr
John Heesome deft

    a deed of 125 acres of land in fee dated the 10th day of the 12th month 1688 was acknowledged and Delivered by Henry Paxſon grantr to William Plumley grantee

    a deed of 100 acres of land in fee dated the 10th day of the 12th month 1688 was acknowledged and delivered by William Plumley grantor to Henry Paxson grantee

    a deed of 310 acres of land in fee dated the 8th day of the 7th month 1689 was delivered and acknowledged by Richard Noble — grantor to moses Masley Grantee

    a deed of mortgage for 310 acres of land in fee dated the 9th day of the 7th month 1689 was delivered and acknowledged by — moses Masley grantor to Richard Noble Grantee

    a deed of one Tract of land about 100 acres in fee dated the 10th day of the 7th month 1689 was acknowledged and delivered by Thomas Coverdale Grantor to Henry Siddall Grantee

Constables appointed for the Succeeding yeare

ffor {
the upper part of the River Peter Worral
the falls Joseph Chorley —
the Lower part of the river Thomas Green
the middle lotts John Rowland atteſted
the upper part of neshaminah James Paxſon
the lower part of Neshaminah John White
}

Estreat   Thomas Revel convicted before Joſeph Growdon of Curſing
197   by his owne Confeſſion & therefore fined for the ſame 5^s
action   The action between John Swift plt & Philip Conway deft the
         declaration read

         Anſwer read

requeſt was made by the plt that the deft might purge him ſelf of the Treſpaſs whereof he Stands accuſed wᶜʰ the defetd to Conde

Anſwer cendd to
deft Philip Conway atteſted declared that he had Said he knew who had kild the Colt of John Swift (declared for) but upon him atteſtation declared that he knew nothing neither directly nor Indirectly of the killing of the ſd Colt neither did he ever of his owne knowledg know that John Swift had any Colt Kild

Iſſue ⎧ & for Tryal he the ſd deft put him on the Cuntry & ſo did
Joyned ⎨ the plt wherefore the Sherrife is Commanded to return
venire ⎩ 12 honeſt & lawfull men &c.

Jury Joſuah Hoops   Jon Palmer   william Dark ⎫
      Joſeph English Tho Tunneclif Samuel Daik ⎬ atteſted
      John Naylor   James Paxson John Hough ⎪
      Joſeph milner John Rowland John Wood — ⎭

witneſſes to the declaration

            Edmund moore ⎫
            Job Houle   ⎬ attested
            Philip Parker ⎭

requeſt made to the Court that a wittnes to a will made by Daniel Hawkins might be examined it haveing relation to a Tract of land left by Said Hawkins unto Thomas Coverdale wᶜʰ ſaid land was by Said Coverdale Conveyed to Henry Siddall & the deed thereof this day acknowled

Anſwer -ged in Court to which the Court gave
attestation John Clement being atteſted doth Say that he Saw the Said will bearing date the 30ᵗʰ day of the 10ᵗʰ month 1688 Sealed & delivered by Said Hawkins & further Saith that the ſd Hawkins did give his land to the Said Coverdale & his heires forever

adjourned the Court for one houre

ordered by this Court that Richard Ridgway or his aſſignes do Receive the mony due from Joſeph Growdon & Stephen Newel upon the account of the negro
            & that the ſd Richard Ridgeway have an order Signed by Some one Juſtice for to Impower him

to receive the Same, the Said Ridgway haveing this day in open Court promifed to anfwer all the Charges that has been out upon the negro & allowed by the Court

198

ordered that a requeft be drawn to the Govrnr that a regifter may be appointed in this County for the probat of wills and granting letters of Administration that people be not put to the extrordinary Charge of going to Philadelphia

a deed of 50 acres of land in fee dated the firft day of the 7th month 1689 acknowledged and delivered by Richard Wilfon grantor to John Gibbs Grantee

a deed of about 90 acres of land in fee dated the 8th day of the 4th month 1688 acknowledged and delivered by Luke Brindley — grantor to Peter Worrall Grantee

Isaac Burges being Calld none appearing agt him the Court difcharges him paying his fees

Jury returned Calld over Say they are not agreed therefore were returned back againe

Grand Jury Ezra Crosdel James Sutton James Crosley

John Clement Stephen Beakes Luke Brindley
Jon: Brearley Rich Wilfon Tho: Stakehoufe attefted
fenr:
Henry Siddal Andrew Heath

petit Jury return againe not agreed wherefore the Court returned them back

Recognizance John Swift being bound by Recognizance to —— appeare at this Court appeared accordingly & nothing appearing agt him the Court discharges him

Recognizance Philip Conway being bound to appear at this Court & to be of good abearing in the meane time appeared — accordingly & nothing appearing agt him the Court difcharges him paying his fees

action John Swift plt
      agt } both appeared
  Philip Conway deft

Jury verdict } Returned do Say they find for the deft

adjourned the Court untill to morrow morning at 8 a Clock

action Tho: Revel plt——————————
     agt
Richard Thatcher & Ifrael Taylor defts } Revel & Taylor appeared ——— }

declaration was

Iffue Anfwer read the plt defends & for tryal puts him felf Joyned on the Cuntry & So doth the plt wherefore the Sherrif is venire Commanded to Caufe to Come i2 honeft & Lawfull men &c.

199

witneffes to prove the Said declaration

    Grace Lang horn Thomas Preift Corin
    Benjemain Jones Ezra: Crosdel ———— } attefted
    Richard Thatcher Senior ——— ——— ———

Recognizance Richard Thatcher appeared according to Recogniz

grand Jury brought in a bill agt: Richard Thatcher Junior
    Ignoramus

grand Jury prfented Richard Thatcher for bringing in a dead hog to the houfe of Ifrael Taylor upon the firft day of the weeke

over Seeres of the High was nominated & appointed for the Succeeding yeare

for the { the upper part of Neshaminah Henry Paxson
the lower part Henry Bircham ————
the other Side of nefhaminah Tho: Hardin
the Lower part of the River John Cook ————
middle lotts Randle BlackShaw ————
the upper part of the River Wm: Clows ———— }

Judgmt given & it is adjudged that John Swift in the action he brought agt: Philip Conway Shall pay Coft of Court

Judgmt given & it is adjudged that Philip Conway for the lye he

Eſtreat   told in Jon Swifts Case whereof he was Convicted by his owne Confeſſion before this Court that he Shall pay — 2ˢ : 6ᵈ

grand jury brought in presentments about the roades in this County

ordered that the over Seers of the high ways take Care to repair the roads preſented by the grand jury

action   Tho Revel agt Ric Thatcher & Iſrael Taylor

Jury verdict } Returned Say they find for the plt thirty Shillings damage with Coſt of Suite

Iſrael Taylor abuſed the Jury being examined about it he made Submiſſion & acknowldgmt of his fault wherefore the Jury deſired the Court to paſs it by

Comitment   for Contempt of the Court by Rich Thatcher Junior & abuſes by him done to Tho: Revel & for Suſpition of takeing a hog that was none of his owne the Court Commits him into the Sherrifs Custody untill he finds Sufitient Suerties for his appearance at the next Court & to be of good abearing in the meane time

Charles Brigham being Calld none appearing agt him the Court diſcharges him paying his fees

a deed of 50 acres of land in fee dated the 10ᵗʰ day of the 7ᵗʰ mo: 1689 acknowledged & delivered by Nicholas waln grantor to William Hearſt grantee

200

Judgment given & it is adjudged that Richard Thatcher and Israel Taylor Shall pay to Thomas Revel 30ˢ damages with Coſts of Suite according to jurye verdict & that Execution Issue accordingly

10ᵗʰ   adjourned the Court to the 11ᵗʰ month next

The 11ᵗʰ day of the 10ᵗʰ month 1689 Several Juſtices met but no busines preſenting no Court was then held

action   Isaac Burges plt
                agt   } deferred untill another Court by
          Randle Blackſhaw deft   Conſent

County Court Bucks ſs:
Penſylvania

At a Court of Quarter Seſſions Held by the authority of William & Mary king & Queen of England &c in the name of William Penn Proprietor & govrnr of the afforeſd Province & Countys annexed at yᵉ: Court houſe for the Said County the 12ᵗʰ day of the first month 1689 being the 10ᵗʰ yeare of the — Propryetors Govermt

The Juſtices Present

Joſeph Growdon   Willm Biles
willm yardley   Henry Baker
Nicholas waln   John Brock
wm: Beakes   Sherrife
Phinehas Pemberton   Cl: Com:

actions

John Shippey plt
        agt   } plea of Caſe
Israel Taylor deft

Jos Growdon plt
        agt   } plea of Caſe
Tho Hutchins deft   demurred

Tho Revel plt
        agt   } plea of debt
Israel Taylor deft

Arthur Cook plt
        agt   } plea of Caſe
Joſeph Croff deft   withdrawn

Gilbert wheeler plt
        agt   } plea of Caſe withdrawn
Luke Brindley deft

Grand Jury

201

Rich Hough Joseph Clows John Palmer ⎫
Nathaniel Harding James Moone Thos Brock ⎪
Rich Ridgway Sam^ll Dark Andrew Ellot — ⎬ attefted
Jeffry Hawkins Andrew Heath Jofeph Englifh ⎪
wm Dark Jofeph Milner Henry Pointer ⎭

Estreat Thomas Coverdale for Comeing into Court drunk the Court fines him in 5ˢ

Commitment Paterick Conway & Philip Conway being Calld and Security required of them to anfwer the Several Complts — brought agt them wch they refufed wherefore the Court Commits them into the Sherrifs Custody untill further ordr

a deed of 200 acres of land in fee dated the 24 day of the 3 month 1689 was acknowledged & delivered by Samuel Burges & Randle BlackShaw grantors to Rich Lundy Grantee

a deed of 100 acres of land in fee dated the 10th day of the 12th month 1688 was acknowledged & delivered by Jofeph Growdon Grantor to Claws Jonfon Grantee

Complt being made by Derick Clawson that formerly he delivered to Arthur Cook and James Harrifon three wolves two of them bitches & one dog & that he hath but Received in part towards them 7ˢ the Court being Satiffyed of the truth hereof by Arthur Cooke one of the Juftices of peace for this County

ordered that the fd Clawson be paid what remaines due to him out of the firft mony that Comes to hand to the Receivors of the publique Stock

notice from John Blackwell not to pay Quit Rents to any but Robt Turner or his Subftitutes read

adjourned the Court for one hour

A deed of Some land for a mill pond in fee dated the 20th day of the 9th month 1689 was acknowledged & delivered by william Beakes attorney to John otter Grantor to — ffrancis Roffill Grantee

Conftables nominated & appointed for the lower part be tween Nefhaminah & Popueffin Samuel Allen Junr: for the upper part thereof Jon: purflone attefted

Estreat William Clows & Thomas Kirle being Summonced to appeare on the jury this Court the Sherrif being attefted declared they had lawfull Summonce they not appearing accordingly the Court fines them in 3ˢ apeice

202

Causual death of Ann Hawkins prſented by yᵉ Corronor to this Court to be by a fall from a mare She rid upon occationed by another horſe that was tyed to her tayle going by the way on the Conterary Side of A tree wᶜʰ Cauſed the mare Suddenly to Stop So that Shee fell from the ſd mare & was killd

prſentments brought in by the Grand Jury

agt Rich Thatcher for abuseing his father

Iſrael Taylor for abuseing the Jury Caling them for Sworn Rogues & saing to Tho: Tunneclif that he wold knock him on the head

Wmⁱ Beakes for keeping bad fence

the High Way between the fferry houſe & newtowne

Andrew Ellot for ſelling bear without Lycence

Henry Marjorum for Selling Liquors

Thats its neceſſary the County be devided into Townſhips

that the former Tax be gathered & that there be another Tax raiſed for defraying Such neceſſary Charges as the former Shall fall Short

adjourned to 8 in the morning

grand jurys prſentmt agt: Paterick Conway & Philip Conway

Bucks ſs: 12ᵗʰ i 1689
       mo

(1) The Jurrors for the propryetory & Govrnr by the king & Queens authority do prſent Paterick Conway & Philip Conway of the afforesaid County that on or about the laſt day of the iiᵗʰ month laſt paſt did breake open the houſe of Wm ffisher in the County of Philadelphia and from thence did take Steale and Carry away — Several goods to the value of foure pounds and fiveteen — Shillings agt the king & Queens peace & againſt the ſtatute law in that Case made & provided

   John Swift proſecutr

Wm ffisher } witnesses attested
Samuel Vose }

pleading   A true bill

upon wich they were arrained & pleaded not guilty & for tryal put them Seves upon the Cuntry

(2)   Bucks fs: The 12th $\frac{i}{mo}$ $\frac{1689}{90}$

The Jurrors for the propryetory & Govrnr by the king & queens authority do prsent Philip Conway for fraudulently takeing & stealing one mare being the goods of the propryetory & govrnr about the 13 day of the first month last past to the value of foure pound agt the king & queens peace & agt the Statute law in that Case made & —
Provided
                John Swift profecutor

Pleading   nicholas Randle Micheal Bucher witnesses   A true bill
to wch he pleaded not guilty & for tryal put him felf upon the Cuntry

Bucks fs: The 12th $\frac{i}{mo}$ $\frac{1689}{90}$

203

(3) The Jurrors for the propryetor & govrnr by the king & queens authority do prsent Paterick Conway of the afforesaid — County for fraudulent Takeing & Stealing one half hide of lether to the value of Ten Shillings in or about the 10th month last past being the proper goods of Charles thomas of the County of Philadelphia agt the king & queens — Peace & Conterary to the Statute law in that Case made & Provided   Charles Thomas profecutor } attested
              William ffisher witnes }

pleading   a true bill

To which he pleaded not guilty & for tryal put him Self upon the Cuntry

Bucks fs: The i2th $\frac{i}{mo}$ $\frac{1689}{90}$

(4) The Jurrors for the propryetory & govrnr by the king & queens authority do prfent Paterick Conway and Philip Conway of the County aforefaid for that on the Second day of this Inftant by violent affault & force they took away from the perfon of william ffisher one Colt to the value of Twenty Shillings being the proper goods of william Penn Propryetory & govrnr agt the king & queens peace & Conterary to the Statute law in that Cafe made & provided

        william ffisher profecutor ⎱
        John Swift ——————— ⎰ wittneffes attefted

    The evidence of George Burton taken before William Markham
Secretary & one of the Juftices
    of peace for Philadelphia County

    A true bill

pleading

To which they pleaded not guilty & for Tryal put them Selves upon the Cuntry

(5) Bucks fs: The i3 day of the $\frac{i}{mo}$ $\frac{1689}{90}$

The jurrors for the propryetory and govrnr by the king & queens authority do prfent Richard Thatcher Junior of the afforefaid County for fraudulently takeing and Stealing one hog being the proper goods of John Purflone in or about the 4th or 5th month laft paft to the value of one pound agt the king and Queens peace and Conterary to the Statute law in that Cafe made & provided

        John Purflone profecutor ⎱
        Thomas Revel ——————— ⎰ witnesses attested

pleading   A true bill

To which he pleaded not guilty & for tryal put him felf on the Cuntry

204

motion being made by william Biles the Receivor of the Publique Stock

of the County that there was Several neceſſary Charges of the County
to defrayed as the fees of the Councell & assemblymen
killing of wolves &c: & that he had no Effects in his hands
whereupon the grand jury prſented the neceſſity of haveing a
new Tax raiſed

Jury ====== Joſuah Hoops John wood william Ellet ⎫
     Thomas Stakehous John Allen Stephen Beaks ⎬ atteſted
     Henry Hulestone wm: Paxson wm Taylor ⎪
     Rich: Lundy Tho: Hardin Ezra Crosdel ⎭

no Chalenges made by the priſoners agt any of them

witnesses upon the firſt Indictmt agt Paterick Conway & Philip Conway

william ffisher atteſted doth Say that about the latter End of Janu
-ary being at the houſe of Philip Conway in order to ſeek a
mare of his that was loſt after he found he he returned
home againe at which time he found his houſe broken up and
his Cheſt unlocked & the key in the lock wch key at his going
away he hid under his beds tead and none knew of the —
hideing of it there Save Paterick Conway who was prſent —
when the key was hid & that upon Search for his Goods
he found part of his goods in Philip Conways houſe viz: one
Inke horn

Samuel voſe atteſted doth Say that on the laſt day of January
at night being to have the hay of william ffisher went to the ſd
ffishers houſe for Some of the hay where he found all
well on the next morning he went againe for more hay
where he found a man & horſe had been about the houſe
he followed the Track in the Snow between 3 & 4 miles
& as he did apprehend the Track did lead towards the houſe
of Philip Conway & further Saith not

James Paxson atteſted Saith that he being Conſtable Searched
the houſe of Philip Conway where was found an Inkhorn
which william ffisher owned to be his & futher Saith not

Grand Jurys prſentmts i3 day $\frac{i}{mo}$ $\frac{i689}{90}$ adjourned for i houre

Bucks ſs: wee the jurrors for the body of the County do prſent it
to the Court thats its neceſſary that a Tax be forthwith made
for the defraying the requiſit Charge of the County as paying the
Councel & aſſembley.mens fees what is allready due to them &
allowed by law & for killing of wolves &c.

jury returned do Say that Paterick Conway & Philip Conway is not guilty of breaking up the houſe of william ffisher

205

(3) agt Patrick Conway for ſtealing half a hide of lether

Charles Thomas atteſted doth Say in decemb laſt paſt Paterick Conway & he Came to walter fforeſt mill with lether at which time he Sold the Said Paterick i Side of lether & the remameing pte of his lether he left out of doores for Some time 2 or 3 days & ſaid Thomas Telling over his lether he miſt one ſide there of & after Some time willm ffisher told Said Thomas he Saw 2 ſides of lether in Philip Conways houſe & that Paterick Conway told Said ffisher that Charles Thomas gave him one & Sold him the other

willm ffisher atteſted doth Say he Saw 2 ſides of lether in Philip Conways houſe & that Paterick Conway told him that he bought one of them of Charles Thomas & that he gave him the other

Jury returned Say Paterick Conway is guilty of ſtealing the ſide of lether from Charles Thomas

action

John Shippey plt ⎫
          agt ⎬ both appeared
Iſrael Taylor deft ⎭

declarat read

Anſwer read

Iſsue Joyned for tryal both put them Selves upon the Cuntry
  venire   wherefore the Sherrifeis Commanded to Cauſe to Come i2 honeſt & Lawfull men &c —

Jury ——— John wood William Ellet Tho: Stakehouſe ⎫
             John Allen Stephen Beakes Henry Hudlestone ⎬ attested
             Willm Paxson Willm Taylor Rich Lundy ——
             Thomas Hardin Gilbert wheeler Ezra Croſdel ⎭

william Biles Joſeph Croſſe atteſted for the plant

Richard Thatcher Junr: John Purstone atteſted for the deft

adjourned untill tomorrow morning at 7 a Clock

Grand Jury bring in theire prſentments

The ſ4ᵗʰ day of the i 1689 / mo 90

prſent Iſrael Taylor for Receiveing a Stolen hog from Rich Thatcher Junʳ on the firſt day of the weeke

alſo prſent Henry Marjorum for ſwearing by god the ſ3 day Inſtant

Iſrael Taylor being Calld into Court upon the prſentment for the abuſe done to Thomas Tunneclif he Confeſt the fact whereupon the Court ordrs he give bond for his appearance at next Court & to keepe the peace in the meane time

206

Recognizance Iſrael Taylor oblidges him Self in 8 £ to be payd to the — propryetory & govrnr his heires & Succeſſors to be levyed on his lands & tenements goods & Chattles & this upon Condition yᵗ: the ſd Taylor appeare at the next Court of Quarter Seſſions to be held for this County & to keepe the peace in the meane time

action John Shippey agt Iſrael Taylor

jury returned do Say they find for the plt with 4ᵈ damages & Coſt

verdict   of Suite

a deed of ſ50 acres of land in fee dated the ſ0ᵗʰ day of february ſ689 / 90 was acknowledged and delivered by Robt Heaton attorney to Henry fflower grantor to Thomas Harding grantee

Henry Marjorum being Calld to anſwer the grand Jurys prſentmts for Selling Liquors deſired to have what was done paſt by & for the future he wold for beare

Henry Marjorum upon the prſentmt of the grand Jury for Swearing by god Submitted to the Court for wᶜʰ the Court fines him
Eſtreat   in 5ˢ

(2)   Indictmt agt Philip Conway for ſtealing a mare of the propryetors

Jury calld over objected agt Gilbert wheeler

Jury ——— John Wood Robt Haton Tho: Stakehoufe ⎫
Stephen Beakes John Allen wm Paxfon ⎪
Anthony Burton wm: Taylor Tho: Hardin ⎬ attefted
Rich Lundy Wm Ellot Henry Hudelfon — ⎭

John Swift attefted doth Say that he tooke up a mare Suppofed to be about 3 yeares of age unmarked of Colour mealy mouthed about 4 yeares paft in the 2nd month next of wch mare he gave notice to the raingers but he refufed to take her & that he fpoke to James Harrifon the Govrnrs Steward to have bought her to wch James Harrifon gave way but put no price upon her upon which he eare marked her with a half peny cut on the under fide of the nearror eare wch Said mare he Saw Several times — Since in Philip Conways Cuftody but more perticulerly about 3 weeks ago & about the i3 day of the $\frac{i1688}{mo9}$ & that Since then he Saw the Same mare with her Eare marke Changed —

Nicholas Randle attefted doth declare the aforefd markes & takeing up of the fd mare unmarked & of the Ear marke John Swift gave her & of his aquainting the raingers with her & further Saith that about a yeare after the mare Strayed away from

from the Said Swifts House Philip Conway told him he wold have the fd mare & Several times after that he Saw the faid mare in Said Conways Cuftody & perticulerly about 2 weekes ago or 3 weekes in harnes at Philip Conways house & Since then in Philip Conways feild & further Saith that when he Spoke with Conway about the Said mare he the fd Conway Said he wold have her

Micheal Bucher attefted doth say that he was prfent at the takeing up of the fd mare by Jon: Swift as aforefaid & y^t: Shee had the marks & Colour as before teftefyed & y^t: he Saw the fd mare feveral times in Said Conways — Cuftody & that he Saw fd Conway ride on her about 2 yeares ago & that he Chalenged the mare & fd Conway thereupon rid away from him that John Swift marked her with a half peny Cut as aforefd

(4th) Indictemt agt Paterick Conway & Philip Conway for forceably takeing a Colt from willm ffisher being the Propryetors

Jury attefted being the Same laft mentioned
william ffisher attefted doth Say he has order to take up a Colt
-by Capt: Markham belonging to the govrnr which he according
-ly he did & when he had the Colt in his yard the 2nd day of
this Inftant Paterick Conway & Philip Conway Came to his
houfe & demanded the Colt the Said ffifher refuseing to deliver
it Paterick Conway knoct him over in the meane time
Philip Conway tooke away the Said Colt

George Burfton attefted before william Markham Secretary the
3 day of the firft month $\dfrac{1689}{90}$ Saith that yesterday he was at the
houfe of willm ffifher and that he Saw a Colt tyed in the
yard the fd ffifher telling the deponant that he had taken up
the fd Colt & was ordered by Capt = Markham to bring him to towne
being unmarked after wch Came into the yard one Paterick
Conway & Philip his brother & said the Colt was theires &
though they were Charged to the Conterary yet they let the fd
Colt loofe & Carryed her away & the fd ffifher going to —
prvent them by putting up the barre either Struck or thruft
him backward over the fence & forced the mare & Colt
over him

Taken before Wm Markham Secretary
the day above faid

whereas the Sherrife wm Beakes & Phine: Pemberton Clark hath
made it appeare that there is due to them for fees three pounds
nine Shillings foure pence from Richard Thatcher & that he the
fd Thatcher refufed to pay the Same

208
jury returned
do say that Philip Conway is Guilty of Stealing one mare whereof he
ftands

verdict Indicted

They alfo Say Paterick Conway & Philip Conway are Guilty of takeing
forcably one Colt from wm ffifher whereof he ftands indicted

(5) Indictmt agt Richard Thatcher for Stealing one hog the goods of
John Purflones

Jury attefted

John Purflone attefted Saith that he loft a hog of Colour neare White abo
about 2 yeares of age with a Slit in the further eare & that
he doth Sufpect Ricnard Thatcher Junr Stole the Said hog &

that about the Same time he loft the Said hogg another hog of his Came home cut Crofs the nofe

Thomas Revel attefted doth Say that about the beginning of harveft laft Richard Tatcher Junior brought a hog to the houfe of — Ifrael Taylor of Colour neare white Some what red on the Sholders but whether it was Sanded or blood he knows not one of the eares had a Slit in it whether he knew not wch hog the fd Richard Thatcher told him was two yeares old or upward

Ifrael Taylor attefted doth Say that Richard Thatcher Junr did bring to his houfe a hog of white Colour with one or both — Sholders Sanded Some time afore harveft & that he told fd Taylor he wifht he had not brought the fd hog for he doubted it was his fathers hog

A deed of 250 acres of land in fee dated the i3 day of the firft month i689 was acknowledged and delivered by Ifrael Taylor — grantor to william Biles for the ufe of John Coates Grantee

Jury returned
verdict ——— do find Richard Thatcher guilty of ftealing a hog

action

Thomas Revel agt Israel Taylor

declara read

Iffuing ⎱ Anfwe read
Joyned ⎰ the deft him Self on the Cunty & So doth plt therefore the

venire Sherrife is Commaned to Caufe to Come i2 honeft & Lawful men &c:

Jury attefted

Joseph Growdon Ezra Crofdel ffrancis Roffill witnefes attefted

Jury ⎱ returned do Say they find for the plt with 6^d damages & Cofts
verdict ⎰ of fuite

adjourned for one houre

adjourned untill tomorrow morning at 8 a Clock

Judgment given & it is adjudged that Richard Thatcher for Stealing one hog Shall make 3 fold Satiffaction to the owner & be whipt on his bare back 2i Stripes

Judgmt awarded in the Cafe Shippey agt Taylor that the Said Ifrael Taylor Shall pay the Said John Shippey 2 £ 10ˢ with 4ᵈ damages & Cofts of fuite

Thomas Revel in open Court declared that Ifrael Taylor had Satisfyed him what was awarded him by the Jurys verdict & defired Judgment in the fd Case to be fufpended

ordered that Execution Iffue agt the goods of Richard Thatcher for the aforefd fees due to the Several officers aforefd if he does not take Speedy Courfe to Satisfye the Same

Recognizance Richard Thatcher Junior oblidges him felf in 20 £ to the propryetory & govrnr his heires & fucceffors to be levyed on his lands & Tenemts goods & Chattles & this upon Condition that he be & appeare at the next Court of Quarter Seffions to be held for this County & to be of good abearing in the meane time

Recognizance Thomas Hutchins became bound to the proprye tor &c in the Sum of Ten pounds before Jofeph growdon for the appearance of one Ellenor Manarte (a vagrant woman) at this Court but Shee appeared

Estreat not wherefore the fd Hutchins forfeited his recognizanc

Judgment awarded upon the 2ⁿᵈ Indictment & it is adjudged that Philip Conway for Stealeing one mare being the goods of Govrnr Penn Shall make three fold Satisfaction being i2 £ to be levyed on his goods or Lands & be whipt on his bare back 39 Stripes & be banifhed out of this Govrmt not to return againe on penalty of one hundred pounds it being the 3 offence whereof he is Convicted

Judgmt Given & it is adjudged that Paterick Conway & Philip Conway for takeing away by force and violent affault from William ffisher one Colt the proper goods of Govrnr Penn Shall make foure fold Satisfaction being foure pounds — to be levyed on theire goods or lands & that Paterick — Conway be whipt on his bare back i5 Stripes & Philip Conway one Stripe both in the Sight of the people

Judgmt given & it is adjudged that Paterick Conway for — Stealing one half hide of lether the proper goods of Charles — Thomas Shall make 3 fold Satisfaction being 30ˢ to be Levyed on his goods & Chattles & for want of goods & Chattles

to be & remame bondman unto ſd Charles Thomas untill he
be Satisfyed the ſaid 30ˢ & to be whip on his bare back 15
Stripes in the ſight of the Court & people

ajourned to the 20ᵗʰ day of this Inſtant month

210

Bucks ſs: At a Court held by adjournment the 26 day of
the firſt month 1690

Justices pr̲ſ̲e̲n̲t̲

Arthur Cook   william Biles
willm yardley   Nicholas waln
Henry Baker   John Br̲o̲c̲k̲
willm Beakes Sherriſe
Stephen Beakes Deputy Sherriſc
Phinehas Pemberton   Cl: Com:

Several acctts & requeſts this day brought in from
them that have Served in Councill & aſſembley that they
may be Satisfyed what the law allows them for theire —
attendance this Court with the approbation of the Grand jury —
have Thought good to order that a Tax be raiſed for —
the defraing the neceſſary Charge of the County & it is

ordered   therefore ordered that a Tax be forth with raiſed of 300 £
on the males and lands according as the law directs & that
the Collectors after named Collect the Same with in theire —
Several diviſſions as may be rated on them for theire ſhares
& give an acctt of theire lands & males within theire Several
deviſions viz

for { above the falls to John woods: Joſeph Milner
thence to the Govrnrs Stephen Beakes
thence to ne ſhaminh & up the ſame to Robt Halls plantation
James Boyden junior
thence up the Creek to the upper moſt land taken up ton —
Neshamina Thomas Rowland
middle lotts william Dark
Between neshaminah & poqueſſin to the upper part of —
Joſeph Growdons land Samuel Allen junior
thence to the upper moſt lands taken up Henry Pointer

ordered that an acctt of lands & males be returned to the Juftices the 23 day of 2ⁿᵈ month next at the Court houfe

adjourned the 23 day of the 2ⁿᵈ month next

no Court held according to adjournmt the 23 day of the 2ⁿᵈ month

Pennsylvania

County Court Bucks fs:

211

action

wm: Thomas
  agt } plea of
Andrew Heath } Cafe
  with drawn

At a Court of Quarter Sessions held by the king and Queens authority in the name of Willm Penn Propryetor and govrnr of the afforesaid Province & Counties annexed at the Court houfe for the Said County the iith day of the 4th month 1690

The Justices prfent
Wm Biles   Nicholas Waln
Henry Baker   Jon: Brock
Wm yardley   vic: Com:
Phinehas Pemberton   Cl: Com:

returned the death of John ackerman that he was drowned accidentely the iith 3 mo 1690

Recognizance Israel Taylor being bound to appear at this Court appeared accordingly & none appearing agt him the Court difcharges him

a deed of 6 acres of land in fee dated the 4th day of the 4th month 1690 acknowledged & delivered by william yardley attorney to Samuel Burges grantor to willm Biles & Jofuah Hoops grantees for the ufe of them Selves & Tho: Janney and Richard Hough Grantees

a deed in fee for 300 acres of land dated the 18th day of the 12th mo: 1689 acknowledged and delivered by willm Beakes grantor to Thomas Tunnclif attorney to Jon worrilow & walter ——— worrilow in Truft for the ufes therein expreffed

meffage from the affembley that there is due from this County to the Clarks of the affembley 1: £ 7^s 0^d & defired that Care be taken to anfwer the Same ordered that the Same be pd out of the County ſtock when it comes in

whereas Tho: Rowland as ordered laſt Court to bring in an acctt of the lands & males within his deviſion appointed & that he is Since dead & now that deviſion now thought too large for one man its therefore

ordered that wm Hearſt from the lower ſide of Robt Halls —— plantation to new Town & Shadrach walley from thence to the upper moſt land taken up do give an acctt of the lands & males Taxable

agreed that if Iſrael Taylor bring in an acctt of all lands ſurveyed Seated or unſeated with in the limits of this County att or before the next Court & the Same acctt be Juſt & true faire drawn out that then the ſd Iſrael Taylor have 20^s for his paines diſcounted out of the Tax to be raiſed

whereas there is occation for a Cuiionor a boy being lately drowned & none being Commiſſionated for this County

ordered that wm Biles Ar: Cooke & wm yardley take Care to Endeavor y^t a Corronor & Regiſter be appointed in this County

212

ordered that the Said prſons request the Councill that the upper Roade for the upper moſt plantations in this County be layd Through Philadelphia County

Complt being made by John Cartor that his brother Edward Cartor doth not allow him meate & apparrel

ordered that Arthur Cook & wm: Biles forthwith take Care about it & ſee for what time the ſd Jon was placed to him by the orphans Court & endeavor to redreſs the Complt

18 4 1690 execution granted agt Paterick & Philip Conway in wm ffiſhers
   mo   Caſe re turnd

adjourned to the 10th 7th mo next execut the 30 4 1690 p wm
                                                          mo   yardley

30th 4 90 execution in Swifts Caſe dated
         mo

for 10 £: 3^s: 3^d returnd executed ſame day
p wm yardley

Pensylvania
County Court Bucks fs:

actions Entered
7ᵗʰ day 6 1690
mo

John Jones by his attorney Samuel Carpentr
Paterick Robinſon Joſhu ffuller & Jon: Swift plt
agt
Joſ Holden deft in an acctt of debt 66 £ : 8ˢ : 06ᵈ

Attachmt granted the i9ᵗʰ day of the 6ᵗʰ month i690 agt the goods of Joſeph Hold in the Caſe afforeſaid by Arthur Cook

Return thereof executed the 2iᵗʰ day of the 6ᵗʰ month i690 p wm yardley Sherrife

action Entered
23 day of the 6
mo
1690

John Duplovie plt
agt
Joſeph Watson deft

in an action of debt 15 £ : 16ˢ : 07ᵈ

Attachment granted the 2i day of the 6ᵗʰ month i690 agt: the goods of Joſeph Holden in the Caſe afforeſaid by Arthur Cook

Return the 30ᵗʰ 6 i690 executed p wm yardley Sherrife
mo

action Entered
23 day of 6
mo
1690

Philip Richards plt
agt
Joſeph Holden deft

in an action of debt

Attachment granted the 2i day of the 6ᵗʰ month i690 agt: the goods of Joſeph Holden in the Caſe afforeſaid by Arthur Cooke

Return 30ᵗʰ 6 1690 executed p wm: yardley Sherrife
mo

action Entered
24 6 1690
mo

Iſrael Taylor plt
agt
Tho: Brock Ralph Boome
John Stetton ffrancis Roſſill
mathew miller
defts

in an action on the
Caſe Sum 8 £

Summonce granted 26th 6/mo 1690 agt: ſd defts p John Brock

Return 30th 6/mo executed the ſd Summonce p wm: yardley ſherrif

action Entered 26th 6/mo i690 } Policarpus Roſe plt
agt
John Pidcock deft }

Summonce granted in ſd Caſe 26th 6/mo i690 agt ſd deft p Jon Brock

Return 29th 6/mo 1690 executed ſd Summonce p wm yardley ſherriſe

Summonce for witneſſes in ſd Caſe granted 26th 6/mo 1690 for

213

John Lee & his wife Rachel martha Lee & Robt Benſon

Return 28 & 29th 6/mo 1690 Summonced the ſd p wm yardley Sherriſe

action Entered 26th 6/mo 1690 } Gilbert wheeler plt
agt
John Pidcock deft } in a plea of Caſe

Sumonc granted in ſd Case for ſd deft 26th 6/mo i690 p Jon Brock

Return the 29th of the 6/mo 1690 executed p wm yardley Sherrif

Action Entered the 26th 6/mo i690 } Iſrael Taylor plt
agt
John Shippey deft } in a plea of Caſe

Sumonc granted for ſd deft: 26ᵗʰ 6/mo i690 p Jon Brock

Return 29ᵗʰ 6/mo i690 executed p wm yardley ſherriſe

Summonce granted for wm Roles witnes in ſd Case the 26ᵗʰ 6/mo i690

Return 29ᵗʰ 6/mo i690 executed the ſd ſum p wm yardley ſherrif

action Entered the 28ᵗʰ 6/mo 1690 } John wood plt agt: John Butler deft } in a plea of Caſe

attachment granted the 28ᵗʰ day 6 mo in ſd Caſe p Jon Brock

Return 29 & 30 day 6/mo i690 executed p wm yardley ſherrif

action Entered the 28 6/mo 1690 } mary Beakes Adminiſtratrix to her late huſband wm: Beakes by her attorney

Samuel Beakes plt
agt
Jonathan Eldridge deft }

Arreſt granted agt ſd deft the iiᵗʰ 4/mo 1690 p wm Biles

Return the iiᵗʰ 4/mo i690 Taken into Cuſtody

action Entered 28ᵗʰ 6/mo i690 } John wood plt agt John Swift deft } in a plea of Caſe

Sumonce granted the 28ᵗʰ day 6ᵗʰ month 1690 p Jon Brock

return 29th 6/mo 1690 executed p wm yardley

Pensylvania

Bucks ſs: 214

At a Court of Quarter Seſſions held by the king & Queens authority in the name of Willm Penn Propryetory & Govrnr of the afforeſaid Province & Counties annexed at the Court houſe for the afforeſaid County the 10th of the 7th month 1690

The Justices Present

Joseph Growdon Wm Biles
nicholas Waln Henry Baker
John Brock
Wm: yardley Sherrife
Phinehas Pemberton Cl Com:

Comitment William Evans for Suspition of being Conferate with Joseph Trivitham in a felonious act the Court Commits into Safe Cuſtody untill further ordr

adjourned untill 9 o Clock in the morning

action Jon Jones by his attorneys
      agt   } plea of debt
Joſeph Holden

appearance Paterick Robinson & Jon Swift Attorneys to ſd Jones appeared & the deft by his attorney Hugh Marſh appeared

declaration Read

A Coppy of the ſd Attorneys power & a Certificate of the back thereof Read

Bonds Read & proved

bill read & proved by atteſtation of John Swift & Henry Pointer

defts attorney declared he had nothing to bject why Judgmt might not paſs

Judgmt awarded & it is adjudged that Joſeph Holden ſhall pay to Jon Jones or his attorneys the ſum

of thirty pounds Silver monys
as alſo the Sum of Six pounds eight Shillings Six pence
with Intreſt for the thirty pounds from the firſt day of the
3 month 1690 with Coſts of ſuite to which the defts attorneys
aſſented

ordered by the Court that Paterick Robinson becom bound
upon Record in Court in 100 £ that Jon Jones Shall ratiefye
what he and other attorneys has done in relation to the
afforeſaid action

obligation 215

Patrick Robinson oblidges him Self his heirs executrs
and administrators to the Juſtices now on the —
bench being Joſeph Growdon William Biles Tho: Janney
Nicholas waln Henry Baker & John Brock theire
Executors and adminiſtrators in the Sum of one —
hundred Pounds to be levied on his lands Tenements
goods and Chattles Conditioned for the procureing of
an authentick power from Jon Jones or that the ſd
John Jones his heires Executors or adminiſtrators in
12 months time do Rate fye what ſd Paterick ——
Robinſon & the reſt of the attorneys of John Jones
has done or Shall do in relation to an action of
debt for 36 £ : 8ˢ : 06ᵈ now brought agt Joſeph
Holden **PAT: ROBINSON**

Action John Duplovie ⎫
      agt   ⎬ plea of debt
  Joſeph Holden — ⎭

plt appeared by his attorney Paterick Robinſon
his letter of attorney to Impower him produced
deft appeared by his attorney Hugh marſh
his letter of attorney to Impower him produced

debt accknowledged by the defts attorney

Judgmt Given & it is adjudged that Joſeph Holden Shall
pay to John Duplovie the Sum of thirtteen pounds
pounds eighteen Shillings Seven pence half peny
13 £ : 18ˢ 7½ᵈ (the Said attorney haveing promiſed to
allow what Shall be further made appeare paid upon
acctt)
if any be & that Execution Iſſue accordingly to ſd
Judgmt

Action   Philip Richards plt ⎫
                agt   ⎬ in a plea of debt
      Joſeph Holden deft ⎭

      Paterick Robinſon his attorney appeares letter of attorney produced to prove the ſame

      Hugh marsh attorney afforeſd appeares

      declaration read

      Anſwer the ſaid defts attorney acknowledges the debt

      Judgmt Given & it is adjudged that Joſeph Holden ſhall pay to Philip Richards the ſum of Ten pounds Two Shillings & three pence 10 £ : 2ˢ 3ᵈ (the ſd plts attorney promiſeing to allow what Shall be further made appeare paid on acctt) & that execution Iſſue accordingly

216

action   John wood plt ⎫
             agt   ⎬ in a plea of Caſe both appeared
    John Swift deft ⎭

declaration read

Anſwer he doth owe the takeing up the negroes

the matter refferred to the bench

Judgmt given and it is adjudged that John Swift Shall pay to John wood one pound five Shillings & that ſd Swift ſhall alſo pay Coſt of ſuite

action Samuel Beakes attorney to Mary Beakes plt ⎫ both
                         agt ⎬ in a plea of debt ⎬ appeared
     Jonathan Eldridge deft ⎭

declaration read

Anſwer he ownes the debt

Judgmt Given & it is adjudged that Jonathan Eldridg Shall pay to the plt the Sum of Two pounds Three ſhillings Seven pence with Coſts of Suite

which Said Sum of Two pounds three ſhillings Seven pence

willm Embley in open Court declared he wold pay to the plt or attorney in three months time

willm Biles promifed to pay the fee of the fd Cafe

a deed of 72 Square Rods of land in fee dated the 4th day of the 7th month 1690 acknowledged & delivered by Thomas Janney grantor to Jofuah Hoops & wm yardley for the ufe of them Selves & the reft of the grantees

adjourned for one houre

a deed in fee of 200 acres of land dated the 10th day of the 12th month 1689 by Phinehas Pemberton grantor unto mary Radclif widow of the grantee

a deed in fee of 250 acres of land dated the 8th day of the 7th month 1690 acknowledged & delivered by willm Clows & marjory Clows Grantors to Jofeph Clows Grantee

a deed in fee of 250 acres of land dated the 8th day of the 7th month 1690 was acknowledged & delivered by Joseph Clows grantor to willm Clows Grantee

grand jury attefted

Samuel Dark wm Ellot wm Hayhurft
Tho: Tunneclif Shadrach walley John Palmer
Jofuah Hoopes Andrew Heath Joseph Clowes
Jonathan fcaife Andrew Ellot Jon Lee
Jonathan Walters Henry Paxfon peter Worral
Jon white

Indictmt Bucks fs: the jurrors for the body of this County do prfent

Thomas Brock for extortion in ferriage the 8th day of this Inftant

the 7th month Conterarly to the ftatute law in that Cafe made & provided

to wich prfentmt he pleaded Guilty

217

a deed of 500 acres of land in fee dated the 9th day of the 7th month 1690 acknowledged and delivered by John Rowland grantor to Gilbert wheeler Grantee

a deed of 360 acres of land in fee dated the 15th day of

November in the firſt yeare of the reigne of willm & mary king & Queen of England &c: acknowledged & delivered by wm Biles attorney to John Cuff grantor to Samuel Beakes grantee

a deed of 60 acres of land in fee dated the 20th day of the 6th month 1690 acknowledged & delivered by Joſeph Growdon grantor to Thomas Scot grantee

action Iſrael Taylor plt

agt:

Thomas Brock ffrancis Roſſill John Stedon
Ralph Boome & mathew miller defts

Iſrael Taylor appeared

Thomas Brock ffrancis Roſſill & Jon: Stedon appeared on behalt of them Selves & the reſt

declaracon read

Anſwer they Confeſt to the declaracon & Sayd that they wold pay the plt. 5 £: 10^s: 00^d with Coſt of ſuite

replye Iſrael Taylor ſaid it Shold Content him & Craved Judgmt for the Same

Judgmt given & it is adjudged that the ſd defts Shall pay to ſaid plt Iſrael Taylor 5 £: 10^s: 00^d with Coſts of Suite & that execution Iſſue accordingly

Cornelius Empſon Craved in open Court that wm: Embley might be his attorney to proſecute an action of debt agt Joſeph Holden for 8 £ Silver mony

allowed the ſd request

wm Evans being examined about a hors found in the Cuſtody of Joſeph Trivetham Said that he lent the ſd Trivetham the horſe

adjourned untill 8 a Clock tomorrow morning   £   s   d

Execution drawn to be ſigned for John Jones for the levying of 36 : 8 : 6 & 2 £ : 3^s: i^d Coſts on the Goods & Chattles of Joſeph Holden

action   Cornelius Empson
                    agt   } Caſe of debt for 8 £ Silver mony
         Joseph Holden

appeares by his attorney wm: Embley

Joseph Holden appeares by his attorney Hugh Marſh declarcon Read

Anſwer he ownes the declaracon & Confeſſes the debt

218

Judgment Given and it is adjudged that Joſeph Holden Shall pay to Cornelius Empſon the Sum of eight pounds Silver mony with Coſts of Suite & that Execution Iſſue accordingly

Iſrael Taylor
         agt   } plea of Caſe both appeared
John Shippey —

declaracon Read

Anſwer that he owes the plt 33ˢ & will pay Coſts of Suite plt declared that the Same pd to him will Satisfy him

Judgmt Given & it is adjudged that John Shippey Shall pay Thirty Three Shillings with Coſts of Suite & that execu-tion Iſſue accordingly

grand Jury prſents Joſeph Trevithan formerly of this County for fraudulently takeing and Carrying away from the houſe of Joſeph Growdon the 8th day of this Inſtant the 7th month one broad Cloth Coate i paire pluſh breeches one womans Cloake being the proper goods of the ſd Joſeph Growdon to the value of five pounds Conterary to the king & Queens peace & the Statute law in that Caſe made & provided &c:

Pro ſecutor Joſeph Growdon

wittneſſes Tho: ffox John Hawkins atteſted

This bill found

Joſeph Trevithan to the Said Indictmt pleaded not Guilty & for Tryal puts him Self upon the Cuntry wherefore the Sherrife is
venire   Commanded to Cauſe to Come i2 honeſt & Lawfull men &c:

Jury—Thomas Stackhouſe Senr Joſ. milner Stephen Beakes ⎫
   wm Paxson   John Croſdel   Edmund Lovet ——— ⎬ atteſted
   wm:Taylor   wm: Dark Henry Marjorum ——— ⎬
   John Penquoit   Henry Pointer   Jon: Swift ——— ⎭

Thomas ffox atteſted Saith that upon the 8th day of this Inſtant
   month the ſd Trevithan Came to the houſe of Joſ: Growdon
   & Said Joſ: Growdon had ſent him for Cloths for he & his
   wife had faln in the River meaning the ſd Joſ: Growdon &
   wife & that they wanted them & thereby obteined from
   the negro woman i Cloth Coate i paire pluſh breeches i —
   Cloake for a woman & further Saith not

219

John Hawkins atteſted Saith that upon monday laſt being the 8th
   Instant he Saw the Said Trevithan at the houſe of
   Joſ: Growdon & that He Saw the ſd Trevithan have
   upon his horſe i Cloth Coate i paire of pluſh breeches &
   one womans Cloak wch under pretence of Joſeph
   Growdons being wet in the River he had obtained from t
   the negro woman

action   policarpus Roſe ⎫
          agt   ⎬ with drawn by order of the plt
   John Pidcock   ⎭

Conſtables   ⎧ above the falls Joſuah Hoops
                | below to penſberry Joſ: Chorley
                | middle Lotts wm: Duncan
                ⎨ the upper pte of Neſhaminah John white
ffor | the upper pte of the other ſid of Neſhaminah Jon:
                | purſley
                | the lower pte on the other side Sam^{ll} Allen Junr
                ⎩ the lower pte of the River Tho: Green

Jury returned do Say the find Joſeph Trevithan as he is
   Charged in the prſentment

prſentmt agt Tho: king for de fameing Joan the wife of
   ffrancis Searl found to be a true bill to wch ſd king
pleaded not guilty & for Tryal put him Self upon the Cuntry

venire where the Sherrife is Commanded to Caufe to Com &c. i2 honeſt
& lawfull men &c

Jury before mentioned Attefted

Hugh Marſh Attefted doth Say that in or about the 3 month laſt paſt Says he heard Thomas king Say there was a witch neare by being askt who it was Said he Suſpected Francis Searls wife for She was an ugly ile favored woman & he did beleive her to be one

Robt marſh attefted Says he heard Tho: king Say that there was a witch hard by

action John Wood   ⎫
        agt   ⎬ plea of debt plt appeared
       John Buttler   ⎭   deft appeared not

declaracon Read

Rich Richway attefted doth Say that he knows that John wood did deliver a Confiderable Quantity of Wheate & that he beleives

220

ſd Buttler owed John wood at his going away above 20 £ : to the beſt
of his knowledge 2i or 22 £ as he heard John Butler Say & further
Saith John Buttler promifed Cattle for the Said Corn

Joſeph wood attefted proved every article of the acctt

Judgmt Given by default & it is adjudged that John Buttler Shall pay to John wood the Sum of five pounds ii^s with three pounds damages & Coſts of Suite & that Execution Iſſue accordingly

Jury Returned finds Thomas king Guilty of defameing Joan the wife of ffrancis Searl in Saying he beleived She was a witch

Gilbert wheeler in open Court promifed to pay the fees of pollicarpus Rose action

action Gilbert wheeler plt ⎫
           agt   ⎬ plea of Cafe both appeared
         John Pidcock   ⎭

declaracon Read

Anſwer he defds & Saith he owes nothing & for Tryal puts him Self upon the Cuntry & plt Likewiſe wherefore the — venire Sherriſe is Commanded to Cauſe to Come &c: 12 honeſt & lawfull men &c

Jury before mentioned atteſted

acct brought & in & atteſted to by the plt & plea of debt proved by Jos: Hollinshead atteſtation

jurys
verdict we find for the plt with Coſt of ſuite

adjudged that John Pidcock Shall pay to Gilbert wheeler 2 £ : 14ˢ : 00ᵈ with Costs of Suite & that Execution Iſſue accordingly

a deed in fee of 296 acres of land dated the 12ᵗʰ day of the firſt month 1689 was acknowledged and delivered by Henry —
90
marjerum grantor to John Clark Grantee

Judgmt Given & it is adjudged that Thomas king Shall pay Coſts of ſuite & be bound to keep the peace & to appeare at the next Court of Quarter Seſſions

Recognizance Thomas king acknowledges him Self Indebted to the propryetor & govrnr in the Sum of Ten pounds to be levied on his lands & Tenements Goods & Chattles &

that upon Condition that he Shall appeare at the next Court of Quarter Seſſions & to keepe the king & Queens peace in the meane time

adjourned to 8 a Clock in the morning

none appearing agt Wm Evans the Court diſcharges him paying his fees & Costs

221

Judgmt given and it is adjudged that Joſeph Trevithan upon his Indictment Shall make double Satiſfaction which is he Shall Pay to Joseph Growdon Ten pounds and that Joseph Growdon Shall pay the Coſts and fees the Goalers fees excepted and whereas the Said Trevithan hath not eſtate to anſwer the ſd Judgmt it is adjudged that the ſd Trevithan for the Same Shall Serve the Said Joſeph Growdon one yeare and a Quarter except he doth Serve very well & faithfully

one yeare then to be free at the yeares End to wich
Judgment both Joſeph Growdon & the ſd Trevithan declared
theire Satiſfaction

John Pidcock being Called appeared and declared Pollicarpus Roſe
had made him Satiſfaction

Policarpus Roſe appeared & nothing appearing agt him the
Court discharges him paying his fees

over ſeeres of the High ways

    above the falls Ruben Pownal
    below to the Govrnrs Joſeph Chorley
    the Lower part of the River Richard Wilſon
    the Lower part of Neſhaminah Derick Clawſon
    the upper part of Neſhaminah wm Hayhurſt
    the middle lotts ——— ——— John Webſter
    the Lower part beyond Neſhaminah walter fforrest
    and Sa. Allen
    for the upper part of the Same Tho: Harding

Adjourned to the 7th of the 8th month next

Executions agt the Goods and Chattles of Joſeph Holden Jon
Duplovies Caſe in Philip Richards Caſe in Cornelius Empsons Caſe
were granted the 19th day of the 7th mo: 1690

no Court then Held no buſines prſenting & Returned by the Sherrif
          the 29th of the 7th mo 1690

action peter Jenings plt ⎫
     agt   ⎬ plea of Case no goods or Chattles to
   Tho. Fox deft ⎭   be found wm yardley

Sumonce dated the 12th day 7 mo 1690 granted by Jon Brock
return that the ſum was executed the 20th day 7/mo 1690 by
          wm: yardley Sherrife

action John Teft plt ⎫
     agt   ⎬ in a plea of Caſe
   Thomas ffox deft ⎭

  Sumonce granted 20th day 7/mo 1690 p wm Biles
  return

action Joseph ffarrington plt
    agt   } in a plea of debt
 John Thatham deft

Sumonce Granted 27th day $\frac{7}{mo}$ 1690 p wm Biles

return Sumonced the 29th $\frac{9}{mo}$ 90 p wm yardley Sherrife

                222

action Thomas Tunneclif plt
    agt   } in a plea of Case
 John Lee deft

summonce Granted 27th $\frac{9}{mo}$ 1690 p wm Biles

return executed the 20th day of $\frac{9}{mo}$ 1690 p wm yardley Sherrife

Execution granted agt: the Goods & Chattles of John Pidcock the 29th $\frac{7}{mo}$ 1690 by Jos: Growdon to Satisfye a Judgmt obteined by Gilbert wheeler the 10th day of the 7th mo aforesd

execution granted agt the Goods & Chattles of John Buttler the 14th day of the 9th month 1690 by John Brock to Satisfye a Judgmt obteined by John wood agt sd Butler the 10th day of the 7th month last past

Bucks ss:

  At a Court of Quarter Sessions held by the king & Queens authority in the name of Willm Penn Propryetor & Govrnr of the afforesd Province & Counties annexed at the Court house for the sd County the 10th day of the 10th month being the 2nd yeare of the king & Queens Reign & 10th yeare of the propryetorys govrmt 1690

    The Justices Present

    Tho: Janney willm Biles
    Nicholas waln Henry Baker
    John Brock
    John Cook Corronor
    wm yardley Sherrif
    Phinehas Pemberton Cl: Com:

Grand Jury atteſted

Jonathan Scaiſe   John Hough   James Paxson
John Smith   Henry Pawlin   Stephen Newell
John Towne   Tho: Stakehouſe ſenr   Tho: Stakehouſe Jnr
wm Hearſt   Ezra Croſdel   John Croſdel
Henry Hudleſtone   Shadrach walley   Jos: Milner
Henry Marjerum   Richard Lundy

action   Peter Jenings
       agt } Cald but neither appeared
    Tho: ffox

223

action   John Teft
       agt: } both Called but neither partie appeared
    Tho ffox

action   Jos: ffarrington
       agt } J: ffarringto appeard
    John Tatham   Jon Tatham appeared not

Requeſt being made by John Tatham to reſpite the action makeing it appear that he was Sick & Indiſ-poſed & not able to make his appearance Edward Hunlock & Rich Baſnet engaged for his appearance at the next Court to anſwer the action without further Summonce or proceſs

accidental death of John Stotton returned & read

adjourned the Court for one houre

action   Tho: Tunneclif
       agt } both appeared
    John Lee   action with drawn

Tho: Tunneclif agreed to pay half the Charge

Grand Jurys prſentmt agt Iſrael Taylor

Penſylvania

County Court Bucks ſs:

The Jurrors for the body of this County do prſent Iſrael

Taylor for takeing Stealing killing & Converting to
his owne ufe about the beginning of 9th month in
the yeare 1689 one heifer of Colour red the end of
her taile white haveing a Crop on the further eare
being about one yeare and a half old & worth about
forty Shillings being the proper goods of John Naylor
Conterary to the king & Queens peace & the ftatute
Law in that Cafe made & provided
John naylor profecutor

    Richard Thatcher } witneffes attefted
    Bartholemew Thatcher

we the jurrors do find this bill
to wch Said Taylor pleaded not Guilty & for Tryal put
pleading him Self upon the Cuntry wherefore the Sherrif is
venire   Commanded to Caufe to Come before the Court 12
    honeft & Lawfull men &c:

224

Jury   Jofuah Hoops Stephen Beakes Sam: Dark
      John wood wm: Ellet — Henry Paxson
      wm Dark Jacob Hall — wm: Beakes } attefted
      wm Paxson Samuel Beakes Andrew Ellet

  Rich Thatcher attefted doth Say that being at work at Ifrael
    Taylors in the fall Laft was 12 months he Saw Ifrael
    Taylor give the heifer of Jon naylor bread Several
    times & he the Said Taylor Sd: to the fd Thatcher Come
    let us kill this heifer: but at that time he left the fd
    Taylors houfe for want of provifions & in a few days after
    Ifrael asked the fd Thatcher to Come againe for he had
    Provifions enough & he Came there & Saw in the Celler
    of fd Taylor in a brl Several peices of Smal meate
    & he Saw then the hinder part of A hide of Colour red &
    the end of the taile white & he Saw the fd Taylor bury the
    fd piece of a hide & that about 10 or 12 weekes ago the
    fd Thatcher underftanding that he was under Suspition
    of being Guilty of affifting in the killing of the fd heifer
    he the fd Thatcher went to the fd Taylors houfe and afked
    the fd Taylors wife what heifer it was that was killed
    and who killed it & She Said Benjemame Jones & Israel
    kill'd her & that Shee beleived it was naylors heifer

Bartholomew Thatcher attested doth Say Last fall was Twelve
months he Stayd at Israel Taylors al night & he Saw
Israel Taylo's wife drefs Some meate wch he Thought
was young heifer beefe & before that time the heifer of
John Naylor was wanting

The will of Rich Thatcher being delivered into Court it was
ordered that Phinehas Pemberton Should keep it till
further ordr

adjourned the Court for one houre

verdict Jury Returned do Say Israel Taylor is not guilty
of the fellony whereof he ftands Indicted

a deed in fee of 200 acres of land dated the 3 day of the 9th
month 1690 acknowledged & delivered by Jofuah Hoops
attorney to Jofeph Englifh Grantor to Samuel Dark
grantee

Grand Jury prfents the want of Standard for Juft weights &
meafures
& the want of the County to be devided in to Town fhips &c

The Executions before mentioned both returned Satiffyed

225

Wm: Biles acknowledged in open Court that he had Received
full Satisfaction from Derrick Jonfon for one bl
mare with a long Taile & dule back with Some —
white haires in her forehead & a half peny Cut on the
further eare, wch Said mare the fd Derrick is allowed
to take up when he Can find her & her Increase that
Shall Lawfully appeare to be long to her & that he the
fd wm: Biles will warrant the fd mare & her Said
Increafe to the fd Jonfon & defend from all perfons

Reported to this Court by John Brock that Richard Thatcher
did Confefs he owed to Derrick Jonfon the fum of
one pound eight Shillings & that it was to be pd in good
wheate & that it was adjudged by the fd Jon
Brock that the fd Sum Shold be accordingly pd
with Cofts wch fd Judgmt is approved of by this
Court & thereupon ordered that execution Iffue accordingly

Judgmt Given & its adjudged that John Naylor Shall pay Cofts
of Suite & that execution Iffue accordingly

Israel Taylor promifed to pay the fees in both actions —
wherein Revel was Concerned agt: him to the officers

adjourned the Court to the 20th day of this month to the
houfe of Thomas Janney

8th $\frac{io}{mo}$ 1690

Execut agt: Thater for fees 3£ 9ˢ: 4ᵈ returned i3 $\frac{io}{mo}$ 90

i2 $\frac{io}{mo}$ i690 execu agt fd Thatcher & Taylor for 14£ 14ˢ: 6ᵈ returnd —

i6th $\frac{io}{mo}$ 1690

i2 $\frac{io}{mo}$ 1690 execu agt fd Thather for 1 £ i6ˢ returnd

At A Court held by adjournmnt the 20th day of
the ioth month i690 at the houfe of Tho: Janney

Tho Janney: wm: Biles
Nicholas Waln Jon: Brock
wm yardley Sherrife
Phinehas Pemberton Cl: Com:

Richard Thatcher being bound in 20 £ to appear at this
Court none appeareing agt him the Court difcharges him

action John Brock plt
   agt   } act of debt plt appeared
 Gilbert wheeler deft } the deft appeared not ——

decl read

bill read

wm Biles appeared on fd Wheelers acctt & Said that
Gilbert Wheeler was before him this day & Confeft the
bill mentioned in the declaration

226

John Brock Confeft he had Red in pte of the fd bill 1 £ : 10ˢ 9ᵈ

Judgmt Given & it is adjudged that Gilbert wheeler Shall pay
to John Brock 4 £ : 5ˢ: Dt & 5ˢ damages with Cofts of fuite
& that execution Iffue accordingly

whereas the Sherrif hath mad return of the executions out agt the goods & Chattles of Jos: Holden for the Several Sums obtained by John Duplovie Philip Richards & Cornelius Empſon that there is no Goods or Chattles to Satiſfye the debts & that the perſons have requeſted to have execution agt the ſd Holdens Land it is ordered by this Court that execution Iſſue agt: the lands of the ſd Holden to Satiſfye the Several Judgmts: obteined by the affore ſd perſons

whereas the Grand Jury did prſent the neceſſity of haveing the County devided into Town Ships it is ordered that Henry Baker Thomas Janney wm: Biles Phinehas Pemberton Arthur Cook Edmund Bennet James Boyden Nicholas waln Joſuah Hoops John Rowland Jos: Growdon Sam[ll] Allen & that they meete together the day before the next Court at the Court house & then & there devide this County into Town ſhips that the Same may be prſent to the next Court to have the approbation thereof

whereas the Grand Jury prſented the neceſſity of haveing weight & meaſures Equall according to law its referred to be further Conſidered of

adjourned to the ii[th] day of the firſt month next
the 3 executions aforesaid granted agt Holdens Land dat the 20th day ii 1690 / mo

Bucks ſs: County Court the ii[th] 1 1690 / mo 1

Action Entered the 20th 9 1690 / mo

Joſeph ffarrington plt
    agt:
John Tatham deft
} plea of Debt for tryal at the 10th / mo Court but the tryal was reſpited

untill this Court becauſe of the deft then Sickneſ
action Entered the i 12 1690 / mo

1690

John Smith plt } 15th day ii/mo an arrest granted at the fuite
agt of wm Biles agt John Pidcock
Thomas Peirce deft 15th ii/mo 1690 attachmt granted at the
fuite of wm Biles agt the goods of
John Pidcock

action Entered 16th i2/mo 1690   Thefe withdrawn againe by wm Biles

Zacharia Whitpaine plt
agt } plea of debt
Gilbert wheeler deft

227

Sum Granted 16th i2/mo 1690

return executed the 16th 12/mo 1690 p wm yardley Sherrife
with drawn

action Entered the 23 i2/mo 1690

Thomas Revel plt agt Israel Taylor deft plea of Cafe

Summonce granted 23 i2/mo 1690

return 27 i2/mo 90 p wm yardley

Sum for wittneffes dated 24th i2/mo 1690
return

action Entered 24th i2/mo 1690

Andrew Heath plt
agt } in a plea of Trefpafs
wm Beakes deft

Sum granted 24th 12/mo 90

return 25th 12/mo 90 p wm yardley

Sum for witneſſes dated 4th i/mo 1690 return 10th i/mo 90

action Entered 25th 12/mo 90

wm yardley plt
   agt
Hugh Marſh deft } & Robt Marſh } in an action of debt

Sum granted 20th 12/mo 1690 return 27th 12/mo 90 p w: yardley

action Entered 25th 12/mo 1690

Thomas Janney by his attorney Jon: neild plt
   agt
Jon Lee & Joſeph Milner defts in a plea of debt }

Sum granted the 25th 12/mo i690 return 25 i2th/mo 90

with drawn by ordr of Tho: Janney

action Entered 25th 12/mo i690

Tho: peirce plt
   agt
Jon pidcock deft } in a plea of Caſe

attachmt. granted 22 ii/mo 90 .

return buck ſkin 3 doe ſkins 2 Guns 30lb of red Lead

Penſylvania 228

Bucks ſs: At a Court of Quarter Seſſions held by the king & Queen

authority in the name of wm Penn propryetory & govrnr
of the Said Province & Counties annexed at the Court
houſe for the ſd County the iith day of the $\frac{i}{mo}$ 1690 being
the iith yeare of the propryetorys Govrmt

    The Justices then prſent

      Arthur Cooke Joſeph Growdon
      Nicholas waln & Henry Baker
      wm yardley Sherriſe
      Phinehas Pemberton Cl. Com:

action Joſ: ffarrington plt ⎫
    agt   ⎬ both appeared & deſired
John Tatham deft   ⎭ one houres time beſore
  the matter be brought to tryal allowed by
  the Court

action Thomas Revel agt Israel Taylor neither appeared

action Andrew Heath ⎫
  agt   ⎬ both appeared decl read
 wm Beakes ————⎭

deft defends the force for tryal puts him Self upon the

Anſwer
  Cuntry & ſo doth the plt wherefore the Sherriſe is Commanded
venire to Cauſe to Come i2 honeſt & Lawfull men &c

  Jury—John Swift Henry Pointer wm: Dark   ⎫
    Joſuah Hoops Tho: ſtackhouſe ſen^r Henry Paxſon ⎬ atteſted
    wm Paxſon James Paxſon John Rowland ⎪
    Edmund Lovet wm Taylor Joſ kirkbride ⎭

action wm yardley agt Hugh & Robt marſh plt appeared the
 defts appeared not wherefore the Court ſuſpends the action untill
 to morrow

action Andrew Heath agt: wm Beakes

decl proved by the Evidence of James Sutton Joseph } attested
Henbry Tho: kirle george Cockrum Joseph
Stewards Tho Tunneclif Ann Ellot Sarah Biles
Jon Wood Andrew Ellot all of them ⎬ attested

adjourned for one houre

adjourned untill tomorrow morning at 9 a Clock

verdict Jury finds for the plt Andrew Heats 3 £ damages & Costs of Suite

229

action Jos: ffarrington agt John Tatham both appeared
declarat read Answer read for Tryal put them
Selves upon the Cuntry
wherefore the Sherrife is Commanded to Cause to Come
12 honest & Lawfull men &c

The Jury afforesd attested

decla: read

Answer read

obligation read & Confest by the deft

award read & Confest by the deft

Jury do say they find for the plt_____

John Tatham Craved an appeale

adjourned the Court for one houre

A deed of Mortgage of 400 acres of land by John Pidcock grantor to Edward Hunlock Grantee dated the 10th of the 12th mo: 1690 with a Schedule thereunto annexed was tendered in open Court by sd Hunlock to Said Pidcock to be acknowledged according to law in open Court wch Said Pidcock refused to do without Shewing any Cause for his so refuseing

action John Smith agt Tho: Peirce both parties appeared & refferred the Case to the bench

action Tho: Peirce agt John Pidcock both appeared

declaracon read

Anſwer he ows nothing & for tryal puts him Self upon the Cuntry & ſo doth the plt wherefore the Sherriſe is Commanded to Cauſe to Come 12 honest & Lawful men &c

Jury atteſted

declaration proved by the atteſtations of Tho: peirce gilbert wheeler Policarpus Roſe

Jury finds for the plt 20ˢ with Coſts of ſuite

adjourned the Court to 9 to morrow morning

wm yardley agt Hugh & Robt marſh both appeared

declaracon read bill obligate read

Answer the defts ownes the bill to be theire acts & deeds

Thomas Peirce produced a diſcharge under Jon Smiths hand in full & the Said Peirce promiſed in open Court to pay & discharge all Coſts & fees

230

adjudged by the Court that the action agt ſd Peirce be with drawn

Judgmt given in Heaths Caſe agt Beakes according to verdict and that execution Issue accordingly

Judgment given & it is adjudged that John Tatham pay to Joſeph ffarrington 50 £ & Coſts of Suite

Difference

after Judgmt Given both parties Refferred to the Juſtices on the bence what Shall be adjudged in Equity to be abated on the penalty

Judgmt given & it is adjudged that John Pidcock Shall pay to Tho Peirce 20ˢ & Coſts of Suite & that execution Iſſue accordingly

Tho: Revel agt Iſrael Taylor both Calld but neither appeared

adjourned for one houre

13 i 1690 whereas Joseph ffarrington & John Tatham ——
mo
refferred to the Justices on the bench what the Judg in ——
Equity the sd John Thatham Shall pay to the sd ffarrington
in full Satisfaction of the afforesaid Judgmt whereupon the
sd Justices do Judg award & determine that the sd Jon
Tatham Shall pay to the Said ffarrington Twenty eight
Pounds in Silver mony or in good merchantable wheate
at Silver mony Price in one months time after the day
of the date hereof & further that the sd John Tatham
Shall pay to the Respective officers the ffees due to them by
reason of the afforesaid Judgment & upon payment of the
Said mony that the Said Parties Shall Seale each other General
releases & y^t if the Said John Tatham Shall faile payment of the
Said mony as above expressed that then execution Issue ——
according to the Judgment first obteined & further it is expressed
that the sd John Tatham Shall make payment to the sd Joseph
ffarrington or his attorney at the ffurry house over agt Bur
-lington

george Browne being Calld upon his Recognizance being
bound for assaulting & abuseing wm Biles one of the Justices
of peace for this County upon his examination Confest that
he pushed him twice with his hand whereupon the Court gave
Judgmt & it is adjudged that the sd george Brown Shall give
bond for his appearance at next Court & to be of good ——

231

abearing in the meane time & Shall pay a fine of 20^s
to be disposed of as the Justices hereafter Shall think
fit

George Brown acknowledges him Self Indebted to the
Propryetor & Govrnr in 10 £ to be levyed on his lands &
tenements goods & Chattles & this upon Condition for
his appearance at the next Court & to be of good ——
abearing in the meane time

adjourned untill tomorrow morning at 9 a Clock

whereas the persons appointed to devide the County have
not done it is ordered that the sd persons meete to
gether on the 20th day of the 2nd month next to devide
it into town ships

adjourned the Court unto the 20th day of the 2^d month next

23 i/mo execut agt Rich Thather in Ifrael Taylors Cafe dated &
1690/i returnd

no bufines prfenting there was no Court held in the 2nd month

County Court Bucks fS:

action Entered the 20th i/mo 169i/2

Daniel Cox by his attorney John Tatham ⎫
     agt plea of debt ⎬
Gilbert wheeler ⎭

Summonce dated 26th 3/mo 169i return — 29th 3/mo 169i

action entered 2i i/mo 169i

Gilbert wheeler plt ⎫
   agt   ⎬ in a plea of Slander
John Tatham deft ⎭

Summonce dated the 26th 3/mo 9i

arreft granted the 14th 3/mo i69i agt Henry Boucher at the fuite of Jofeph knight

Returnd the 29th 3/mo i69i not to be found p wm yardley Sherrife

action Entered the 23 3/mo i69i ⎫ Arreft dated 25 3/mo 9i
Jofeph England plt   ⎬ Returnd 5th 4/mo 169i taken
   agt   ⎭
Lawrence Parker deft into Custody by Wm Yardley Sherrife

the above action with drawn by Philip England i0th 4/mo 9i

action Entered the 25th 3/mo 169i

Thomas Hudſon by his attorney Jon white plt
agt } Summons dated the 26th 3/mo 1691
Jacob Hall deft return dated the 29 3/mo 169i
withdrawn by ordr of wm Biles

232

action Entered the 25th 3/mo i69i

Joſeph Chorley plt ⎫
    agt ⎬ in a plea of Case ⎰
marjery Claws deft ⎭ Summonce dated 26th 3/mo i69i ⎱ withdrawn by order of Joseph Chorley

action Entered the 25 3/mo i69i

John Tatham plt ⎫   ⎧ Summonce dated the 26 3/mo 169i
    agt ⎬ plea of Caſe ⎨
Joseph Growdon deft ⎭   ⎩ Return dated the 30th 3/mo 169i

action Entered the 25th 3/mo i69i

Thomas Revel plt ⎫   ⎧ Sum: Dated 25th 3/mo 169i
    agt ⎬ action of debt ⎨
ffrancis Roſſill deft ⎭   ⎩ Return dated 30th 3/mo i69i

action Entered 25th 3/mo 169i

John otter plt ⎫   ⎧ Summonc dated 25th 3/mo 169i
    agt ⎬ action of debt ⎨
ffrancis Roſſill deft ⎭   ⎩ return dated 30th 3/mo 169i

action Entered 26th 3/mo 1691

Thomas Brock plt
agt:
ffrancis Roffill deft
} in a plea of Cafe {
Summonc dated 25th 3/mo 1691
Return dated 30th 3/mo 1691

arreſt granted the 25th 12/mo 1690 agt Ralph Sidwell at Tho Brocks Suite

returnd the 29th 3/mo 1691 not to be found p wm yardley Sherrife

County Court Bucks ſs: Penſylvania

at a Court of Quarter Seſſions held by the authority of wm: & mary king & Queen of England &c: & in the name of wm Penn Propryetor & Govrnr of the Said Province & Countys annexed the 10th day of the 4th month 1691

The Justices then Prſent
Arthur Cook   Joseph Growdon   wm Biles
Nicholas waln   Henry Baker   John Brock
John Cooke Corronor
wm yardley Sherrife
Phinehas Pemberton Cl: Com:

George Brown Continued on Recognizance untill next Court

233

Judgment Given by wm Biles one of the Juſtices of Peace for this County between Iſrael Taylor plt & Richard deft: whereupon it was adjudged that Richard Thatcher Shold pay Israel Taylor 3s 9d & thirty apple trees or for want of the apple trees the Said Thatcher to pay Ten Shillings Inſtead thereof wch Judgment by this Court is allowed & its adjudged that execution Iſſue accordingly

action John otter agt: ffrancis Roffill both appeared

declaracon read

bond read

Anſwer deft owned the bond

plt declared that he deſired nothing but Ten pounds with the Intreſt Since it was due

A proclamation agt vice from the Govrnr read

action Tho: Revel agt ffrancis Roſſill both appeared

declarcon read

bill read

Anſwer the deft owned the debt but not the damages

reply the plt declared that the debt without damages wold Satiſfye him

action Tho: Brock agt ffrancis Roſſill both appeared

declaracon read

Ansſer the deft owned the debt but not the damages

reply the plt declared that the debt without damages wold Satiſfye him

Judgmt given and it is adjudged that ffrancis Roſſill pay to John otter Ten Pounds with Intreſt Since it was due & Coſts of Suite & that execution Iſſue accordingly

Judgmt Given & it is adjudged that ffrancis Roſſill pay to Thomas Revel Seven pounds one Shilling three pence & Coſt of Suite & that execution Iſſue accordingly

Judgment Given & it is adjudged that ffrancis Roſſill pay to Thomas Brock Ten pounds nineteen Shillings & five —— pence with Coſts of ſuite & that execution Iſſue accordingly

action Daniel Cox agt Gilbert wheeler deft appeared the plt by his attorneys Ed: Hunlock george Hutchinſon

declaration read   & Tho: Revel ——

Anſwer the deft & defends & Says he owes nothing upon the bond & for tryal puts him Self on the Cuntry & so doth the plt wherefore the Sherrif is Commanded to Caufe to Come i2 honeft & lawfull men &c

Jury John Swift Henry Pointer Jonathan Scaife ⎫
   Jofuah Hoops
   Stephen Beakes wm Beakes Tho: ⎬ attested
   Stakehoufe Andrew Ellot
   Sam^{ll} Dark wm: Dark wm: Paxfon James
   Paxfon ⎭

Bond read & owned by the deft

234

george Hutchinfon James Hill & Bernard Devonifh attefted Prove bond to be fealed while the fd Deft in Dures

action John Tatham agt Jofeph Growdon plt appeared

John Tatham appeared by his attorney Edward Hunlock

george Hutchinfon & Tho: Revell aforefaid who Say they are not Informed any thing Concerning the fd action & therefore defired a Continuation thereof untill the next Court

deft Craved a non fuite with Cofts

wherefore it is adjudged that John Tatham not appearing nor Informing his attorneys Concerning the fd action he Shall be non fuited & pay the Cofts

Jury returnd in the Cafe Cox agt wheeler finds for the deft with Cofts of Suite

Judgmt Given & it is adjudged that Daniel Cox pay Cofts of Suite

action Gilbert wheeler agt John Tatham plt appeared & deft by his attorney aforefaid & both plt & deft defired the fd action to be Continued untill next Court

adjourned for one houre

adjourned to the i6th 7 next
               mo

County Court Bucks fs: Penfylvania

action Entered for Tryal Last Court but Suſpended by
Conſent
untill this

Gilbert wheeler plt ⎫
            agt: ⎬ in action of ⎰ withdrawn
John Tatham deft ⎭   Slander ⎱ by the plts ordr

action Entered the 29th $\frac{6}{mo}$ 169i

Stephen Beakes agt George Brown in an action of Caſe

Summonce granted 29th $\frac{6}{mo}$ 169i return dated 4th
day $\frac{7}{mo}$ 9i

action Entered the 29 day $\frac{6^{th}}{mo}$ i69i ⎫
                                   ⎬ in an action oſ
Stephen Beakes agt Joſeph Steward ⎭ Caſe

Summonce dated 1^{ſt} of the 7th mo 169i return dated 3
                                                   day $\frac{7}{mo}$ 169

action Entered the 31: $\frac{6}{mo}$ 169i

John Tatham plt agt Gilbert wheeler deft in an action
on y^e Caſe

Summonce dated i $\frac{7}{mo}$ i69i return dated 4: day $\frac{7}{mo}$ 169

235

action Entered the 3i $\frac{6}{mo}$ i69i

John Tatham plt agt Joſeph Growdon deft action of the Caſe
Summonce dated the i $\frac{7}{mo}$ 169i return dated 3 $\frac{7}{mo}$ 169i

action Entered the 3i $\frac{6}{mo}$ 169i

Jame Bleake by his attorney Chriftopher Snoden plt ⎫
                        agt   ⎬
John Clawson in a plea of Cafe ——————— ⎭

Summonce dated the i 7   9i return dated the 3 day 7   9i
                     ———   ———
                      mo   mo

Bucks fs: Penfylvania
            At a Court of Quarter Seffions held by the
            king & Queens authority in the name of
            wm Penn Propryetor & Govrnr of the
            afforesaid Province & Counties annexed
            at the Court houfe for the afforefd County
            the 16th day of the 7th month being the 3
            yeare of the king & Queens reigne &
            iith yeare of the propryetorys Govrmt i69i
                The Justices prfent
                        Arthur Cook   Joseph Growdon
                        Thomas Janney   Henry Baker
                        Wm yardley Sherrif
                        Phinehas Pemberton Cl: Com:

a deed of a peice of meadow land about five acres in fee
dated the 14th day of the 7th month i69i was delivered
and acknowledged by James Moone Senior & James Moon
Junr: grantors to Samuel Dark grantee

Grand Jury
            Henry Margerum   Tho: Stakehoufe   wm Buckman
         Thomas Rogers   Shadrach walley   James Paxfon   wm Paxfon
         Andrew Heath   Jos: kirkbride   Hugh Marfh   Andrew Ellot
         Abraham Cox   John white   Samll Burges all attefted

action Gilbert wheeler agt John Tatham both appeared &
   defired the action to be Suspended for one houre wch was
   allowed by the Court

                                236

action Stephen Beakes agt Jofeph Steward plt appeared but
   the deft appeared not but it was alleadged by Richard Hough

that the occation of his abſence was by reaſon of a
refference of the Caſe had been diſcourſed between the
Parties wherefore by Conſent it is refferred untill another
Court

Stephen Beakes aſſigne to Jon Jonſon agt George Brown both
appeared the declaration read

Anſwer read alleading the plt had no power by law to bring the
Said action & therefore Craved anon Suite wch was
granted by the Court

Judgmt given & it is adjudged that Stephen Beakes Shall
Suffer anon Suite & pay Coſts of Court

george Brown acknowledged what there was owing to Jonſon aforeſd
being 26 buſhells of wheate with Intreſt & promiſed to pay the
Same to Stephen Beakes before the next Court of Quarter
Seſſions

adjourned for one houre

grand Jurys prſentments

we prsent wm: Beakes for Stoping the paſſage by the river ſide
that doth damnifye the neighbours

we allſo prſent the high way from the falls to South hampton to
be Cleared & the bridge by James Paxſons allſo the bridge tha
Comes from wm: Bians to be repaired

we prſent Abraham wharley for keeping unlawfull ——
Swine that hath damnifyed the Inhabitans of new Town

we allſo prſent the neceſſity of way from new Town to the
mill & Burlington fferry

      Henry Margerum fforeman

over ſeers of the high ways

for above the falls	————————	Ruben Powna
from { thence to the govrnrs	————————	Edward Lucas
thence below to neſhaminah	————	Richard Wilſon
for { the Lower pte of neſhaminah		James Paxson
the middle Lotts	————————	James moone
the other ſide of neſhaminah	Jon: Gilbert & Sam: Allen Jur
South hampton	————————	Tho: Hardi

Tho: Brock attefted Saith that Chriftopher Snoden defired the action agt John Clawfon to be Stayed this Court

237

Apprizers appointed untill further order

Sam^{ll} Dark Jofeph kirkbride & John Rowland

george Brown being bound to appeare at Laft Court was Continued & therfore defired this Court to difcharge who was accordingly difcharged from his recognizance

action Gilbert wheeler agt John Tatham with drawn by ordr of fd plt

action Daniel Cox by his Attorney John Tatham with — drawn by ordr of fd Tatham

Conftables for this County are ftill Continued untill further order

action John Tatham agt Jos: Growdon both appeard & Jofeph Growdon made Claime of the benefit of the law for magiftrates & Councillmen becaufe the time was but Short & therefore was not prepared for tryal & therefore time was allowed untill next Court

adjourned untill 8 a Clock tomorrow morning

whereas the grand Jury prfented at a Court held the i2th day of the firft month 1689 the neceffity of haveing a Tax raifed to pay the Councill & affembly men for theire attendance already paft & other publique Charge of the County it was accordingly ordered by a Court held the 26 1/mo 90 that a Tax of 300 £ be raifed according to Law on the lands & males of this County for the ufes aforefd & that returns be perfected according to former order of lands & males & now ordered that duplicites be made thereof to every Collector for
raifeing the fd mony

george Philips being taken up for a run away by Tho: Brock & brought before this Court being Searched was found in his Pocket one purs in wch was foure pounds 9^d Silver

mony & one bras 9^d bit who upon his examination ―――
Confeſt that he had taken the ſaid mony in the night time
out of the Cloſet of Denis Linſtone with whom he had
lived about 3 months as alſo one paire of gloves wch ſd
gloves he the ſd Philips Confeſt the tooke out of the ſd Cloſet

Judgmt Given & it is adjudged that the ſd George Philips Shall
make Satiſfaction to the parties greived as the Law requires
by Servitude that he the ſd George Philips have 15 ſtripes
on his bare back well layd on now in Sight of the Court
& that he be Confined in the Sherrifs Cuſtody (untill his ―
maſter have notice hereof) & that he be not delivered

238

to his Said maſter without ordr from Joſeph Growdon to whom
this Court referrs the ſd Denis Linstone to treat about the ſaid
George Philips freedom or Servitude being obteined as is ſd
Conterary to law

ordered that the ſd mony be kept by the Clerk as alſo the Gloves
& that after all Charges fees & Coſts are deducted that the
remaineing part be delivered to the owner thereof

adjourned to the 9th : 10th month next

action Suſpended Laſt Court untill this Court } with drawn by the
John Tatham agt Jos: Growdon plea of Caſe } plts ordr ―――

action Entered 23 9 169i
　　　　　　　　　mo

Joſeph Growdon agt John Grey alls Tatham　} with drawn by
　in a plea for Treſpaſs done ――― ―――　} the plts ordr
Summonce Granted 23　9　i69i ―――――
　　　　　　　　　　　mo

action Entered 23　9　169i
　　　　　　　　mo

Joſeph Growdon agt John White in a plea of Treſpaſs } with draw
　　　　　　　　　　　　　　　　　　　　　　　　　　　by the pl
Summonce Granted 23　9　i69i　―――――――　} order
　　　　　　　　　　　mo

action Entered 23 9/mo 169i

Joſeph Growdon agt Edward Cartor in a plea of Treſpaſs } withdrawn by the plts ordr
Summonce Granted 23 9/mo 169i

action Entered 23 9/mo 169i

Joſeph Growdon agt: Henry Hudleſton in a plea of Treſpaſs } with drawn by the plts ordr
Summonce granted the 23 9/mo i69i

action Entered 23 9/mo 169i

Joſeph Growdon agt Tho: Stakehouſe Ju^nr in a plea of Treſpaſs } withdrawn by the plt ordr
Summonce granted the 23 9/mo i69i

County Court Bucks ſs: Penſylvania

  At a Court of Quarter Seſſions held by the authority of wm & mary king & Queen of England &c & in the name of wm: Penn Propryetor & govrnr of the province of Penſylvania & Counties annexed at the Court houſe for the afforeſd County the 9th day of the i0th month being the 3 yeare of the king & Queens Reigne & ii^th year of the Propryetors Govrmt i69i

  The Juſtices Preſent

Thomas Janney wm Biles Henry Baker Jon Brock
wm yardley vice Com:
Phinehas Pemberton Cl: Com:

239

The mony found upon George Philips wch was delivered to Phinehas Pemberton to be kept for the owner there

of untill the owner was known being Two pounds ten
Shillings nine pence & one bad 9ᵈ bit being what —
remamed of the whole Charges being deducted out of
the whole for takeing him up & other fees then Contracted
was delivered to Arthur Cook by the Said Phinehas
Pemberton which this Court doth allow of & difcharges
the fd Phinehas Pemberton of the faid Sum of 4 £ 9ᵈ &
one bras bitt the fees & Charges being 30ˢ & payd as
appeares in Court by fd Phinehas Pemberton
whereas there has none Com'n to Complaine agt geo:
Philips for any mifdemeanor Committed by him the
Court by Confent of the boy has put him to Henry Baker
for 6 months time to See in the meane time what
may be alledged agt him

  adjourned to the 9ᵗʰ $\frac{i}{mo}$ next

28 $\frac{ii}{mo}$ 169i Jofeph Holdens land taken in execution to Satifye the deb
  & Cofts

       of Jon: Duplovie Philip
              Richard
       & Cornelius Empfon

County Court Bucks fs: Penfylvania

Juftices prfent

Jos: Growdon
wm Biles
Nicholas waln
Henry Baker
wm yardley fherrif
P. Pemberton Cl Com

    at a Court of Quarter seffions held by the king
& Queen authority in the name of willm Penn
Penn Propryetor & Govrnr of the afforefd
Province & Counties annexed at the Court
house for the afforefd County the 9ᵗʰ day of the
firft month being the 3 yeare of the king and
Queens Reigne over England &c & i2ᵗʰ yeare
of the propryetors Govrmt i691

Atteftation of Samˡˡ overton attefted doth Say that he lent
2 Chaines to John Clows & that he never Re but one of

the said Chaines either from the Said Clows or any other
perfon directly or indirectly Since that time
Dunkin williams & his Son william william williams being
bound over to this Court upon Complt of Jofeph Growdon
& his baile defireing to be difcharged declareing they will
not Stand bound any longer & the fd Dunkin williams
Craveing untill another Court to prepare him felf for
tryal wch is allowed the Court Commits them into Cuftody
untill they Shall give Suffitiont fuerties for theire appearance
at next Court & to keep the peace in the meane time
John Bown & Ralph Boome Complt of george Philips
It appearing that Sd Philips by John Bown and fd Boome unto Denis
Linck who lives out of the Province its ordered that Jon: Bowen
Shall difcharge Ralph Boome & Reinburs what Denis Linck
has pd towards the price he was to give for him & that Ralph Boone
difcharge the Linck & that the fd Geo: Philips Shall ferve the fd
John Bowen two yeares from this day in Confideration of

240

the damage done to him by Sd Philips & that he the fd John Bowen
Shall pay to Henry Baker for what Cloths he hath bought for
him what they may be Judged to be reafonably worth & to this
the parties declared theire Satiffaction

adjourned to the 8th day 4th month next

2nd 3 month i692 the Land of Jofeph Holden taken in execution was
appraifed by

County Court Bucks fs: Penfylvania   i2 men at eighty pounds

   At a Court of Quarter Seffions held by the authority of
   wm & mary king & Queen of England &c and
   in the name of Willm Penn Propryetor and
   govrnr of the Said Province & Counties annexed
   at the Court houfe for the Said County the 8th day
   of the 4th month i692 being the 4th yeare of the
   king & Queens Reigne & i2 yeare of the propry
   etors Govrmt

     The Justices Present

      Jofeph Growdon   w^m Biles
      Nicholas waln   Henry Baker
      John Cook   Corronr
      Phinehas Pemberton Cl: Com.

a deed of 27 acres of Land in fee dated the 6th 2/mo i692
acknowledged & delivered by Phinehas Pemberton attorney
to Joſeph English Grantor to Thomas Brock Grantee

a deed of 500 acres of land in fee dated the 8th day of the
i0th month i69i was acknowledged and delivered in open
Court by John Rowland Grantor to Henry Baker Grantee

a deed of Two hundered acres of Land in fee dated the i0th day
of the 4th month i692 was acknowledged and delivered in
open Court by John Cook attorney to Samuel Allen Grantor
to John Baldwin Grantee

a deed of five hundered acres of land in fee dated the 16th day of
the 7th month i69i was acknowledged and delivered by
Joſeph Chorley attorney to Jacob Hall grantor to william Biles
attorney to Thomas Hudson grantee

a deed in fee for Two hundered acres of land dated the 8th day of
the 4th month i692 was acknowledged and delivered by —
Samuel Allen Grantor to Samuel Allen his Son grantee

7th 4/mo 1692   a deed in fee for 200 hundered acres of land was acknowledged and
delivered unto John Balwin by Samuel Allen grantor for the uſe
of his grand daughter Elizabeth Pegg dated the 7th day of the 4th
month i692

241

Complt being made agt Ralph Boome for Some extravagant
Speeches he Submitting to the Court it was ordered that
he Shold pay to the wittnes foure Shillings & other Coſts
of Court

Willm Dunken being bound to this Court to appeare to anſwer
the Complt of Joseph Growdon deſired the ſd Court to —
Suſpend the tryal untill another Court for that his
wittneſſes were not in readines wch was aſſented to by
Joſeph Growdon

a deed of one hundred and Twenty acres of land in fee
dated the 8th day of the 4th month i69i & of two rods
through the Land added in breadth to the lines mentioned

was acknowledged and delivered by Richard Ridgway grantor to Samuel Beakes grantee

Corronors Inquest Concerning the death of Ellizabeth Chappel taken before John Cook Corronor the 15th day of the 3 month 1692 was this day returned into this Court that her death was Cafual by falling of her horfe into the water or nefhaminah Creek

Corronors Inqueft Concerning the death of an unknown perfon found neare the mouth of nefhaminah Creek the 8th day of the 3 month 1692 taken before John Cooke Corronor the 12th day of the fd 3 month laft returned into this Court willfully murthered Suppofed to be ———— murthered about 6 weekes afore the fd veiue

upon a due examination of things it appeared that a Confiderable Quanty of blood on the wall and on the bed of one — Derrick Jonfon als Clawfon about the Suppofed time that the above murthered perfon loft his life was difcovered & the Said Derrick refufed to give any account how the Said blood Came there whereupon this Court Commits him the fd Derrick Clawfon als Jonfon into Safe Cuftody of the Sherrif untill he Shall be delivered by due Courfe of Law

Derrick Jonfon als Clawfon being examined Saith he ———— Shewed the blood on the wall to Edward Lane & his brother Claws Jonfon & to mary Boydon he also Saith there was no blood on the bed but what was bled by a man that Came to Thrafh for him 3 yeares ago & that he had Spoke of the blood fully as much as it was

Corronor John Cook Saith that when he went to veiue the blood he perceived that it had run in Several Streames down the boords on the wall wch Streames Continued untill they went behind the planks that lay on the ground floore

242

Brighta the wife of Said Derrick Saith that the blood Seen on the wall was difcovered between day and sun rifeing & that there was a Sheete hanged on the out Side of the bed in manner of a Curtaine & that there was no blood on the bed being asked when the put frefh Straw in the bed Shee Said Shee was not Certaine but Shee thought about the latter end of march or beginning of apprill laft

Adjourned the Court to the 14th of the 7th month next

action Entered the 29th 6/mo 1692

wm Biles agt Gilbert wheeler in a plea of Cafe } with drawn
Summonce granted ditto return date 2 7/mo 92 } by the
plts order

action Entered the 29th 6/mo 1692

Stephen Beakes agt Gilbert wheeler in a plea of Cafe } withdrawn
Summonce Granted ditto returnd dated 2 7/mo 1692 } by the
plts order

action Entered the 30th 6/mo 1692

Edward Antill Leasor to Jon whitpaine by his attorney willm Nichols plt
  agt
John Teft oufter deft } in an action ejectione firme the endorfement & declaraction Served & Read on the premifes the 2d 7/mo 1692

Penfylvania County Court Bucks fs: P Saml Beakes Sherrife
At a Court of Quarter Seffions held by the king & Queens authority in the name of willm Penn propryetor & govrnr of the afforefaid Province & Counties annexed at the Court houfe for the Said County the 14th day of the 7th month being the 4th yeare of the Reigne of willm & mary king & Queen of England &c & 12th yeare of the propryetors govrmt 1692

The Justices Present

Arthur Cook   Joseph Growdon
wm: Biles   Nicholas waln   Henry Baker
John Cook Corronor
Samuel Beakes vice: Com:
Phinehas Pemberton Cl: Com:

Willm: Nichols Letter of attorney from Edward Antill proved

action Edward Antill Leaſor to John whitepaine appeared by his attorney willm Nichols —

It appearing that this action was not brought according to for-mer method the Court was not willing to admit the tryal but

243

but Gilbert wheeler then poſſeſt of the premiſes prayed that he might be admitted deft & that the action might be brought on not with Standing they had varyed from the former method & So did plts attorney whereupon the Court gave way & ordered the Tryal accordingly Shold be permitted to Paſs & thereupon the Iſſue was Joyned

defts–⎫ pleaded not Guilty as to Come with force & armes but as
anſwer⎭

as to the Trepaſs defends the force for that the ſd Antill Leaſor did Enter upon the premiſes as a diffeiſor

replye And the Said Edward Antill by his Said Attorney replyes that he did not Enter as a diffeisor & this he deſires may be enquired of by the Cuntry & So doth the deft in like manner where

venire for the Shrriſ is Commanded to return a Jury ——

Jury — Richard Hough Robt Heaton James Paxson ⎫
John Rowland Edmund Lovet Joseph Kirkbride ⎪
John white Samll Dark Stephen Beakes —— ⎬ atteſted
Joſeph Milner Job Bunting Thomas Brock —— ⎭

declaracon read

Anſwer read

a deed from Gilbert wheeler unto Edward Antill of the prmiſes read & owned by Gilbert wheeler

Two letters read Said to be from Gilbert wheeler to Said Edward Antill owning mony due to be payd to Said Edward Antill but the Said Letters were not owned nor disowned by ſd Wheeler the one dated Decemb the 18th 1686 the other dated august the 10th 1689

a deed for 200 acres of land in fee dated the 20th day of the — 9th month 1690 was acknowledged and delivered by ——

Hugh marſh & Anthony Morgan grantors to Joſias Hill grantee

A Mortgage dated the 20th day of the 9th month 1690 for the ſd 200 acres of Land acknowledged and delivered by Joſias —— Hill grantor to Anthony Morgain grantee

adjourned the Court untill tomorrow morning at 8 a Clock

Petition of Evan Prothera Concerning George Philips servitude read

Petitioner refferred to treat with John Bown for the Said Philips time of Servitude & if done to Content of all parties the Juſtices will ratefye the agreement

ordered that it be aſſented to that if the Said Evan Prothera do make reaſonable Satiſfaction to John Bowen his peſent maſter & that the Said John Bowen & George Philips be agreeing to the Same that then the Said Evan Prothera have him the remainder of the time he is to Serve the Said John Bowen by order of Court or for what leſs time the ſd George Philips & Evan Prothera Can agree for

244

Thomas Bowman atteſted doth Say that after Edward Antill had attached the goods of Gilbert wheeler to his knowledg Gilbert wheeler Stood in So much feare of Edward Antill that he durſt not Come at York for a time except privately untill that he had given him a mortgage of his land

Conſtables above the falls Ruben Pownall ——		over ſeeres of the highways for the ſd Places
from { thence to the govrnrs Edward Lucas —		Peter worrall
thence below Neſhaminah Rich Wilſon		Stephen Beakes
		wm: Dungan
Neſhaminah Tho: Stakehous ſenr —		Henry Pawlin
for { middle lotts — Edmund Lovet ——		Abraham Cox
the other ſide neſhaminah Jon: Gilbert		Samll Allen

Jury return in Antill agt wheeler Caſe brought in theire verdict for the plt

an appeale preſently there upon requeſted by the deft to the next Provincial Court in Equity wch was then by the Court allowed of &

adjudged that he the ſd deft giveing Security to profecute the ſd appeale & pay Coſts ought to have an appeale

By Confent & on requeſt to the Court of both plt & deft that the ſd appeale might be deferred to the Provincial Court in equity wch Shold happen in Spring next wch was allowed of by the Court & ordered that Security be taken accordingly

Recognizance memorand that Gilbert wheeler & Robt Cole both of the afforeſd County Came before this Court & acknowledged them Selves to be Indebted to Edward Antill of new York Gent in the Sum of fifty pounds Currant mony of this Province to be payd to the ſd Edward Antill for true payment whereof they grant for them felves theire heires executors & administrators that the Said Sum be levyed & recovered from their lands & tenemts goods Chattles & hereditaments of them the Said Gilbert wheeler & Robt Cole theire heires executors & administrators & affignes whereever they be found

Condition and this upon Condition that the Said Gilbert wheeler Shall appeare at the provincial Court wch Shall be held for this County in the Spring next & then & there Shall profecute his appeale wch is taken in equity with effect & if he be Caſt in the Said Court Shall not only pay all the Coſts and damages he Shall be Caſt in at the faid Court but alſo all the Coſts & damages of this prſent Court

a deed in fee of 240 acres of land dated the 8 day of the 4th month 1692 was acknowledged & delivered by Henry Baker grantr to Job Bunting grantee

A deed in fee of 60 acres of land dated the 7th day of the 4th month 1692 was acknowledged & delivered by Robt Heaton attorney to Jon Auſtin grantor unto Nicholas waln grantee

245

Roads whereas the former ordr for laying out the road from the upper plantations upon Delaware to the Landing at the ferry houſe agt Burlington was not obſerved & that Some of the pſons ordered are removed its therefore now —

ordered that Henry Baker Ruben Pownal Joſeph Milner Enoch yardley Jacob Janney Richard Hough Abraham Cox & Edmund Lovet or any 6 of them do lay out the ſaid Road & give an acctt thereof to the next Court

Town Ships whereas there was encouragemt formerly (for the deviding of this County into Town Ships) from the Councill

& that thereupon there was an ordr from the Court to pti
culers for deviding the Same & that it was not pformed accord
ingly its therefore now ——

ordered that Arthur Cook Joſeph Growdon John Cook Tho:
Janney Richard Hough Henry Baker Phinehas Pemberton
Joſuah Hoops wm Biles Nicholas waln Edmund Lovet
Abraham Cox & James Boyden or the greater number of
them meete together at the meeting houſe at neſhami
-nah the 27th day of this Inſtant & devide this County
into Town Ships

adjourned this Court to the meeting houſe at Neſhaminah
to the 27th day of this Inſtant month i692

    At a Court held at the meeting houſe at Neshaminah
    the 27th 7 1692
      mo

      Justices Present

    Arthur Cook Joseph Growdon
    Thomas Janney Nicholas waln Henry Baker
    Samll Beakes vic Com:
    Phinehas Pemberton Cl: Com:

whereas it was ordered formerly that this County Shold
be devided into Town ſhips according to ſd ordr the ſd perſons
by this Court ordred did this day meete & devided the
Same as ffolloweth

the upper moſt Town Ship being Calld makefeild to begin at
the upper moſt plantations & along the river to the upper
moſt part of John woods Lands & by the Lands formerly belong
-ing to the Hawkinses & Jos: kerkbrid & wid Lucas Land &
So along as neare as may be in a ſtreight line to fetch in Joſuah Hoops
 land

the Town ſhip at the falls being Calld *
begin at Penſbery & So up the River to the upper ſide of Jon
woods Land & then to take in the Hawkins Jos kerkbride & the
wid: Lucas Land & So the land a long that Creek Continueing
the ſame untill it takes in the land of Jon Rowland &

---

* Pemberton omitted to say what it was called.

246 †

& Edward Pearſon & so to Continue till it Com with Penſbury
Land then along Penſbury to the place of begining
Then Penſbury as its layd out
below Penſbury its calld Buckingham & from Penſberry to to follow the river
to neſhaminah then up neſhaminah to the upper ſid of Robt
Halls plantation & to take in the Land of Jon Town Edmund
Lovet Abram Cox & So to Penſbery & by the ſame to the
place of beginning
the middle Town to be Calld middleton to begin at the upper ſide of
Robt Hall Land * * * inah to New Town & from
thence to take in * * * John Hough Jonathan
Scaiſe & John * * * Jon * * * Land & ſo to take
in the back part * * * by theire land to the
place of begining * * *
new Town & wrights * * * one Town Ship
all the Lands between Neshaminah & Poqueſſin & So to
the upper ſide of Joſeph Growdons Land in one & to be
Called Salem
South Hampton & the Lands about it with warminſter one

Whereas there was a Tax formerly ordered its now ordered
that the ſame be forth with raiſed & that warrants be Iſſued
to the Conſtables of every deviſion for the doing thereof
& that when Rec it be pd to Arthur Cook Joſeph Growdon ——
Nicholas walne and Sam: Beakes that the publique Charges of
the County may be defrayed

ordered that the Receivors be accountable to every Court of
Quarter Seſſions from time to time as they Rec any mony

adjourned to the next 3 day at the Court houſe

Penſylvania 247

Bucks ſS: the 4th day of the 8th/mo 1692 at a Court of Quarter

Seſſions held by adjournmt

---

† The lower third of pages 246 and 247 have been clipped away.

Derrick Clawſon als Jonſon deſired that he might have
libertie on baile for his appearance

whereas it was Suppoſed in the beginning of this Court y^t:
the Said Derrick Shold have been brought to Tryall
forth with but the Judges beleiving it to be more diſcretion
—all to deffer the Tryall untill Spring to See if Some
thing further might not be diſcovered Concerning the
Suppoſed murther & * * * winter Seaſon &
the prison Inconvenienced * * * Seaſon Thought good
to ordr that baile be * * * his and his wifes appearance at the
next Court of Quarter Seſſions to be held for this County

____N____

memorand: that Derrick Clawſon als Jonſon acknowledges him
Self Indebted to be propryetor & govrnr in 100 £ and
Claws Jonſon in 50 £ & Peter Rambo in 50 £ to be levyed
on theire goods & Chattles Lands & tenements where
ever they be found

and this upon Condition that the ſd Derrick Clawſon & his
wife Shall appeare at the next Court of Quarter Seſſions
to be held for this County in the firſt month next &
to be of good abearing in the meane time

14th day of the 8th month 1692
adjourned to the tenth of the firſt month next

action Entered the 23 day 9   1692
                           ―――
                            mo

Sold to Joseph
the land of Joſeph Holden taken in execution
growdon at
Seventy Seven
pounds by
Sam Beakes Sherriſ

John Nichols by his Attorneys Phinehas
    Pemberton & Henry Baker

           agt

Bartholemew Joſeph & Amos Thatcher executors
of theire ―――
father Richard Thatcher in a plea of debt― ――― ―

248

Summonce * * *
Summonce for Joſ * * * 9   1692
                       ―――
                        mo

action Entered the 2 * * * proven by witnesses dated 29th $\frac{9}{mo}$ 1692

Tho: Brock plt * * * with drawn
  agt
Richard Bartho * * *
Sum Dated 26th * * * Thatcher defts } in a plea of debt

Sum: for Jon * * * & white & Anthony Banks witnesses dated to 29th $\frac{9}{mo}$ * * * drawn

action Entered 23 $\frac{9}{mo}$ * * *

wm: Biles plt _ _ _ _ * * *   dated 28th $\frac{9}{mo}$ 1692
  agt
Ralph Boome deft   witnesses ditto 29th

action Entered 26th $\frac{9}{mo}$ * * *

Joseph Chorley plt ⎫ * * *
  agt   ⎬* * * Sum dated 29 $\frac{9}{mo}$ 1692
Edward Lucas deft ⎭

Arrest granted agt Henry Greenland dated 4th $\frac{9}{mo}$ i692 at the suite of Richard Thather plea of Case returnd executed the 4th day 9 month i692 & baile taken p Sa: Beakes vic: Com:

    Pensylvania
County Court Bucks ss:

  At a Court of Quarter Sessions held by the king and Queens authority in the name of Willm Penn ——— Propryetor & Govrnr of the afforesaid Province and Counties annexed at the Court house for the Said County The i4th day of the $\frac{i0}{mo}$ 1692

   The Justices Present
    Wm: Biles Nicholas Waln Henry Baker
    Samll Beakes Sherrif
   Phinehas Pemberton Cl: Com:

Adjourned to the houſe of Joſeph Chorley

a deed in fee for 340 acres of Land dated the 2ⁿᵈ day of the
9ᵗʰ month 1692 acknowledged & delivered by wm Biles
attorney to Ellizabeth Bennet grantor to Nicholas waln grantee

[249] *

action Entered Jos: * * * Lucas both appeared

declaracon read
Anſwer not guilty & for * * * ſelf on the Cuntry
& So doth the plt wher * * * 3ʳ &c:
Cauſe to come i2 honeſt * * *

Jury John Rowland * * * Samˡˡ Dark Peter Worral
James moone John Pan * * * wm: Paxson ⎫ all
Andrew Ellot Joseph Cr * * * wm: Dungan ⎭ attested

wittneſes to the ſd * * *
Robt Cole = * * * John Clark * * * Tho: peirce wm: Taylor
James yates Tho: Cole * * * Poole all atteſted
adjourned the Court * * *

verdict the Jury retu * * * by deft with Coſts

A deed in fee of * * * dated the i2ᵗʰ day of the
7ᵗʰ month 1692 was acknowledged & delivered by Rich
Lundy grantor to ff * * * grantee

An appeale requeſted by Joſeph * * * Chorley But the pretended
damages not being 10 £ Sterling the Jury declaring they
had veiued the ox & that he was so little harmed by the
Shot that the Said Chorley needed not to have loſt 2 days
work for any harm the ox had Received by the Same
as alſo the deft: Craved the Benefit of the law that
where the debt or damage is pretended to be above —
five pounds & it prove undr that in Such Caſe the plt
Shall Looſe his action wherefore the Court Saw no Cauſe
to grant him an appeale

Judgmt Given & it is adjudged the Joſeph Chorley pay Coſts
& that execution Iſſue accordingly

---

* Page 249 is numbered at the bottom of the page.

Richard Thatcher
      agt } both Calld but neither appeared
Henry Greenland

adjourned the Court to the 8th day of the firſt month next

Penſylvania County Court Bucks ſs:

> At a Court of Quarter Seſſions held by the authority of wh & mary king and Queen of England &c: & in the name of wm Penn Propryetor and & Govrnr of the ſd Province & Countyes —— annexed at the houſe of Samll Beakes the 8th day of the i month 1692 being the 4th yeare
>   3
> of the king & Queens Reigne & i3 yeare of the Propryetors Govrmt ——

[250]*

* * *

* * * berton Cl: Com:

adjourned the C * * *

Wm: Duncan being * * * appeared * * * ance none appearing agt him the Court * * * paying his fees

Robt Benſon being bound * * * Recognizance appeared none appeareing * * * the Court discharges him paying fees

Stephen Newell being summonced to Court for Selling a Servant out of the province alleadged that he had not Sold him but lent him to Service for Some time & that he wold bring him back in 3 months

a deed of 5½ acres of land in fee dated the 8th day of march 1692 acknowledged & delivered by Thomas Green and — Rachel his wife grantors to Thomas Brock Grantee

a deed of 5½ acres of land in fee dated the 8th day of march 1692 acknowledged and Delivered by Thomas Green and Rachel his wife Grantors to Anthony Burton Grantee

---

*Page 250 is numbered at the bottom of the page.

Richard Thatcher being Committed into Cuſtody on Suſpition of ffelony being Calld requeſted his Tryal might be defferred untill further time & that in the meane time he might be let to baile wch is left to the diſcretion of the Juſtice wch Thatcher Shall applye him Self to with his baile

Job: Houle being bound by Recognizance to this Court further Comp Comeing agt him by Tho: Brock he is Continued untill the next Court

Job Houle acknowledges him Self Indebted to the propryetor & govrnr in Ten pounds to be Levyed on his lands & tenemts goods & Chattles & this upon Condition that he appeare at the next Court & Anſwer the Complt of Tho: Brock

adjourned to the i0^{th} Inſtant at i0 a Clock in the morning

250

[251]*
* * *
* * * that wm: * * *
ke Care ab * * *

adjourned the * * *

At * * * nment at the Court houſe * * * unty the i4^{th} day 2
                                                              ──
                                                              mo
i693 * * *

* * * Present
* * * on Wm Biles
* * * Henry Baker
Sam * * * kes Sherrif
Phin * * * Pemberton Cl: Com:

action John Addington plt ⎫
          agt   ⎬ in a plea of Caſe withdrawn by
John Hewett def _____ ⎭ the plts ordr

A deed in fee for 250 acres of land Dated this i4^{th} day of the 2nd month i693 acknowledged & delivered by Israel

---

*Page is numbered at the bottom of the page.

Taylor Grantor to James yates Grantee

Tho Lacy being bound by Recognizance to appeare here being Charged with geting mary Roles with Child appeared accordingly

mary Roles being examined about the Same declared that Thomas Lacy had got her with Child & Said he lay with her Several times one time was the firſt day afore Iſaac page dyed wch is Said to be about the middle of the 9th month laſt & that he lay with her but once afterwards & that was about i3 or i4 weekes from this time

ordered that the ſd Thomas Lacy give bond to anſwer the ſd Complt at the next Court

N

memorand Thomas Lacy acknowledges him Self Indetted to the Propryetor in 10 £ & Iſrael Taylor in 5 £ to be levyed theire lands & Tenements goods & Chattles & this upon Condition for the appearance of the ſd Tho: Lacy at the next Court to anſwer the aforeſd Complt of mary Rowles

Hugh marſh declared that Iſrael Taylor had arreſted him — and that he deſired a Special Court wch was granted him he being about to depart out of the province

[252]*

[The upper 2/5 of the page is missing]

agt him the Court * * * paying his fees

adjourned for one * * *

Bucks ſs: Penſy * * *

The Jurors * * * pryetor & Govrnr by the king and Queens authority * * * Richard Thatcher for that he Some time before 18th day * * * of the 12th mo: laſt paſt did Steale and fraudulen^t
-ly take away one * * * mare with a blaze in her face & a Snip on her noſe & one of Colt of a black Colour belonging to the ſd mare being the proper goods of ffrancis white being worth foure pounds

---

*Page 252 is numbered at bottom of the page.

Conterary to the king and Queens Peace & the Statute law in that Cafe made & provided

ffrancis white Profecutor
Robt Benfon   Jon Clark
Jon Crofdel   Jon: Penquoit
Jofeph Chorley ——— ———
} witneffes attefted

a True bill

grand Jury Joun Swift Thos Hardin Jofuah Hoops geo: Brown
Jos: Milner Job Bunting Abraham Cox Samⁿ Dark
Henry Paxfon Jonathan Scaife Jofeph kirkbride
ffrancis Roffill James Paxfon wm: Beakes Jon: Palmer
} attefte

Richard Thatcher being Calld appeared according to recognizance ordered that he be taken into the Sherrifs Cuftody untill ——— further ordr

adjourned for one houre   252

[Upper 1/3 page missing]

[253]*

* * * the fd Thatcher * * * e mare that was in
* * * fdels pafture
Robt Cole attefted doth * * * Saw Richard Thatcher
when he brought a black * * * the River with a mare
Colt of blackifh dun * * * ge Starr in her face
and a Snip on her nofe & * * * further eare & fome
notches in the other but what he * * * Certaine & he afked
Said Thatcher where he had the Said mare and he Said he bought
her of an eaft Jerfey man on the road between Daniel
Brinfons & Doctor greenlands & that Jon Richardfon and
John Houghton were prefent when he bought her & the
Said Thatcher Confeffes it was the Same mare that he
sold to John Clark

John Crofdel attefted doth say Richard Thatcher Came to fee the mare in his brothers pafture & that Said Thatcher Confeft it was the mare he Sold to John Clark & that he knowns that ffrancis white or his mother bought the Said mare of Thomas-Stakehoufe Junr

---

*Page 253 is numbered at the bottom of the page.

Jon Penquoit attefted Saith the Same

Derrick Clawfon appearing to this Court according to recognizance the Court difcharges him & his Suerties of the fd recognizance

John Gilbert being accufed with begating a baftard Child on a negro girl of the widow fforreft wch fd Gilbert deneyed & it appearing by the examination of the fd girl that Shee is disagreeing in her relation both as to the time & Cercum ftances its therefore ordered that She be whipt & have i5 Lafhes on her bare back   253

[All the foregoing pages are in the hand of Phineas Pemberton. Beginning with 254 the hand changes to that of Robert Cole.]

            Pennfilvania   254
Bucks vid:

    At a Courte of Quarter feffions held by ye king & Quens Authority at the Courte houfe of the sd County the 14 day of June 1693 beinge ye ffifte yeare of thayer Maggestis Reigne

     The Justices psent   Gilbard Wheeler
                Jos: Woode
                John Brocke
                 Robt Cole Clarke

Ordered That Cloufe Johnston & Mary Boydon beforth wth sent ffor to give in Bonnds ffor thayer apearance at ye Next Coarte to Teftifie all they now Consearing ye Blood that was seene upon Derick Johnstons Wall in May 92

  Tho: Leacy Caled to Answar ye Complaynt of Mary Roales Leacy not apeared

  Mary Roales Caled to procute ye Complaynt against Tho: Leacy Not apeared
       Ordered
    That ye Complaynt stand upon Record till next Coarte

Ordered That Wm Tayler Putt up Rayles about ye Courte houfe stayers & Rayles about ye Table ffor wch he is to have 16/ to be pd by sd Wheeler

Ordered a New Table to be made by Wm Taylor for
wch he is to have 15/ to be pd by Robt Cole

The. Courte rajornes tell ye 13 of Sept 93

Bucks vid: 255   Pennsylvania

Att a Courte of Quarter Sesions held by the kinge &
Quens Authority at the Courte houfe of ye County aforesd
the 13 day of Sept 1693 Being ye iiii of thayer maigestys
Reaigne

The Justises Present	Gilbart Wheeler
John Brocke	Jo: Wood
John Swifte	Henry Poyntar
Tho: Brock Shreefe	Robt Cole Clark

Grand
Jury   The Grand Jury attested Wm Doyles fforeman
James Paxton   Henry Paxton   Wm Paxton   Wm Hofte
John Crosdall   John Pinck White   Jobe Buntinge
Sa: Coatts   Wm Darke   Shadraich Woolly   Jos: Millenor
John Parseley   Henry Hudelston

Tho: Brocke } Complaynent
Jos: Chorly   Chorly Apearing according to his racognefens
and Nothing Ap'ing against him is Clered

Jo: Wood } Complaynent
Mary Chorly   Jos: Wood makes Complaynt of seavaroll abuses
done him by Mary Chorley ye Courte suspends thayr

Judgment   at this tim & rajourns for 2 owers
The Courte seetts & ye Grand Jury Caled noa present
ments Courte rajourns tell next moring

Sept 14   The Courte seets & Chofes Petar White Constable
ffor Middletown Antho: Burton for Buckinham
An: Heath for mackefeld Nick: Randalph for Southhampton
John Clarke ffor Crockhorne

overseeyers Tho: Williams Buckingham & ffrances Rosale
highways Gorge Brown for Crockhorne Wm Paxton for —

Midd Sam: Aleine for Bensalame Jo: Webstar
for Southhampton John Clowefe for Mackfeld

deed Abraham Beake grantor acknowledges a deede of Land
bearing date ye 13 of Sep^t 1693 of 300 ackars of Land
* * *
* * *

Bucks vid: 256 Pennsivania

Att a Courte of Common Peafe held by ye kinge & Queens
Authority at ye Courte Houfe of ye sd County Sep^t ye 14 day
1693 and ye 1111i yeare of theyer Maytis Reaigne

 The Justises Present Gilbart Wheeler John Brocke
 Jos: Wood John Swife Henry Poyntor

Jos: Wood } plt in an actyon of Debt
Henry Hudellston } Deft ye actyon Caled thay boath apered

Henry Hudelston in open Court acknowledgs Judgment
ffor his Bonnd

Lewifs Lavally } plt
John Pownd } Dff boath apered ye Declarcyon read

The Daf^t saith hee is not Guilty in manner & fforme
& soa puts himselfe upon ye Country Jo: White atorney
for plt

The plt in Licke manor Pettar morow saith y^t John pownd
did ack: y^t hee had ye bill of Lews
Lavally &
Left it weet in his window Rodger
Murfey swore ye same

Iffue } The Jury atested Henry Marjoron John White
Joyned} Edward Carter Tho. Green An: Burton James Moon se^r
Tho: Shackhars Henry Hudelston Bartho: Thathar
Wm Darke Jo: Millner Ruben Pownar

Wm Biles } plt upon two acktyons they Boath Comm to Courte
Jo: Pidcock } Dff and desaireth y^t ye actyons may Continew upon
racord tell next Courte of Comon pleafe

Jo: Pidcock } plt
Wm Biles } Dff ye actyon Caled they boath Com in to Courte &
desiareth y^t ye actyon may Continew upon racord
tell ye next Courte of Comon pleafs

The Jury raturned & ffind for ye Dtt John Pound
John White Atorney for ye plt moved ffor an apell
to ye present Courte
wch was Granted & ye plt & Deff in ye meane time agreefe
Wm Beaks Coms into Courte & John Murfyn his Sarvaint
& Wm Beaks doas acknowledg y^t provided his man Murfen
dufe behave himselfe dutyfully he will give him one yeare
of his sarvice & Murfeyn doas declear he has 4 years
from ye 15 day of Mo: Next but on is to be alowed

Mary Beaks } Coms in to Courte & acknowledges a deed in ffee of
Steven Beaks } 300 Akars of Land to Wm Beaks bearing date ye 9 day

Sam: Beaks } of ye 11 moth ye 4 yeare of kinge James ye 2^d Reaigne
Abra: Beaks } The Court rajorns tell ye 2^d day of ye 7th month

257

Bucks fs: At a Court of Quarter Sefsions held by ye kinge &
Quens authority at ye Courte houfe neare ye ffalls
the seconde Wednsday of ye monnth of Decr 1693
and ye ffifte yeare of thayer Majestis reigne

The Justices Present   Gilbart Wheeler

             John Brocke   Jos: Woode   John Swifte
Tho Brocke   Tho: Lacy stood bound by racognefence to answar ye
             Com of M Roles Cald Not
Shrefe   apeared Isarale Taylor security
             ffor Lacy Cald Not apered for wch they forfeett thayer
Robt Cole   Racognisence
Clarke

The Grand Jury Caled & atested Johnathan Scafe
Jos Millar John Pamar John White Tho: Cearll
Tho: Tannclefte John Hugh ffrances Rofell
Wm Cluse Wm Darke James Paxton Henry Paxton
Jobe Bownton John Pursly Tho: Thakorf

Adiorned the Court tell 8 acloke in ye moring

1 The Grande Jury raturns caled & all
answar they doa prasent grate Nafsity of a Carte
Roade to be laid out from Newtowne to ye ferry
houfe Tho: Stackhoufe Senior Sam: Coate Steven
Willson Jobe Bunting Wm Buckman Wm Smith

John Cowgell being men ordred by this Courte to
Leay out ye roade

2 The Grand Jury have in discorsed ye Leate trasurar
doa finde savarall Just debts due to ye County & y^t thare
are savarall persons in arare of ye late tax thay doa
prasent ye Nefsity of Collecting the same & alsoa
raqueste ye Court y^t warrants be Isued forth for ye
parfecting of it

3 According to ye Leat acte of Genarall afsembly ffor ye
defraying of Nefsary Charges as ye provincall Judges
& allsoa ffor ye destroying of woolfes wee thare fore do
present ye Nefsity of Raifen the some of Thirty pounds
to defray ye Same & wee raqueft this Courte that two
Safe and honest men be chofen to putt ye s^d Some
* * *

258 And that the s^d two men be accountable to this Court
and the Country viz: ye grandiury Soa often as nede shall
requiar

4 wee do^e alfoa p^rsent ye nefsesity of a road to be laide
out ffrom Henry Bakers to John Pidcoks
Ordared y^t men be apoynted to Leay out a roade from
the uper side of Jos: Woods Lande to Henry Bakers —
& Soa to ye Linkers poynte men apoynted by ye Courte
John Pidcoke Henry Maryorom John Brocke Jacobe
Jeney Wm Clufe Tho: Tanyclefte
The Grand Jury doa prefent Gilbart Wheeler for
takeing extortion for ferrige

The Courte mets and apoynts a privat seisons to Consider
of ye Bill delivered by ye Grande Jury to be
at Gilbarte Wheelers ye ffirste day of January
Next

A deed in ffee of 50 Akars of Lands dated ye 10 day
of ye 10 Month 1689 was acknowledged & delivered in
open Coarte by John Gibbs Grantor to Rich: Willson
Grantee

Att a Coarte of Common pleafes held by ye kinge &
Quens athourity at ye Courte houfe of ye s^d County
Buks fs ye 13 day Decr 1693

Justis Present   Gilbart Wheelar
Jos: Woode   John Brocke   John Swifte
                    Robt Cole   Clarke

Mary Beaks plt   ⎫   The action caled thay Both apeare y^e —
Jos: Charlly Defts   ⎬   daclaratyon rad ye Bonde read ye Covenan^t
& Mary His wife   ⎭   in ye daclaratyon ye patten of ye Land mentyoned
in ye Covenante and it was proved
in Courte y^t ye D^{tt} hade Noa Afsetts of Akarm
ans In his hands save y^e Tracte Lande
mentyoned in y^e Morgadg

Thare ffor y^e Dft acknowledge Judgment in open
Coarte for 48 £ deb^t & fourten pounds in trest wth
Cost of sute to be Leavied on y^e Lande of Akarman
According to Lawe

259

Buks fs   At a privat sesions held at Gilbart Wheelars Jenuary
the 1 day $\frac{4}{93}$ by y^e Justis of the County whear it is
ordered that the Clarke gives publique Notife to
the in habitents of this County by Nayleing up 4
Bills at y^e most publique pleafses of y^e County to
deasiar all parfons y^t are Consarned in y^e County
to apear y^e 2^d wednsday of March next at ye
Courte houfe of ye s^d County to put a finell end and
to deschardg the arrears layd to ye Charge of ye
County by ye fformar Councell and afsembly
That thare be awarant Isued out for ye Collecting
the arears of ye ould tax of this side & ye ffarthar
side Neashamony & y^t thare be anew tax of 7^d p
pounde upon ye reall & parsonall eastate & 6/ by y^e
Powlle of all Not Capable of beinge othar ways
taxed from 16 years to 60 years to be Collected by
Tho: Brocke High Shrefe ye County & Broug^t
in to ye Next County Courte
And that Notis be given to y^e in Habitents of
the siteing of ye orphants Coarte
John Caws Ralfe Bons & wife ye Hayers of Rich
Thathar Nick: Walen James Delworth —
And: Hearth
Att a Courte of Quorter Sisins hild by y^e

Kinge & Quens athourity at ye Courte
Courte houſs of the County aforſ^d 14th of 1 mo 1693/4

The Juſtis present Gilbert Wheeler
Joſ: Woode John Brocke John Swife
Henry Poyter Tho: Brocke Shreefe
Robt Cole Cla

Stephen Nowell Being being bounde by
racogneſence to appear to ye Complaynt of
ralfe Cowgell upon his Complaynt y^t hee did
ſuspecte ye s^d Nowell to have ſtolene a mare
Cowlte of his ye sd Nowell apears & ye Grande
Jury being Impeneled & ateſted did not find
ye bill where upon Nowell was Clered payin
fees

(260)

The Names of the Grande Jury as they was
Ateſted Was Joſ: Whoops fforman
Johna: Scaſe Wm Beaks Tho Curll
Jon- Hugh And: Eliott Tho Rodgers
Jon Rowland ffrances Roſalle
Wm Dungan Wm Eliott Wm Darke
Ruben Pownor Enocke yardly
John Gilbart John Baldwn
Wm Clowſe John Palmar

Danill Gardnar Being bound by racogniſence
by Gilbert Wheeler Juſtis to anſwar ffor his
Contempt against John Clarke when hee Came
to ſarve awarant one hime, upon Gardners
Submiſion ye Courte Clears him payin his
ffees   The Courte Calls & ratiurns tell ye 2^d
Weednsday of Mon^th of June 94

Att acurte of Com pleaſs held at ye Courte
houſs ye 14 day 1th Month 1694 by ye Kinge &
3
Quens authority The Juſtis Present
Gilbart Wheeler Joſ: Woode Jo: Brocke
Jo: Swifte Henry Poynter Tho: Brocke
Shreefe Robt Cole Clark

The Coarte caled & raiurned to yᵉ 2ᵈ Weednsdy
of the Monᵗ of June 1694
June yᵉ

Noa Courte this month ——— ————
Sepᵗ the   Noa Courte by rason of yᵉ Shrefe
Leay very secke at Philidalph
Decʳ ye   Noa Courte by rason of Exterordnary Beade Weathar *

Bucks ſs:

261†   At a Court of Quarter ffeſſions held by the kings authority in the name of William penn abſolute proprietary & Governor: of the province of penſylvania and Counties annexed the i2ᵗʰ day of the fourth month 1695 being the 7 yeare of the kings Reign &   of the proprietarys govermt over the ſd province &c.

The Juſtices preſent
Gilbert wheeler Joſeph Wood
John Brock   John Swift
John Cook Corroner
Tho: Brock Sherrif

a deed in fee for 300 acres of land dated the 20 $\frac{1}{mo}$ 1694 was acknowledged and delivered by Saml Beakes attorney to William Beaks & his wife Ellizabeth Beaks grantors to John ſnowden grantee

a deed of Joynture dated the i8ᵗʰ $\frac{i2}{mo}$ 1689 made by Wm — Beakes of the above mentioned three hundred acres of land to John worrilow & walter worrilow in truſt

---

*This is the last entry in the hand of Robert Cole.

† Beginning with this entry Phineas Pemberton resumed his county clerkship and so continued until the 14ᵗʰ day of the first month 1699 , the last entry in his hand.

1700

for Elizabeth worrilow theire fifter & now wife of the fd
wm: Beakes was furrendered in open
Court by Saml Beakes
attorney to John worrilow aforefd furviveing truftee
unto the above named John fnowden by order of fd
wm Beakes & Ellizabeth

Mary fcaife being examined about her haveing of a baftard
born on her body acknowledged the fame & faid
James Heaton was the father of it

ffined The Court adjudged to pay a fine of three pounds for
Commiting fornication

payment of the fame was promifed by Jonathan fcaife
father of the fd Mary

adjourned to the 7 mo next
at ufual day

262

Grand Jurys prfentmts brought in

we of the Grand Jury do prfent the kings roade through the
Timber Swamp neare Saml Burges & fo along the road to
middle Towne

and James Heaton for haveing a baftard Child by Mary
the daughter of Jonathan Scaife —

And the neceffity of haveing a ftandard in this County for
wett and dry meafures and alfo for weights

and Tho Brock for not bringing in his acc^{tts} to this Court
Concerning the late tax for which he was made Collector

And the roade between Henry Bakers and the ffalls
a return made of the Roade from the upper planation to the — —
ferry againft Burlington
ffirft from Richard Houghs Plantation by a line of marked
trees
to the falls meeting houfe and from thence to the Cold
Spring —
by a line of marked trees & fo down the old Road to the fferry

By Richard Hough   Ruben Pownal   Jofeph Milner
Enoch yardley   Henry Baker formerly appointed to
lay out the fame

Action	ffrancis Jones plt agt Robt Cole deft	plt appeares deft being Calld appeared not

Joſeph Wood Soninlaw to the ſd Defte haveing formerly had an attachment upon the pipe ſtaves mentioned in the plt Declarcon being upon the land of the ſaid Jos Wood he the Said wood here in Court declares that the action Grounded upon the ſd attachment is with drawn and that he diſclaimes any property in the ſd pipe Staves and that the said plt may take them away when he pleaſes according to the ſd Deft Robt Coles deſire Certeſyed to this Court by the afforeſd wood and Gilbert wheeler

Judgmt   Therefore it is Conſidered that the ſd plt Shall recover agt the ſd deft the ſd pipe staves or value thereof with Coſts of ſuite

action	wm Rakeſtraw plt agt Tho Terry deft	both appeared the deft made anſwer he had not ſeen or heard that any Compl^{lt} was Entered agt him whereupon the Court Granted the deft a non ſuite

action	wm Rakeſtraw plt agt Robt Cole deft —	both appeared but the plt withdraw his action

Court adjourned untill the 4th day 9 month next

263   Bucks ſs: Att a Court of Quarter ſeſſions held by the kings authority in the name Willm Penn Proprietary & Governor of the Province of Penſylvania at the Court houſe for the ſaid County the iith day of the i0th month being the   yeare of the kings reigne   of the Proprietarys — govrmt i695

The Juſtices preſent

Willm Biles   Richard Hough
John Swift — — — — — — —

Samll Beaks Sherriff
phinehas pemberton Clerk Coun:

The Court adjourns into the house of Joſeph Chorley

a deed of Two hundered thirty Six acres of land in fee dated the 12 day of the 6th month 1694 acknowledged and delivered by Joſeph Chorley attorney to Charles Biles Grantor to Abell Janney Grantee

a deed of foure hundered and eighty acres of land in fee dated the 20th day 12 mo: 1693 acknowledged and delivered by — Abel Janney Atorney to John Hornor to Grantor Phinehas Pemberton Grantee

a Certificate of Joan the wife of James Moones being alive Signed in Court Shee being then Preſent

The preſentment agt James Heaton Continued untill next Court and ordered that a warrant Iſſue that he be apprehended to give bond for his appearance at the next Court ——

Accounts of Tho: Brock late Sherrife this day preſented but not being perfected and no grand Jury preſent they are returned and ordered that they be brought to the next Court and That a warrant Iſſue from Some of the Juſtices to Impower the said Tho Brock to levye What is in arreare of the County Taxes

ordered that the Clerk write to Joſeph wood to bring or ſend the County records that he hath in his hands

Sent the Said order by Andrew Heath Conſtable who being returned brought three paperbooks 2 of them Covered with Sky-Coloured paper marked No: 1: 2: and another paper book of Robt Coles writeing in ffo: haveing thereon write only ſeven ſides all the reſt blank and Said that the ſaid Joſeph wood Said that was all that was in his Cuſtody

The Court adjourns for one houre

(264)

Reported to this Court by John Swift that the land of Philip Conway was formerly taken in Execution to Satiſfye the Several Judgments of Court and that the Same has not been ſold and diſpoſed of So as to aſſure thoſe now poſſeſt of it a ſuitable — title Its therefore ordered that Execution be againe Iſſued

Comley—Robt Heaton with his Son in law Henry Comley appeared in Court this day and declared the ſaid Comley to be of age &

desired to have in those bonds given to Court on his behalf —

ordered thereupon that the Clark make search after the bonds & records yet remameing in the late Clerk Robt Coles hands & when the bonds relateing to Said Comley are had and — obtained that he deliver them to Robt Heaton to be — disposed of to his use as soone as may be —

Reported to this Court by Tho Brock that ffrancis Rossill left to the poore of this County Certaine Sums of mony to be payd by his Executor Samll Carpenter & that the said Samll Carpenter is willing to pay it to Such from time to time as this Court Shall recommend to be necessitous & therefore its —

ordered that the Clerk write to Said Samll Carpenter ——— acquaint him that Edward Doyal & James Sutton are necessi -tous & that if he please to lett them have fifty Shillings — a piece that they have need of it

a deed in fee of 248 acres of land dated the i0th day i0 1695
                        mo
acknowledged and delivered by Job Bunting Grantor to Stephen Twineing Grantee

    adjourned untill the iith 1 next
               mo

— — — — — — — — — — —

Bucks ss:

265

At a Court of Quarter Sessions held by the kings authority in the name of Willm Penn absolute proprietarie and governr — of this province and Territorys thereunto belonging at the Court house of the said County the i1th day of the i mo: i695
                   6

The Justices present

    Joseph Growdon Willm Biles
    Henry Baker Richard Hough
    Samll Beakes Sherrife
    Phinehas Pemberton Cl: Com:

—a deed in fee from Thomas William Grantor of Two hundered — acres of land in fee dated the 2 day 9th month —

i695 was by him acknowledged and delivered
unto Abraham Cox Grantee

a releafe from the Governor of a fine Impofed by
the Court on mary the daughter of —
Jonathan Scaife produced in Court by her father
as ffolloweth

Penfylvania

Locus whereas the daughter of Jonathan Scape of Bucks
figil   County Stands ffind upon Record of the Said County in
the Sum of three pounds I do forgive Releafe and —
acquit her of the Said fine witnefs my hand & seale
this 26 day of october i695

       Wm Markham Govr
       undr wm Penn abfolute
Recorded by order of Court Proprietor

prfentmt agt: James Heaton for haveing a bastard Child

Bucks fs: 9th 8 i695
     mo

The Jurrors for the proprietary and
govrnr by the kings authority do prfent James
Heaton for haveing a baftard Child by mary —
daughter of Jonathan Scaife Conterary to the kings
peace and the Statute law in that Cafe made and
provided &c.

pleaded not Guilty & for tryal put him felf upon the Cuntry whereupon

venire   the Sherrife was Commanded to return a Jury wch according
=ly he did

Jury   Peter Warrall Henry Marjorum John Crofdell ⎫
  James moon John Smith Edmond Lovet   ⎬ attefted
  Ruben Pownal wm Dark John Palmer   ⎭
  Edward Pearfon ffrancis Tunneclift Ed: Lucas

prefentmt proved by mary Scaife Thomas Stakehoufe Junr —
and Jonathan Scaife

    Court adjourned for an houre & a half

action Arthur Cooke plt
       agt } in a plea that he render to ſd plt
  ffrancis Collins deft Seventy pounds damage for want
                         of pforming Sundry Covenants about
                         building both plt & deft appeared
declaracon Read

  Anſwer   the deft anſwered the Complt was true & deſired Judgmt —
               might be entered accordingly

  Judgmt — Therefore it is Conſidered that the Said plt recover agt
              the ſd deft the Said Sum of Seventy pounds with Coſt
              of Suite

— a deed of Two hundered acres of land in fee dated the
             Tenth day of the firſt month i695   acknowledged and
             delivered by Nicholas Waln grantor to John ſtakhouſe
             grantee

   verdict Jury returned give in verdict we do find James =
           Heaton guilty of begeting a Child of mary Scaiſe

   a deed-of-one hundered acres of Land in fee dated the fourth
           day of the eleventh month $\frac{i695}{6}$ acknowledged and
           delivered by prudence Betridge grantor to George
           willard Grantee

   a deed of Elleven acres of land in fee dated the Twentieth
           day of the Twelfth month $\frac{i695}{6}$ acknowledged
           and delivered by Phinehas Pemberton
           Attorney to Joſeph Engliſh Grantor to Thomas —
           Brock & Anthony Burton Grantees

   a deed of Elleven acres of land in fee dated the Twentieth
           day of the Twelfth month $\frac{i695}{6}$ acknowledged and —
           delivered by Phinehas Pemberton attorney to Joſeph
           Engliſh Grantor to Peter white Grantee

           William Rakestraw plt:
action {   agt: } in an action of detenuce }
           Gilbert Wheeler deft.   both appeared ———

  a deed of   of land in fee dated the   day

	of the month i69 acknowledged and delivered by John Rowland Grantor to Arthur Cook Grantee
decleracon	read Complaineing agt Gilbert G wheeler for detaineing of 33 bufhells of barley & 6i bushells of oates of the plts
Anfwer venire —	he detaines it not & of this put him felf upon the Cuntry & fo doth the plt whereupon the Sherrife is Commanded to return a Jury wch he accordingly did

267

Jury—	Henry Marjorum John Crosdell James Moone — — John Smith Edmund Lovet willm Dark ——— — Jofeph Kirkbride Edward pearfon ffrancis Tunneclift Edward Lucas Enoch yardley John fiddall attefted
declaracon:	proved by the Evidence of Phinehas Pemberton Richard Hough Peter Worrall Thomas Janney Jnr Ruben Pownal John Palmer ——— Thomas Brock all attefted
a deed–	of Two hundred acres of land in fee dated the firft day of february i695 acknowledged & delivered by Jofeph wood attorney to Thomas ffaireman grantor to John Swift Grantee ———
a deed	of Sixty acres of land in fee dated the 29th day of May i695 acknowledged and delivered by Jofeph Wood attorney to Ifrael Taylor Grantor to John —— Swift Grantee
a deed–	of one hundered Seventy three acres of land in fee dated the i4th day of the 2 month i693 acknowledged and delivered in open Court by willm Biles Grantor — to Samuel Beakes Grantee
a deed–	of one hundered acres of land in fee dated the Tenth day of the Sixth month i695 acknowledged & delivered by willm Crofdel & John Crofdell Grantors to Jonathan Scaife Grantee
a deed	of one hundered and Seventy acres of land in fee dated the i2th day of the Tenth month i694 acknowledged and delivered by william Crofdell & John Crofdell —— Grantors to Robt Heaton Junr Grantee
a deed–	of Two hundered acres of land In fee dated the 20th

day of the 9th month 1693 acknowledged and ——
delivered by John Cook attorney to John Green Thomas
Green & katherine
Green Grantors to Thomas Brock attorney to Joseph Large
grantee

a deed of Sale & mortgage for Two hundered acres of land in
fee dated the 2nd day of the 9th month 1694 ——
acknowledged & delivered by Phinehas Pemberton
attorney to Joseph Large grantor to John Cook ——
attorney to Samuel Carpenter grantee

a deed of one hundered and Twelve acres of land in fee dated
the first day of the first month 1694 acknowledged and
$$\overline{5}$$
delivered by Phinehas Pemberton attorney to Randel
Blackshaw Grantor to Ralph Cowgill Grantee

a deed of fifty acres of land in fee dated the Tenth day of the
first month 1695 acknowledged and delivered by
$$\overline{6}$$
Clement Dungan grantor to Joseph Large Greantee

Judgment given upon the verdict brought in against James
Heaton for haveing a child by Mary Scaife & it is
fine adjudged that he pay a fine of three pounds & ffees

Court adjourns to the house of Joseph Chorley

268

Complt being made by the overseer of the high way of Make
feild that peter Worral neglected to bring his
teame to the high ways when he had notice so to do by
the sd officer & that the makeing a bridg was there
order–by left undone its therefore ordered that Peter ——
worral do lead the wood for the bridg & help to
lay it up or pay a fine of 25ˢ

order——   whereas divers attempts have been made to bring
about   the arrears of assembley & Councell mens
the fees   fees to Some Certainty & that Som Compensati-
of   on may be made to Such as have been at an ——
members extrordinary Charge by theire long attendance there
of   -in its ordered that the Justices meete together
Council   at the Court house the 18th day Instant to treate
&   with those Concerned & see what will Satifye them

Aſſembly	& give an acc[tt] thereof to the next County Court to be then further Conſidered of by the Grand Jury.
Complt request	being made by Joſph Large of his poverty requeſted the Courts recomendation to Saml Carpenter —— Executor to ffrancis Rossill late of this County deceaſed to have a Share of the Legacy left by Said Roſſill to the poore of this County whereupon
order–	it was ordered that the Clerk do write to ſaid Saml Carpenter to let him have three pounds of the ſd Legacy
verdict	The Jurys verdict in the action wm Rakestraw agt Gilbert wheeler was find for the plantf with coſts of Suite
Judgmt:	whereupon the Court awards Judgment that the deft pay to the Said plaintſ & that Execution Iſſue the ſaid ſum of 4£ with Coſts accordly
Complaint	being made that Some perſons do oppoſe the laying out the Cart way from the mill Dam to the landing at the fferry in Buckingham its there fore ——
ordered	that Henry Baker Peter worral nicholas waln and John wilfford & Enoch yardley or any three of them do lay out the ſame upon a Straightline & make return thereof to the next Court

    Adjourned the Court untill the i8[th]
    day Inſtant at the Court houſe

— — — — — — — — — — — —

269 At a Court held by adjournment the i8 day of the
   firſt month i695
        6

    The Juſtices preſent

  William Biles Richard Hough John Swift
  Samuel Beaks Sherrife
  Phinehas Pemberton Cl: Com:

  adjourned to the houſe of Joſeph Chorley

addreſs being made to this Court by Phinehas Pemberton

about the
Sale of
Adkiſons
land

on behalf and at request of Jane formerly the
wife of Thomas Adkinson but now wife of Willm
Biles requeſting the
approbation of this Court for the diſpoſeing & Sale of three
hundered acres of land given to her by her Said
late huſband Thomas Adkiſon by his laſt will and
Teſtament dureing her natural life & after her ——
deceaſe to his three Sons Isaac william & Samuel
Adkiſon alſo acquainting the Court how that the ſame
might be ſold for a full value & the aforeſaid william
Biles declared that at the requeſt of his ſd wife Jane
& for the benefit of her ſd three ſons had by her firſt
huſband he had Condicended to quit his Claime and
Intreſt in it dureing his ſd wifes life & wold Raise for
the Same ninety pounds and Intreſt for the
reſpective Sums or Shares due to the ſd Sons of ——
Tho: Adkinſon as they Shold Severaly attaine to theire
ſeveral ages   They ſeveraly
acquiting theire Claime or title to the ſaid land and
premiſes as they shold severaly Re: theire parts & ——
shares of the ſaid mony & Intreſt viz: To Iſaac Adkinſon
at the age of 2i yeares thirty pounds & the Intreſt thereof
to william Adkinſon the like ſum of thirty pounds with the
Intreſt thereof when attained to the age of 2i yeares
to Samuel Adkinſon the like ſum of thirty pounds with
the Interest thereof when attained to the age of 2i yeares
and this Court haveing fuly Conſidered that the ſaid
ninety pounds is a full value for the lands & that the
Sale there of will much Conduce to the bettering and ——
Improveing the ſaid Childrens Eſtate & be divers ways
advantagious to them this Court adjudged that the
Said Land be ſold and the mony Secured as aforeſd

270

what was
done about
the members
of Council
& assembleys
fees

Whereas it was ordered laſt Court that the Juſtices Shold
meet this day and aſſertaine the Councill and
aſſembley mens fees that have been at extrordinary
Charge in theire Long ſervice & have as yet had
no Compenſation for the Same which they accordingly
did but few made appearance here this day to make demand & therefore it was beleived much was not
expected but haveing difcourſt with thoſe preſent they
were found to be moderated & ſeemed Rather to

Seek to have an end put to the Said affaire then
theire own Intreſt & Cold not perceive but that if
the Grand Jury wold make Some ſuitable preſents
to thoſe that had been at an extrordinary Charge
by Reaſon of theire long Continuance in the ſaid
places that it wold put an end to it
adjourned to the 10th of the 4th month next

Bucks ſS:

At a Court held by the kings authority in the —
name of william penn abſolute proprietarie and
govrnr of the province of penſilvania and Counties
annexed at the Court houſe for the aforeſaid — —
County the 10th day of the 4 month 1696

The Juſtices preſent

Joseph Growdon   William Biles } Juſtices
Henry Baker   Richard Hough }

John Cook Corronor
Sam¹ Beaks Sherrif
Phinehas Pemberton Cl: Com:

Eſtreat

John Snowden being Summoned to ſerve on the
Jury this Court & for his non appearance according
to Summons the Court fines him in five shillings

grand Jury
atteſted —

Jonathan Scaife   Joſuah Hoops   Samuel Dark
James paxſon   John Brock   Joſeph Wood
Henry Marjorum   Joſeph millner
           Thomas Hardin
willm Paxſon   John palmer   Richard wilſon
Joſeph Clows   Andrew Ellot
           Thomas ſtakehouſe Jnr
william Smith   Joſeph kirkbridge   all atteſted

271

—A deed of partition of the moiety of Twenty Two acres of land in
ffee dated
the Sixteenth day of the firſt month 1695 was acknowledged
and delivered by peter white & Ellizabeth his wife grantors
to Anthony Burton & Thomas Brock grantees

—a deed of portion of the other moiety of the fame Twenty acres of Land in ffee dated the faid fixteenth day of the firft month 1695 was acknowledged and delivered by Anthony Burton & Thomas Brock grantors to peter white Grantee

—A deed–in ffee for fifty acres of Land dated the 30 day of decemb 1695 acknowledged & delivered by Thomas Brock attorney to Matts kan Hance Loyke Elizabeth Johnfon and ―― katherine Johnfon Grantors to Breta Johnfon grantee

—A deed–in ffee for one hundred acres of land dated the 4th day of feptember 1695 was acknowledged and delivered by Thomas Brock attorney to Thomas ffaireman Grantor to Dunken ―― williams grantee

—A deed in ffee for Two hundred forty six acres of land dated the 17 day of the 3 month acknowledged and delivered by John Town Attorney to Ralph ward & Thomas Jenner grantors unto Thomas Stakehoufe Unior Grantee

—An Indenture of partion for the moiety of ii acres of land in ffee dated the 8 day of the 4 month 1696 was acknowledged and delivered by Thomas Brock grantor to Anthony ―― Burton grantee

—An Indenture of partion for the other moiety of the faid ii acres of land in ffee was acknowledged and delivered by Anthony Burton grantor to Thomas Brock Grantee

—A deed–in ffee of foure hundred and fifty acres of land taken in Execution to
fatifye the debts of Jofeph Holden bearing date the eighteenth day of the 2 month was acknowledged and delivered
in open Court by Samuel Beaks the then fherrife Grantor to Jofeph Growdon Grantee

—A deed ffor the abovefaid foure hundered and fifty acres of land in ffee dated the 30 day of the firft month 1694 was acknowledged and delivered by Jofeph Growdon grantor to John naylor Grantee

—A deed of Two hundred thirty fix acres of land in ffee dated the 8 day of the fourth month 1696 was acknowledged & delivered by Samuel Beaks grantor to John ―― neild grantee

—The former Record of Court againe allowed and approved in Relation to Thomas Adkifons Lands & fecurity given in Court at the fame time for the Confideration mony by william Biles unto Phineas Pemberton & Richard Hough in truft for the heires of faid Akdifon —— ——

—A deed of Three hundred acres of land in ffee dated the Tenth day of the fourth month one Thoufand fix hundered ninety fix acknowledged and delivered in open Court by william Biles and Jane Biles his wife grantors to george Biles grantee

Execution agt Gilbert wheeler in willm Rakeftraws Cafe returned fully Levyed according to the Contents thereof by Samuel — Beaks fherrife

272

Complaint being made by Jofeph Chorley & mary his wife of feveral abufes done to them by Richard Thatcher & Bartholemew Thatcher as that they did ftrike the faid Chorley & his wife in the faid Chorley's houfe to the fheding of Blood which fact the faid Richard Thatcher & Bartholemew — Thatcher Confeft to be true & fubmited to the Court where upon the Court fines them Richard Thather in in forty
ffine fhillings & Bartholemew Thather in Twenty fhillings to be paid to the proprietor & govrnr & that they be bound to theire good behaviour for one yeare

Recognizance Richard Thatcher acknowledged him felf Indebted to the proprietor & govr willm Penn the fum of Twenty pounds & the faid Bartholemew Thather acknowledged him felf Indebted to the faid proprietor in Ten pounds to be Levied on theire Lands & tenements goods & Chatles under Condition that he the faid Richard Thatcher Shold be of good abearing towards the faid proprietarie & all the kings fubjects for one whole & yeare

requeft George Heathcoat & John fiddal defired the matter in diference between them might be fufpended untill the next Court

Recognizance Bartholemew Thatcher acknowledged him felf Indebted Twenty pounds & Richard Thatcher in Ten Pounds to the proprietor & Governor willm pen to be
levied on theire lands & tenements goods & Chattles under Condition that fhold be of good abeareing towards the fd proprietarie & all the kings fubjects for one whole yeare

adjournment adjourned untill 9 a Clock to morrow morning

Holdens Estate — whereas the eftate of Jofeph Holden was formerly taken in Execution to fatiffye the feveral debts due from the faid Holder to his Creditors and the accts thereof are not as yet brought in of the faid eftate by Samuel Beakes Sherrife it is therefore ordered that the said fherrife do bring in an acctt thereof & of what monys is in the hands of Jofeph Growdon & how much is paid out of the faid eftate to anfwer the feveral Judgments of the Court

adjournment — adjourned the Court for one houre

Grand jurys prefentments

(1) we the jurrors for the body of this County do prefent the great neceffity of a roade to be layd out from new Towne to the landing at Gilbert Wheelers for the fervice of Inha bitants both of new Town & the neighbourhood on this fide

(2) we do prfent the overfeer or fupervifor for the falls townfhip for neglecting the high roade to mend the fame—(viz:) the road leading from Gilbert wheers to midle Townfhip —

(3) Alfo we do prefent the neceffity of Clearing & mending the road that's layd out from Henry Bakers to the ferry over agt Burling

(4) Alfo we do prfent the neceffity of a rate to be made through out this County of three half pence per pound & heads according ly according to the law provided in that Cafe viz: after the the manner of one peny p pound and six fhillings p head for the defraying of neceffary Charges of the faid County and alfo that a Collector in every Townfhip be Chofen to Collect the fame & that Two honeft fubftantial men be Chofsen to be receivors in order to — which we propofe Jofuah Hoops william Paxfon Samuel Dark & Jonathan fcaife & that any two of them which the Court fhall think fitt may ferve to Receive and pay all fuch mony as fhall be Collected & payd to them by the order of the Court & grand jury and that the faid Receivors Shall be accountable when & fo often as the Court & grand jury fhall fee meet.

(5) alfo we do prefent Ralph Boome & Jofeph Croffe for unlawfull takeing & Carrying away a black walnut Logg of Claws Jonfon Edward Lane and Willm

	Howard & John Jonſon from John Bowens Landing at the bottom of neſhaminah Creek
road —	prſent-ment of a road from Wrights Town to the Landing at the ferry agt Burlington brought in
roade —	The road from the mill pond to the Landing at the fferry afforeſd agt Burlington prſented to be Layd as ſtraight as may be
order —	upon the prſentment of the neceſſity of a Cartroad from newtowne to the landing at Gilbert wheelers the Court appoints willm Buckman Joſuah Hoops Jonathan ſcaife william Dark & Jon Hough to lay out the ſame
petetion	of Iſaac Burges declareing his want of releiſe
ordered	that Juſtice Growdon Inſpect his neceſſity & —— allow him what is fit for a preſent ſupplye
preſentmt	upon the Grand jurys prſentmt of Ralph Boome & Joseph Croſſ unlawfull takeing away of a black walnut Logg belonging to Claws Jonſon Edward Lane wm Howard & John Jonſon from John Bowens Landing at the bottom of neſhaminah Creek
deftes	pleaded not guilty & for tryal put them ſelves on the Cuntry
venire	ſherrif is Commanded to return a jury wch was accordingly done
jury	ptr worrall Robert Heaton Henry Hudleſtone willm Croſdell peter White willm Buckman John pidcock Jeremiah Langhorn Wm Taylor John neild Andrew Heath Abraham Cox all
atteſted	John Bowen Lucy Boare Henry Bowen Margret matthews atteſted for the plants:
ordered	by the Court that the Juſtices meet the 22 day of this Inſtant to aſſeſſ the Tax at the Court houſe prſented by the grand jury neceſſary to be raiſed.
A deed 274	of Two hundered and fifty acres of land in fee dated the eight day of the fourth month one Thouſand ſix hundred ninety ſix acknowledged and delivered by Henry —— marjorum Grantor to Henry Baker grantee

verdict	jury finds for the plt Twenty fhillings with Coft of fuite
Judgmt	Given and it is adjudged that the faid Jofeph Crofs and Ralph Boome pay accordingly & that Execution Iffue accordingly
ordered	that peter worral & Enoch yardley & Henry Baker or any two of them lay out the road from the mill dam to the Common Landing at the ferry
adjournment	adjourned to the 22 day of this Inftant month

Bucks fs: At a Court held by adjournment the 22 day of the $\frac{4}{mo}$

1696

Juftices then prefent

william Biles Henry Baker Richard Hough

Sam^{ll}: Beakes Sherrife Phineas Pemberton Cl. Com:

accounts	of Thomas Brock hath been in pte examined but find the orriginal Tax book is wanting that was made under the Commif -fion of Benjamaine fletcher & no Recipts of any mony paid by the faid Brock late Sherrife to be found therefore the faid acc^{ts} are defferred untill — an other time and its
ordered	that Sam^{ll} Beakes the prfent Sherrife do fpeake to John Swift one of the Juftices under that Commiffion and enquire of him for
to	the orriginal Tax book & the Acc^{tts} brought in by faid Brock the grand jury that the faid acc^{tts} may be brought in & pfected at the next Court
Tax	whereas the grand jury laft Court prfented the neceffity of raifeing a — Tax of three half pence pte on the Clear value of real & pfonal eftates & 9^d p pole on thofe that are not otherwife rated according as the law directs in that Cafe for the defraying of neceffary Charges of the aforefaid County
ordered	& agreed that the feveral Inhabitants be valued as they were in the laft tax except where there is manifeft Caufe

to the Conterary & that all such as are Taxable that have
beene heretofore omitted be entered in this Tax & that
this be regarded & altered by the Clerke as he fhall find
any error or omiffion made now in this Court in the
tranfcribeing of the faid Tax

petition of Ifaac Burges in relation to a debt due to him from
his brother Sam^{ll} Burges was read and the Court ——

appoints Jofeph kirkbride to fpeake to faid faml Burges & advife
him to reffer the mater in diferenc to Indiferent men to
be by them Chosen but if he fhall refufe the faid advice then
then willm Biles & Richard Hough do take what further
Care is fitt to accomodate the matter in diference as may
be found moft expedient & expeditious

   adjourned for one houre

ordered that the Clerk write the Tax faire over agt next Court
275 & after allowance thereof to draw out duplicates of every
Townfhips Tax respectively

Collectors ordered for the feverall Townfhips

for
- Buckingham   Anthony Burton
- ffals — — — — Samll Beakes
- makefeild — — Jofeph milner
- middle Town ——⎫
- new Town —— ⎬ wm Crofdel
- wrights Towne ⎪
- & Lands adjacent ⎭
- Benfalem — — John Gilbert
- fouth hampton & Lands adjacent } John Cuttler

ordered that Jonathan Scaife & Samll Darke be receviors
of the County Tax to be difpofed of as the Court fhall
appoint

—A deed of Several lotts of land (in Buckingham) in fee dated fixteenth day of the fourth month 1696 acknowledged and
delivered by willm Crofdell attorney to Thomas Brock
  Anthony Burton peter
white & Elizabeth his wife grantors to phineas pemberton
grantee

—A deed of one lott of land in fee (in Buckingham) dated the Twenty
ſecond day of the fourth month one Thouſand ſix hundred
ninety ſix acknowledged and delivered by Anthony Burton
grantor to phineas pemberton Attorney to ſamll Bowne
grantee

—A deed of one lott of land in fee (in Buckingham) dated 22 day of
the 4 month 1696 acknowledged and delivered by ——
Anthony Burton grantor to willm Croſdel grantee

—A deed of one lott of land in fee (in Buckingham) dated 22
day of the 4 month 1696 acknowledged and delivered
by Anthony Burton grantor Henry Baker grantee ——

A deed — of ſeveral lotts of land in fee (in Buckingham) dated the
ſixteenth day of the fourth month 1696 was acknowledged
and delivered by Anthony Burton Attorney to the
peter white & Elizabeth white his wife grantors
to Phineas pemberton Attorney to ſaml Carpenter —
grantee

adjournment   adjourned to the 9th day of the
7 month next

Bucks ſS: 276
At a Court of Quarter ſseſſions by the kings
authority in the name of william penn abſolute
proprietarie and govrnr of the province of
penſylvania and Territories thereunto belong
-ing at the Court houſe for the Said County the
9th day of the 7th month 1696.

The Juſtices present

Joſeph Growdon   Henry Baker ——
Richard Hough   John Swift
Samll Beaks Sherrife
Phineas Pemberton Cl: Com: —— ——

roade — peter worrall Enoch yardley &c make return —
that they have laid out the road from the mill —
Dam in Buckingham to the Common landing
by the fferry houſe upon a ſtraight line

roade — 3 day of the 7 month 1696 we whoſe names are
hereunder written being appointed by order of the

laſt Court to lay out a roade (viz a Cart roade from
new Town to the fferry at Gilbert wheelers pur-
ſuant to the ſaid order we accordingly have met —
together and Layd it out according to the beſt of
our underſtanding (viz) from new town to the Creek
Commonly Called the old mans Creek or Core Creek by
a line of marked trees from thence to James ſutton
by a line of marked trees from thence to ſtony hill —
by a line of marked trees from thenc by the houſe
of widow Lucas or ſome of that familys by a line
of marked trees from thence by a line of marked
trees into the kings roade that leads to philadel-
-phia from Gilbert wheelers & from thence to the
ffalls along the kings roade

requeſt   In order to effect the ſaid roade we deſire
the Court wold be pleaſed to give out ordr that the
ſaid road may be Cleared with as much expedition
as may be for the uſe & benefit of all the ——
Inhabitants Concerned

witnes our hands

   will Buckman
   Joſhua Hoops
   Jonathan ſcaiſe
   John Hough

Tax   againe allowed and a warrant signed for the ——
277   Collecting thereof

Conſtables Choſen

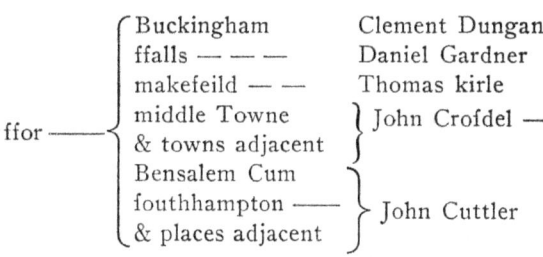

ffor — Buckingham   Clement Dungan
    ffalls — — —   Daniel Gardner
    makeſeild — —   Thomas kirle
    middle Towne   } John Croſdel —
    & towns adjacent
    Bensalem Cum
    ſouthhampton —— } John Cuttler
    & places adjacent

overſeers of the high ways

304   RECORDS OF THE COURTS OF QUARTER SESSIONS AND

for —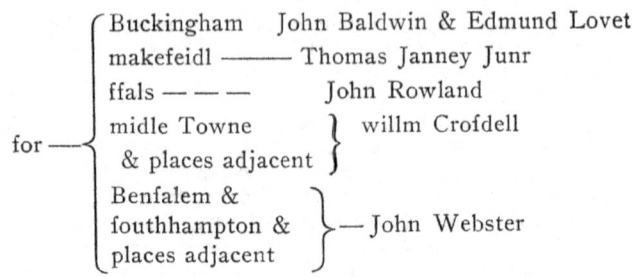
⎧ Buckingham   John Baldwin & Edmund Lovet
⎪ makefeidl ——— Thomas Janney Junr
⎪ ffals — — —   John Rowland
⎨ midle Towne   ⎫ willm Crofdell
⎪ & places adjacent ⎭
⎪ Benfalem &   ⎫
⎪ fouthhampton &   ⎬ — John Webster
⎩ places adjacent   ⎭

—A deed— of Two hundered and fifty acres of land in ffee —
dated the fourth day of the fourth month 1694
acknowledged and delivered by Jofeph Chorley —
Attorney to John otter grantor to Henry Baker
grantee

—A deed— of Two small parcells of land in ffee dated the
14 day of the 12th month 1693 acknowledged &
delivered by phineas pemberton attorney to
Randle Blackfhaw grantor to Jofeph kirkbride
grantee

—A deed   of five hundred acres of land in ffee dated the
23 day of july 1696 acknowledged and delivered
by Jofeph kirkbride grantor to phineas pemberton
for the ufe of Gideon ffreborn grantee —

adjourn ment   adjourned to the 9th of the 10 next
                                               ——
                                                mo
                                                                    278

Bucks fs: At a Court of Quarter feffions held by the kings
authority in the name of william Penn abfolute
proprietarie and Govrnr of the province of
penfylvania & Territories thereunto belong
-ing at the Court houfe for the faid County the
9th day of the 10th month being **the 8 yeare**
of king willm: the 2nd of his raigne over —
England &c. annoquoe dm: 1696

         The Juftices prfent

Jofeph Growdon willm: Biles Henry —
Baker Richard Hough John Swift ——
Sam1 Beakes Sherrife
Phineas pemberton Cl: Com:

—A deed— of Two hundred thirty five acres of land in fee dated the firſt day of the 10 month 1696 acknowledged and delivered by willm Darke grantor to John Dark grantee

—A deed of five hundred acres of land in fee dated the Twenty seventh day of the 4th month 1696 acknowledged and delivered by phineas pemberton attorney to Samll Bown grantor to Samll Beakes attorney to Richard willits gardian to Hannah willits his daughter grantee

—A deed— of one lott of land in fee (in Buckingham) dated the 8th day of the 10th month 1696 acknowledged and delivered by peter white & Elizabeth white wife of the Said peter grantors to Joſeph Growdon Grantee

An Indenture of ſale & mortgage in fee for Two lotts of Land in Buckingham dated the 9th day of the 10th month 1696 acknowledged and delivered by —— Thomas Brock grantor to Stephen nowel Grantee

—a deed of fifty acres of land in fee dated the 9th day of the fourth month 1696 acknowledged and delivered in open Court in the ſaid County by Clement Dungan grantor to Edward Doyle grantee

—a deed of one hundred fifty five acres of land in fee dated the ninth day of the 10th month 1696 acknowledged and delivered by John webſter grantor to ſamuel Burges Junr grantee

—a deed of fifty acres of land in fee dated the firſt day of the 10th month 1696 acknowledged & delivered by Thomas Dure grantor willm Darby grantee ——

—A deed of one hundred and ſix acres of land in fee dated
279   the fourth day of September 1694 acknowledged and delivered by phineas pemberton Attorney to Henry Burcham and margret Burcham his wife grantors to James Boyden Junr attorney to willm Hughs — grantee

—A deed–of the ſaid one hundred and ſix acres of Land in fee dated the 9th day of September 1696 acknowledged & delivered by James Boyden attorney to Willm Hughes grantor to Daniel Done Attorney to Thomas Bills — grantee

action — Arthur Cook agt Tho. Rogrs they both appeared and defired the fame might be fufpended untill next Court

adjournment   adjourned untill tomorrow morning at 9 a Clock

certificate of Jofiah Blackfhaws being alive Signed — —

Richard Thatcher being Committed for breaking the peace was Called & Confeffed the fact & fubmitted to the Court — whereupon the Court ordered ordrs that he give fureties for his appearance at the Court to be held in the 10th month in the yeare 1697 & to be of good abearing in the meane time and to be Comitted to prifon untill he pforme the fame
The Court alfo awards judgment that he had forfeited his former recognizance

grand jury Jofuah Hoops wm Paxfon Ezra Crofdel James paxfon Jofeph kirkbride George Brown Willm Biles Jof: wood ftephen Sands Richard wilfon Ralph Cowgill John fmith John Snowden wm Dark all attefted ——

grand juries prefentments } we present Jofeph Smalwood for prophane fwearing

we prefent the bridge on Widow Lucas land in the roade leading from the falls to new Towne

we prefent the neceffity of a bridge over Core Creek leading from new Town to the fferry

we prefent the neceffity of mentaineing the way from middle towne to the falls

Bucks fs: The jurors for the proprietarie & govrnr by the kings authority do prfent ftephen nowel for entering into the houfe of peter white the 2i day of 7 month laft paft & did then and there violently affault with Batterie the wife of faid peter white & the wife of the faid ftephen nowell & did alfo open a Cheft & ffelonoufly take out of the faid Cheft about five pounds of filver mony and one filver fpoone & one filver Chaine the Chaine & fpoone

280*

|280| the proper goods of peter white Conterary to the kings peace and the ftatute laws in that cafe made & provided

peter white profecutor   Ellizabeth white } wittneffes
                         Ellizabeth nowel }

vera billa   we find this bill

pleaded — not Guilty & for tryal put him felf on the Cuntry where

venire   upon the fherrife was Commanded to return a jury wch was done as ffolloweth

Jury — Gilbert wheeler   Henry Marjorum   Jeremiah Langhorn — Stephen Beakes   ffrancis Tunneclift   James moone fenr — John Brock   faml Coates   Wm Darby   james Yates   Saml Hough   James moone junr   all attefted

wittneffes Ellizabeth white & Ellizabeth nowel proved the prfentmt agt ft nowel

Complaints about the Tax redreffed

ordered   that phineas pemberton examine the accts of Tho: **Brock**

Recognizance   Richard Thatcher did acknowledg him felf Indebted to the proprietary & govrnr in the fum of 20 £ & Jofeph Thatcher in the fum of 10 £ to be levied on theire lands and tenements goods & Chattles and this upon Condition that the faid Richard Thatcher Shall appeare at the Court of Quarter feffions to be held in the 10th month in the yeare 1697 and not to depart the Said Court untill he Shall have licence fo to do & to be of good abearing in the meane time

verdict — we of the jury do find Stephen nowell guilty of ftrikeing of Elizabeth white in the houfe of peter white figned in the behalf of the jury by Gilbert wheeler foreman

judgment   given and it was adjudged that Stephen nowell Shold pay the Coft of Court & that Execution iffue accordingly and that he give fuerties for his appearance at the next Court of Quarter feffions to be held for this County & to be of good abearing in the meane time

---

*This page is numbered twice.

Recognizance   Stephen nowell acknowledged him felf Indebted
to the proprietarie & govrnr wm Penn in the fum of
20 £ & george Duncan & James moone Junr each in
10 £ to be levied on theire lands and tenements goods &
Chattles and this upon Condition that the faid ftephen
nowell Shall appeare at the next Court of Quarter —
feffions to

petition —of Edward Doyal Read feting forth his want of releife

ordered   that Samll Beakes pay him out of the County Levie
the fum of

fatiffaction on a Judgment obtained by willm Rakeftraw againft
Gilbert wheeler was made appeare in Court by a rect
under faid Rakeftraws hand dated the 2 day of the $\frac{5}{mo}$
i696 in Samull Beakes the fherrifs Cuftody

ordered   that the Several Collectors do pay the mony they
$\underline{281}$ Receive on the late County Tax to Saml Dark
or Jonathan Scaife & take theire or either of
theire Receits for So much mony as they pay and
that the faid Saml Dark & Jonathan fcaife —
bring the Said mony to the next Court then and
there to be difpofed of by the Court for the —
defraying the neceffary Charges of the County
to what other ufes it was raifed

adjourned to the 9th day of the firft month next

Bucks fs:
At a Court of Quarter feffions
held by the kings authority in the
name of willm penn proprietarie
and governr of the province
of penfylvania and Territories
thereunto belonging at the Court
houfe for the aforefaid County the
10th day of the firft month being
the 8th yeare of the king reigne
and 17 yeare of the proprietaries
govrmt over the faid province $\frac{1696}{7}$

The Juſtices present
william Biles   Henry Baker
Richard Hough
Jonathan Scaife Corronor
Samll Beaks Sherrife
Phineas Pemberton Cl: Com:

Commiſſ Corronors Commiſſion read

—A deed— of five Thouſand acres of Land in fee dated the ninth day of the firſt month 1696/7 acknowledged and delivered by willm Biles Attorney to Thomas — Hudſon grantor to Stephen Beaks attorney to willm Lawrence John Talman Joſeph Thorn Samuel Thorn & Benjemaine ffeild grantees

—A deed of Two hundred and fifty acres of land in fee dated the 5th day of the firſt month 1696/7 was acknowledged and delivered by phineas pemberton Granto unto Stephen Beakes for the uſe of william kenerley and his heires Grantee

—A deed —of one hundred and Twenty five acres of Land in ffee dated the eight day of the Tenth month one Thouſand Six hundred ninety Six acknowledged and delivered by Joſuah Hoops grantor to Daniel Hoops Grantee

+A deed of Six hundred and Sixteen acres and Two thirds of an acre in ffee dated the Twenty firſt day of the eleventh month one Thouſand Six hundred ninety Six was acknowledged and delivered by Henry Baker — Grantor to peter worral Attorney to John Harriſon Grantee

A deed of Twenty five acres of land in fee dated the — Twenty firſt day of the Eleventh month one Thouſand Six hundred ninety Six acknowledged and — delivered by william Biles attorney to Thomas Hudſon Grantor to peter worral Attorney to John Harriſon Grantee

—A deed of foure hundred acres of land in fee dated the
Twentieth day of the eight month one Thouſand
Six hundered ninety Six acknowledged and
delivered by John Smith Attorney to Arthur Cooke
and John Cook Grantors to John Circuit grantee

—A deed of one Thouſand and fifty acres of land in ffee dated the
Twenty firſt day of the eleventh month one Thouſand
Six hundred ninety Six acknowledged and —
delivered unto peter worral Attorney to Matthias
Harvie grantee by william Biles Attorney to
Thomas Hudſon grantor

—A deed of Two hundred ninety Six acres of land in ffee
dated the firſt day of the Tenth month one Thouſand
Six hundred ninety Six acknowledged and delivered
by Joſeph Chorley Attorney to John Clark grantor
unto Joſeph milner Grantee

—A deed of one hundred and Seventy acres of land in fee
dated the Tenth day of the firſt month one Thouſand
Six hundred ninety Six acknowledged and delivered
by Robert Heaton Junior Grantor to Jonathan
Scaiſe Grantee

—A deed of Two hundred Thirty Six acres of land in ffee
dated the Sixth day of the firſt month one Thouſand
Six hundred ninety Six acknowledged and
delivered by Abel Janney Grantor to Richard
Hough Grantee

—A deed of Two acres of meadow land in fee dated the
ninth day of the fourth month one Thouſand ſix
ninety Six acknowledged and delivered by
Enoch yardley grantor to Ruben pownal grantee

—A deed of fifty acres of land in ffee dated the fifth of
283 the firſt month one Thouſand Six hundred ninety
Six acknowledged and delivered by Joſeph Chorley
Attorney to Elixabeth Bennet grantor to Thomas
yardley Grantee

—A deed of eighteen acres and a half of land in ffee
dated the Sixth day of the firſt month one Thouſand
Six hundred ninety Six acknowledged and
delivered by John white Grantor to John Smith
grantee

—A deed of nine acres and a Quarter of land in fee dated —
the eighth day of the firſt month one Thouſand Six
hundered ninety Six acknowledged and delivered
by John Smith grantor to John Town Grantee

—A deed of about foure acres and a half in fee dated the
eight day of the firſt month one Thouſand ſix
hundered ninety Six acknowledged and delivered
by John Smith Grantor to Phineas pemberton
Attorney to Thomas muſgrave grantee

—A deed of a Small lott of land in ffee dated the ninth
day of the firſt month one Thouſand Six hundered
ninety Six acknowledged and delivered by John
Town Grantor to Henry Baker partner to ſamuel
Carpenter grantee

—A deed of Two hundered and ninety acres of land in ffee
dated the firſt day of the firſt month one Thouſand
Six hundered ninety Six acknowledged and —
delivered by Randol Blackſhaw
grantor Joſe: kirkbride grantee

—A deed of eight hundered acres of land in ffee dated firſt
day of the firſt month one Thouſand Six hundered
ninety Six acknowledged and delivered by Randol
Blackſhaw grantor to Joſeph kirkbride for the
uſe of nehemiah Blackſhaw Son to the
Said Randol grantee

—A deed of Two hundered acres of land in ffee dated the
firſt day of the firſt month one Thouſand Six hundered
ninety Six acknowledged and delivered by Randol
Blackſhaw grantor to Joſeph kirkbride for the uſe of Abraham
Cowgill and nehemiah
Cowgill ſons of Ralph Cowgill grantees

ordered & the ſaid Randol Blackſhaw ordered the ſaid deed
after recorded to be delivered to the ſaid Joſeph
kirkbride to be by him kept untill the Said Abraham
and nehemiah Shold Come of age

—A deed of one hundered and Twelve acres of land in ffee
dated the firſty day of the firſt month one Thouſand
Six hundered ninety Six acknowledged and —
delivered by Ralph Cowgill grantor to Joſeph kirkbride
grantee

284

A deed— of four hundred and eighty acres of land in fee acknowledged and Delivered being dated the fourth day of december one Thouſand Six — hundered eighty nine by Henry pawlin grantor to Richard Burges Grantee
and the ſeale of the ſaid deed being Imperfect & broken he the ſaid Pawlin did amend and new make the Said ſeale in open Court before the delivery there of

the death of Richard Atthary returned by the corronor to be a natural death

aſſeſſors choſen for the ffollowing yeare John Gilbert Jonathan Scaiſe Joſeph milner
Edmund Lovet Samuel Dark Henry Baker

Complaint being made by John Siddal that George Heath coate had taken out of his houſe ſeveral goods by vertue of a warrant of ſearch and refuſed to proſe cute or bring the ſaid matter to A hearing the he was bound ſo to do neare a yeare agoe by recog -nizance and that he the ſaid ſiddal had given his Attendance at Every Court to make his defence & therefore Craved an order from this Court to have his goods reſtored to him againe whereupon

its ordered the Said Complaint appeareing to be true that the Conſtable in whoſe Cuſtody the ſaid goods are do reſtore the ſaid goods ſo taken to the ſaid John ſiddal he the ſaid ſiddal paying the ffes was Cleared by proclamation —

ordered that the Collectors and Receivors of the County Tax give theire Attendance here and pay in the mony Collected by them the firſt day of the 2 month next adjourned the Court to the firſt day of the of the Second month next enſueing

At a Court held by adjournment the 1ˢᵗ day of the 2/mo 1697

The Juſtices preſent

william Biles   Henry Baker
Richard Hough   John Swift
Samˡ Beakes   Sherrife
Phineas Pemberton Cl: Com:

adjourned the Court to the houſe of Joſeph Chorley

Grand Jury Joſuah Hoops   John palmer   Edmund Lovet
Abraham Cox John Rowland   James Boyden Junr
Robt Heaton   Henry Hudleſtone   Enoch yardley
William Duncan   Stephen Beakes   James moone
Joſeph Milner   John Gilbert   Samuel Dark
John Grifith   all Atteſted

$\overline{285}$ accounts made up in open Court with divers perſons about wolf heads

adjourned the Court for one houre

accounts more made up with divers perſons about wolfs and the accounts returned to Saml Dark

accounts about wolves Ballanced about Wolves with Joſuah Hoops John palmer Henry * * *

accounted with John Swift & he was then debtor to the County as may appear by the account in Saml Darks hand 1 £ i5ˢ 3ᵈ and that Jos Growdon had detained in his hand from John Gilbert the Collector of Benſalem Tax 5 £ –9ˢ –0ᵈ

makefeild Tax amounted ii £ : i4ˢ : 3ᵈ being a * * * made the $\frac{4}{\text{mo}}$ 1696 to defray the neceſſary Charges of the County

Recognizance Stephen newel & George Duncan * * * diſcharged therefrom being bound to appeare at this Court

Stephen newel appeared to proſecute in a Caſe agt Claws Johnſon according to a recognizance as he Saith Taken before Joſeph Growdon and it being the Second time of his appearance & no recognizance returned the Court difcharged him from the fame

—a deed of Two hundered and fifty acres of land in fee dated the Twelfth day of the i month $\frac{1696}{7}$ acknowledged and delivered by John Cartor grantor to John Smith grantee

—a deed of a lot of land in Buckingham in fee dated the 25 day of october acknowledged & delivered by John Smith grantor to Richard Burges grantee

—a deed of Two hundered & ninety acres of land in fee dated the 22 day of March $\frac{1696}{7}$ acknowledged and delivered by Saml Beaks attorney Ifrael Taylor grantor to John Grifith grantee

—one Indenture of mortgage and fale of the above mentioned Two hundered and ninety acres of land was acknowledged and delivered by John Grifith aforefaid mortgageor to Abraham Cox attorney to the aforefaid Ifrael Taylor mortgagee

presentments of the Grand Jury (286)
we of the Grand Jury of the County of Bucks do prefent the neceffity of repaireing the bridge between this County & the County of philadelphia on poquefin Creek

The i day 2 mo 1697

we do alfo acquaint the Court that we wold have phineas pemberton and Arthur Cook each of them to have eight pounds paid them out of the County Tax in full for theire Service and Attendance in Council & affembley or any difburfements thereupon provided they give difcharges to the County in full upon the acceptance & Receipt there of

we alfo wold have Jofeph Growdon to have Six pounds payd accordingly he accepting the Same & difchargeing the County accordingly in full for his fervice attendance

& other disburfements in or about the Council or —
assembley
phineas pemberton declared then in Court that he
wold accept the Same & accordingly difcharged the
County whereupon it was

ordered that william Crofdel Collector of the Tax in the
middle Townfhip Should pay to the faid phineas pem
berton eight pounds out of the Said Tax —

ordered that Saml Beaks Collector of the Tax in the
ffalls Town Ship pay to the administrators of wm
Beaks eight pounds fourteen Shillings foure pence
being the ballance of an acc^{tt} due to faid Beaks
in his life time for difburfements about the
building the Court houfe &c:

The petition of the Inhabitants of Benfalem about laying
out of a road to the fferry at Dunk williams deffered
for the prefent

—a deed one hundered & fifty acres of land in fee dated the
10th day of the $\frac{3}{\text{mo}}$ 1689 acknowledged & delivered by
phineas pemberton Attorney to Edward Smith grantor
to Jofeph kirkbride grantee

ordered that Arthur Cook be payd out of the County levyes
the Sum of eight pounds according to the grand Juries
requeft he difcharging accordingly

and That Jofeph Growdon be payd Six pounds on
the fame Terms

adjourned untill the 9th of the 4 month next

Bucks ff: 287

At a Court held in the name of William — — —
penn proprietarie of the province of penfylvania
and Counties Annexed at the Court houfe for the — —
aforefaid County the 9th day of the 4th month 1697

Juſtices present

Joſeph Growdon william Biles Henry Baker
Richard Hough John Swift
Jonathan Scaiſe Corronor
Samuel Beake Sherriſe
Phineas Pemberton Cl: Com:

The Grand Jury Joſua Hoops foreman

Anthony Burton Edmund Lovet Abraham Cox Stephen wilſon
Henry Margerum John Brock John white Thomas Brock —
Peter worral Thomas Stakehouſe William Hayhurſt James moon
John palmer ffrancis white John Snowdon Shadrach walley
William Duncan willm Dark Ruben pownal John Stakehouſe

} all Atteſted

26ᵗʰ 3 / mo   Action Entered

Iſaac merriot plt
    agt
Samuel Jerrom deft
} in an action upon the Caſe

Bucks ſſ   Theſe are by the kings authority in the name of william penn
Locus   proprietarie and govrnr to require thee to Arreſt the body of
Sigilli   Samll Jerrome if found in they Balywick and him Safely keep
Arreſt   and have at the next Court to be held at the Court houſe for the
           aforeſaid County the 9ᵗʰ day of the 4ᵗʰ month next as well to anſwer
           the Complt of Iſaac Merriot of Burlington in weſt Jerſey merchant
           in a plea on the Caſe as to abide the Judgmt of the ſd Court
           and make return hereof and of thy doings herein at the sd Court
           faile not at thy perril and for thy ſo doing this Shall be thy —
           ſuffitient warrant given under my hand and Seale of the County
           the 27ᵗʰ day of the 3 month 1697

To Samll Beakes Sherriſe of the ſaid   William Biles
County of Bucks theſe

Bucks ſſ By vertue of the within the body of Samuel Jerrome was return } Arrested the 27th day of the 3 month 1697 p

Samll Beakes sherrife

Declaracon Bucks ff

Isaac merriot plt
agt
Samuel Jerrome deft
} in a plea upon the Case

Isaac Merriot of Burlington in west Jersey Complts agt Samll Jerrome for that whereas the Said deft Stands Justly Indebted to the sd plt in the Sum of Six pounds Six shillings and ten pence half penny Currant Silver mony being due to the Said plt for divers goods wares and merchandizes by him

290* Sold to the Said Defte for which he the Said Jerrome did assume and faithfully promise to pay all which the sd plt aver notwithstanding the
Said deft: his promise and Assumption not regarding but Endeavoring
and fraudulently Intending him the Said plt in this behalfe Craftely and Subtilly to deceive and defraud hitherto hath refused and Still doth refuse the Same to pay whereupon action doth accrew to the sd plt and Craves Judgmt of this Court agt the sd Samll Jerrome for the sd Sum of Six pounds Six shillings and ten pence half peny with thirty Shillings damages and Cost of suite &c:

action Called both plt and defend appeared

declarcon read

Judgmt
Confest
} The Said Samuel Jerrome Confessed he owed unto the Isaac merriot the Said Sum of Six pounds Six Shillings ten pence half penny

Judgmt &
Execucon
awarded
accordingly
} { whereupon Judgmt was awarded for the Said Sum and that Execut
Issue accordingly & for Cost of suite

A deed in ffee of Three hundered acres of Land bearing date the the 15th

---

*There is no page numbered 288 or 289. Page 290 follows page 287.

day of the firſt month 1696 was delivered by John Smith grantor / 7
unto Henry Baker grantee

A deed in ffee of foure hundred acres of Land dated the 17th day of the third month 1697 was delivered by John Shaw and George Willard
grantors unto Phineas Pemberton Attorney to william Smith grantee

A deed in ffee of Six hundred and   acres of Land dated the firſt day of the 2nd month 1697 was delivered by Joſeph Growdon grantor to william Duncan grantee

Adjourned   Adjourned the Court unto the houſe of Joſeph Chorley at 10 a Clock in the morning   wm: Markham govrnr preſent

A deed in fee of five hundred acres of Land dated the 4th day of the 10th
month 1696 was delivered by Joſeph Chorley Subſtitute Attorney to
Thomas ffaireman Attorney to his brother Robt fairman grantor
unto Joſeph Growdon grantee

A deed in fee of one hundred acres of Land dated the 6th day of the firſt month 1696 was delivered by Joſeph Chorley Attorney to Edward Evans grantor unto Joſeph Growdon grantee

A deed in ffee of ninety acres of Land dated the 9th day of the 4 month 1697 was delivered by Phineas Pemberton Attorney to grace Langhorn Jeremiah Langhorn william Biles Junr and his wife Sarah Biles grantors unto William Paxſon grantee

A deed in ffee of three hundred acres of Land dated the 17th day of may 1695 was delivered by John Rowland Attorney to Robert webb and his wife Elizabeth webb grantors unto william Buckman
grantee

Action entered the 26 day of the 3 month 1697

Joſeph Engliſh peter white Elizabeth his wife
Thomas Green and Rachel his wife plts —
againſt
Richard noble defendant - - - - - - - -
} in an action upon the Caſe

291

Action being Called peter white one of the plts appeared and produced
A letter
of Attorney from the Reſt to appeare on theire behalfs
defendant Called but appeared not

Complaint being made agt John Rowland for neglecting his duty
in Collecting the Tax he being made Collector of A provincial
Tax for the Townſhip at the ffalls

Exam: he being Called to anſwer to the Said Complt Confeſſed that he
had not Collected any part thereof nor paid in the monys as
the Law in that Caſe directs and that he was not ffree to Collect
it

ffine whereupon the Court fines in three pounds to Levied on his
goods
and Chattles

ordered thereupon that Samuel Beakes Sherrif be Collector of
the Said Tax for the Said Townſhip at the ffalls

John Rowland in his defence about not Collecting the ſd
Tax haveing Spoke an untruth in the Court and for telling
one of the Juſtices that he Spoke falsly the Court demanded
of him to appear at the next Court to —
make anſwer to the Same and he acordingly promiſed
to appeare

action Entered the 26th day of the 3 month 1697

Iſaac Norris plt
agt } in an action upon the Caſe
Samuel Jerrome deft

Arreſt thereupon granted the 27th of the ſd mo 1699
3

Return of the Sherrife thereupon

Bucks ff By vertue of the within the body of Samll
Jerrome was Arreſted the 27th day of the 3 month 1699

Action } Iſaac norris & ptner plts } appeared by his Attorney
Called- Saml Jerrome deft appeared

declaracon being read Bucks ff Iſaac norris plt } in a plea
agt } upon the
Saml Jerrome deft Caſe

Isaac norris of philadelphia merchant Complains agt —
Samuel Jerrome for that whereas the sd deft Stands Just
-ly indebted to the plts in the Sum of Ten pounds five
teen Shillings nine pence half peny Currant silver mony
of the province of pensylvania being the ballance of an —
account of divers goods wares and merchandizes Sold by the
Said plts to the sd deft an acc^{tt} whereof under the plts hand
herewith in Court to be produced may appear all wch the
sd plts do aver And tho the plts have often requested the said
deft to have made payment to them of the said Sum in full —
ballance of the sd account never the less the sd deft hath refused
neglected and deneyed the Same to pay Still doth whereupon –

292

action doth accrew to the sd plts and Craves Judgmt of this —
Court agt the Said Samuel Jerrome for the Said Sum of Ten
pounds fiveteen Shillings and nine pence half peny with forty
Shillings damages and Cost of Suite &c:

Judgmt } The Said Samuel Jerrome Confessed that he owed to the sd
Confest } plts the aforesd Sum of Ten pounds fiveteen Shillings nine
pence half penney

Judgmt
&
Execution
awarded
accordingly } Whereupon Judgmt was awarded with Cost of Suite and that
Execution Issue accordingly

Adjourned the Court for one houre

obligation
to pay mony
to Isaac
norris &c:
pt of the } Joseph Growdon and John Swift promised in open Court to
pay to Isaac norris & partner theire Executors or
Administrators
the Sum of Eight pounds on account of the Samll Jerrome
in the ninth month next Ensueing
And the sd Joseph Growdon and John Swift did likewise

Judgmt—
obligation
to pay—
mony on the
aforesd Judg
mt to Isaac
merriot } promise to pay to Isaac merriot his Executrs or Administrate
the Sum of Six pounds and Cost of Suite in three yeares
time to be paid Quarterly by Equal portions

obligation to serve in Confideration of the afore fd mony—

In confideracon whereof the Said Saml, Jerrome obliged him felf to ferve the Said Jofeph Growdon and John Swift or theire Affigns Two yeares for the Said mony by them fo to be paid

we of the grand Jury for this County do by feverall Complts for want of the ferry at Gilbert wheelers not being kept do prfent the neceffity of haveing A ferry kept at Jofeph Chorleys which is a Convenient place and he doth promife to keep and Attend the Said ferry and A flat and Cannoes always ready for to Attend the fd ferry fo that there be no other place of ferriage allowed within three miles of the fd Jofeph Chorleys

grand Jurys— prefentments

Likewife we prefent the neceffity of A ferry at nefhamina Creek to be kept at John Baldwins which is nearrer to philadelphia from the ferry at Buckingham by 2 or 3 miles then the other ferry or way of rideing and John Baldwin will keep a flat for to ferry horfes at reasonable termes as the Cuntry Shall think fit he haveing the priveledg aforefaid alowed him

we Likewife prefent the bridg and the Roade that comes from new town to the falls for want of repaire

we Likewife prefent the neceffity of gathering the arrears of Taxes due from the County by the next Court and to be paid into the Court or to whom they fhall authorize to Receive the fame

we Likewife prefent the necessity of John Brock haveing his mony that is due to him from the County Several yeares—

293

we Likewife prefent that no perfon or perfons Shall Sell rum or any other Liquor by Small meafures to be drunk in theire houfes without A license from the govrnr

grand Jurys prfent mts –

we Likewife prefent Andrew Heath for Selling of Rum by Retaile and Richard Burges for the like offence of felling Liquor by Small meafure

It was Likewife prefented as neceffary and A petition drawn that we might have a Town layd out at Bucking ham neare the old ferry and was prefented to the govr

-nr and Council being Signed by all the grand Jury and by about 20 pſons more

    The Court adjourns to 2nd weekly fourth day in the 7ᵗʰ month next

Actions Entered for the 7ᵗʰ month Court next

24ᵗʰ 6 1697 ffrancis white plt
  mo
     agt   } in an action upon the Caſe
  Stepehn newel — →

25ᵗʰ 6 i697 Summonce granted agt ſd newell ditto a ſummonce for witneſſes
  mo
     with drawn by the plts order

24ᵗʰ 6 1697 John Town plt — —
  mo
     agt   } in an action upon the Caſe
  Stephen newell deft

25 6 Summonce granted agt ſd newel in ſd action
  mo

24ᵗʰ 6 1697 — — Thomas Hudſon plt
  mo   agt   in an action upon the Caſe
25 6 Sumonce } Samll Hough deft } This action with drawn by ordr
  mo
  in ſd Case —

of the plts attorney wm Biles

26 6 mo 1697 Gilbert wheeler plt
     agt   } in an action upon the Caſe —
  John Heeſum deft

26 6 1697 Arreſt granted agt John Heeſum
  mo
by vertue whereof the Sherrif returned him Arreſted the 27ᵗʰ 6 9
                     mo

Action Entered the 26ᵗʰ 3 1697
       mo

peter White &c: plts ⎫
  agt   ⎬ in an action upon the Cafe —
Richard noble deft ⎭

Attachment was thereupon granted then Returnable to the next Court
 by Saml Beakes then Sherrife dated 26th day 3 month 1697
return thereupon was made in the following words or words to
 the fame Effect viz

Bucks ff by vertue of the abovefaid the Land of Richard noble
 Lying in the Townfhip of Buckingham Conteineing about
 300 acres was Attached the 26th day of the 3 month 1697
      p Samll Beakes fherrife

Bucks ff At a Court of Quarter Seffions held in the name of
294 william penn proprietarie and Govrnr of the pro-
 -vince of penfylvania and the Counties annexed
 at the Court houfe for the aforefd County the 8th
 day of the 7th month 1697

    Juftices prefent
 Henry Baker Richard Hough John Swift
 Jonathan Scaife Corronr
 Samll Beakes Sherrife
 Phineas Pemberton Cl: Com..

Apprizors ⎰ appointed Jofeph milner Edmund Lovet Anthony Burton all
Attefted ⎱

Action peter white and as Attorney ⎫
Called to Jofeph Englifh Thomas green ⎬plts ⎫ appeared
   and his wife Rachel — — — ⎭ ⎬
      agt   ⎪
   Richard noble — — — — defts ⎭ appeared not

A Deed In fee of about Ten acres of Land dated the firft day of
   the Seventh month 1697 was delivered by —
   matthias Harvie grantor to Jofeph milner grantee

A Deed in fee of one hunered Ten 110 acres of Land dated
   the 30th day of the 6th month 1694 was delivered by —
   Phineas Pemberton Attorney to Charles Read and Anne his

wife grantors unto John Rowland Attorney to Thomas Rogers Grantee

A Deed in fee of the above ſaid one hundred and Ten acres of Land Dated the i2ᵗʰ day of the i0ᵗʰ month 1694 was delivered by John Rowland Attorney to the above named Thomas Rogers grantor unto Edmund Lovet grantee

A Deed in fee of A lott of Land in Buckingham dated was Delivered by Thomas Brock grantor unto Jonathan — Scaiſe Attorney to walter pomphray grantee

A deed in fee of one hundred ninety three acres of Land dated the 10ᵗʰ day of the firſt month 1694 was Delivered by Samuel Beakes Attorney to John Rowland and his wife priſcilla grantors unto Phineas Pemberton Attorney unto Arthur Cook grantee

A Deed in fee of Six hundred acres of Land Dated the 3 day of the Sixth month i697 was Delivered by Jonathan Scaiſe Subſtitute Attorney to Samuel Carpenter and Phineas Pemberton Attorneys to Thomas Muſgrave grantor unto Samuel Beakes Attorney to valentine Hudleſtone grantee

A Deed in fee of one hundred and Ten acres of Land dated the 7ᵗʰ day of the 7ᵗʰ month 1697 was Delivered by Edmund Lovet grantor unto John Rowland grantee

Court adjourns untill the 5ᵗʰ day of the 8ᵗʰ month next

Action — David powel plt
Entered — agt
9ᵗʰ 7/mo 97 — Richard Davies deft
} action Treſpaſe upon the Caſe

Attachment thereupon granted i0ᵗʰ 7/mo i697

return that the Lands of ſd Davies was Attached the 25ᵗʰ day 7/mo 1697

(295)

At A Court Held by Adjournment the 5ᵗʰ day of the eight month 1697

9th $\frac{7}{\text{mo}}$ 1697 action Entered David powel plt agt Richard Davies deft action Trefpafe upon the Cafe ———	Juftices prfent Joseph Growdon william Biles Henry Baker Richard Hough John Swift Samuel Beakes Sherrife Phineas Pembert Cl: Com:

grand Jury Attefted — —

A Deed in ffee of eighty acres of Land dated the firft day of the 6th month 1697 was Delivered by Jofeph Growdon Grantor unto Thomas knight grantee

A deed of foure hundered acres of Land in fee dated the firft day of the 6th month
i697 was delivered by Jofeph Growdon grantor unto francis Searl grantee

A Deed of Twenty five acres of Land in fee Dated the firft day of the 8th month i697 was Delivered by william Biles Attorney to Thomas — Hudfon grantor unto Richard Hough grantee

A Deed of Sixty one acres and A half of Land in fee dated the 5th day of the eight month 1697 was Delivered by Thomas Stakehoufe Junr grantor unto Ezra Crofdel grantee

A Deed of fifty one acres and A half of Land in fee dated the 8th day of the 10th month 1696 was delivered by Jofeph kirkbride grantor unto peter webfter grantee

A Servant boy his name being Neel Grant was prfented to the Court by his mafter Jofeph kirkbride to have his age adjudged and the Court according
-ly did adjudg him to be thirteen yeares of age the firft day of the fifth month Laft paft and that he Serve his Said mafter according to Law
And the Said Jofeph kirkbride promifed to give to his Said Servant at the expiration of his terme as the Law directs

A Servant boy his name being John Weire was prfented to the Court by his mafter John Duncan to have his age adjudged and the Court — accordingly did adjudg him to be thirteen yeares of age from this day and that he Serve his Said mafter according to Law

And the Said John Duncan promiſed to give to his Said Servant at the Expiration of his terme of Servitude as the Law directs

Court adjourns for one houre

A Deed of three hundered acres of Land in fee dated the 7th day of the 7th month 1697 was Delivered by william Buckman grantor unto John Shaw grantee

A Deed of two hundered and three acres of Land in fee dated the firſt day of the 8th month 1697 was by william Croſdel grantor Delivered unto John Croſdel grantee

ordered that Duncan Williams have A Lycence to keep ordinary to pay 24s

ordered that Thomas Brock have A lycence to keep ordinary to pay 24s

A Deed of one hundered acres of Land in fee unto william Smith and of Two hundered acres of Land in fee unto Ralph Boome bearing date the firſt day of the Sixth month 1697 was Delivered by — Samll Beakes Attorney to Samuel Carpenter grantor unto the Said william Smith and Ralph Boome grantees

ordered that Joſeph Chorley have a Lycence to keep an ordinary & to pay 24s

296

A Deed of Two parcels of Land Conteing foure hundered and ninety acres in fee
dated the fourth day of Auguſt 1696 was Delivered by Phineas Pemberton Attorney to James wood grantor unto Joſeph Growdon Attorney to Joſeph kirle grantee

A Deed of Two hundered and forty Six acres of Land in fee dated the i day of the 6th month 1697 was delivered by Phineas Pemberton Attorney to Joſeph paul grantor unto John Shaw Attorney to George willard grantee

A Deed of a lot of Land in Buckingham In fee dated the i day of the 7th month 1697 was Delivered by Thomas Brock grantor unto Saml oldale grantee

A Deed of a Lot of Land in Buckingham in fee dated the i day of the 7th month 1697 was delivered by Thomas Brock unto Edward mayos grantee

grand Jurys prſentments { we the grand jury do prſent James Alman for breaking the peace on Saml Beakes & John Addington Sherrife & Conſtable in Executing a warrant on the goods of John Rowland

| Action Called | John Town plt agt Stephen newel deft | in an action upon the Caſe | plt appeared —— deft appeared not |

| Action Called | Gilbert wheeler plt agt John Heeſum deft | in an action upon the Caſe | plt appeared —— deft appeared not |

Action was continued at the plts requeſt untill another Court

| Action Called | David powel plt agt Richard Davies deft | in an action upon | plt appeared · deft appeared not |

grand Jurys prſentmts Adjourned the Court untill tomorrow morning at 9 a Clock

we the grand jury do prſent the neceſſity of raiseing a Tax of one peny p pound to defray the County Charge   Joſuah Hoops foreman

John Heeſum being accuſed of Swearing by the name of god upon his Examination Confeſſed the fact

ffine   whereupon the Court fines him in Ten ſhillings

Conſtables   appointed to Serve for the Succeeding yeare

for —
- Buckingham — — — — John Baldwin
- ffalls — — — — — — Samuel Burges
- makefeild — — — — — John Dark
- middle Town, new Town & wrights Town — — — ffrancis white
- Benſalem — — — — — nicholas vandegrieft
- Southhampton & warminſter — — — — Henry walmsley — —

overſeers of the High was for the enſueing yeare

for
- Buckingham — — — — Thomas Brock
- falls — — — — — — - Edmund Lovet
- makefeild — — — — Joſeph kirkbride
- middle Town ⎫
- new Town & ⎬ — — — Joſeph milner
- wrights Town ⎭ — — — Henry Hudleſtone
- Benſalem — — — — — ffrancis Searle
- South hampton & ⎫ — — — John Eaſtbourn
- warminſter — — ⎭

grand Jurys prſentmt

we the grand Jury do prſent the neceſſity of the executing a warrant directed to
phineas Pemberton bearing date the 28th day of may 1697 for the laying out of a conve
nient Road from the falls to philadelphia and from wrights town to Dunk williams on —
delaware river and that Reasonable Charges be paid him out of the ſtock —

297

ordered That phineas pemberton Survey and Lay out the Road between the falls and John Gilberts and alſo the Town of Buckingham according
to the warrant to him directed with the aſſiſtance of John Surket Samuel Beakes Joſeph Chorley Thomas Brock John Baldwin Saml Allin John Gilbert nicholas vandegreiſt and as many of the Juſtices as Can well be there

ordered That phineas pemberton Survey and Lay out the Road from wrights Town to neſhaminah meeting houſe and from Thence to Joſeph Growdons and thence to branch out the one way to — — the ford at Allin foſters over penipecce the other from — Joſeph Growdons to Duncan williams according to a warrant to him Directed from the Govrnr

ordered that william Smith william Buckman James yates Robert Heaton Henry Huddleſtone Jeremiah Langhorn aſſiſt him therein

ordered that the Said Phineas Pemberton be paid for Surveying and Laying out the Said Roads and Town out of the County Levies after the Same is done

Adjourned the Court for one houre

accounts of the County when Thomas Brock was made Collector of the Tax was by Said Brock made up in open Court and it then — appeared there was due to Said Brock from the County 12^s: 3^d

action Robt Lucas plt
    agt
Richard Thacher deft
} whereas Complt was made to william Biles one of the Juftices of the peace for the aforefd County how that Richard Thatcher was Indebted to him

the fpliting of foure hundered of Railes whereupon the fame being made appeare to the faid juftice of peace he gave Judgmt that the Said Thatcher Shold Split the Said Railes wch being — Judgmt reported to this Court upon further Examination thereof did Confirm the Said Judgmt

A Deed of one hundred two and a half acres of land in fee dated the 1st day of the 7th month 1697 was Delivered by mahlon Stacy and Henry Baker Attornes to John nichols and Elias nicholas grantors
unto Jofeph Chorley grantee

ordered that Gilbert wheeler have a lycence to keep ordinary & to pay 30^s

Adjourned to the 2nd weekly 4th day in the 10th month next

Action Entered the 2i day of the 9th month 1697

Saml Beakes plt
    agt
Richard Thatcher deft
} in an action upon the Cafe

Arreft granted thereupon agt the fd deft the 22 day 9/mo 1697

Return Bucks ff by vertue of the within the body of Richard Thatcher was Arrefted the 30th day of the 9 month 1697 p me
                              Samll Beekes Sherrife

Bucks ff

298

At a Court of Quarter Seffions held in the name of william penn proprietarie of the province of penfylvania and Territories thereunto belonging at the Court houfe for the aforefaid County the 8th day of the i0th month 1697

The Juftices prefent

Jofeph Growdon william Biles Richard Hough
Samuel Beakes Sherrife
Phineas Pemberton Cl: Com:

Court Adjourned to the houfe of Jofeph Chorley

Affault & Battery	Thomas Archer being Committed to prifon for affaulting & beating Thomas Brock being Examined thereupon Confeft the fact and Submitted to the Court whereupon the Court Commits
Submitted to the Court	him into the fherrifs Cuftody untill give Suerties for his appearance the next Court and to be of good abearing in the meanetime and also the Court fines him
fine	Twenty Shillings

A Deed in fee of Two hundered forty five acres of Land dated the 7th day of December 1697 was delivered by Jofeph Growdon grantor unto Claws Jonfon grantee

A Deed in fee of Two hundered forty one acres of Land dated the firft day of the 5th month i697 was Delivered by Jofeph Growdon grantor unto Leonard vandegreift grantee

A Deed of Two hundered and fifteen acres of Land in fee dated the — firft day of the 5th month 1697 was Delivered by Jofeph Growdon grantor unto nicholas vandegrieft grantee

A Deed of one hundered and Six acres of Land dated the firft day of the 5th month i697 was Delivered by Jofeph Growdon grantor unto — ffrederick vandegreift grantee

A Deed of Two hundered Seventy one acres of Land in fee dated the firft day of the 5th month 1697 was Delivered by Jofeph Growdon grantor unto Johannes vandegreift grantee

A Deed of one hundered and Six acres of Land in fee dated the firft day of the 5th month i697 was Delivered by Jofeph Growdon grantor unto Jacob Groesbeck grantee

A Deed of one hundered and Six acres of Land in fee dated the firft day of the 5th month 1697 was delivered by Jofeph Growdon grantor unto Barndt virkirk grantee

A Deed of Three hundred acres of Land in fee dated the 3 day of the 10th month 1697 was Delivered by John Rowland grantor unto Daniel Burges grantee

A Deed of a lot of Land in fee lying in Buckingham dated the 7th day of the 10th month 1697 was Delivered by John Town — grantor unto Saml Beakes Attorney to Rebecca wilfford grantee

ordered that Phineas Pemberton Send the will of Richard Thatcher unto the Govrnr being Regifter general

Action David powel plt } the plt appeared by his Attorney
agt } Andrew Heath
Richard Davies Deft } the Defendant appeared not — —

299

Action } peter white for him Self and as Attorney for Jofeph } appeared
Englifh
Called — } Thomas Green and his wife Rachel plts — — —
Richard noble deft appeared not — — — — — —
default haveing been made three times

Adjourned the Court untill 9 tomorrow morning

Declaracon being read is as follows

Bucks ff Jofeph Englifh peter white and Elizabeth his wife Thomas green and Rachel his wife complaines agt Richard noble of the Said County yeoman Adminiftrator of the Eftate which was of — Saml Clift late of the Said County hufbandman deceased of A — plea that whereas the Said Saml Clift in his Lifetime (to wit) on the 23 day of the 9th month in the yeare of our Lord 1682 being very weake in body but of perfect Sence and memory did make his laft will and Teftament in writeing and after he had bequeathed Some Legacyes he thereby declared that as for his proper Eftate and houfeing and alfo his goods liveing & dead he freely gave unto his Son Jonathan Clift whome he left his Executor defireing Chriftopher Taylor and Richard noble to be his Truftees and over Seers for his Said Son as by the Said Laft will and Teftement more fully appeares and fhortly after dyed after whofe deceafe the Said Chriftopher refufing to meddle with the Said Truft Adminiftracon of the Said Teftators goods & Chattles with his will annexed was Committed to the Said Richard noble by vertue whereof he the fd deft did — poffefs him Self of the Said Teftator Samll Clifts Eftate real — and perfonal to the value of above Seventy Six pounds but

hath not diſtributed the Said Eſtate according to the direction
of the Said will nor rendered any account of his Adminiſt
ration Either to the ordinary or Regiſter general as he —
ought to have done and the plts in fact Say that the ſaid
Jonathan Clift Dyed Inteſtate haveing no Iſſue now Living
after whoſe deceaſe the Said Samll Clifts Eſtate ought of
right to be diſtributed amongſt the plts being the next of
—kin or relation to the ſd decedents Samuel and Jonathan
Clift nevertheles the ſaid deft (Though often requeſted —
hath not delivered or given up the Said Eſtate to be diſtributed
as aforeſaid but detained and doth detaine the ſame in
his own hands and Converted to his own uſe to the plts damage
of 200 £ and thereof they bring Suite &c:

The will of Samll Clift and ⎫ by which it appeared that there was due
 the Inventory read ⎭ to the —
to the plts from the ſd Defts as he is Adminiſtrator of the ſd Clifts
Eſtate the Sum of thirty five pounds eight Shillings Six pence

Ralph Boome being then upon the plantation and Lands of Richard noble
the plts Crave that he may be Called into Court and ordered to
ſhew
if anything for Self he hath to Say or knoweth wherefore the
ſd plts ought not to have execution of the Lands of Richard
Noble then in

300 the poſſeſſion of the Sherriſe as in the return of the Attachmt
So as
afore mentioned Attached
whereupon the Said Ralph Boome came and Said that he held the aboveſd
plantation and premiſes by vertue of an agreemt made by his
wifes
former huſband (namely John Allen) with one moſes maſley to
whom the ſaid premiſes was Sold by the ſd deft noble and by the
ſd masley mortgaged and reconveyed to the ſd deft for ſecurity of
the Conſideracon mony
whereunto the plts replye and produce A letter which the ſd Deft
Sent from
England unto <u>Edmund Bennet</u> intimateing that the ſd maſley
had not
wherewith to pay the Said mortgage mony therefore he the ſd
Deft
was Conſtrained to take back the Land and plantation aforeſd
inſtead
of his mony and So gave order to ſd Bennet to ſell the Same

All which being Seen by the Juſtices here fully underſtood

It was Conſidered by the Court that the Said plts Shall recover agt the deft the Said 35 £ : 8ˢ–6ᵈ with Coſt of Suite and Shall have Execucon for the Same to be Levied on the lands Tenements and plantation (of the ſd Deft in the Townſhip of Buckingham according to the Sherrifts return of the Attachment) So as aforeſd Attached

And the Said peter white for him Self and the reſt of the plts did find Suffitient Security to reſtore the ſd Lands unto the ſd Deft if he with
    in one yeare and a day Shall and will come and verefie by due —
Courſe of Law that the aforeſd plts theire action aforeſd ought not
    to have and mentaine (as ffolloweth)

Be it remembered that peter white for him ſelf and Elizabeth his wife and for Joſeph Engliſh his father in law and for Thomas Green & Rachel his wife did produce ffrancis white and John Smith for his Security who recognized them ſelves (to wit) the ſaid peter white in —
Sixty pounds and the Said ffrancis white and John Smith in —
Twenty pounds apeice to be levied on theire Lands and Tennemts goods and Chattles for the uſe of Richard noble Adminiſtrator of Samll Clift Deceaſed
upon Condition that if the Said Richard noble Shall come intoany of the County Courts that Shall be held for the ſd County of Bucks with
    in one yeare and A day now next enſueing and diſprove or by due Courſe of Law avoyd the damages So recovered by the ſaid Joſeph Engliſh peter white and Elizabeth his wife Thomas Green &
Rachel his wife as aforeſaid that then the Said Recoverers theire heirs Executors or Aſſigns Shall reſtore the Lands and Tennemts goods and Chattles which hath been Attached as aboveſaid and Shall be taken and ſeized in Execucon to Satiſfy the ſaid recovery

A mortgage of the Lands and plantation Henry Baker now lives upon was —
    delivered by ſaid Baker mortgagor
    unto phineas pemberton Attorney to Richard walter of Barbadoes mortgagee

A Deed of Two hundered fifty Two acres of land in fee dated the firſt day of the 8th month 1697 was Delivered by Henry Baker grantor unto Stephen wilſon grantee

Action Called } John Town plt agt Stephen newel deft } plt appeared and deſired the action to be with drawn

Adjourned the Court to the Court houſe

301

A Reconveyance of a Tract of land in fee of Six hundered and Sixteen acres and
 Two thirds of an acre wch was formerly granted by Henry Baker to John
Harriſon was by the Said Harriſon reconveyed in fee and the Said Reconveyance was delivered by Joſeph milner Attorney to the ſd
John Harriſon grantor unto the Said Henry Baker grantee

A Conveyance of Twenty five acres of Land in fee wch was formerly Conveyed to
John Harriſon by Thomas Hudſon was reconveyed in ffee by ſaid Harriſon to Said Hudſon wch reconveyance was Delivered by — Joſeph milner Attorney to Said John Harriſon reconveyor unto the Said Thomas Hudſon by his Attorney william Biles

Action Called } Gilbert wheeler plt agt John Heeſum deft } in an action upon the Caſe { the plt appeared the deft did not appeare when Called but francis Tunneclift his ſecurity appeared and petitioned

to the Court as followeth that whereas he according to the baile – given did Attend with the deft & the action was Continued at the requeſt of the plt & the deft being now of the province prayed that the
action might be Continued untill another Court

But it appearing by the Records of the Court that the ſd deft did not appeare when the action was Called and the plt Craveing Judgmt the Court rejected his petition

Declaracon being read as ffolloweth viz

Bucks ſſ Gilbert wheeler Complaines agt John Heeſum in a plea that he render unto him Ten pounds foure ſhillings & one penny wch he unjustly detaines from him and for that whereas the ſaid John – Heeſum gave his bill under his Hand dated the 20 day of the 5th month 1697 to pay to the Said Gilbert wheeler the Said Sum of Ten pounds foure Shillings and one penny upon demand as may appeare by the Said bill herewith in Court to be produced as alſo he the Said John Heeſum hath bought and had at Sundry times Since the date of the Said bill in meate drink and Lodging from the ſd Gilbert wheeler to the value of Seventeen ſhillings foure pence yet not withſtanding the Said mony being in the whole — Eleven pounds one ſhilling and five pence hath been divers times demanded from the Said John Heeſum yet he hath hitherto refuſed

to pay the Same and ſtill doth refuſe whereupon the Said Gilbert wheeler brings this action and Craves Judgment of this Court – agt the ſd John Heeſum for the Said Sum of Ten pounds foure Shillings and one penny as alſo for the ſaid Sum of Seventeen Shillings and foure pence with damages and Coſt of Suite &c:

The bill mentioned in the aforeſd declaracon read

witneſes Richard Bull } atteſted to the truth thereof
william Taylor

The Account alſo read and Gilbert wheeler Atteſted to the truth thereof and that he Cold not give any Credit towardd the ſd bill or the ſd account

It was Conſidered by the Court that the Said plt Shall recover agt the Said John Heeſum the Said Sum of Eleven pounds one Shillings and five pence with Coſt of Suite and that Execution Iſſue accordingly

Action } Samll Beakes plt
Called } agt
Richard Thatcher deft

both appeared and deſired that the action depending between them might be reffered to be arbitrated by william embley Joſeph wood and George
Brown and both declared they wold ſtand to theire award or the award of any two of them to wch the Court aſſented

302 whereupon the Said Arbitrators takeing upon them the Said Charge report

to the Court that they have awarded the Said Richard Thatcher Shall pay to
the Said Samll Beakes the Sum of Two pounds and both plt and deft — declared theire Satiffaction therewith

whereupon the Said Samuel Beakes defired Judgmt of the Court for the Same and that Execution might Iffue accordingly

wherefore It being Confidered by the Court that the Same Judgment of the arbitrators was done according to theire request and Satiffaction the Court awarded Judgmt that the Said Richard Thatcher Shold pay to the Said Samll Beakes the Said Sume of forty Shillings and that Execution Iffue accordingly

Richard Burges being brought into Court Selling of his wife and other mifdemeanors and Contempts

The Court Committs him the Said Burges into the Sherrifts Cuftody untill he Shall find Suerties for his appearance at the next Court and to be of good abearing in the meane time

James Alman being prefented by the grand Jury Laft Court for — hindering the Sherrife and Conftable in the due execution of theire office and the Said Alman being brought before the Court and the Said prefentment read to him he Submitted to the Court

whereupon the Court difcharged him paying his fees

Recognizance Richard Burges acknowledges him Self Indebted to the proprietarie
in the Sum of thirty pounds and Henry Margorm of the aforefd —
County and Andrew Heath of the Same in Ten pounds apeice to be —
Levied on theire Lands and Tennements goods and Chattles
And this is upon Condition that the Said Richard Burges Shall appeare at the next Court of Quarter Seffions to be held for this
County then and there to anfwer Such matters of mifdemeanor as
Shall then and there be objected againft him and to abide the Judgmt
of the Said Court and to be of good abearing in the meane time

A Deed of the moiety of the Land plantation and other premifes in fee mentioned

in the Said deed Dated the 4th day of the 10th month 1697 was—
Delivered by Robert Lucas grantor unto his brother Edward Lucas
grantee

A Deed of Two hundered forty foure acres of Land and premifes with Some exceptions in the Same in fee dated the 6th day of the 10th month
1697 was Delivered by Elizabeth Lucas Giles Lucas and Edward Lucas
grantors unto Robert Lucas grantee

ordered that the Sherrife get the Court Staires repaired or made new and Two of the windows of the Court houfe glazed and one of them Shut up and the north end plaftered and that the Same be pd
for out of the County ftock

Recognrz Thomas Archer Acknowledges him felf Indebted in Twenty pounds and Edward
Doyl in five pounds unto the proprietarie to belevied on their Lands
and Tennements goods and Chattles

And this is upon Condition that the fd Thomas Archer Shall appeare
at the next Court of Quarter Seffions to be held for this County and to
be of good abearing in the meanetime

upon Complt of Samll Beake Sherrife agt Richard Thatcher how that the
Said Thatcher Stood in debted to him the fum of Two pounds – Seventeen Shillings and eight pence due to him for fees in fundry Cafes

303

before this Court and Craved Judgmt of this Court
whereupon the Court being full Satiffyed of the Same Iwas Confidered that
the Said Samuel Beakes Shold recover the Said Sum of 2 £ : 17s : 8d and
that Execution Iffue accordingly

ordered that phineas pemberton write to Samuel Carpenter Executor of

ffrancis Roffill that it is the Courts requeft that he wold
pay to Edward Doyl Twenty Shillings and to James Sutton
Twenty
Shillings out of the Legacy left to the poore of this County
by the
Said ffrancis Roffill

Adjourned the Court unto the Second weekly fourth day in
the firft month next

Action Entered the 2i day of the i2th mo: $\frac{1697}{8}$

Richard Burges plt agt Henry paxfon deft in a plea

Summonce thereupon granted the 22 day of the i2th month 1697/8

Bucks ff   At a Court of Quarter Seffions held in the name
of William Penn proprietarie and Govrnr of the
province of penfylvania and Territories thereunto
belonging at the Court houfe for the aforefaid
County the 9th day of the firft month i698 $\frac{7}{}$

Juftices prefent

Jofeph Growdon william Biles   Richard Hough

Samuel Beakes Sherrife and deputy Cl: Com

Action   David powel agt Richard Davies Continued untill next Court
at the requeft of plt and
deft   Court ajourns to the houfe of Jofeph Chorley one hour
hence

whereas there was an Ececution granted ffor the Leviing of th
fum
of Eleven pounds one Shilling five pence which Gilbert
wheeler —
recovered by Judgmt in a Court of Quarter Seffions held fo
the afrefd
County the 8th day of the 10th month laft paft with 2 £ : 11^s :
with Coft of
Suite

Return upon the Said Execution was made viz

Bucks ff There is no Effects of goods nor Chattles of ye with
John —

Heefum to be found with in the aforefd County

The 9th of i/mo 1697/8   p me Saml Beakes

whereas execution was granted agt John Rowland for the Leviing of A
fine of three pounds Impofed upon him the 9th day of the 4th month laft
paft dated the 20th day of the fd 4th month

Return was made upon the fd Execution as followeth

Bucks ff by vertue of the within there is taken one Cow of the Goods of
John Rowland the 7th day of the 6th month 1697
p Saml Beakes fherrife

Bucks ff The above faid Cow was Sold at an out cry unto Thomas Brock
for Two pounds and Two fhillings the 9th day of the 10th month 1697
p Saml Beakes Sherrife

grand Jury Jofuah Hoops John palmer willm Dark John Crofdel
Jeremiah Langhorn John Smith Stephen Beakes Samll Hough —
Daniel Done Enock yardley willm Duncan Stephen Twineing —
Thomas kirle James moone — all of them Attefted

304

A Deed of A Certaine Tract of Land in fee dated the 14th day of february 1697
was Delivered by Jofeph wood Attorney to Elizabeth Bennet grantor
unto Jofeph Taylor Subftitute Attorney to Barbery Blayden grantee

A Deed of Sixty acres of Land in fee Dated the 9th day of the firft month
1698 was Delivered by John Scarbrough grantor unto Thomas Bayns grantee

Action } Richard Burges plt }
Called }   agt   } in A plea { both appeared
        Henry paxfon deft }

declaracon Read

Anfwer the plt Saith he is not Guilty and thereof for tryal puts him
felf

venire   upon the Cuntry and So doth the plt whereupon the fherrife is
         Commanded to return A Jury

Jury Thomas Stakehoufe Jofeph kirkbride   ⎫ all
    Edward Lucas   ⎪
James yates John Scarbrough Robt Heaton   ⎬
    Thomas Bayns   ⎪
Clement Dungan Jofeph milner Samuel Dark   ⎪
    wm: Dark Jos: Wood   ⎭ attefted

Declarcon againe Read

Action Continued at the requeft of the plt & by the Confent of the
    Deft untill
the next Court

Complt was made by Henry paxfon that Richard Burges Did not take
    Suitable Care to mentaine his wife

Anfwer the Said Burges promifed the Court to allow his wife such &
    So much as this Court Shall order him towards a mentainance

A Deed of about Sixty acres of Land be it more or lefs in fee dated
    the 9th day of the 8th month 1697 was Delivered by Jofuah Hoops
    Attorney to James Dilworth grantor unto Thomas Stakehoufe
    Attorney to
martin wildman grantee

Information being given to the Court agt Richard Thather the he had
    Sworn and Curfed & otherwife broke the kings peace
ordered that A warrant be Iffued out to apprehend the faid Thatcher
    to make anfwer to the Same

Court Adjourned untill 8 a Clock in the morning

grand Jurys prfentment brought in agt nathaniel walton
    nathaniel walton being Called appeares
    Barndt virkirk profecutor appeared

prefent ment as follows being read

Bucks ff we the grand Jury for the body of the County do prfent nathaniel
walton for takeing and Converting to his own ufe onw Sow Swine
of the proper goods of Barndt virkirks the i8th day of the i2 month
i697 Conterary to the kings peace and Law of this province
Jofuah Hoops foreman

prifoner being Arraigned pleased not guilty and for tryal put him
felf upon the Cuntry whereupon the Sherrife was Commanded to
venire return Twelve honeft men of the neighbourhood
Jury Thomas ftakehoufe Jofeph kirkbride Edward Lucas James Yates
John fcarbrough Robert Heaton Thomas Baines Clement
Dungan
Jofeph milner Samuel Dark william Dark Jofeph Wood
all Attefted

The prfentment proved by Barndt virkirk and John Gilbert both Atteft
Jury Returned Adjourned the Court for one houre
prifoner brought to the barr

305

Jury } delivers in theire verdict we find the prifoner guilty as he ftands —
verdict- } Indicted

It is therefore Confidered by the Court that nathaniel walton pay to
Barndt virkirk Twenty foure Shillings he being therewith fatiffyed
and the Coft of Suite and that Execucon Iffue accordingly

Andrew Heath being prfented by the Jury fubmits to the bench
whereupon
the Court fines him 10ˢ and Discharges him paying the fees

nathaniel walton Discharged by proclamation

Adjourned the Court untill the i4th day of the 2 next
mo

10th day 1 1697 Execucon granted agt the Land of Richard noble in Englifh
mo 8
and whites Cafe returnable to Seventh month Court next

Action Entered the 26th i 1698
mo

Thomas kirle plt }
agt } in an action of Trefpas upon the Cafe
Andrew Heath deft }

Arreſt thereupon granted agt the body of Andrew Heath the 29th day 1 1698
                                                                    ―――
                                                                    mo

return made by Samll Beakes Sherrife that he had taken the body of the ſd
    Heath the 30th day of the 1   1698
                              ―――
                              mo

At a Court held by Ajournment the i4th day of the 2nd month 1698

Juſtices preſent

Joſeph Growdon   william Biles   Richard Hough
Samuel Beakes Sherrife and Deputy Cl: Com:

Action Called

Thomas kirle plt ⎫   ⎧ plt appeared ⎫
    agt   ⎬ in an action of Treſpaſe   ⎨   ⎬
Andrew Heath deft⎭ upon the Caſe   ⎩ deft appeared⎭

Declaracon read

Anſwer that the plt did not pforme on his pte whileſt he the deft was in a Capacity to pforme and that he is now diveſted of his Truſt and Cannot performe the Conditions menconed in the ſd Declaracon and of

Iſſue – this puts him Self upon the Cuntry and So doth the plt whereupon the

venire – Sherrife is Commanded to return Twelve honeſt men of the vicinage by whom the Truth of the matter may be the better known –

Jury – Samuel Dark   Robt Heaton   Thomas Stakehouſe ⎫
    John palmer   ⎪ all
    Jeremiah Langhorn   william Dark   Stephen Beakes⎬
    Ralph Cowgill   ⎪
    william Duncan   John neild   william Croſdel   ⎪ Atteſted
    Joſeph Chorley   ⎭

Declaracon Read as follows

Action of Treſpaſs in Caſe agt Andrew Heath Treſpaſſer to Thomas kirle plt and the Said Thomas kirle Compts that the ſd Andrew Heath by his promiſe and agreement made with the Said Thomas kirle the 9th day of the 10th month 1697 did bargaine and Sell unto the Said Thomas – kirle his Heirs and Aſſigns forever Two hundered and fourteen acres of Land part of the Land on which the Said Andrew Heath did then live to be Laid out at the back part of the aforesd Lot for and in Consideracon of the Sum of forty five pounds Currant silver mony of this province of pensylvania to be paid unto the Said Andrew Heath his Heirs or Assigns and untill the Said time of payment to pay Lawfull Intrest for the Same from the 25 day of the first month Called march last past in part of which Sum of forty five pounds the sd Thomas kirle did then and there pay the Said Andrew Heath the Sum of Six Shillings which he the sd Andrew Heath

306 Received as Such and promised he wold make unto the Said Thomas kirle a good title to the Said 214 acres of Land all which the Said Thomas kirle is ready to prove and make appear in Court yet notwithstanding the promises the said Andrew Heath Craftily and fraudulently Intending to Deceive the said Thomas kirle hath refused and hitherto doth refuse to layout the said Land or suffer it to be done unto the sd Thomas kirle or to make him a title to the same though often thereunto required whereby the sd Thomas kirle saith he is worse and hath damage to the value of ninety pounds and therefore &c: Craves Judgmt of this Court for the sd Sum with Cost of suite

Answer
Andrew Heath } for his plea agt kirl Saith

That being requested by his Daughters in Law to sell the Said 214 acres of Land &c: he acknowledges the Conditions in sd Declaracon menconed and was accordingly on sd 25th day of march last past ready to have pformed the Conditions but sd kirle the plt — brought neither deed to be signed nor Consideracon mony nor — offered any Security for the same and since the sd Andrew is — divested of his Trust and is in no Capacity to pforme the Conditions &c: and of this put himself upon the Cuntry and so doth the plt

witneſes Atteſted Andrew Ellot & Joſeph Henbery } for the plt – { John Gilbert Jonathan ſcaiſe
Edmund Lovet ſtephen Beaks
Andrew Ellot wm Buckman }

Aſſeſſors appointed for this preſent yeare – – –

  Court Adjourned for one houre

Recognizance Richard Thatcher being Called upon his Recognizance appeared not
  the Court being informed that he was Sick ordered that he —
  appeare at the next Court

  one Letter of Attorney from Thomas Hudſon to Impower william Biles to ſell his Land in this province bearing date the 18 day of Auguſt was brought before the Court and was there approved and allowed

  Jury returned
    verdict finds for the plt 15 £ Damages with coſt of ſuite
    Appeale from which verdict the deft appealed to the next provincial Court in Equity

Recognizance Andrew Heath and Richard wilſon became bound unto Thomas kirle in the Sum of fifty pounds on Condition that the ſd Andrew Heath Shall proſecute his appeale at the next provencial Court and pay the Charge of the ſd Court if he Shall be Caſt

Action Called } David powel agt Richard Davies neither plt nor deft appeared when Called
  Court Adjourns untill the 2ⁿᵈ wekly 4ᵗʰ day in the 4
  next   mo

  action entered the 31 day 3 1698 Joſeph Chorley agt Henry warwin
  action upon   mo
  the Caſe Replevin thereon granted

Bucks ff

Sherrifs return that he had replevined on horfe of sd warwins and fummonced fd warwin to appear at the next Court — dated the 1 day of the 4th month 1698 —

} At a Court of Quarter Seffions held in the name of william penn proprietarie and Governor of the province of penfylvania and Territories thereunto — belonging at the Court houfe for the aforefd County the

8th day of the 4th month 1698

The Juftices present

8th month 1698

Samll Jerrome plt
agt
Andrew Heath deft

william Biles   Henry Baker   Richard Hough
John Swift
Jonathan Scaife Coronor
Samuel Beakes Sherrife
Phineas Pemberton Cl: Com:

Arreft granted
with drawn

Juftices Commiffion Read

proclamation from the Govrnrs for the Apprehending of all pirates privateers and Sea rovers was read

307

A Deed of one hundred acres of Land in fee dated the firft day of the — 10th month 1697 was Delivered by Jane Chapman grantor unto willm Smith grantee

Adjourned the Court for one houre

order

petition of James kirkham agt his mafter Samuel oldale read the fd Samll oldale being Called in Court and Examined upon the Same and the Juftices being fully informed thereof the Confidered the premifes and ordered that Said oldale Receive his Said fervant kirkham againe into his Service and defray his Charges dureing his Sickness and pay the Said kirkham wages for the time he — Served according to his agreement

A Deed of three hundred acres of Land in fee Dated the iith day of the 10th month 1697 was Delivered by Jonathan Scaife attorney to Richard Burges and his wife Elizabeth grantors unto Israel morris and Edmund Cowgill grantees

A Deed of Two hundred forty foure acres of Land in fee Dated the 12th day of the 8th month 1697 was Delivered by william Crosdel Attorney to James Dilworth grantor unto Robert Heaton grantee

A Deed of three hundred and forty acres of Land in fee Dated the first day of the 10th month 1697 was Delivered by Saml Beakes – Attorney to nicholas waln grantor unto Robert Heaton grantee

A Deed of Two hundred eighty Six acres of Land in fee Dated the 8th day of the fourth month 1698 was Delivered by James paxson grantor unto his william paxson grantee

A Deed in of five hundred acres of Land in fee Dated the 12th day of the 8th month 1697 was Delivered by Samuel Beakes Attorney to Daniel Jones grantor unto Daniel Smith grantee

Joseph Smalwood being bound over by Recognizance to Appear at this Court for beating and abuseing his wife and it appearing to this Court that he had since threatened her to do her further misheife

Comitmt the Court Commits him into the Sherrifs Custody untill he give — Security for his appearance at the next Court and to be of good abearing in the meane time

Richard Thatcher being Called into Court upon his Recognizance it being made appeare by the Testemony of James mills & John Clark that he Swore 4 times by the name of god the

fine Court fines him in 20ˢ and orders that he pay Costs

Action ⎫ Joseph Chorley plt ⎫ in an action upon ⎧ plt appeared ⎫
        ⎬   agt   ⎬ the Case   ⎨   ⎬
Called ⎭ Henry warwin deft ⎭   ⎩ deft appeared not ⎭

Action Continued untill the next Court being the first default

Adjourned the Court unto the house of Joseph Chorley

Same Examinations taken about venables and Barrets Land

Adjourned the Court untill the 14th day of the 7th month next

308

Actions Continued untill the next Court

Action Joseph Chorley plt
       agt   } in an action upon the Case
       Henry warwin deft

Actions entered for the next Court 20th day of the 4th month 1698

       ffrancis white plt
       agt   } in an action of Trespas upon the Case
       James Alman deft

Replevin thereupon granted the 20 day of the 4 month 1698

Sherrifs return that he had Attached one gelding

   Entered the 13 day 6th month 1698

       Thomas Gardiner plt
       agt   } in an action of Trespass and Assault
       Samll oldale deft --

Arrest thereupon granted the 13 day of the 6th month 1698

   return made Samll oldale was Arrested the i3 day 6 1698
                                                     mo

       p Samll Beaks sherf

   Entered the 13 day 6 i698
                       mo

       Thomas Gardiner plt
       agt   } in an action of Trespas upon
       Christopher Snowdon deft   the Case

Arrest thereupon granted the i3 day of 6th month i698

Return Christopher Snowdon was Arrested the 16th day of the
    6   i698
    mo

   Entered the 30 day of the 6th month 1698

       Edward Hunlock plt
       agt   } in an action of Trespass upon the
       John pidcock deft   Case

   Summonce thereupon granted

return that he was Summonced

Entered the 30th day 6th month 1698

John grey als Tatham plt
        agt
Robt Cole &
Joſeph wood   defts
    } in an action of Debt

Summonce thereupon granted

return that Joſeph wood was ſummonced Robt Cole not to be found

Entered the 30th day 6th mo 1698

John Grey also Tatham plt
      agt
Joſeph Growdon deft –
} in an action upon the Caſe

Summonce thereupon granted the 2 day 7th mo 1698

returned ſummonced

Entered the 1 day of the 7th mont 1698

James Alman plt
    agt
John Rowland deft
} in an action upon the Case

Summonce thereupon granted

return that he was Summonced

309

Bucks ſſ   At a Court of Quarter ſeſſions held in the name of william penn proprietaries and — Govrnr of the province of penſylvania and Territories thereunto belonging at the Court houſe for the aforeſaid County the 14th day of the 7th month 1698

The Juſtices preſent

Joſeph Growdon william Biles Richard Hough John Swift

  Jonathan Scaife Corronor
  Samull Beakes Sherrife
  Phineas Pemberton Cl: Com:

grand Jury Joſhuah Hoops Peter worral John Surket willm Duncan
John Croaſdel Robt Heaton Ruben pownal william Buckman
atteſted   Samll Coates Jeremiah Langhorn John white Giles Lucas –
Thomas kirle william paxſon william Hayhurſt all atteſted

Return of an Execution granted agt the Goods Chattles and Land of
Richard Thatcher to Satifye Two Judgmts obtained by Samll –
Beakes as ffollows –

Bucks ff by vertue of the within Execucon the Land of Richard
Thatcher Lying neare neſhaminah Creek at or neare the pines –
was taken the 3 day of the 7ᵗʰ month 1698

p Saml Beakes ſherrife

Return of an Execution granted agt the Lands of Richard noble
to Satiffie A Judgment obtained in A Court held for this –
County the 8ᵗʰ day of the 10ᵗʰ month Laſt paſt as follows
by Jos Engliſh peter white and Elizabeth Thomas Green and Rachel

Bucks ff Theſe are to Certefie that I have Cauſed the meſſuage
Land and plantation with in mentioned to be apprized by –
Twelve honeſtmen of the neigh bourhood as within I
am Commanded which meſſuage Lands and plantation remaines
unſold for want of buyers and I am ready to Deliver the ſame
premiſes to the Creditors as within I am required the Reſidue of
the Execucon of this writ Lyes in a schedule Certefied under
my hand the Twenty ninth day of auguſt 1698

valued by the apprizors at 200£   Samuell Beakes ſherrife

A Deed of three hundered acres of Land in fee Dated the 1 day of
the fifth month 1698 was Delivered by Joſeph Chorley Attorney
to william Smith grantor unto Thomas Brock grantee

A Deed of a lot of Land in Buckingham about eight acres in fee
Dated the 1 day of the 6ᵗʰ month 1698 was Delivered by –
Thomas Brock grantor unto Phineas Pemberton Attorney
to Samuel Carpenter grantee

Adjourned the Court for one houre

310

A Deed of Two hundered acres of Land in fee Dated the 2 day of the
2ⁿᵈ month 1698 was Delivered by Clement Dungan

Thomas Dungan Jeremiah Dungan and John Dungan
grantor unto walter pomphray grantee

A Deed of one hundered acres of Land in fee Dated the 22 day of the 5th month 1698 was Delivered by Clement Dungan Jeremiah Dungan and John Dungan grantor unto Thomas Dungan theire brother grantee

A Deed of five hundered eighty Two acres of Land in fee Dated the 7th day of the 11th month 1698 was Delivered by John fwift Attorney to Thomas ffaireman grantor unto James plumley grantee

A Deed of Two hundered and fifty acres of Land in fee Dated the 28th day of the 3 month 1698 was Delivered by John Swift Attorney to James Jacob grantor unto nicholas Randol grantee

A Deed of Two hundered and fifty acres of Land in fee dated the 30th day of July 1696 was Delivered by John Swift Attorney to phillip Howel mary peart and Thomas peart grantors unto James Jacob grantee

A Deed of Two Lotts of Land in ffee Lying in Buckingham Dated the 5th day of the 5th month 1698 was Delivered by Anthony Burton grantor unto Jeremiah Dungan grantee

Recogniz: Jofeph Smallwood appeared in Court according to his Recognizance but the Court did not think fitt to difcharge him untill they had further Considered of it

Action Called

John Tatham plt
agt
Robert Cole & Jofeph Wood
deft

in an action of debt

plt appeared
Jofeph wood appeared

Judgmt

The Declaracon being Read the Said Jofeph wood one of the plts Confeffed that there was due to the Said John – Tatham from his father in law Robt Cole for which he the fd wood ftood bound with his fd father in law to the fd plant the Sum of Sixty five pounds fiveteen fhillings foure pence It was Therefore Confidered by the Court that the Said plt Shold recover agt the fd Defts the Said Sum of 65 £ : 15ˢ : 4ᵈ with Coft of fuite and that Execution Iffue accordingly

Action Thomas Gardiner plt
        agt   in an action of Trespaſs   plt & deft   appeared
        Samuel Oldale deft   & aſſault — — —

declaracon Read whereupon the defts Attorney Inſtits upon the ſtatute 2i James i2 but waived pleading the general Iſſue as the ſtatute directs but after Some debate both parties agreed to deferr any further proceedings untill tomorrow morning

Adjourned the Court untill 9 a Clock in the morning

311

At which time the ſd plt and Deft being Called and both appeared and Some things being offered agt the Tryal the Caſe In this Court the Court thereupon Continued the action untill the Juſtices Shold adviſe thereupon and the Defts baile is Continued to anſwer to the action and to abide the Judgmt of the next Court

Action   Thomas Gardiner plt
Called   agt   in an action   plt & deft   both—
         Chriſtopher Snowden deft   upon the Caſe   appeared

The Same things being offered agt the Tryal of the ſd action in this Court as in the other this action was alſo Continued untill the Juſtices Shold adviſe thereupon and the baile in like manner Continued Except they put in other baile

Action   John Grey alis Tatham plt
Called   agt   in an action   plt & deft   both appeared
         Joſeph Growdon deft - -   upon the Caſe

Declaracon being read and the action depending upon Some accts both plt and deft requeſted that the accts might be firſt audited and Requeſted that Thomas Revel and willm Biles may have the auditing of the ſd accts and that if they Cannot agree thereupon Edward Shippen may have the Concluſion thereof of wch the Court Allowed and
ordered accordingly and that they make report of theire doings therein unto the next Court to be held here in the next 10th month –

action   Edward Hunloke plt
Called   agt   in an action of Treſpas   plt & deft   appeared
         John pikcock deft   upon the Caſe

Declaracon read and the deft acknowledged that he had the goods &
Chattles declared for of the Eſtate of Bowmans and promiſed
to yeild up the Same to the plt he the ſd plt paying the funeral
Charges of the ſd Bowman and Attendance in his Sicknes and
The Court haveing heard the premiſes Conſidered that the
plt Shold recover agt the deft the Eſtate of the ſd Bowman
that Came to the hands and poſſeſſion of the ſd deft in the life
time of the ſd Bowman and at his deceaſe and that the plt
Shold pay to the ſd deft nine pounds five Shillings Six pence
for funeral Charges and that the deft deliver up all writeings
books papers or accounts that were in his hands or poſſeſſion
or that he Cold get into his poſſeſſion that did any way relate
to the ſd Thomas Bowman deceaſed and that the deft pay Coſt
of ſuite

And the ſd deft promiſed to yeild and deliver up what he had in
his poſſeſſion to the plt or his order Except the books papers or
other writeings which he had and thoſe he promiſed to deliver to
willm Biles one of the Juſtices of peace then upon the bench
for the uſe of the ſd plt

Court adjourns for one houre

A Deed of Three hundered and fifty acres of land in fee dated the 25th
day of April 1698 was Delivered by Samll Beakes Attorney
to Henry flower grantor unto Thomas Hardin grantee

312

Action ⎱ James Alman plt ⎫ in an action of Treſpas ⎧ plt ⎫ appeared
Called ⎰   agt   ⎬ upon the Caſe   ⎨ & ⎬
           John Rowland Deft ⎭   ⎩ deft ⎭

declaracon Read the plt and Deft deſired that the actions depending might
be arbitrated by Joſeph kirkbride and James paxſon to wch the –
Court Conſented and appointed Richard Hough as umpire to End
what they Cold not agree upon viz the arbitrators and they
promiſed
to pforme what they Shold award (viz the plt and deft) relateing
to the ſaid Complt then brought into Court by the plt & deft And
the Court
ordered that the ſd awarders make report of theire doings therein
unto the next Court to be held in the 10th month next

| Action Called | ffrancis white plt agt James Alman deft | in an action of Trespas upon the Case | plt & deft | appeared |

Declaration read as follows

ffrancis white Complaines agt James Alman of the County of Bucks aforesaid in an action of Trespafs upon the Case for that whereas the Said ffrancis white was possessed of one nag or gelding about foure yeares of age neare a Chestnut Coulour with a Small blaze down
his face being parted neare the middle with other Coloured haire a little white Spot on the sitlock upon the right foot behind –
a Smal half penny Cut neare the middle of the right Eare upon the under side and branded whilest he was out of the Custody of the sd plt: worth three pounds Ten shillings which nag or gelding
doth properly belong to the said plt
and Altho the said deft was sufitiontly
informed thereof yet notwithstanding
the Said James Alman deviseing to deceive the sd plt: of the sd nag or gelding
him did take keep use and Convert to his own use Conterary to the statute Laws of this province whereupon the sd plt Saith he is damnified three pounds Ten
Shillings and thereupon produceth this suite and Craves Judgmt of this Court for the sd damages and Cost of suite &c:

Answer the deft pleaded not guilty and for tryal puts him self upon the Cuntry and so doth the plt whereupon the Sherrife is Commanded venire to return Twelve honest men of the neighbourhood by whom the truth of the matter may be the better known

Jury returnd Attested
Joseph milner   Anthony Burton   Henry Margerum   Edmund Lovet
Edward Lucas   walter pomphray   William Dark   John Shaw –
John Stakehouse   Jacob Janney   Thomas Janney   all attested

wittnesses Attested for the plt

Elizabeth white Attested doth Say as to the horse declared for She knew him from a Colt and that Shee knew his Sucking of her Son ffrancis Whites mare

peter white Attested doth Say that he knew him from a Sucking Colt and that he hath a Small blaze down his face and a Smal

White Spot upon his nofe of a Chefnut Colour about the latter End of this Summer foure yeares of age

John Cartor Attefted doth say he knew the fd horse from about a month old and that he hath know him all along untill this time being about foure yeares of age of a Chefnut Colour with a blaze down his face parted in the middle of the face with haire of the Colour of his body

313

william Codery Attefted doth Say that he being Servant to the fd plt he knew of the takeing up the mare and the Colt the Colt being the horfe now declared for and that he took Care of it and gave it meale one – winter, and that he helped to marked it with a Smal half peny cut under the right Eare and to the Colour and blaze as above

John plumley Attefted doth Say that he knew the horfe from a Colt and that he was always Called by the name of ffrancis white Colt and afterward by his horfe and alfo Spoke to the Colour and blaze as above

witnefes Attefted for the deft

william Biles Junr: Attefted doth Say that he Chalenged the horfe when he was a Colt and that he had fo done and known him yearly Ever fince and did take him up and brand him and that he – heard ffrancis white Say that the horfe that he now Claimes to the beft of his knowledg had Two half peny cuts

John Biles Attefted Say that he Eare marked a Colt which is as – likely to be the Same horfe now in Controverfie as its poffible a Colt Can be like to a horfe

Samll Beakes Attefted doth Say that about the 22 or 23 day of the 5th mo: laft paft being at ffrancis whites there was A young mare that fd white told him was marked at the fame time when the aforefd horfe was Eare marked which marked with Two half peny cuts and he afked why they were diferently marked and Said white Said that he might know them the one from the other

Jeremiah Dungan Saith that he knew george Biles mare and knew

Shee was Drowned and Saw the Colt and it was lame & poore

Edward Mayos Attefted Saith he and John Cook riding up Cooks run found a Colt that was fo weak and poore it Cold not Stand tho they helped it up whereupon faid Cook Said it was George Biles Colt and knockt it on the head and kild it becaufe they thought it Cold not live

John Addington Attefted Saith that william Biles Chalenged a horfe at grace Langhorns of about 3 years of age that was then unearemarked

Richard Thatcher Attefted Saith that George Biles Told him his Colt had mealy Sides and muffel

verdict Jury returned finds for the deft:

Grand Jury Complaines that Clement Dungan and John Gilbert Collectors of the late Tax have not brought in theire duplicates and made up theire accounts of the Tax its therefore

ordered that warrantes be Iffued for bringing in the fd Collectors to this Court to anfwer the fd neglect

A Deed or Indenture } of the moiety of Sundry Lots and parcels of Land mils and buildings premifes and appurtenances therein mentioned in fee Dated the 3 day of the 7th month 1698 was Delivered by — Phineas Pemberton Attorney to Samuel Carpenter grantor unto Henry Baker grantee

The Counter part thereof was Likewife delivered by the aforefaid – Henry Baker unto the aforefaid Phineas Pemberton for the ufe of the aforefaid Samuel Carpenter

314

Action Called } Jofeph Chorley plt– agt Henry warwin deft } in an action upon the Cafe { plt appeared deft appeared not

It being the Second Default

A Deed of Three hundered acres of Land in fee Dated the firft day of the 7th month 1698 was Delivered by Henry Baker grantor unto william Biles grantee

Recogniz: george Randol being Called upon his Recognizance appeared nothing further appearing againſt the Said george Randol the Court diſcharges him paying his fees

grand Jurys preſentmts

Ralph Boome prſented for aſſaulting the Sherriſe and Conſtable in the Execution of theire office

Bucks ſſ we the grand Jury haveing veiued the County accounts and do find the County in debt and do preſent the neceſſity of raiſeing one peny the pound Tax for defraying the Charge

Joſuah Hoops foreman

The neceſſity of A road from Thomas kirls houſe to the kings road

The neceſſity of Every freeholder to have a diſtinct Eare mark

Bucks ſſ we the grand Jury for the body of this County do preſent ffrancis white for ſtrikeing John Addington one blow

Joſuah Hoops foreman

A Deed of one hundred and fifty acres of Land in fee dated the 25th day of the 4th month 1698 was Delivered by Samll Beakes Attorney to Bartholemew Thather and Joſeph Thatcher grantors
unto Robt Heaton grantee

Complt – Samll Beakes Complaines againſt John Stork how that he was taken up as A run away and has made an Eſcape from him and
how that there was fees due to him and others for the takeing of
him up to the value of 2£ -5ˢ -6ᵈ as p his pticulers wᶜʰ was allowed of by this Court and the Court awarded Execution
agt: the goods and Chattles of ſd Stork for satisfyeing the ſd Charge

over ſeeres of the high ways appointed for the Succeeding yeare

Buckingham	Thomas Brock
ffalls _ _ _ _ _ _ _	Joſeph kirkbride
makefeild _ _ _ _	Joſeph milner
middle Town _ _ _	Henry Hudleſtone

new Town
&
Wrights Town } James yates

Benfalem _ _ _ _ ffrancis fearle

Southhampton
&
Warminfter } John Eaftbourn

Conftables for the fucceeding yeare

Buckingham — — — Thomas yardley
ffalls — — — — peter webfter
makefeild — — — Thomas Janney
middle Town — — Edward Cartor
new Town
&
wrights Town } _ _ _Samll Hough

Benfalem — — — nicholas vandegreift
Southhampton & warminfter John Eaftbourn

ffrancis white being prfented for Strikeing John Addington one blow

Submitted to the Court

Whereupon the Court difcharged him paying his ffees

Court Adjourns untill the Last Inftant

Actions Continued untill the next Court

Action John grey als Tatham plt
        agt
   Jofeph Growdon deft } in an action upon the Cafe

    Thomas Gardiner plt
        agt
   Chriftopher Snowdon deft } in an action upon the Cafe

Thomas Gardiner plt
    agt — in an action of Trefpafs & affault
Saml oldale deft –

Jofeph Chorley plt
    agt in an action upon the Cafe
Henry warwin deft –

Action Entered the i day i0 month 1699 Wm Biles Junr plt
    agt in an action upon the Cafe
Summonce granted iith day   Elizabeth Burges deft

with drawn the 14th day by the plts ordr

Bucks ff –   At a Court of Quarter feffions held in the name of william penn proprietarie & Govrnr of the province of penfylvania and Territories thereunto belonging at the Court houfe for the aforefaid County the i4th day of the i0th month 1698

    The Juftices present

        Jofeph Growdon william Biles Richard Hough
        Jonathan Scaife Corronor
        Samuel Beakes Sherrife
        Phineas Pemberton Cl: Com:

    Court Adjourns to the Houfe of Jofeph Chorley

grand Jury Robt Heaton Peter worral John Hough Henry paxfon Stephen Twineing John Surket Thomas Stakehoufe Andrew–
Attefted – Ellot Enoch yardley Jeremiah Langhorn Thomas knight – Thomas Bayns william paxfon John palmer Jofuah Hoops all Attefted

Jofeph milner Anthony Burton walter pomphray Thomas Janney
william Dark Edmund Lovet Edward Lucas Jacob Janney — John Shaw Henry Margerum John Stakehoufe James moone — being bound by Recognizance to appear at this Court to Anfwer

theire Illegal proceedings being Impaneled on a Jury the Laſt — Court for tryal of a Caſe then depending between ffrancis white plt and James Alman deft
being Called they all appeared

316 And upon their Examination thereupon they acknowledged and Confeſſed
that being devided in theire oppinions Cold not agree upon a verdict haveing debated the Caſe part of A day and the moſt part of the night they Condecended to See which way it Cold go by Lot and thereupon Cauſed the Conſtable John Dark to Caſt a peice of mony in his hat but deney'd that the verdict was brought in upon the Lott but that they afterward agreed upon the verdict and accordingly brought the Same verdict in to Court which Caſting of the lot had been agreat trouble to them that they had ſuffered Such a thing amongſt them and that they had payd So much money as had given Satiſfaction both to the plt and deft and parties Concerned whereupon ffrancis white George Biles &c: were Called into the Court and declared the Jury had given them ſatiſfaction and that they were no way hurt or damnifyed by the said verdict

Adjourned the Court for one houre

Adjourned until tomorrow morning at 8 a Clock

The Said Jury men being againe Called in to court they declared as before and Submitted to what the Court wold do to them for the Said offence and So they did all being Called anſwered one by one that they ſubmitted to the Court
John Dark the Conſtable who Attended the Jury at the Same time and Caſt the mony in the hat being bound by recognizance to — appeare at this Court being Called appeared Likewiſe and Confeſt the fact and Submitted to the Court

It was Confidered by the Court that they Sold be fined as followeth

Joſeph milner Shold pay a fine of 2£ — 10ˢ — 0ᵈ
Anthony Burton—a fine of _ _ _ _ 2 — 10 — 0
Henry Margerum a fine of _ _ _ _ _ 2 — 10 — 0
Edmund Lovet a fine of _ _ _ _ _ _ 2 — 10 — 0
Edward Lucas a fine of _ _ _ _ 2 — 10 — 0
walter pomphray a fine of _ _ _ _ _ 2 — 10 — 0
James moone a fine of _ _ _ _ _ _ 2 — 10 — 0
willm Dark a fine of _ _ _ _ _ _ 2 — 10 — 0
John Shaw — a fine of _ _ _ _ _ 2 — 10 — 0

John Stakehoufe a fine of	2	10	0
John Stakehoufe a fine of	10	10	0
John Stakehoufe a fine of	2	10	0
Jacob Janney — a fine of	2	10	0
Thomas Janney a fine of	2	10	0
in all — 30			

And the Court fines the Said John Dark in 10ˢ

And alſo awards that they and Every of them pay theire respective ffees

A Deed of five hundred acres of Land in fee with divers goods and Chattles Dated the 10th day of the 10th month 1698 was Delivered by Henry paxſon and Elizabeth Burges grantors unto James plumley and John plumley grantees

A Deed of foure hundred ninety Two acres of Land in fee dated the 10th day of the 10th month

Abigaile Milles being bound over by Recognizance to appear at this Court being Called appeared accordingly
And be accuſed by Stepen Beakes for felonioufly takeing from him ſundry goods to

317

the value of foure Shillings Sixpence and upon her Examination Confeſſed
the fact and Submitted to the Court
whereupon the Court considered that the Said Abigaile miles Shold pay to the Said Stephen Beakes foure fold being 18ˢ and fees of Court

| Action Called | John grey als Tatham plt agt Joſeph Growdon deft — | in an action upon the Caſe | plt appeared deft appeared not |

The Deft Said he ought to have a non Suite but being he beleived that the River being frozen was the occation of his not being there he therefore wold not take the advantage but is Contented it may be Continued whereupon the Court Continued the ſd action untill the
next Court

Adjourned the Court for one houre

Action } Thomas Gardiner plt — } in an action { plt appeared by his Attorney David Lloyd
Called }   agt   upon the Case
Christopher Snowdon deft   deft appeared not

The Deft baile Craved that in as much as they lived on the other side of the River and the River being frozen up that he Cold not Come over that the action might be Continued untill the next Court

wch was accordingly Continued by the plts Attorneys Consent and the baile was likewise Continued

Action } Thomas Gardiner plt } in an action { plt appeared by his Attorney David Lloyd
Called }   agt   of Trespass
Samll oldale deft   and assault   deft appeared

But the action was Continued at the request of the plt & deft —

Action } Joseph Chorley plt } in an action upon { plt appeared —
Called }   agt   the Case
Henry warwin deft   deft appeared not

The declaracon Read as ffollows

Joseph Chorley Complaines agt Henry warwin of East Jersey in a
plea of Case for that whereas the Said Henry warwin did take one brown bay stone horse to the value of foure pounds being the proper goods of the Said Joseph Chorley which horse the said
warwin did Convert to his own proper use whereupon the said plt Commences his Suite and Craves Judgmt of this Court for the sd horse with damages and Cost of suite &c

The Declaracon proved by Richard Thatcher James Acreman and Saml Beakes

The Justices haveing heard and understood the premises it was Considered that Joseph Chorley Shold recover the horse declared for with Cost of Suite

John Grifith being Chosen Constable for Southhampton &c:
 pleaded
his age and desired to be excused and the Court accordingly — Excused him

John Eastbourn appointed in his stead for the succeeding time
Grand Jury, brought in theire presentments

Bucks ss we the grand Jury for the body of this County do prsent Henry Baker for not repaireing the way where the wast water runs neare bucks mill dam being intolerable passing both for foot and horse

318   we also present Joseph kirkbride for being defective in his office in not repaireing the way that Leads from the falls to neshaminah
in the falls Township

upon the Complt of peter webster we prsent the necessity of his haveing Convenient way from his house to the kings road
                                             Robt Heaton foreman

we also do prsent Joseph Smalwood for violently beating and Intolerably abuseing his wife

we also do prsent Geo Randol for beating and Intolerably abuseing
of his grand Child

we also prsent the necessity of A bridg to be made over the Creek Commonly Called Cooks Creek on the road from the falls to Buckingham
                                       Robt. Heaton foreman

we do also prsent the necessity of another house of Entertainemnt
and accomodations for man & horse at the Court time to be kept at Saml Beakes house

we do also prsent Joseph Chorley for Selling beare by unlawfull measure
                                       Robt Heaton foreman

Joseph Chorley being prsented by the grand Jury for Selling beare by unlawfull measure Submitted to the Court
Samll Beakes allowed to keep ordinary

Gilbert   Joseph Gilbert being brought before the Court upon the Complt of nicholas williams was ordered to give Security for
Recogniz   his appearance at the next Court to answer the sd Complt
Joseph Gilbert acknowledge him self Indebted to the proprietarie in the Sum of Twenty pounds and John Gilbert his father in

Ten pounds to be Levied on theire Lands and Tenemts goods & Chattles

And this is upon Condition that the Said Joseph Gilbert Shall appeare at the next Court of Quarter Seffions to be held for the aforesd County to answer the Complt of nicholas williams

willms Recogniz
nicholas williams acknowledged him self Indebted to the proprietarie in the Sum of Ten pounds to be Levied on his goods and Chattles Lands and Tennemts

And this is upon Condition that he appeare at the next Court of Quarter Seffions to be held for this County to profecute his — Complt agt Joseph Gilbert

Judgmt and Execut awarded
Samll Beakes requested the Court to grant him Execution for ffees due to him and the Jury about Serveing the Execution in the Cafe Englifh white & green agt noble his Demand according to his account being 6£ –10^s –6^d whereupon the Court awarded that Execution be Iffued agt the sd plts for foure pounds in pte of the Said ffees

upon the prfentment of peter webfters neceffity of a road from his Houfe to the kings roade The Court appoints Saml Dark Henry margerum willm Dark James paxfon & John Rowland to Lay out the fame

The Court adjourns to 2nd weekly 4th day in the firft month next

Actions Continued untill the next Court   319

John grey als Tatham plt
    agt
Joseph Growdon deft – –
} in an action upon the Cafe

Thomas gardiner plt
    agt
Samll oldale deft
} in an action of Trefpafs and Affault

Thomas gardiner plt
    agt
Chriftopher Snowdon deft
} in an action upon the Cafe

Actions Entered agt the next Court

Action Entered the 4th day of the 12th month 1698

mahlon Stacy plt
    agt } in an action of debt
Joſeph Chorley deft

Summonce granted thereupon

Action Entered the 4th day of the i2th month 1698

Samll oldale plt
    agt } in an action upon the Caſe
Joſeph Chorley deft

Attachment granted thereupon the 4th day i2 month i698

Action Entered the 4th day i2 month 1698

william Biles plt
    agt } in an action upon the Caſe
Joſeph Chorley deft

Attachment thereupon granted the 4th day i2 month 1698 with drawn the ſd action by the plts ordr the 20th day of the ſd month

Action Entered the 4th day i2th month 1698

John Scarbrought plt
    agt } in an action upon the Caſe
Joſeph Chorley deft

Attachment thereupon granted the 4th day i2th month i698 with drawn the ſd action by the plts ordr the 20th day of the ſd month

Action Entered the 4th day i2 month 1698

Joſeph kirkbride plt
    agt } in an action upon the Caſe
Joſeph Chorley deft –

Attachment thereupon granted the 4th day i2 month 1698 with drawn by the plts ordr the 20th day of the ſd month

320

Action Entered the 6th day of the i2th month 1698

Gilbert wheeler plt
   agt   } in an action of debt
Joseph Chorley deft

Attachment granted thereupon the 6th day of the 12th mo $\frac{1698}{9}$

with drawn by the plts ordr the 20th day 12 month

Action Entered the 6th day 12th month 1698

John Scarbrought plt –
   agt   } in an action upon the Case
Joseph Smalwood deft

Attachment thereupon granted the 6th day 12th month 1698

Return Attached one bright bay mare and a Colt about 2 yeares the 27th 12 month $\frac{1698}{9}$

p Saml Beakes sherrife

Action Entered the 6th day 12th month 1698

willm Embley Thomas Lambert & ffrancis Davenport
Executrs of John Lambert deceased plts agt   } in an action of debt
Joseph Chorley deft — — — — — — — — —

Attachment granted thereupon the same Day

with drawn by the plts ordr the 20th day of the sd month

Action Entered the 7th day 12 month 1698

James Acreman plt
   agt   } in an action upon the Case
James Alman deft

Arrest thereupon granted the same day

Action Entered the   day of the   month 1698

Peter worral plt
   agt   } in an action upon the Case
ffrancis Tunneclift deft

with drawn

Action Entered the 9th day 12th month 1698

John Snowdon plt
    agt } in an action upon the Cafe
Jofeph Chorley deft

Attachment granted thereupon the fame day

with drawn by the plts ordr the 20th day 12
                                          mo

Action Entered the 15th day 12th month 1698   321

Phineas Pemberton plt
    agt } in an action upon the Case
Jofeph Chorley deft

Arreft granted thereupon the Same day

with drawn by the plts ordr the 20th Inftant

Action Entered the 17 day of the 12 month 1698

John and Elias nichols plts } in an action upon the Cafe for a
    agt   fum
Jofeph Chorley deft   under forty Shillings

warrant granted thereupon to apprend the Said Jofeph Chorley to bring him
before a Juftice of the peace to anfwer the fd Complt: the 17th day 12
                mo

The fame day the fd Chorley was brought before Richard Hough one of
the Juftices of peace for the aforefd County where fd Joseph — Chorley owned that he owed the mony to the plt mentioned in the warrant aforefd

whereupon the Said Juftices of the peace ordered payment thereof to the Complainant

Action Entered the 14th day 12 month 1698

Ifaac Norris plt
    agt } in an action upon the Cafe
Jofeph Chorley deft

Arreſt granted thereupon the Same day

 return the body of Joſeph Chorley was Arreaſted the i5th day of the ſd month

  by Samll Beakes Sherriſe

Action Entered the 17th day i2th month 1698

 John nichols and Elias nicholas Leaſors to Anthony Burton Leaſee by theire Attorneys mahlon Stacy and Henry Baker } plts

   agt

 Thomas Brock auſtor in an action Ejectione firme

Summonce & Declaracon of the Ejectmt read and delivered to Joſeph Chorley

the 17th day of the ſd month by Samll Beakes ſherriſe

Action Entered the i5 day i2th month 1698

 Jeffery Hawkins plt
   agt   } in an action upon the Caſe
 Joſeph Chorley deft

Arreſt granted thereupon the i5th day of the Same month
with drawn the 20th of the ſd month by the plts ordr

322

Action Entered the i5th day i2th month 1698

 Stephen Beakes plt
   agt   } in an action upon the Caſe
 Joſeph Chorley deft

Arreſt granted thereupon the Same day

with drawn by the plts order the 20th Inſtant

Action Entered the i5th day i2th month 1698

 Samll Jennings plt
   agt   } in Caſe under forty Shillings
 Joſeph Chorley deft

warrant granted the i5th day of the ſd month to anſwer the ſd Complt and the debt he owned to be due before Richard Hough one of the Juſtices of peace for the ſd County who ordered payment thereof the ſd day

with drawn by the plts ordr the 20th Inſtant

Action Entered the 15th day 12th month 1698

    Iſaac Merriot plt
        agt   } in Caſe under forty Shillings
    Joſeph Chorley deft

A warrant granted thereupon the Said day month & yeare to anſwer the ſd
Complt and the ſd debt he the ſd deft owned the Same day to be
due to the ſd plt before Richard Hough one of the Juſtices of peace
for the ſaid County who at the ſame time ordered payment thereof

with drawn by the plts ordr the 20th Inſtant

Action Entered the 16th day of the 12th month 1698

    James ffox plt
        agt   } in an action upon the Caſe
    Joſeph Chorley deft

Arreſt thereupon granted the ſame day

with drawn by the plts order the 20th day of the ſd month

Action Entered the 17th day 12th month 1698

    Andrew Ellot plt
        agt   } in an action upon the Caſe
    Joſeph Chorley deft

Attachment granted thereupon the Same day

with drawn by the plts order the 20th Inſtant

Action Entered the   day   month 1698

    Joſeph Chorley plt
        agt   }
    Samll Beakes deft

with drawn by the plts order the 9th $\frac{i}{mo}$ $\frac{1698}{9}$

Action Entered 18th day 12th month 1698

> John Cartor plt
> agt
> Bartholomew Thatcher deft
> } in an action upon the Cafe

Arreſt granted thereupon the 21 day of the ſd 12th month
return not to be found

Action Entered the 21 day 12th month 1698

> Joſeph kirkbride plt
> agt
> Bartholomew Thatcher deft
> } in an action upon the Cafe

Arreſt granted the Said day

Return not to be found

Action Entered the 21 day 12 mo 1698

> Joſeph Chorley plt
> agt
> Elizabeth Burges deft
> } in an action upon the Cafe

Summonce granted thereupon

with drawn by the pls order

Action Entered the 8th day of the 1 month 1698

> Joſeph Chorley plt
> agt
> John Hornor deft
> } in an action upon the Cafe

Arrest thereupon granted the ſame day

Bucks ſſ   At a Court of Quarter Seſſions held in the name
of william penn proprietarie of the province
of penſylvania the 8th day of the firſt month
at the Court houſe for the aforeſaid County
Anno Dij $\frac{1698}{9}$

The Juſtices prſent

willm Biles   Henry Baker   Richard Hough   John ſwift

Jonathan Scaiſe Corronr

Saml Beakes Sherriſe

Phineas Pemberton Cl: Com:

grand Jury Joſuah Hoops   John Surket   Edward Lucas   william Smith   Stephen Twineing   John Cowgill   John Croſdel   Thomas Hardin   Henry Margerum   John Rowland   John Smith   Robert Heaton   Saml Allin   willm Hayhurſt   Saml Coates all Atteſted

Ralph Boome being Called upon his prſentment Submitted to the Court whereupon the Court Diſcharged him paying his fees

Henry Baker being prſented Laſt Court for not repaireing the road where the waſt water of the mill dam at Buckingham overflowed promiſed to repair the Same when the weather prſented but ſaid he expected the Cuntrys Affiſtance

324

Joſeph kirkbride being prſented Laſt Court for neglecting to get the high
ways repaired in the ffalls Townſhip promiſed to take Speedy Care to get them repaired

upon the prſentment of the neceſſity of A bridg over the Run Called Cooks
Run or Creek the Court ordered that the overſeers of the high ways Summonce the inhabitants of the Townſhips of the ffalls & Buckingham to make a bridg over the ſd Run

Joſeph Chorley being prſented Laſt Court for ſelling beare or ale by Small meaſure Submitted to the Court and thereupon the Court diſcharged him paying his ffees

Adjourned the Court for one houre

A Deed of A Tract of Land about Two hundered and fifty acres in fee dated the Twenty ninth day of the 10th month 1698 was Delivered by Peter white grantor unto John Headley grantee

A Deed of Three hundered acres of Land in ffee Dated the 28th day of the 10th month 1698 was Delivered by Samuel Beakes Attorney to John white ffrancis white willm White Joſeph White and

Benjemame white grantors unto theire brother peter white grantee

A Deed of Two hundered and fifty acres of Land in fee Dated the ii day of march 1695 was Delivered by John white grantor unto peter white Attorney to his mother Elizabeth white grantee

grand Jury prſented John pidcock for beating and wounding James verrier

pleaded not guilty and for Tryal put him ſelf upon the Cuntry whereupon the Sherrif is Commanded to return 12 honeſt men of the neighbourhood whereby the truth of the matter may be the better known

Jury william paxſon Joſeph Clows Enoch yardley willm Duncan
Stephen Beakes Andrew Ellot Henry Hudleſton Ruben pownel
Jeremiah Langhorn wm Biles Junr: willm Ellot John Hough
} all Atteſted

bill read as ffollows

County of Bucks for the Court held in the ſd County the 8th March 1698/9

we the grand Jury for the body of ſd County do preſent John pidcock
of the ſd County yeoman for that he the ſd pidcock did on or about the 2i
day of January Laſt paſt wilfully and malitiouſly in his own houſe within
the Juriſdiction of this Court violently aſſault knock down beate & abuſe
James verier of the Said County maſon So that his head was extreamly
Swelled Cut and battered to the great hazard of his Life and very much to his
damage all which is againſt the peace of our Soveraigne Lord the king his
Crown and Dignity and againſt the Laws of this province in that Caſe made &
provided

A true Bill Joſuah Hoops foreman

peaded not guilty

willm Smith Attested Saith that John pidcock Struck James verier on the
head first with a peice of a Loafe of bread and after broke a stoole upon
him and after gave him a blow upon the head with a stoole & further
Saith not

325

A Deed of Two Tracts of Land being three hundered acres in fee dated the 29th day of the 4th month 1698 was Delivered by peter —
white Attorney to John white
and wife grantors unto ffrancis white grantee

A Deed of Two hundered acres of Land in fee Dated the 29th day of the 4th month 1698 was Delivered by Samll Beakes ———
Attorney to Elizabeth white peter white ffrancis white Joseph white Benjemaine white and william white grators unto ———
John white grantee

A Deed of Two hundered and fifty acres of Land in fee Dated the 5th day of the
3 month 1697 was Delivered by Samuel Beakes Attorney to Sarah Clows and her husband Edward Bennet grantors unto Richard Hough
grantee

A Deed of Six hundered acres of Land in ffee dated the 14th day of the 3 —
month 1684 was Delivered by John Swift Attorney to Allin ffoster and his wife mary grantors unto James plumley Attorney to Thomas
ffaireman grantee

A Deed of five hundered eighty Two acres of Land in fee Dated 26th day of the
iith month 1698 was Delivered by James plumley grantor unto John   9
Swift Attorney to John morris grantee _____

A Deed of one hundered and eighteen acres of Land in ffee dated the —
6th day of the i0th month 1697 was Delivered by Samll Allin —
Attorney to Nicholas waln grantor unto John Town grantee

A Deed of one hundered acres of Land in fee dated the i2th day of the 7th month 1692 was Delivered by william Hayhurst Attorney to
Thomas

ffaireman grantor unto Samuel Allin grantee

Adjourned the Court untill 9 a Clock tomorrow morning

A Letter of Attorney from Samel Beakes to his brother willm Beakes acknowledged by the Said Samel Beakes to be his act & deed

A Deed of Twenty five acres of Land in fee Dated 8th day of the i2th month 1698 was Delivered by willm Biles Attorney to Thomas 9
Hudſon grantor unto Richard Hough grantee

A Deed of Twenty five acres of Land in ffee dated the 7th day of the i2th month i698 was Delivered by willm Biles Attorney to Thomas Hudson grantor unto Henry Baker grantee

A Deed of five hundred acres of Land in ffee dated the 6th day of the firſt month 1688 was Delivered by phineas pemberton 9
Subſtitute Attorney to Richard Davies grantor unto Joſeph — Growdon grantee

A Deed of Two hundered acres of Land in fee dated the 10th day of the 8th month i698 was Delivered by Joſeph Chorley Attorney to Iſabel Cutler grantor unto william paxſon grantee

A Deed of a Smal peice of Land about three acres in fee Dated the 12th day of the 10th month i698 was Delivered by Barndt virkirk grantor unto Leonard vandegreift grantee

A Deed of about thirty Two acres of Land in fee dated the i2th day of the 10th month i698 was Delivered by ffrederick vandegrieft grantor unto Barndt virkirk grantee

(326)

A Deed of one hundred ninety Seven acres of Land in fee Dated 20th day of
the i2th month 1698 was Delivered by william Hayhurſt Attorney to 9
william Croſdell and John Croſdell grantors unto John Cowgill grantee

A Deed of one hundred acres of Land in fee Dated the 6th day of the i2th month 1696 was Delivered by Richard Thatcher (Attorney Samuel Beakes) grantor unto John Scarbrough grantee

Edward Hunloke Complained agt John pidcock how that according to A former Judgmt of Court wch he the Said Hunloke obtained agt the Said pidcock he had not performed neither to deliver the affets of Thomas Bowman deceafed nor to pay the Court Charges and — Therefore Craved Execution agt the fd pidcock whereby the Said Judgment may be fullfilled

whereupon the Court ordered that Execution Iffue agt the eftate of the Said John pidcock for one pound eight Shillings and Ten pence half peny charges of Court and for all the bookes papers writeings or other Eftate the faid John pidcock hath got in his Cuftody of the faid Thomas Bowman

Jury Returned and Called over

John pidcock Called appeared

verdict we find John pidcock guilty of the Crime whereof he ftands Indicted

Judgmt It was therefore Confidered by the Court that John pidcock Shold pay
fine A fine of Ten fhillings to the Govrnr and give Security for his good abearing toward James verier and all the kings fubjects

Jofeph Chorley being Called upon his Recognizance appeared and the
Court orders that he give Security for his appearance at the next Court and for his good abearing in the meane time and —
Commits him into the Sherrifs Cuftody untill he Shall performe the fame

Adjourned the Court for one houre

A Deed of   of Land in fee dated the day of the month 169   was Delivered by Jofeph Growdon grantor unto James Bond grantee

A Deed of one hundred acres — — — of Land in ffee dated the — 3 day of the i month 1698 was Delivered by Jofeph Growdon grantor unto Stephen Sands grantee

A Deed of Two hundred and Two acres of Land in ffee with fome Exceptions dated the 16th day of the 12th month $\frac{1698}{9}$ was Delivered by Jofeph Growdon grantor unto william Beale grantee

A Deed of Two hundered and fifty acres of Land and premifes in fee Dated the 10th day of the 12th month 1698/9 was Delivered by Samuel Beakes Attorney to Jonathan Scaife grantor unto John Hough grantee

A Deed of Two hundered and nine acres of Land in fee dated the Tenth day of the 12th month 1698/9 was Delivered by Samuel Beakes Attorney to John Dawſon and his wife martha and Ann Clarke grantors unto Henry Bowen grantee

A Deed of three parcells of Land in fee Dated the 1 day of the firſt month 1698/9 was Delivered by Joseph kirkbride grantor unto his father in law Randol Blackſhaw grantee

327

A Deed of the aforementioned three parcells of Land in ffee with Some proviſoes Dated the 2nd day of the 1 month 1698 was Delivered by Randol Blackſhaw unto his Son nehemiah Blackſhaw — grantee

The Counterpart of the Said Deed or Indenture bearing Equal date therewih was Delivered by nehemiah Blackſhaw unto his father Randol Blackſhaw

A Deed of one Thouſand and fifty acres of Land in fee Dated the 8th day of the 12th month 1698 was Delivered by willm Biles Attorney to Thomas Hodſon grantor unto matthias Harvie grantee

Joſeph Gilbert being prſented by the grand Jury for felonrouſly takeing Sundry goods out of the houſe of nicholas williams

    pleaded to the Said preſentment not guilty and for tryal put him ſelf

        upon the Cuntry whereupon the Sherrife is Commanded to return —

venire 12 honeſt men of the neighbourhood whereby the truth of the matter may be the better known

Jury returned william paxſon Enoch yardley william Duncan Stephen Beakes Andrew Ellot Henry Hudleſton Jeremiah Langhorn william Biles Junr

William Ellot Ruben pownal John Hough John Snowdon all
 Atteſted

bill read

 *we the Jurrors do find Joſeph Gilbert guilty of ffelonioufly entering into the houſe of nicholas williams and from thence takeing and converting to his owne uſe several goods to the value of foure Shillings — Eleven pence

Bucks ff we the Jurrors for the body of this County do prſent Joſeph Gilbert for going into the houſe of nicholas williams and takeing away — Several goods thence Conterary to the kings peace and Statute Laws of this province &c

 a true bill — Joſuah Hoops foreman

preſentment proved by the affidavit of Joſeph Saterthwait

Jury returned and Called over & the ſaid Joſeph Gilbert brought to the barr delivered theire verdict in writeing as ffollows

verdict we the Jurrors do find Joſeph Gilbert Guilty of ffelonioufly entering into the houſe of nicholas williams and from thence takeing and Converting to his own uſe Several goods to the value of foure Shillings Eleven pence

 willm paxſon foreman

Commitm^t Court Commits Joſeph Gilbert into the Sherrifs Cuſtody untill further order

Judgmt The Court thereupon Conſidered that nicholas williams Shold recover agt Joſeph Gilbert foure fold the value of the Said goods being i9^s — 8^d and Coſts and that the ſd Gilbert be at Liberty

prſentmt we the Jurrors for the body of this County do prſent the neceſſity of a way to be Layd out from James Bonds Stephen Sands and Iſſabel Cutlers to the mill and meeting

---

*This paragraph crossed over in original record.

prſentmt we do prſent James Alman and Benjamain Cook for tyeing of Straw to the tayle of Joſeph Large Horſe and Setting it on fire and Samuel Smith Suffering it to be done in his ſight and upon his plantation

         Joſuah Hoops foreman —

they all pleaded not guilty and for tryal put them ſelves upon the Cuntry The Sherrife is therefore Commanded to return i2 honeſt men of the neighbourhood by whom the truth of the matter may be the better known

328 Thomas Terrey   Jury willm paxſon Enoch yardley
   Jaſper Terrey   willm Duncan Stephen Beakes
   Lawrence pearſon }all Atteſted Andrew
   Enoch pearſon   Ellot Henry Hudleſtone
                 Jeremiah Langhorn
                 willm Biles Junr: willm Ellot John
                 Snowdon Tho ſtakehouſe Ruben pownall
                    all Atteſted

 Jury Returnd give in theire verdict they donot find Benjemaine Cook and Samuel Smith guilty

 Iwas Conſidered by the Court that James Alman Shall pay a fine of Twenty Shillings to the Govrnr and pay Coſts

Action { John grey als Tatham plt } action Continued att the plts requeſt
     agt   & by the defts Conſent
   Joſeph Growdon deft - -

Action { Thomas Gardiner plt } the action Continued neither plt nor
     agt   deft appearing but requeſt that the
   Samll oldale deft   Same may be Continued

Action { Thomas Gardiner plt } the action Continued according to
     agt   requeſt untill the next Court
   Chriſtopher Snowdon deft

Recogniz John pidcock acknowledges him ſelf indebted to the proprietarie in the Sum of Twenty pounds and Richard Wilſon and John Scarbrough in Each Ten pounds to be Levied on theire goods & Chattles Lands and Tennements

And this is upon Condition that the Said John pidcock Shall be of good abeareing towards James verier and all the kings fubjects untill the Juftices Shall think fit to difcharge him or untill the next Court of Quarter Seffions

Jofeph Chorley acknowledged him Self indebted to the proprietarie in the Sum of one hundred pounds and willm Crofdel in the fum of forty pounds to be levied on theire goods and Chattles Lands and tennements

And this is upon Condition for the good behavior of Jofeph — Chorley to wards John Hornor and all the kings Subjects & that he appear at the next Court of Quarter Seffions or untill the Juftices Shall think fit to difcharge him

A Deed of part of Two hundered acres of Land in fee Dated the 16th day of the 9th month 1697 was Delivered by Samll Beakes Attorney to Job Houle grantor unto Hugh Ellis grantee

Adjourned the Court untill the 23 Inftant

Action Entered the 9th day of the firft month 1698

Jonathan oldham plt
    agt } in an action upon the Cafe
Jofeph Chorley deft

Attachment granted thereupon the fame day

Action Entered the 9th 1 mo 1698

John Swift plt
    agt } in an action of debt
Jofeph Chorley deft

Attachment granted the fame day

Bucks ff   At a Court held by Adjournment the 23 day of the 1 month 16 8/99

Juftices present william Biles Henry Baker Richard Hough John Swift
Samuel Beakes Sherrife
Phineas Pemberton Cl: Com:

COMMON PLEAS OF BUCKS COUNTY, PENNSYLVANIA 379

A Deed of one Thousand acres of Land in fee Dated the 18th day of November 1697 was Delivered by phineas pemberton Attorney to Israel Taylor Joseph Taylor John Busby and mary Busby grantors unto Robt Heaton grantee

A Deed of one hundered acres of Land in fee Dated the 17th day of the 12th month 1698/9 was Delivered by John Shaw grantor unto George willard grantee

A letter of Attorney from Anthony Burton to his brother John Burton was acknowledged to be the act and deed of the said Anthony Burton bearing date this day and the Same Certefied under the hands of the Justices and County Seal

petition of Julian kirle Read about away from her house to kings road refferred to the next Court

Return of the Road from peter websters house to the kings road read and report made to the Court that it was not layd out to satisfaction

ordered that Henry Baker and Richard Hough do veiue the place as it is returned and if it donot Satisfie all parties Concerned that then they appoint how it Shall be layd out

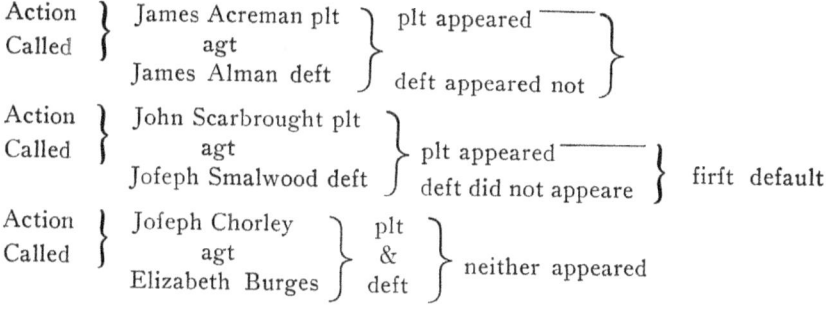

Action Called	James Acreman plt agt James Alman deft	plt appeared deft appeared not	
Action Called	John Scarbrought plt agt Joseph Smalwood deft	plt appeared deft did not appeare	first default
Action Called	Joseph Chorley agt Elizabeth Burges	plt & deft neither appeared	

Adjourned the Court for one houre

acctt   Gilbert wheeler presented his account in Court and there appeared to be due to him 5 £ – 10s which the Court orders that he have payd to him by the Treasurror out of the County Stock

Samuel Beakes Requested the Court to grant him Judgmt for the — remaineing part of the fees due to him in the Case peter White &c:

agt Rich noble and the Court thereupon Confidered that the Said-Beakes Shold have 20ˢ more then what was formerly allowed him and that Execution Iffue accordingly and that he take no more —

Adjourned the Court untill the 1 day of the Second month next

Bucks ff
───
330

At a Court held by adjournment the firft day of the Second month 1699

The Juftices prfent
william Biles   Henry Baker   Richard Hough
Samuel Beakes Sherrife
Phineas Pemberton Cl: Com:

Action Called– { mahlon Stacy plt agt Jofeph Chorley deft } { plt appeared deft appeared } action debt

Declaracon read

Jofeph Chorley did acknowledge and Confefs that he then Stood Indebted unto the Said mahlon Stacy the Sum of forty pounds mentioned in the Said Declaracon

Anfwer made by the plt that he wold not take the advantage of the forfeiture of the obligation but defired only the forty pounds principal mony

All which being fully underftood by the Juftices

It was Confidered by the Court that the fd plt Shold recover agt the — deft the Said forty pounds with coft of Suite and that he Shall — have execution for the Same — to be Levied on the goods and — Chattles of the fd deft the aforefd Judgmt was not given untill the 4 mo Court and may be seen in the minuts of the fd Court

Action Called { John nichols and Elias nichols by theire attorneys Mahlon ftacy and Henry Baker —— agt Thomas Brock deft — — — — — — — — — — — — — } Leafors to Anthony Burton Leffee plts

Jofeph Chorley Came into Court and defired that he might be admitted deft which was allowed by the court & plts — —

plts & deft appared both   action Ejectione firme

Declaracon read

        Joſeph Chorley did acknowledg and Confeſs that he had Executed a Certaine deed of Sale and mortgage unto the ſaid John and Elias nichols which proviſoe in the Said deed or Indenture is not performed on his part and that there is 64 £ i3ˢ –0ᵈ due to the Said plts for which mony the Land mentioned in the Said declaracon lyes — mortgaged to the ſd plts

Action Called { Abra Hardman & Iſaac Norris } by theire Attorneys plts

Joſeph kirkbride — — agt
Joſeph Chorley — — — deft

{ plt appeared by his ſd Attorney deft appeared -- } action upon the Caſe

Declaracon Read

    Anſwer made by the deft Joſeph Chorley that he did Confeſs and acknowledg that he is and ſtands Indebted to the Said plt the Sum of fifty foure pounds thirteen Shillings being the Sum declared for — defferred in the foregoing Caſes untill the next Court

Judgmt

action under 40ˢ-- upon the Caſe
{ John and Elias nichols plts agt Joſeph Chorley deft — — }
Richard Hough one of the Juſtices of peace reported to this Court how that Joſeph Chorley acknowledged him ſelf debtor the plts 39ˢ ii ᵈ ½ due for rent of a Certaine parcel of Land and that he had given it as his Judgmt that the ſd Chorley ought to pay the ſame and the ſd Chorley againe Confeſſed the ſd Debt to be due to ſd plts The Court Confirmed the ſd Judgmt and ordered Execution to Iſſue accordingly

*[331]

---

*Page 331 is not numbered in the record book.

action under 40ˢ -- upon the Cafe
: Thomas Coleman acknowledged that he was Indebted unto John – nichols and Elias nichols thirty nine Shillings and Eleven pence half peny It was therefore confidered by the Court that the fd nichols Shold recover — agt: the Said Thomas Coleman the fd 39ˢ ii½ᵈ and Cofts and that Execution Iffue accordingly

Adjourned the Court to Samll Beakes houfe an houre hence

Action Called : Jofeph Chorley plt agt Elizabeth Burges deft } plt appeared & defired the action to be with drawn

Action : Jonathan oldham plt agt Jofeph Chorley deft } plt nor deft } neither appeared

ordered that phineas pemberton have paid him by the Treafurror five pounds towards what is due to him for Laying out the Roads

Adjourned the Court untill the 14ᵗʰ day 4 next
                                            mo

Actions Continued untill the next Court

Action John grey als Tatham plt agt Jofeph Growdon deft } in an action upon the Cafe

Action Thomas Gardiner plts agt Samuel Oldale deft } in an action of Trefpafs and affault

Action Thomas Gardiner plt agt Chriftopher Snowdon deft } in an action upon the Cafe

Action John Scarbrough plt agt Jofeph Smalwood deft } in an action upon the Cafe

Action James Acreman plt
          agt } in an action upon the Cafe
       James Alman deft

Action John and Elias nichols
       by theire Attorneys ──
       Henry Baker & mahlon ſtacy } plts
              agt } in an action Ejectione firme
       Joſeph Chorley defts ── ── ──

Action Iſaac Norris plt
           agt } in an action upon the Cafe
       Joſeph Chorley deft

Action mahlon Stacy plt
           agt } in an action of debt
       Joſeph Chorley deft

Action Joſeph Chorley plt
           agt } in an action upon the Cafe
       John Hornor deft

Action John Swift plt
           agt } in an action of debt
       Joſeph Chorley deft

332

Action Entered for the fourth month Court next

    Action   Joſeph kirkbride plt
entered the   agt } in an action upon the Cafe
10ᵗʰ 2 1699 Bartholomew Thather deft
    mo

Attachment thereupon granted the Same day

Return there was Attached the 14ᵗʰ day of the 2ⁿᵈ month 1699 in the hand of
Robt Heaton the Sum of thirty pounds being due upon bond the 25ᵗʰ day
of the 4ᵗʰ month 1698 as alſo one Tract of Land Lying and adjoyneing

to the Land of willm Hayhurſt and one Tract of Land Lying over the
Creek the Quantyty unknown to me was Attached the 10th day of the 3
$$\overline{mo}$$
1699 p e Samll Beakes ſherriſe

Action Entered the 17th day of the 2 month 1699

Edmund wells plt
    agt } in an action of debt
ffrancis white deft

Summonce thereupon granted for the deft appearance at the next Court to be
held for this County

Action Entered the 1 day of the 4th month 1699

Joſeph Chorley
    agt } in an action upon the Caſe
James Alman deft

Attachment granted thereupon the Same day

Execution granted Samll Beakes for fees due to him in the Caſe peter white &c
agt Rich noble dated the 5th day of the 3 month 1699

Return there was taken the mony of peter white the Sum of five pounds thirteen Shillings in full p me

                                  Samll Beakes ſherriſe

Action Entered the 25th day of the 3 month 1699

Richard Thatcher plt
    agt } in an action upon the Caſe
willm Huntley deft

Arreſt granted the Same day

Bucks ff   At a Court of Quarter Seſſions held in —
the name of william penn proprietarie of
the province of penſylvania and territories thereunto
belonging At the Court houſe for the aforeSaid County

the 14th day of the 4th month 1699

The Juftices prfent

Jofeph Growdon william Biles Henry Baker Richard Hough

Samll Beakes Sherrife and deputy Cl: of the County

proclamation from the govrn^r about the Scoth Laws made the Laft Affembley read

Adjourned the Court for one houre

Action Called } Edmund wells plt agt ffrancis white deft } plt & deft } both appeared

333

deft did Confefs that he owed the plt Thirty pounds and Intreft for the Same

It was therefore Confidered by the Court that the plt Shall recover

agt the deft thirty pounds with Intreft for the Same & Coft of Suite

being what the plt defired and that he Shall have Execution for the

Same to be Levied on the goods and Chattles of the Said Deft

Action John grey als Tatham plt agt Jofeph Growdon deft - - } in an action upon the Cafe { plt appeared not deft did appeare }

and Said he ought to have a non Suite but however tho he had often

appeared to the Said action yet he was not unwilling that the action

might be Continued untill the next Court to fee if the plt might then make

his appearance and profecute his action whereupon the Court Continues

the action untill the next court

Action Ifaac Norris plt agt Jofeph Chorley deft } in an action upon the Cafe {

whereas the Laſt Court held the firſt day of the 2ᵈ month Laſt paſt the deft
Confeſſed that he was Indebted to the plt fifty foure pounds thirteen
Shillings

It was Conſidered by the Court that the Said Iſaac norris Shold recover
agt the Said Joſeph Chorley the Said Sum of 54£ : 13ˢ : 00ᵈ and Coſt of
Suite and that the plt Shall have execution for the Same to be Levied on
the goods and Chattles of the Said deft:

Action Mahlon Stacy plt }
    agt   } in an action of debt
Joſeph Chorley deft }

Joſeph Chorley in a Court held the i day of the 2 month Laſt paſt
did Confeſſ he owed & Stood Indebted unto mahlon Stacy the Sum of
forty pounds

It was Conſidered by the Court tha the Said plt Shold recover agt the ſd deft the
Said forty pounds with coſt of Suite and that he Shall have execution
for the Same to be Levied on the goods and Chattles of the ſd deft:

Joſeph Chorley being bound by Recognizance to appeare a this Court
appeared accordingly and was diſcharged paying his fees

Action John nicholas and Elias nichols plts } plt appeared by their
    agt   } ſubſtitute Attorney
Joſeph Chorley deft — — — — — } Samuel Beakes who
declared that he had Received 66£ –13ˢ –00ᵈ and Coſt of Suit in full
Satiſfaction of what was due to the Said plts and thereupon Cancelled
the mortgage & Sale of the Land Sued for in this Court by the ſaid
plts and Delivered up all patents writeings or other evidence Concern

ing the Same unto the deft Joſeph Chorley

A Deed of Three hundered and od acres in fee dated the 22 day of the 3ᵈ month 1699 was Delivered by Joſeph Chorley and mary his wife James Acreman James Heyworth and mary his wife grantrs
unto Samuel Beakes Attorney to John Harriſon grantee

Adjourned the Court untill 8 a Clock in the morning

| Action Called | Joſeph Chorley plt agt John Hornor deft plt declared his willingness to Continue the action untill next Court | plt appeared — — — deft appeared not | Court Continued it accordingly |

334

| Action Called | John Swift plt agt Joſeph Chorley deft | in an action of debt | plt appeared by his Attorney Samuel Beakes deft appeared |

And the Said Deft Confeſſed that he owed to the ſd plt Six pounds
and Intreſt for the Same the plt declared his Satiſfaction therewith

It was Conſidered by the Court that the Said plt Shold recover agt the Said deft the Said Sum of Six pounds and Intreſt due thereupon and Coſt of Suite and that he Shall have execution for the Same to be Levied on the goods and Chattles of the ſd deft

| Action Called | Joſeph Kirkbride plt agt Bartholemew Thatcher deft | in an action the Caſe | plt appeared by his Attorney Samll Beakes deft appared not |

Declaracon Read and the account therein mentioned likewiſe proveing the ſd Declaracon

whereupon the Court ordered that Robt Heaton Garniſhee be ſummoned to Court to ſee if he have any thing to ſay why the mony Attached in his hands Shold not pay what is due to the plt

| Action Called | Joseph Chorley plt agt James Alman deft | both appeared and defired the Continuation of the action untill the next Court and it was accordingly Continued |

| Action Called | Thomas Gardiner plt agt Samuel oldale deft | neither plt nor deft appeared whereupon the Court Continues the action |

| Action Called | Thomas Gardiner plt agt Chrifto Snowdon deft | neither plt nor deft appeared whereupon the Court Continues the action |

| Action Called | John Scarbrough plt agt Jofeph Smalwood deft | plt appeared deft appeared not | Second default |

| Action Called | Richard Thather plt agt willm Huntley deft | action Continued |

mahlon Stacy appeared in Court and acknowledged he had Received
ffull Satiffaction from Jofeph Chorley for the Judgmt he obtained this Court being forty pounds & Coft of fuite

Samll Beakes Attorney to Ifaac norris declared that he had Received 54£ 13ˢ and Coft of fuit being in full Satiffaction of the Judgmt the faid Ifaac norris obtained this Court agt Jofeph Chorley

ordered that Samuel Beakes be recommended to the governor as A fit perfon to keep ordinary

Adjourned the Court untill the 17ᵗʰ day of the 7 month next

335

Actions Continued untill the next Court

| John Grey als Tatham plt agt Jofeph Growdon deft | in an action upon the Cafe |

Thomas Gardiner plt
    agt } in an action of Treſpaſs and aſſault
Samuel Oldale deft

Thomas Gardiner plt
    agt } in an action upon the Caſe
Chriſtopher Snowdon deft

John Scarbrough plt
    agt } in an action upon the Caſe
Joſeph Smalwood deft

Joſeph kirkbride plt
    agt } in an action upon the Caſe
Bartholemew Thather deft

Joſeph Chorley plt
    agt } in an action upon the Caſe
John Hornor deft
  withdrawn

Joſeph Chorley plts
    agt } in an action upon the Caſe
James Alman deft

Richard Thatcher plt
    agt } in an action upon the Caſe
willm Huntley deft
non ſuite granted thereupon

Actions Entered for the Court to be held in the 7th month next

Action Entered the 28th day of the 6th month 1699

Enoch yardley plt
    agt } in an action upon the Caſe
Joseph Chorley deft

Attach[mt] granted thereupon
with drawn the declaracon by the plts order

Action Entered he 28th day of the 6th month 1699

Edward Hunloke plt
    agt } in an action of Debt
Walter pumphray deft

Summonce granted thereupon
non fuite

Action Entered the 3i day of the 6th month 1699

Peter worral plt
    agt } in an action upon the Cafe
ffrancis Tunneclift deft

Attachment granted the 3i day of the 6th month 1699
non fuite

336

Action Entered the 25th day of the 5th month i699

John Burradel plt
    agt } in an action of debt
Richard Thatcher deft

Arreft thereupon granted agt the body of Richard Thatcher the 25th day __5__ 1699
          mo

Return he had taken his body the 2nd of the 6th month i699
                                p Samll Beakes
Action Entered the 25th day of the 5th month 1699   Sherrife

George ffifher plt
    agt } in an action of debt
Edward Shaw deft

Arreft granted agt his body the body of the deft the 25th day 5 mo i699

Return Taken the i day of the 6th month i699
non fuite

Bucks ff   At a Court of Quarter Seffions held
in the name William Penn proprietaries of the —
province of penfylvania and Territories
thereunto belonging at the Court houfe of the afore Said County the
13 day of the 7th month 1699

The Juftices present

Jofeph Growdon william Biles   Henry Baker
John Swift
    Jonathan Scaife Corronor
    Samll Beakes Sherrife
    Phineas Pemberton Cl:Com:

Thefe perfons following being Summonced to ferve upon the Jury did not appeare when Called viz John Rowland Stephen Sands Henry pawlin francis white Samuel Smih george Brown James Heaton Thomas Stakehoufe Junr Ralph Cowgill

Edward Doyl the Sherrifs Deputy Attefted that he did Summonce allof them to ferve upon the Jury this Court

ffines   whereupon the Court fines John Rowland in 5ˢ Stephen Sands 5ˢ Henry pawlin 5ˢ francis white 5ˢ Samll Smith 5ˢ george brown 5ˢ James Heaton 5ˢ Thomas Stakehoufe Junr 5ˢ Ralph Cowgil 5ˢ

Return of the Corronors Inqueft of the death of James Hagath the fervant of John Scot that he Received his death by a blow of John Snowdons Horfe that he ftruck him the 5ᵗʰ day of the 7ᵗʰ month 1699 & dyed the day following the boy being driveing the plow when the horfe ftruck him

Action } John Scarbrought plt } plt appeared   }
Called }   agt   }   } it being the 3
         Jofeph Smalwood deft } deft appeared not } default

Declaration Read as ffolloweth viz

John Scarbrough Complaines agt Jofeph Smalwood in a plea that where
as the Said Jofeph Smalwood did Imploy the wife of the Said John Scarbrough
to wafh for him his Linnen &c which shee accordingly did to the value

337

of Twenty Seven Shillings with Several goods delivered to him as may appeare
by account herewith in Court to be produced as alfo the Said Jofeph Smalwood

did agree with the Said John Scarbrough to keep and nurſe his Child for which
the Said Joſeph Smalwood did agree and aſſume upon him Self to pay foure
Shillings for every weeke he Shold So keep and nurſe the Said Child with in
the yeare the Said Child was So put to him thirty Shillings in part where
of the Said Joſeph Smalwood hath paid yet not with ſtanding the Said
John Scarbrough hath often demanded the Said Joſeph Smalwood to —
pay what was Due to him for keeping the Said Child and upon the ſaid
account he the Said Smalwood hath hitherto refuſed and Still doth refuſe
to pay what is due and therefore the ſd plt Commenceth this Suite & —
Craves Judgmt of this Court for the Said Twenty Seven Shillings and
for the nurſing and keeping the Said Child after the rate of foure – Shillings p week untill the time of holding this Court with
damages and
Coſt of Suite &c

The deft Atteſted the truth of the ſd Declaracon and that he Cold not give him
any more Credit

It was Conſidered by the Court that the plt Shold recover what was due to him
for nurſeing the Child & for the goods and waſhing with Coſt of Suite & that
he Shall have Execution for the Same to be Levied on the goods and Chattles of the ſd deft

Action Called } George ffisher plt
agt
Edward Shaw deft } in an action of debt { plt appeared not
deft appeared

whereupon the deft Craved a non Suite for that he had not filed a __ __
declaracon nor appeared to his action

The Court therupon awarded a non ſuite

COMMON PLEAS OF BUCKS COUNTY, PENNSYLVANIA   393

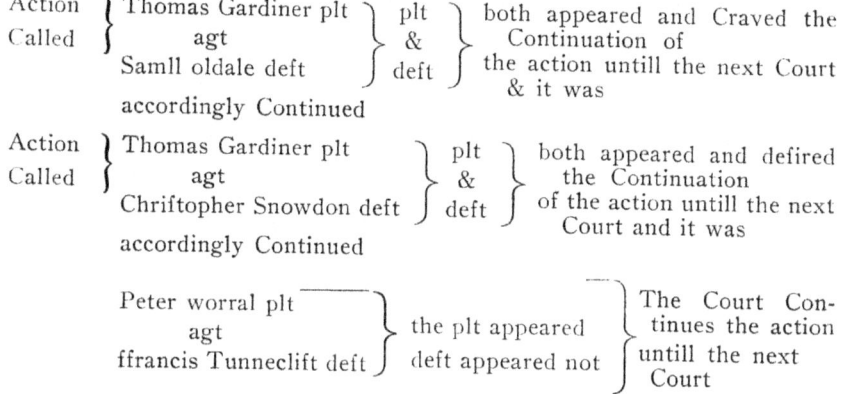

Action } Thomas Gardiner plt } plt } both appeared and Craved the
Called }   agt   } &   } Continuation of
        } Samll oldale deft   } deft } the action untill the next Court
          accordingly Continued   & it was

Action } Thomas Gardiner plt   } plt } both appeared and defired
Called }   agt   } &   } the Continuation
        } Chriftopher Snowdon deft } deft } of the action untill the next
          accordingly Continued   Court and it was

        Peter worral plt   }   } The Court Con-
              agt   } the plt appeared   } tinues the action
        ffrancis Tunneclift deft} deft appeared not } untill the next
                                                       Court

              Adjourned the Court for one houre

A Deed in ffee of 12½ acres dated the 4th day 7 month 1699 was Delivered
       by
       willm Hayhurft grantor unto Henry Hudleftone grantee
A Deed of A parcel of Land be it more or lefs dated the 14th day of the
       4th month 1699 was Delivered by James paxfon Attorney to his fon
       william paxfon grantor unto John Scarbrough grantee
Ordered that Jonathan Scaife have the fees due to him for veiueing the body
       of Richard Athay who was found dead upon the Road payd him
       out of
       the County Stock by the Trefurror
  ordered that John Cook late Corronor have the fees due to him for —
       veiueing the body of John Stotton payd him out of the County
       ftock
       by the treafurror

  John pidcock being Called upon his recognizance Appeared
       & the Court difcharged him

338

A Deed of a Lot of Land in fee Lying in Buckingham Dated the 11th day
       of the 7th
       month 1699 was Delivered by Jofeph Growden grantor unto
       william
       Crofdell grantee

A Deed from John Scarbrough of eighty acres of Land in fee dated the 4th day
of the 7th month 1699 was delivered by him grantor unto Henry Hudlestone
grantee

A letter of Attorney from John Scarbrough of London to the aforesaid John
Scarbrough his Son Dated the 15th day of october 1696 was proven
in Court

A Deed of foure hundered acres of Land in fee was Delivered by Andrew
Heath and his Son in law John Richardson and his wife Joyce
Richardson
grantors unto John Snowdon grantee

A Deed of five hundered acres of Land in ffee dated the 4th day of the 8th month
1696 being Endorsed on A pattent Dated the 20th day of december 1690
was Delivered by John Swift Attorney to Joseph Jones grantor unto —
peter Chamberlaine for the use of him & his wife Lucy grantees

Complaint being made by peter webster that the Road formerly ordered by
the Court to be Layd out from his House to the kings road that is not
as yet perfected

whereupon the Court orders Peter worral John palmer Josuah Hoops —
Thomas Janney Anthony Burton John Siddal to veiue the place
and if there be need to
Lay out the Same according to Law

Complt being made by peter Chamberlaine of the want of a road from
his House to the kings Road the Court orders John Jones, Henry pointer
Thomas Hardin John Naylor John Eastbourne nicholas Randol to veiue
the place and ground and if there be need to lay out the Same according
to Law

Complt of Thomas kirle for the want of Aroad from his House to the kings
road John Palmer Josuah Hoops Thomas Janney Abel Janney
Anthony Burton John Siddal are ordered to veiue the Same and
if there be – need to Lay out the Same according to Law

COMMON PLEAS OF BUCKS COUNTY, PENNSYLVANIA 395

Action } John Burradel plt _____ } in an action of debt { plt & deft } both appeared
Called   agt
              Richard Thatcher deft

The Declaracon Read

Bucks ff   John Burradel Complaines agt Richard Thatcher in an action of
debt for that whereas the Said Richard Thatcher became bound and
obliged to the Said John Burradel in one obligation bearing date the
iith day of the 10th month 1697 in the Sum of Twenty pounds for pay
ment of Ten pounds with Lawfull Intereſt at or upon the 10th day of the i0
month Enſueing the date thereof and not with ſtanding the Said plt hath
divers times demanded the Said mony So due the ſd deft hitherto hath
refuſed and Still doth refuſe the Same to pay whereupon the plt —
Commenceth this Suite agt the Said deft and Craves Judgmt for the
Said Sum of Twenty pounds with Coſt of Suite &c

Anſwer the deft Confeſſed to the truth of the declaracon and Said he had —
nothing to Say agt it

whereupon it was Confidered by the Court that John Burradel Shold recover
agt the ſd Deft: the Said Sum of Twenty pounds and Coſt of ſuite
and that he Shold have Execution agt the body of the ſaid deft
for payment thereof

Zachariah fferries being Called upon his Recognizance appeared and
Confeſt he had taken a ſcread of ſtuf from John Swift to a
Small value nothing further appearing agt him the Court orders him
to pay to ſd Swift 9^s 6^d and Charge of Court and is thereupon
diſcharged

339

Conſtables appointed for the Succeding yeare

ffor —
{
Buckingham — — — Thomas Dungan
ffalls — — — — — John Siddal
makefeild — — — — giles Lucas
middle Town — — — Edward Cartor
Benſalem — — — — Abel Finckſtone
South hampon &- } — — John Eaſtbourn
warminſter - - -
wrights Towne }
  Cum   — Saml Hough -
  new Town -
} all Atteſted

over Seers of the high ways appointed for the Succeeding yeare

ffor
{
Buckingham — — — John Surket
ffalls — — — — — willm Biles Junr
makefeild — — — peter worrall
middle Town — — Ezra Croſdel
Benſalem — — — ffrancis Searle
South hampton }
  cum   — Thomas Walmſley
  warminſter -
new Town }
  cum   — James yates
  wrights Town
}

Adjourned the Court untill the 19th day of the 8th month next

Action Entered the 8 day of the 8 month 1699

John Sutton Executor of Joſeph Burden late of Barbadoes deceaſed by

Samuel Carpenter his Attorney plt ——— }
           agt
Samuel Burden Son and heire of Samuel-
  Burden   } in an action of
deceaſed and ffrancis Rawle Adminiſtrator   Covenant
  of the
goods and Chattles of the ſd Samll Burden
  deceaſed deft

Bucks ſſ   At a Court of Quarter Seſſions held by ——

Adjournment the 19th day of the 8th month 1699

The Juftices present
Jofeph Growdon William Biles
Henry Baker Richard Hough John Swift
Samll Beakes Sherrife
Phineas Pemberton Cl. Com:
Conftables Attefted

grand Jury William paxfon John palmer Stephen Twineing Shadrach walley
william Smith Edward Lucas Thomas Stakehoufe fenr Jeremiah Langhorn —
william Hayhurft Thomas Stakehoufe Junr Ezra Crofdel Henry pawlin John Smith Peter worrall Job Bunting John Penquoit

All Attested

Charge given

340

Return of the Roads from peter webfters houfe to the kings Road as ffolloweth

Bucks ff The 14th day of the 8th month 1699

wee whofe names are under written being appointed by order of Court
to Lay out a road for Peter webfter have Layd it out as ffolloweth from
a Stake Standing by the fence of peter webfter from thence upon a Straight line by the Eaft end of the houfe of Randol Blackfhaw and from thence Straight to the Road Leading from the ffalls to Southampton Two poles wide

Jofuah Hoops   John Palmer
Peter worral   Anthony Burton
Thomas Janney John fiddall

The 14 of the 8 month 1699

we whofe names are hereunder written being appointed by order of Court to Lay out a road for the Conveniancy of Thomas kirle begining at the houfe of Thomas kirle and runing along between Thomas

kirle and Andrew Ellot and then between Andrew Ellot and
 Peter worrall
along theire line unto the Road Leading from the falls up the
 River
being two poles in breadth all along
        Jofuah Hoops John palmer
        Anthony Burton Thomas Janney
        John fiddal Abel Janney
Read allowed and ordered to be Entered the abovefd returns

Dure & Ston } george Stone Came into Court and Confeffed him Self to be debtr to Thomas Dure the Sum of thirteen pounds eighteen Shillings and promifed paymt of the Same

A Deed of five hundered acres of Land in fee dated the 18th day of the 8th
 month
1699 was Delivered by Phineas Pemberton grantor unto george
 ftone
grantee

A Deed of one hundered and fifty acres of Land dated the 10th day of the 12
 month 1698 was Delivered by Jofeph Growdon grantor unto
 Garret
van Sand Grantee

a deed of one hundered and fifty acres of Land in fee Dated the 10th day
 of the
12 month 1698 was Delivered by Jofeph Growdon grantor unto
 Cornelius van Sand grantee

A Deed of ninety acres of Land in fee Dated the 17th day of the 8th month
 1699 was Delivered by Jofeph Growdon grantor unto Thomas
 Stakehoufe Junior grantee

A Deed of one hundred acres of Land in fee Dated the 18th day of the
 8th month 1699 was Delivered by ——————————attorney to
 grace Langhorn Jeremiah Langhorn william Biles and Sarah
 Biles grantors to Thomas Stakehoufe grantee

A Deed of Two Lotts of Land in fee Lying in Buckingham Dated the 18
 day
of the 8th month 1699 was Delivered by Thomas Brock grantor
 unto Phineas Pemberton Attorney to Jofeph kirkbride grantee

A Deed of Two lotts of Land in fee Lying in Buckingham Dated the

5th day of the 7th month 1699 was Delivered by Thomas Brock grantor unto Richard pearce grantee

A Deed of Two hundered fifty two acres of Land and premiſes in fee dated the 17th day of the i2 month i698 was Delivered by ſtephen wilſon grantor unto Stephen Twineing grantee

A Deed of one hundered and eight acres be the ſame more or leſs Dated the 22 day of Aprill 1699 was Delivered by Samuel Beakes Attorney
   to Richard Ridgway grantor unto william Biles Junior Attorney to Daniel
gardiner grantee

(341)

A Deed of the said Tract of Land being about Two hundered and eight acres 10 or 14½ acres be the Same more or Leſs dated the fiiſt day of
the 7th month 1699 was Delivered by william Biles Senr Attorney to Daniel gardiner grantor unto Joſeph Janney grantee

Robert Barry and Iriſh boy Servant to James plumley was brought before the Court to have his age adjudged and the Court accordingly — Judged to be of Ten yeares of age from this day & Serve ——— according to Law and at the expiration of his terme to have allowance accordingly

Adjourned the Court untill 8 in the morning

An Atteſtation of John Bowns read in Court declareing the payment of three pounds to John Pidcock for the Service of negro will done in Eaſt Jerſey after the deceaſe of Thomas Bowman whoſe negro the Said will: was and the John pidcock not makeing it appeare to the Court that he hath payd the Said 3 £ : to Edward Hunlock Adminiſtra
-tor of the Said Bowmans Eſtate

wherefore it was Conſidered by the Court that the Said Edward Hunloke Shold recover the Said 3 £ of the Said John pidcock according to a former Judgmt of this Court which ſd Hunlocke obtained agt the ſd pidcock being aſſets in his hands of the ſd Bowmans Eſtate Except Eleven Shillings which appeared to the Court the ſd pidcock
had Layd out in Shooes and ſtockings for the ſd negro and that he have Execution to Levie the Same on the goods & Chattles of the Said John pidcock for the ſd ſum of 2 £ 9s–

Action Edward Hunloke plt } in a plea { plt & deft } appeared
      agt
walter pomphray deft

The Declaracon read
the affidavit of Robt Stacy read

Henry Grub &   attefted an agree mente or an award made by the awarders —

plt & deft agreed to deffer the tryal of the action to the next Court if the weather wold then permit if not to the next after that neither plt nor deft to take advantage if the weather hindered theire — appearance & it was accordingly Continued

Action Richard Thatcher plt — } plt appeared not
      agt   deft appeared —
willm Huntley deft

whereupon the deft Craved anon fuite which the Court granted him

Action Peter woral plt ——— } plt & deft } both appeared
      agt
ffrancis Tunneclift deft

declaracon read it diferring about three words from the Coppy the deft Craved a non fuite for the Same which the Court granted him

Adjourned the Court to Samll Beakes houfe

Action Jofeph Chorley plt } in an action upon the Cafe { plt & deft } both appeared
      agt
James Alman deft

Declaracon read

342

Anfwer   deft fays he ows nothing of this puts him felf upon the Cuntry
Iffue   and fo doth the plt
venire   whereupon the Sherrife is Commanded to return a Jury
Jury   } Peter worral willm Dungan wm Biles Junr John fiddal
Attefted } Clement Dungan Enoch yardley John fcarbrough Thomas Coleman

Joſeph Janney James moone Junr Geo Biles wm Croſdel all Atteſted

deft offered an account to prove the horſe pd for mentioned in the declaracon

Action depending upon Some accounts the Court appointed wm: Biles Junr and wm Croſdel to audit the accounts and the plt & deft Submitted the whole Caſe to the Arbitration of the ſd Auditors if they think good to take it upon them

grand jury brought in theire prſentments

prſent Edmund Lovet for his difficiency in his office as Collector of the County Tax in Buckingham townſhip

we prſent the neceſſity of a Convenient road from John Croſdells houſe to the kings road that Leads from new Town to Buckingham for the uſe of John Croſdel

we prſent the neceſſity of a road for Ezra Croſdel from his houſe to the kings road which leads from new town to Buckingham

Bucks ſſ The Jurrors for the body of this County do prſent willm Beatridg and James Jolly for runing away from theire maſter John Swifts Service and felonioufly takeing with them Two of theire Said maſters horſes to the value of Twelve pounds Conterary to the kings peace and the Statute Laws inthat Caſe made and provide

we of the grand Jury do find this bill william paxſon foreman

william Beatridge and James Jolly brought to the barr and the preſentment read wm Beateridg
pleaded guilty

The Court thereupon Conſidered that the Said willm Beatridge Shall Serve the Said John Swift Two yeares after the expiration of the term of his prſent Servitue And that he Shall have 7 Laſhes upon his bare back and weare a Roman T on his left arme of A yellow Collour according to Law James Jolly
pleaded guilty

It was thereupon Confidered by the Court that the Said James
Jolly
Shall Serve the Said John Swift Two yeares after the—
Expiration of the terme of his prfent Servitude
And that he Shall be Whipt 7 Lafhes upon his bare back and
weare a Roman T on his Left arme of A yellow Collour accord-
ing to Law

Action Called	John Tatham plt agt Jofeph Growdon deft	in an action upon theCafe	plt & deft	both appeared

Declaracon } John grey als Tatham late of Tatham houfe neare nefheminah
Read —   in the
County of Bucks in Penfylvania merchant Complaineth
againft
Jofeph Growdon of the County aforefd Gent: in an action
upon the

343

Cafe for that whereas in the yeare i685 the fd pltf gave the
faid Deft Credit for
fundyr goods & merchandizes amounting to Seven pounds
Six fhillings and
eight pence which Sum the Said Deft afumed to pay within a
Small time after
the delivery of the Said Goods and merchandizes and lent him
the faid deft
foure books value foure pounds which he promifed Shortly to
reftore and —
likewife lent him fifteen pounds Cafh upon his note or letter
under his
owne hand dated at Benfalem the 7th day of $\underline{9}$ i685 to
repay the faid   mo
fiveteen pounds in filver mony at or before the 6th of the $\underline{i2}$
next   mo
Enfueing the date thereof with Intreft for the Same then due
wch Said
Sums of Seven pounds Six Shillings eight pence and foure
pounds —
Charged for the Said Books and the Said Sum of fiveteen
pounds
Lent and Intreft thereof now due viz fiveteen pounds & eight
fhillings

for Twelve yeares and Ten months at eight p Cent amount to one &
forty pounds fiveteen ſhillings and eight pence And the ſaid pltf hath
often requeſted the ſaid deft the ſaid Several Sums of Seven pounds
Six Shillings and eight pence due for the ſaid goods & merchandizes
and the Sum of foure pounds for the Said books or the books to be
reſtored and the Said Sum of fiveteen pounds with Intreſt due
and accrewing at the Reſpective times when the ſaid pltf demanded
the Same as above Set forth and declared yet nevertheleſs the ſaid
deft hath Still refuſed & doth Still refuſe to pay the Same or any of the
Said Sums or reſtore the Said books whereupon the ſaid pltf brings
this Suite & Craves Judgmt of this Court for the ſaid ſeveral ſums
amounting in the whole (as aforesaid to one and forty pounds —
fiveteen ſhillings and eight pence Currant ſilver mony of the afore
said province with damages and Coſt of Suite

Anſwer read –	I owe unto the pltf nothing to my knowledg only the foure books of a Small value I borrowed wch I am ready to reſtore and of this
Iſſue venire	he puts him ſelf upon the Cuntry & ſo doth the pltf: whereupon the Sherrife is Commanded to reurn 12 honeſt men of the neighbourhood whereby the truth of the matter may be known
Jury Called & Atteſted –	John Surket Henry Hudleſtone John naylor Ralph Cowgill Enoch yardley willm Dungan ffrancis white Richard wilſon willm Biles Junr: Robt Heaton Junr: John Croſdell James plumley

Declaracon againe Read and the pltf produced the letter menconed there in

The letter read as ffolloweth

$$\text{Bensalem } 7^o \ \frac{9}{mo} \ 1685$$

my Good friend

    presumeing that it may not discomode thee I shall requeſt the favore of thee to spare me fiveteen pounds which be pleased to send me by the bearror my Servant Philip Daniel and these Shall oblige me to repay thee againe in silve mony at or before the 6th of $\frac{12}{mo}$ next ensueing with Intreſt and be acknowledged as a great — kindnes done unto thy much obliged friend   Joseph Growdon

$$1685$$

my Respects to thy good wife the same to thy self } Idem J G
pray please to send 6^{lb} of sugr by the bearror —

Receipt for }   7th of november 1685 Received then of John Grey for the use
the same — }   of my mr Joseph Growdon the abovementioned fiveteen pounds witnes my hand

         philip **X** Daniel
         his   mark

witnessed by us will myers John Tomlinson

344

The which letter and the Receipt of the mony the deft owned but pleaded that at the same time the mony was borrowed the sd pltf was Indebted to him the said deft more then the mony mentioned in the sd Letter amounted to upon the account of a Certaine tract of Land he the said deft sold the sd pltf

The pltf replyed he had payd for the Said Land & produced Receipts for the Same

The which Receipts the deft owned but pleaded they signed at the requeſt of

the pltf before all the mony was paid he the ſd pltf aleadging that it was requiſit the ſaid Receipts Shold be given at the ſealing and delivery of the deed or Conveyance of the said Lands and that what
was wanting the ſaid Conſideracon mony he the ſaid pltf promiſed he wold pay or be accountable for the ſame and that he the ſaid deft upon the pltf promiſe did ſeal the ſaid Receipts

whereupon the ſaid pltf for proofe of payment of the ſaid Conſideracon mony to have been made in full according to the ſaid Receipts & that there was nothing due thereupon to ſd deft produced the following account

The acctt read as ffolloweth

A porticuler

of the hundered pounds worth of Engliſh goods which I did pay & Deliver to Joſeph Growdon gent. for one Thouſand acres of Land (by vertue of an agreement verbaly Concluded between him and me for the ſame) in July 1685 the Reſidue of that purchaſe (wch was one hundred pounds more) being payable in Caſh upon the Coſts & Charges of which Goods till they were houſd at my Settlement
neare neſhaminah River I was to have allowed me Twenty pcent: ſterling profit by the ſaid agreemt & no more

		£	s	d
1	Imprims 4 pr mens wofted hofe at 2ˢ: 4ᵈ p pr	—	-9	-4
2	It: i4 pr ditto Coarfer at i8ᵈ p p —	-1	-1	—
3	It. i ps of fine bengall att — —	—	16	—
4	It: 1 ps ditto Courfed at — — —	—	14	—
5	It: 2 ps plaine ditto at 12ˢ 6ᵈ p ps	-1	-5	—
6	It: i ps wᵗ Callicoe at — — — —	—	i0	-6
7	It: 1 ps. ditto — — —	—	-9	-6
8	It: Ifarees — — — — — —	—	i2	—
9	It: i ps wide blew callico — — — -i	—	-3	—
i0	It: i ps blew callico — — —	—	i0	—
ii	It: 2 ps blew linnen at 18ˢ p ps — -i	—	i6	—
i2	It: i ps wᵗ Linnen at - i	—	ii	-3
i3	It i ps wᵗ Ticklingberge —	—	i5	.2
i4	It: 24¾ yrds of Hartfords at 6ˢ p yd — —	—	i2	.4½
i5	It 37 Ells Canvas at iiᵈ p Ell — — -i	—	13	-ii
i6	It: 12 yrds broad Cloth at 5ˢ p yrd	-3	—	—
i7	It 2 ps Duffalls at 6£ -3ˢ -5½ᵈ p ps —	12	-6	ii
i8	It i ps fine Cloth Serge — — — -3	—	13	—
i9	It: 3 ps ditto 5iˢ: 4ᵈ p ps -7	—	14	—
20	It: 6 ps norwich stuff at 20ˢ p ps — —	-6	—	—
	Carrye over	46	i5	5½

		£	s	d
	brought over — 46	i5	5½	
2i	It 2 ps barronits at 30ˢ p ps — — — — -3	—	—	
22	It: 6 pr french fulls at 3ˢ 4ᵈ p pr — —1	—	—	
23	It: 6 pr mens plaines at 2ˢ 3ᵈ p pr — — — —	i3	-6	
24	It: i pr boys & i ditto girls at 16ᵈ p pr — —	-2	-8.	
25	It: i pr boys ditto at — —	-2	2	
26	It: 5 pr pumps at 7ᵈ pr pr — — — —	-2	ii.	
27	It: 2 pr more of girls fhooes at i6ᵈ p pr —	-2	-8.	
28	It: i ps of Canvas Cont: 65½ Ells at 17ᵈ p El -4	12	-9	
29	It: i ps of scotch cloth Cont: 10 yrds at 16ᵈ p yd —	i3	-4	
30	It: i ps of fuftian at —	15	—	
31	It: 3ˡᵇ Coloured thread at 2ˢ p ˡᵇ: i ditto brown 22ᵈ —	-7	i0.	
32	It: i ps Searge Cont: 20½ yrds at 22ᵈ p yrd — -i	i7	-7	
33	It: i grs bell mettal buttons — — — —	-2	-4.	
34	It: 2 brafs kettles — -2	i0	—	
35	It: 13ˡᵇ powder & the brl — — — — .	i3	-8	
36	It: 14ˡᵇ of fhot — — — -i	-6		
37	It: 6 falling axes at i4ᵈ p ps — —	i5	—	
38	It 6 broad hows at i4ᵈ p ps — — — —	-7	—	
39	It 6 tilling hows at 12ᵈ p ps — — — —	-6	—	
40	It i little how at — —	—	10	
4i	It i broad ax at — —	-3	-6	
42	It 3 doz Spoones at 16ᵈ p doz — —	-4	—	
43	It 3 doz more at 20ᵈ p doz — — — —	-5	—	
44	It: 6 Cow bells at 5½ p ps — —	-2	-9	
45	It i Large pewter chamber pot — — —	-3	—	
46	It : 3 doz ditto of Leffor fize — — .	-7	-6	
	Carryed on =	66	-8	—

		£	s	d
	Sum brought over — —	66	-8	-0
47	It 6 Large podding difhes at 9ᵈ p ps		-4	-6
48	It 6 ditto Leffor fize		-4	--
49	It i doz Marjerine plates		i2	--
50	It 3 Small bafons i Large		-8	--
5i	It 3 Quart Tankards 4ˢ p ps		12	--
52	It 2 Large muggs at 12ᵈ p ps		-2	--
53	It 4 Leffor ditto at 10ᵈ p ps		-3	-4
54	It 6 half pt bottles at 9ᵈ p ps		-4	-6
55	It 6 Quart pt bottles at 6ᵈ p ps		-3	--
56	It i pr Large Candlefticks		-6	-6
57	It: i Little Sauce pan		-2	-3
58	It ½ doz tand lether raines at 7ᵈ p pr		-3	-6
59	It 2 pr bl ditto at i0ᵈ p pr		-1	-8
60	It 3 Twifted 3 plaine Snuffles at		-3	-6
6i	It i pr fterrup lether		-i	-6
62	It 4 pr ftirrup Irons at i0ᵈ p pr		-3	-4
63	It 2 more of Tand fterrup lethers		-i	-6
64	It 2 bridle bitts at 20ᵈ p pr		-3	-4
65	It 2 double & 8 fingle girths		-4	--
66	It i plufh faddle with bridle & furniture	1	18	--
67	It 3 hunting fadles with bridles & furniture at i3ˢ p ps	-i	i9	--
68	It 12ˡᵇ of 10ᵈ nailes at 4ˢ 9ᵈ p m		-5	-8
69	It 2 m̄ of 8ᵈ nailes at 3ˢ 9ᵈ p m		-7	-6

345

	£	s	d
Sum brought over — —	77	-3	11
other Cofts & difburfements upon thefe goods for porteridge Cartage Entering at the Cuftome — houfe & duties there paid for the Same for Lighterige to the Ship & fraight being Computed at above 2 Tunn at 4£ & for bringing them up to nefhaminah amount to --	10	--	--
Twenty p cent fterling upon the Cofts of the above goods is	i7	-8	-9
Summa totalis =	i04	12	-8

overpaid

Over paid Mr. Growdon by the within Goods — — — — -4 -i2 -8
as the with in account makes —
Evident

A true Coppy of the faid Account

The above goods were delivered
to Mr. Growdon him felf and by
him Called out of the whole Cargoe
July the i8 and i9th 1685 delivered to his   } - i   i9 -6
fervant July the 28 1685 (vpage P4i)
viz: 2 m̄ 10d nailes at 4s 9d p m̄
& 8 m̄ of 8d ditto at 3s 9d p m wch:
amount to — — — — — — —
It i gouge i hammer i Chiffell —   — — - i -6
It ½ pt bottle — — — — — —   — — - i --

The prime Cofts at the ftores upon   }   77 -3   ii
thefe goods amount to — —

The hundered pounds Cafh which I was further to pay him for the faid Land was thus Difcharged

£   s   d

15 4 1685 pag L:37
  mo
    Then pd Mr. Growdon in ps of   } 10 -- --
    8th Ten pounds fterling — —

ii 5 1685 It pd then more to Mr
   mo
    growdon one hundred ps 8th wch
    he Contentioufly difputed to be no   } 22 10 --
    more then 22£ -10s fterling
    nor wold he otherwife alow for
    the fame tho 30s sterling more

July the 20th i685 then paid Mr
    growdon the refidue of the —
    hundered pounds thus viz fifty   } 53 i9 -2
    Gineas at one & Twenty fhillings
    and Seven pence p ginea wch
    makes the fum of — — — — —

Errors Excepted P me John Tatham

  A true Coppy

pd alfo then to him
  Sixty ps of
  8th more wch: mr
  growdon wold
  not alow to be more
  then — —
  13£ 10s: fterling tho   } i3 10 --
  upon an
  honeft and juft Efti-
  mate of —
  theire value they do
  amount
  to i8s fterling more - -

Then 10d fterling yet
  wanting
  to the ballanceing of
  this
  account according to   } ---- i0
  mr —
  Growdons Calculation
  and
  novel Arithmetick was
  dicharged by a bit and
  a half

                                                100 00 00

overpd in the 2d paymt
  30s in the   } -2 -8 --
  3d payment i8s in the
  whole

over pd as above in
  goods — —   4 -i2 -8

over paid in the whole   7 --- -8
  fterling mony

346

objection by the deft to the foresd acctt } To which the deft answered that they had never pfected any account —
Concerning the same but that the Said pltf had framed the aforesd —
account and that it was a false one that it varied from an account formerly given him by the sd pltf Concering the aforesd Goods and
requested the account menconed in the declaracon might be produced

where upon the sd plt produced the sd account mentioned in the declaracon
which was read and is as followeth

acct mencond in the declacon — — } Joseph Growdon is Debtor unto John Tatham for sundry goods & merchandizes delivered by him unto the sd Joseph Growdon in the yeare 1685 wch the said john was never yet paid for asffollows

	£	s	d
July the 18th 1685 Imprs to a brl of molloses att	–3	–0	–0
It: then to a gallon of Rum		–5	
28 P: 4i – It: to 5 gallon 3 qrts of Rum at 5s p gallon	–1	–8	–9
It: to 1/2 lb sugr	–1	–5	
August ist It to a syth		–4	
Septemr i0th It: to a barr of Iron wt 40lb delivered to ffr: Rush p ordr		13	–4
octob 26 pg R: 43 It to 2lb 30d nailes at 8d p lb		1	–4
It then to 3lb of 20d nailes and 4lb of i0d at 9d p lb		–5	–3
It: to 6lb of sugr delivered to Joseph servant by his note		–3	
It: to 2lb more delivered to Joseph him self at 6d p lb		–1	
novemb 7th It Joseph is debtr to Cash lent him at his request — and upon his promise by his note to repay it with Intrest in three month		15	
It to Intrest for 12 yeares & i0th months now due for the Same at 8 pcent		i5	–8

It to 4 books which he borrowed the fame to be reftored — or theire prices at 20ˢ p booke — — — — —	}	4 — —

                                  Sum Total: 4i – 14 : 8

              Errors Excepted p me John Tatham

      A true Coppy

He owes me likewife for the mony paid and difburfed by me for the furveying of the Thoufand acres of Land he Sold me wch by
bargaine he affumed to pay as is evident by his Letter in PC : 29 and for half of the Charges for the deed for he haveing a Counter part or duplicate ought to pay for it which pticulers I fubmit to your reafonable & Juft Confideracon   John Tatham
due more the 10ᵗʰ of this Inftant September 1699 one yeares Intreft for the i5 £ viz 24ˢ

                        A true Coppy

The deft aleadged that divers articles in the foregoing account were Charged in the account formerly given towards what was due to him for the Thoufand acres of Land

To which the pltf replyed that it was a true account and that he had not Charged any article thereof in any other or former account and that he was ready to be attefted to the truth thereof

                                             347

whereupon the Said John Tatham the pltf was Attefted and upon his Atteftation
declared that the fore going account was Juft and true & that he had not Charged any one article thereof in any former account

The deft thereupon produced an account & afked the pltf whether that was his hand writing

The plt replyed thereto that it was his hand writing he wold not deny it wch Said account so produced by the deft was read & is as ffolloweth

Goods Delivered to Joseph Growdon
as follows

	£	s	d
4 pr fine mens wostet hose at 2s 4d p pr	- -	_9	_4
4 pr mens worstet hose att 18d p pr —	_ i	_1	- -
i ps fine Bengall — — — — — —	- -	16	- -
i ps ditto Coarser — — — — —	- -	14	- -
2 ps plaine ditto — — — — —	_ i	_5	- -
i ps wt Callico — — — — — —	- -	10	_6
1 ps ditto — — — — — — —	- -	_9	_6
1 ps Isarees — — — — — —	- -	12	_6
i ps wide blew calico — — —	_1	_3	- -
i ps blew calico — — — — —	- -	12	- -
2 ps blew linnen — — — — —	_ i	_ ii	_3
1 ps wt Ticklingberge — — —	- -	i5	_2
4¾ hartfords — — — — — —	- -	12	_4½
7 Ells of Canvas at iid p Ell —	_ i	i3	_ ii
2 yrds of broad Cloth at 5s p yrd — — — — — — — —	_3	- -	- -
2 ps Duffalls — — — — — —	12	_6	ii
1 ps fine cloath Searge — —	_2	i3	- -
3 ps Searge — — — — — —	_7	i4	- -
6 ps norwich stuffs — — — —	_6	- -	- -
2 ps Barronets 30s p ps — —	_3	- -	- -
6 pr french ffulls at 3s 4d p pr	_ i	- -	- -
6 pr mens plaines at 2s 3d p pr	- -	13	_6
pr of boys shoes & i of girls at i6d p pr — — — —	- -	_2	_8
Shoes att 7d p pr	- -	_2	_2
1s shoes at i6d p pr	- -	_2	_8
65½ Ells at i7d p Ell	_4	i2	_9½
h Cont: i0 yrds at i6d p yd	- -	13	_4
— — —	15	-	
10 at 2s pd: & 1 brown at 22d	- -	_7	i0
ps of searge Cont: 20½ yrds at 22d p yd	_1	i7	_7
gr bellmetal buttons — — —	- -	_2	_4
brl mollosses — — — — —	_2	_8	- -
fraight & other Charges — —	_3	_8	- -
3 brass kettles — — — — —	_2	i0	- -
3 lb powder & the brl — —	- -	i3	_8
4 lb shot — — — — — —	- -	_ i	_6
6 felling axes — — — — —	- -	i5	- -
6 broad hows — — — — —	- -	_7	- -
6 tilling hows — — — — —	- -	_6	- -
1 little how — — — — —	- -	- -	10
1 broad ax — — — — —	- ..	.3	_6
3 doz spoons 16d p doz — —	- ..	.4	..
3 doz more att 20d p — — —	- ..	.5	. -

Carryed over

his pt of the account was Eaton y rats or mice or uch like it Cold ot be read.

	£	s	d
½ Doz Cow Bells — — — —	- -	_2	_9
1 great Chamber pot — — —	- -	_3	- -
3 little ones — — — — — —	- -	_7	_6
½ doz Large podding dishes —	- -	_4	_6
½ doz of a lesser size — — —	- -	_4	- -
1 doz mazerine plates — — —	- -	12	- -
3 Smal basons 1 Large — —	- -	8	- -
3 Quart tankards — — — —	- -	12	- -
2 Large muggs — — — — —	- -	2	- -
4 lesser ditto — — — — —	- -	3	_4
6 ½ pt bottles — — — — —	- -	_4	_6
	74.13	:	6
½ doz ¼ pt bottles — — —	- -	4	- -
1 pr Large Candle sticks — —	- -	6	_6
1 little sauce pan — — — —	- -	2	_3
½ Doz pare Tand lefer rains —	- -	3	_6
2 pr bl rains — — — — —	- -	1	_8
i pc bl stirrup lethers — — —	- -	- -	10
3 Twisted 3 plaine Snuffles —	- -	3	_6
4 pr stirrup Irons — — — —	- -	3	_4
2 double & 8 single girths —	- -	4	- -
1 plush saddle with holsters &c	1	18	. -
4 bottles of Rum — — — —	- -	5	- -
½ ss sugr — — — — — —	_1	_5	- -
3 lb worth of nailes whereof — delivered 1200 of 10d nailes at 4 s 9d p m & 200 of 8d at 3 s 9d p m — —	_3	- -	- -
delivered more July the 28th — 1685 2 m of 10d nailes at 4s 9d p 8 m of 8d nailes 3 9 — the 1200 delivered before com the 200 10d nailes comes delivered more 5 gallon & 3 qrts of Rum wch at 5 s p gallon comes It i gouge i hammer & i Chiffel	i	10	- -
It ½ pt bottle — — — — —	- -	_ i	- -
	12	_5	_6
	74	13	_6
	86	19	- -

this Eaton as before & Cold not be — read

delivered by my man a syth

348

The Court Compareing the aforegoing accounts together it appeared that —
Several articles in the account mentioned in the declaracon were
Charged formerly by the pltf in the account the deft produced
for and towards payment of the Thoufand acres of Land and that
Some of the articles in the account the pltf produced to prove —
payment for the Land were augmented above what they were
at firſt given in unto the deft

Whereupon the pltf then acknowledged that the account about the Land
was never perfected and was but a Curfory account

The deft aleadged that the Land paid for according to agreement
there wold be nothing due to the pltf and thereupon produced
his objections agt the account firſt given in by the pltf to the
deft and are as ffolloweth

	£	s	d
Imprimis over Charged on nailes Twice fet to account	—	–3	—
overCharged on nailes 200 p m for they ought to be 1200 to each m when as they were but 1000 delivered	—	10	—
over Charged on 5 gallons of Rum being Charged at 5ˢ p gallon the highest rate Sold for here Inſtead whereof I ought to have dollars at 4ˢ 6ᵈ Each or Englifh goods at 20 pcent advance	—	i7	–3
over charged on i brl of molloſſes after the fame manner	—	–i	—
and on 1/2 lb of fugr	—	10	—
and on 4 bottles of Rum	—	–3	—
over charged on fraight &c	—	–i	—
to Damages on 2 ps of Duffalls	–4	–2	–4
to Damages on 2 ps of Callico	—	–5	—
to fo much Loſs by 88£ Received in gineas at 2iˢ 6ᵈ each and other mony Equivalent when as Iought to have by contract Dollars at 4ˢ 6ᵈ each this Loſs at i7ᵈ p £ is	.5	–i3	–4
more loſs on light mony	—	i2	—
to a red leather Chaire lent his ant	—	i5	—
for Timber by him fallen on my land & Converted to his uſe			
	i8	07	ii

After a full hearing of both parties the Jury went out and the next morning returned into the Court and delivered in the following verdict in writeing

Bucks ff

verdict
we of the Jury do find for the deft with coft of fuite as witnes our hands

John furket fforeman Richard wilfon John naylor willm Dungan Enoch yardley Robt Heaton John Crofdell Henry Hudleftone ffrancis white Ralph Cowgill James plumley willm Biles Junr

ffrom which verdict the Said pltf appealed to the next provincial Court to be held for the aforefd County in Equity and entered into — Recognizance according to Law to profecute the fd appeale John Tatham obliges him felf unto william Penn Proprietarie and Govrnr of this province his Heirs and fucceffors in the Sum of fifty pounds to be Levied on his goods and Chattles Lands and

349

Tennemts and This is upon Condition that the Said John Tatham profe
-cute his appeal agt Jofeph Growdon at the next provincial court to
be held for this County in Equity and to pay all cofts & damages that
Shall be decreed in the faid Court agt the Said appealant

grand Jurys prfentmt

Bucks ff the 20th day of the 8th month 1699

we of the grand Jury for the body of this County d prfent John Tatham for Takeing a falfe Atteftation upon the 19th day of the 8th month 1699 Conterary to the kings peace and ftatute Laws made &
provided figned by order of the Jury by

william Paxon
foreman 1699

action

John Sutton
agt
Burden

*merand to Enter
the date of A deed
Jos Growdon grantr
to Abel Hinckſtone
grantee

† Bucks ſS 350

At A Court of Quarter Seſsions held the by the Kings Authority in the Name of William penn propriet^ry & Govern^r of the province: of pensilva^nia and terretories thereunto belonging the 12° day of the first Month Anno Domj: 1700

Juſtices prsent Joseph Growdon   William Biles
John Swift   Richard Hough
Sam^ll Beaks Sherriffe
phenihas pemberton Cl: Com:

The Grand Jury Atteſted which were Bucks ſs the 13° day of the 1st mo: 1 $\frac{700}{699}$

wee the grand jury (upon Complaint) do prsent the Neſseſsity of aroad from the ferry at John Balldwins into the moſt Convenient place of New town Road leading to Neſhaminy Meeting houſe, as it may beſt anſwer y^e Convenency of the Neighbourhood

Wee Likewiſe prsent John Scarbrough for keeing an ordinary without lycence

And allso the Neſseſsity of the placeing a Court houſe Near the Middle of the County which wee eſteem to be Near Neſhaminy Meeting houſe   Signed by
Joſhua Hoops fforeman

---

*A small slip of paper loose between pp. 348 and 349.
† The remaining entries in the record are in a different hand from that of Pemberton, more like that of Jeremiah Langhorn who succeeded him as Clerk of the County.

A deed of   acres of land in fee was acknowledged
   by Anthony Morgan Attorny to Jofias Hill grantor
   unto John Ellett grantee dated the   day of

A deed of   hundred acres of land in fee was acknowledged
   by Samuel Beaks Attorny to Jonathan Scaife grantor
   unto John Rumford grantee dated the   day of

A deed of five thoufand acres of land in fee dated the   day of
         was acknowledged by William Biles Attorney to
   to Thomas Hudson grantor unto William Lawrence
   and Company grantees

A deed of   hundred acres of land in fee dated the day of
   v   was Acknowledged by William Biles junr. Attorny
   to Samuel Richardson grantor unto phenihas pemberton
   Grantee

351

A deed of   hundred acres of land in fee was Acknowledged
   by Joseph Growden grantor unto William Baker grantee
   dated the   day of

A deed of   hundred acres of land in fee was Acknowledged by
   Richard Hough grantor unto John Watson Grantee dated
   the   day of

A deed of Mortgage of   hundred acres of land dated the
   day of   was Acknowledged by John Watson Mortgagor
   unto Richard Hough Mortgagee

           Court Adjurned for one hour

     The Grand Jury's prsentm[ts] brought in

Bucks fs

     The 14th day of ye 1st month $\frac{1699}{700}$

     wee the grand Jurors for the body this County do prefent
     a Nefsefsity of a Road from Joseph Growdon's to the
     Kings Road leading to the falls & Nefhaminy Meeting
     Houfe Signed by   Jofhua Hoops foreman

Bucks ſs the 14th day of ye 1st mo. 1699/700

Wee of the Grand Jurors for the Body of this County do prsent Charles Smith (Sojurnr amongst us) for Entering into the Stable of William paxſon Junr and unlawfully takeing an old pare of Stockings, a bridle and a few old buttons of Samuel Oldale's And allso a horse of ye sd William paxſons out of his Yard without his leave or Conſent Signed by   Joſhua Hoops fforeman

Likewiſe wee preſent the Neſseſsity of building a bridge over Neſhaminy Creeke, And that the Charge thereof, Levied upon our County exceed not eighty pounds, And that the Court apoint Tenn Men for to vew & Make Choice of a place And allso to lett out the worke, And to See the good accompliſhmt. thereof Six whereof agreeing Shall be thought Sufficient
        Signed by
                    Joſhua Hoops fforeman

    Court Adjurned untill Eight a Clock tomorrow
      Morning about wch time being open

Note: The foregoing Court was held on the 12th day of the 1st month Anno Dom 1700. The next court recorded was held on 10th day of 7th mo: 1702. Between these dates are the above presentments and others dated 12th ye first mo 1702/2, and at the end of sundry, similar & other Court record entries appears "This Court adjourns till ye usual time in June."

INDEX OF PERSONS

Only one reference is given to a name on the same page.

Abbott, Samuel, 74, 75, 76, 82, 83, 85, 185.
Abbotts, Answer, 84.
Ackerman, 282.
Ackerman, John, 4, 9, 11, 19, 222.
Ackerman, Mary, 38.
Acreman, James, 361, 365, 379, 383, 387.
Adams, Seemercy, 75.
Addington, 170.
Addington, John, 274, 355, 356, 357, 327.
Adkinson, Isaac, 294.
Adkinson, Jane, 294.
Adkinson, Samuel, 294.
Adkinson, Thomas, 20, 32, 75, 82, 294, 296.
Adkinson, William, 294.
Aleine, see Allen.
Allen, Jedidiah, 66.
Allen, John, 104, 202, 214, 215, 217, 332.
Allen, Nathaniel, 32.
Allen, Neamiah, 91, 191.
Allen, Samuel, 25, 75, 89, 130, 149, 164, 169, 190, 236, 242, 262, 266, 328, 370, 372, 373.
Allen, Samuel, Jr., 91, 112, 122, 147, 158, 164, 191, 210, 221, 233, 256, 262.
Allott, Andrew, 188.
Alman, James, 326, 336, 347, 352, 353, 359, 365, 377, 379, 383, 384, 388, 389, 400.
Alsop, Jon, 57.
Andrews, Elizabeth, 48.
Andrews, Francis, 49.
Antill, Edward, 168, 169, 170, 264, 265, 266, 267.
Archer, Thomas, 330, 337.
Athay, Richard, 393.
Atthary, Richard, 312.
Austin, John, 74, 79, 80, 170, 267.

Bainbridge, John 47.
Bains, Thomas, 339, 340, 341, 358.
Baker, Henry, 20, 22, 25, 41, 47, 59, 86, 90, 92, 93, 100, 101, 105, 111, 121, 123, 126, 130, 133, 138, 139, 152, 157, 159, 161, 162, 163, 167, 170, 171, 172, 174, 176, 178, 185, 190, 192, 193, 199, 200, 203, 209, 221, 222, 227, 228, 237, 242, 245, 251, 255, 259, 260, 261, 262, 264, 267, 268, 270, 271, 274, 281, 285, 288, 293, 295, 298, 299, 300, 302, 304, 309, 311, 312, 313, 316, 318, 323, 325, 329, 333, 334, 345, 355, 362, 367, 370, 373, 378, 380, 383, 385, 391, 397.
Baker, William, 415.
Baldwin, John, 71, 164, 262, 283, 304, 321, 327, 328, 414.
Banks, Anthony, 172, 271.
Bannor, Lawrence, 20, 50, 51, 52, 53, 58, 62, 63, 64, 66, 68.
Bannr, see Bannor.
Barrets, 346.
Barry, Robert 399.
Basnet, Richard, 48, 127, 238.
Bayns, see Bains.
Beake, Abraham, 279, 280.
Beakes, Daniel, 195.
Beakes, Edmund, 84, 85, 184, 185.
Beakes, Elizabeth, 284, 285.
Beakes, Ellenor, 95, 195.
Beaks, Mary, 84, 105, 145, 184, 204, 226, 229, 280, 282.
Beakes, Samuel, 140, 141, 145, 164, 167, 171, 172, 174, 176, 179, 181, 226, 229, 231, 239, 263, 264, 268, 269, 270, 271, 273, 274, 280, 284.

285, 286, 288, 291, 293, 295, 296,
297, 298, 300, 301, 302, 304, 305,
308, 309, 313, 314, 315, 316, 317,
319, 323, 324, 325, 326, 327, 328,
329, 330, 331, 335, 336, 337, 338,
339, 342, 345, 346, 347, 348, 349,
352, 354, 356, 358, 361, 362, 365,
367, 368, 370, 372, 373, 375, 378,
379, 380, 382, 385, 386, 387, 388,
390, 391, 397, 399, 400, 414, 415.
Beakes, Stephen, 85, 99, 121, 156,
157, 158, 165, 167, 168, 169, 185,
187, 198, 203, 206, 214, 215, 217,
221, 233, 239, 253, 254, 255, 256,
264, 265, 266, 280, 307, 309, 313,
339, 342, 344, 360, 367, 371, 375,
377.
Beakes, William, 3, 4, 10, 11, 19, 25,
40, 42, 50, 51, 52, 53, 58, 60, 61,
64, 65, 87, 91, 101, 105, 111, 112,
121, 123, 132, 134, 145, 175, 182,
185, 186, 191, 200, 203, 209, 210,
211, 218, 221, 222, 226, 239, 243,
245, 247, 253, 276, 280, 283, 284,
285, 315, 373.
Beaks, William, Jr., 79, 80.
Beal, see Beale.
Beale, William, 201, 374.
Beatridg, Betridge, see Betrice.
Bennet, Edmund, 10, 15, 19, 24, 31,
32, 40, 49, 58, 62, 64, 65, 123,
130, 242, 332.
Bennet, Edward, 372.
Bennet, Elizabeth, 174, 272, 310,
339.
Benson, Robert, 91, 143, 177, 179,
180, 192, 225, 273, 276.
Betrice, Mark, 88, 107, 125, 188.
Betrice, Prudence, 290.
Betrice, William, 401.
Bians, William, 256.
Bills, Thomas, 306.
Bircham, Henry, 20, 32, 93, 109,
193, 207, 305.
Bircham, Margaret, 305.
Black, William, 82.
Blackwell, John, 112, 210.
Bladen, Barbary, 339.
Biles, Charles, 57, 73, 74, 287.
Biles, George, 297, 354, 355, 359,
401.
Biles, Jane, 297.
Biles, Sarah, 134, 246, 318, 398.

Biles, William, 5, 6, 8, 9, 10, 11,
16, 19, 22, 23, 25, 31, 32, 40, 42,
43, 46, 56, 61, 62, 64, 65, 66, 67,
69, 70, 71, 73, 74, 83, 88, 89, 90,
96, 97, 101, 105, 111, 113, 115,
121 123, 124, 126, 128, 129, 130,
131, 135, 137, 138, 139, 140, 145,
151, 152, 153, 161, 162, 163, 164,
165, 167, 171, 173, 174, 176, 178,
184, 189, 191, 196, 197, 200, 203,
209, 213, 215, 219, 221, 222, 223,
226, 227, 228, 230, 231, 236, 237,
240, 241, 242, 243, 248, 250, 251,
259, 260, 261, 262, 264, 268, 271,
272, 274, 279, 286, 288, 291, 293,
294, 295, 297, 300, 301, 304, 306,
309, 310, 313, 316, 322, 325, 329,
330, 334, 338, 342, 344, 345, 348,
352, 355, 358, 364, 370, 373, 375,
378, 380, 385, 391, 397, 398, 414,
415.
Biles, William, Jr., 318, 354, 358,
371, 375, 377, 396, 399, 400, 403,
413, 415.
Biles, William, Sr., 399.
Blackshaw, Josiah, 306.
Blackshaw, Nehemiah, 311, 375.
Blackshaw, Randulph (Randle or
Randol), 20, 33, 84, 89, 101, 103,
109, 112, 184, 189, 200, 201, 207,
209, 210, 292, 304, 311, 375, 397.
Bleake, James, 156, 255.
Blowers, Joseph, 22, 23, 24.
Boare, Joshua, 20, 40, 57.
Boare, Lucy, 299.
Bond, James, 374, 376.
Bons, see Boone.
Boome, Ralph, 141, 143, 162, 163,
164, 173, 224, 231, 261, 262, 271,
282, 298, 299, 300, 326, 332, 356,
370.
Boucher, Henry, 150, 249.
Bowen, Henry, 299, 375.
Bowen, John, 59, 162, 163, 169, 261,
266, 299, 399.
Bowman, Thomas, 3, 266, 374, 399.
Bowman's Estate, 352.
Bown, Samuel, 305.
Bowns, John, 399.
Bownton, see Bunting.
Boyden, James, 20, 22, 24, 32, 42,
130, 171, 242.

INDEX OF PERSONS 419

Boyden, James, Jr., 121, 221, 305, 313.
Boyden, Mary, 166, 263, 277.
Bradley, Joshua, 67.
Brearley, John, 30, 79, 80, 87, 172, 186, 206.
Brian, William, 191.
Bridgman, Walter, 76, 77, 86, 88, 186, 188.
Brigham, Charles, 103, 110, 202.
Brindley, Luke, 3, 5, 6, 9, 15, 19, 23, 26, 27, 28, 29, 30, 32, 35, 36, 38, 40, 41, 45, 46, 47, 51, 52, 53, 55, 56, 62, 63, 82, 96, 108, 112, 117, 196, 206, 209.
Brinson, Daniel, 4, 11, 16, 17, 32, 34, 37, 59, 68, 180, 276.
Brittan, Lyonel, 10, 20, 22, 32, 47, 58, 63, 99, 198.
Brock, John, 9, 13, 15, 26, 30, 34, 35, 36, 41, 47, 48, 57, 58, 69, 76, 77, 84, 85, 86, 89, 91, 92, 93, 100, 101, 105, 111, 121, 123, 126, 128, 129, 130, 132, 138, 139, 143, 144, 152, 159, 161, 184, 186, 189, 191, 192, 193, 199, 200, 203, 209, 221, 222, 225, 226, 227, 228, 236, 237, 240, 241, 251, 259, 277, 278, 279, 280, 281, 282, 283, 284, 295, 307, 316, 321.
Brock, Thomas, 91, 104, 141, 143, 152, 153, 154, 158, 159, 163, 168, 172, 175, 177, 191, 202, 210, 224, 230, 231, 251, 252, 257, 262, 265, 271, 273, 274, 278, 280, 282, 283, 284, 285, 287, 290, 292, 295, 296, 300, 301, 305, 324, 326, 328, 329, 330, 339, 349, 356, 367, 380, 398, 399.
Brown, George, 32, 137, 152, 156, 157, 158, 182, 248, 251, 254, 256, 257, 276, 278, 306, 335, 391.
Bucher, Michael, 88, 117, 118, 188, 212, 217.
Buckman, William, 76, 77, 93, 193, 229, 255, 280, 299, 303, 318, 326, 328, 344, 349.
Bud, John, 151.
Bull, Richard, 335.
Bunting, Job, 168, 170, 182, 265, 267, 276, 278, 280, 288, 397.
Buntinge, see Bunting.
Burcham, see Bircham.

Burden, 414.
Burden, Joseph, 103, 202, 396.
Burden, Samuel, 97, 99, 100, 103, 104, 197, 199, 202, 396.
Burges, Anthony, 82.
Burges, Daniel, 331.
Burges, Elizabeth, 346, 358, 360, 379, 382.
Burges, Isaac, 108, 206, 209, 299, 301.
Burges, Richard, 178, 181, 312, 314, 321, 336, 338, 340, 346.
Burges, Samuel, 30, 33, 68, 72, 112, 123, 210, 222, 255, 285, 301, 327.
Burges, Samuel, Jr., 305.
Burradel, John, 390, 395.
Burton, Anthony, 98, 177, 197, 217, 273, 278, 279, 290, 295, 296, 301, 302, 316, 323, 350, 358, 359, 367, 379, 380, 394, 397, 398.
Burton, George, 213, 218.
Burton, John, 379.
Busby, John, 379.
Busby, Mary, 379.
Butler, John, 144, 147, 148, 203, 226, 234, 237.

Carpenter, Samuel, 103, 142, 202, 224, 292, 293, 302, 311, 324, 326, 337, 349, 355, 396.
Carter, see Cartor.
Cartor, Edward, 95, 104, 124, 160, 195, 202, 223, 259, 279, 357, 396.
Cartor, John, 70, 71, 124, 223, 314, 354, 369.
Cartor, Robert, 32, 34, 56, 70, 71, 72.
Cartor, William, 56.
Cartr, see Cartor.
Caws, see Clows.
Cearll, Thomas, 280, 283.
Cearll, see Kirle.
Chamberlaine, Lucy, 394.
Chamberlaine, Peter, 163, 394.
Chapman, Jane, 345.
Chappel, Elizabeth, 164, 263.
Chorley, Joseph, 8, 82, 84, 101, 106, 147, 149, 151, 164, 173, 174, 179, 180, 187, 200, 204, 233, 236, 250, 262, 271, 272, 276, 278, 282, 287, 292, 293, 297, 304, 310, 313, 318, 321, 326, 328, 329, 330, 338, 342,

344, 346, 347, 349, 355, 358, 361, 362, 364, 365, 366, 367, 368, 369, 370, 373, 374, 378, 379, 380, 381, 382, 383, 384, 385, 386, 387, 388, 389, 400.
Chorley, Mary, 278, 282, 297, 387.
Circuit, John, 310.
Circuit, see Surket.
Clark, John, 129, 148, 180, 235, 272, 276, 277, 278, 283, 310, 346.
Clarke, Ann, 375.
Clarke's Orphans, 15, 16.
Clawson, Derick, 10, 20, 24, 112, 149, 210, 236, 277.
Clawson als Jonson, Derick, 177, 181, 182, 270.
Clawson, John, 79, 80, 156, 158, 255, 256.
Claypoole, James, 47.
Clement, John, 107, 205, 206.
Clif, Samuel, 44, 331, 332, 333.
Clif, Jonathan, 331, 332.
Clift, see Clif.
Clowes, see Clows.
Clows, John, 7, 8, 32, 47, 57, 162, 260, 279, 282.
Clows, Joseph, 86, 88, 141, 186, 188, 210, 230, 295, 371.
Clows, Margery, 141, 151, 230, 250.
Clows, Sarah, 372.
Clows, William, 98, 109, 112, 141, 197, 207, 211, 230, 280, 281, 283.
Clowse, see Clows.
Cluse, see Clows.
Coates, John, 57, 119, 219.
Coates, Samuel, 278, 280, 307, 349, 370.
Coatts, see Coates.
Cockram, George, 134, 246.
Cockrum, see Cockram.
Codery, William, 354.
Cole, Robert, 170, 180, 267, 272, 276, 277, 278, 280, 282, 283, 286, 287, 288, 348, 350.
Cole, Thomas, 272.
Coleman, Thomas, 134, 135, 382, 400.
Collins, Francis, 290.
Collins, John, 22, 24, 50, 57, 95, 96, 100, 195, 199.
Comley, Henry, 42, 43, 287.
Conway Paterick, 111, 113, 114, 115, 118, 119, 120, 125, 176, 210, 211, 212, 213, 214, 215, 218, 220, 223.
Conway, Philip, 32, 50, 75, 76, 77, 78, 81, 103, 105, 106, 107, 108, 109, 113, 114, 116, 117, 118, 119, 120, 122, 125, 176, 202, 204, 205, 206, 207, 210, 211, 212, 213, 214, 215, 216, 217, 220, 223, 287.
Cook, Arthur, 33, 56, 66, 71, 72, 74, 75, 78, 81, 86, 90, 103, 111, 112, 121, 124, 130, 133, 142, 143, 152, 157, 159, 161, 167, 171, 182, 183, 185, 190, 202, 209, 210, 221, 223, 224, 242, 245, 251, 255, 260, 264, 268, 290, 291, 306, 310, 314, 315, 324.
Cook, Benjamin, 377.
Cook, John, 109, 126, 152, 163, 164, 165, 167, 171, 176, 207, 237, 251, 261, 262, 263, 264, 268, 284, 292, 295, 310, 355, 393.
Cooke, see Cook.
Cotterill, Thomas, 85, 185.
Coverdale, Jane, 75.
Coverdale, Thomas, 105, 106, 107, 111, 134, 135, 204, 205, 210.
Coverdale's wife, 77.
Cowgill, Abraham, 311.
Cowgill, Edmund, 346.
Cowgill, John, 280, 370, 373.
Cowgill, Nehemiah, 311.
Cowgill, Ralph, 283, 292, 306, 311, 342, 391, 403, 413.
Cows, see Clows.
Cox, Abraham, 43, 44, 45, 47, 76, 77, 101, 169, 171, 182, 199, 255, 266, 267, 269, 276, 289, 299, 313, 314, 316.
Cox, Daniel, 150, 154, 155, 158, 249, 252, 253, 257.
Crapp, John, 54, 55.
Crosdel, John, 67, 68, 93, 179, 180, 193, 233, 238, 276, 278, 289, 291, 303, 326, 339, 349, 370, 373, 401, 403, 413.
Crosdell, Ezra, 42, 73, 98, 109, 119, 197, 206, 207, 214, 215, 219, 238, 306, 325, 396, 397, 401.
Crosdell, James, 193.
Crosdell, William, 86, 90, 92, 93, 96, 185, 190, 192, 193, 196, 291, 299, 301, 302, 304, 315, 326, 342, 346, 373, 378, 393, 401.
Crosley, James, 93, 206.

INDEX OF PERSONS 421

Crosse, Joseph, 111, 115, 209, 215, 298, 299, 300.
Crossley, see Crosley.
Cuff, John, 57, 67, 68, 74, 75, 141, 231.
Cuft, see Cuff.
Cutler, Edmund, 25, 49, 59.
Cutler, Isabel, 373, 376.
Cutler, John, 67, 68, 301, 303.
Cuttler, see Cutler.

Daniel, Philip, 404.
Darby, William, 305, 307.
Dark, John, 305, 327, 359, 360.
Dark, Samuel, 6, 10, 11, 16, 41, 42, 79, 80, 93, 99, 128, 157, 158, 160, 182, 193, 198, 205, 210, 230, 239, 240, 253, 255, 257, 265, 272, 276, 295, 298, 301, 308, 312, 313, 340, 341, 342, 363.
Dark, William, 20, 58, 64, 65, 76, 77, 79, 80, 86, 88, 98, 121, 186, 188, 197, 205, 210, 221, 233, 239, 253, 278, 279, 280, 283, 289, 291, 299, 305, 306, 316, 339, 340, 341, 342, 353, 358, 359, 363.
Darke, see Dark.
Davenport, Francis, 365.
Davis, David, 14, 15, 42, 43, 61, 62, 63.
Davies, Richard, 324, 325, 327, 331, 338, 344, 373.
Dawson, John, 375.
Dawson, Martha, 375.
Dennis, Samuel, 67.
Derick's Indictment, 178.
Devonish, Bernard, 154, 155, 253.
Dickerson, Thomas, 50.
Dilworth, James, 49, 50, 59, 163, 282, 340, 346.
Done, Daniel, 306, 339.
Done, Robert, 48, 68, 82.
Dow, Robert, 67.
Doyal, see Doyle.
Doyl, see Doyle.
Doyle, Edward, 305, 308, 337, 338, 391.
Doyles, William, 278.
Druet, Morgan, 33.
Duncan, George, 308, 313.
Duncan, John, 325, 326.
Duncan, William, 147, 164, 177, 233, 262, 313, 316, 318, 339, 342, 349, 371, 375, 377.
Dungan, Clement, 292, 303, 305, 340, 341, 349, 355, 400.
Dungan, Jeremiah, 350, 354.
Dungan, John, 350.
Dungan, Thomas, 350, 396.
Dungan, William, 20, 58, 59, 91, 103, 169, 191, 202, 266, 272, 273, 283, 400, 403, 413.
Dunk, Andrew, 88, 188.
Dunken, see Duncan.
Duplovie, John, 130, 131, 139, 142, 149, 162, 172, 176, 224.
Duplovies, see Duplovie.
Duplovis, see Duplovie.
Dure, Thomas, 305, 398.

Eastbourn, John, 179, 328, 357, 362, 394, 396.
Fire, Mary, 87, 186.
Eldridge, Jonathan, 140, 145, 226, 229.
Eliott, William, 283.
Ellet, see Ellot.
Ellis, Hugh, 378.
Ellot, Ann, 134, 246.
Ellot, Andrew, 42, 88, 93, 134, 193, 210, 211, 230, 239, 246, 253, 255, 272, 283, 295, 344, 358, 368, 371, 375, 377, 398.
Ellot, John, 415.
Ellot, William, 214, 215, 217, 230, 239, 371, 376, 377.
Elly, see Ely.
Ely, Joshua, 84, 87, 186, 192.
Ely, Joshua, Junior, 186.
Ely, Joshua, Senior, 87.
Embley, William, 145, 146, 230, 231, 232, 325, 365.
Empson, 172.
Empson, Cornelius, 130, 131, 145, 146, 149, 162, 176, 231, 232, 236, 242, 260.
England, Joseph, 150, 249.
English, 341, 363.
English, Joane, 63.
English, Joseph, 13, 86, 90, 93, 97, 100, 128, 163, 186, 190, 191, 193, 197, 199, 205, 210, 240, 262, 290, 318, 323, 331, 333, 349.
English, Joseph, Junior, 44.
English, Joseph, Senior, 20, 57, 63.

Evan, see Evans.
Evans, David, 86, 186.
Evans, Edward, 318.
Evans, William, 138, 145, 149, 227, 231, 235.

Fairman, Robert, 318.
Faireman, Thomas, 291, 296, 318, 350, 372.
Farrington, Joseph, 125, 127, 131, 133, 134, 136, 137, 237, 238, 242, 245, 246, 247, 248.
Feild, Benjamin, 309.
Fenbank, Ellenor, 33.
Ferries, Zachariah, 394.
Fisher, George, 390, 392.
Fisher, William, 113, 114, 115, 118, 120, 125, 211, 212, 213, 214, 215, 217, 218, 223.
Fleckney, John, 98, 197.
Fletcher, Benjamin, 300.
Flower, Henry, 116, 216, 352.
Forest, Walter, 149, 215, 236.
Forest, Widow, 277.
Foster, Allen, 328, 372.
Foster, Mary, 372.
Fowler, William, 57.
Fox, James, 368.
Fox, Thomas, 102, 125, 126, 146, 201, 232, 233, 236, 238.
Freeborn, Gideon, 304.
Frezey, Joseph, 67.
Fuller, John, 142, 224.
Furnas, John, 98, 198.

Gabitas, William, 93.
Gardiner, Daniel, 151, 283, 303, 399.
Gardiner, Thomas, 347, 351, 357, 358, 361, 363, 377, 382, 388, 389, 393.
Gardner, see Gardiner.
Garner, Daniel, 134.
George the Negro, 94, 95, 99, 102, 104, 194, 195, 198.
Gibbs, Elizabeth, 41.
Gibbs, John, 108, 206, 281.
Gilbart, see Gilbert.
Gilbert, John, 158, 169, 180, 256, 266, 277, 283, 301, 312, 313, 328, 341, 344, 355, 362, 375.
Gilbert, Joseph, 362, 363, 376.
Glave, George, 38, 60, 67.

Grant, Neel, 325.
Gray, John, 55, 56, 57.
Gray als Tatham, John, 160, 258, 348, 351, 357, 360, 363, 377, 382, 385, 388.
Grayham, James, 68, 69, 70.
Greaves, Jane, 19.
Green, 363.
Green, John, 26, 292.
Green, Katherine, 292.
Green, Rachel, 177, 273, 318, 323, 331, 333, 349.
Green, Thomas, 26, 75, 106, 147, 177, 204, 233, 273, 279, 292, 318, 323, 331, 333, 349.
Greenland, Doctor, 180, 276.
Greenland, Henry, 173, 175, 271, 273.
Griffith, John, 313, 314, 361.
Groesbeck, Jacob, 330.
Growdon, Joseph, 32, 75, 81, 82, 83, 84, 90, 93, 101, 102, 103, 104, 107, 111, 112, 119, 130, 133, 138, 139, 141, 146, 147, 149, 151, 152, 155, 156, 157, 159, 160, 161, 162, 163, 164, 167, 171, 172, 176, 178, 181, 182, 190, 193, 200, 201, 202, 203, 204, 205, 209, 210, 219, 227, 228, 231, 232, 233, 235, 236, 237, 242, 245, 250, 251, 253, 254, 255, 257, 258, 259, 260, 261, 262, 264, 269, 270, 288, 295, 296, 298, 299, 302, 304, 305, 313, 314, 315, 316, 318, 321, 325, 326, 328, 330, 338, 342, 348, 351, 357, 358, 363, 373, 374, 377, 382, 385, 388, 391, 393, 397, 398, 402, 404, 405, 407, 408, 409, 411, 413, 414, 415, 416.
Grub, Henry, 82, 400.

Hagath, James, 391.
Hague, William, 40, 41.
Hall, Jacob, 26, 27, 28, 29, 32, 33, 37, 70, 75, 84, 92, 95, 151, 164, 192, 195, 239, 250, 262.
Hall, Joseph, 72, 73.
Hall, Robert, 41, 42, 49, 121, 124, 269.
Hancock, Edward, 97, 197, 200.
Hardin, Thomas, 109, 158, 182, 207, 214, 215, 217, 256, 276, 295, 370, 382, 394.
Harding, Nathaniel, 210.

Harding, Thomas, 116, 149, 216, 236.
Hardman, Abraham, 331.
Harrison, James, 9, 15, 16, 31, 40, 42, 48, 50, 71, 74, 75, 112, 117, 210, 217.
Harrison, John, 309, 334, 387.
Harvey, Matthias, 310, 323, 375.
Harvie, see Harvey.
Hawkins, 268.
Hawkins, Ann, 113, 211.
Hawkins, Daniel, 83, 91, 107, 192, 205.
Hawkins, Jeffery, 41, 50, 51, 79, 80, 83, 91, 210, 367.
Hawkins, John, 146, 232, 233.
Hawkins, Roger, 39, 40, 41, 59, 66, 95, 99, 195, 198.
Hayhurst, William, 102, 110, 124, 149, 230, 236, 316, 349, 370, 372, 373, 384, 393, 397.
Hayworth, James, 387.
Hayworth, Mary, 387.
Headley, John, 370.
Hearst, William, 201, 223, 238.
Heath, Andrew, 32, 132, 134, 206, 210, 222, 230, 243, 245, 247, 255, 278, 299, 321, 331, 336, 341, 342, 343, 344, 345, 394.
Heathcoate, George, 297, 312.
Hearth, And, 282, 287.
Heaton, James, 285, 287, 289, 290, 292, 391.
Heaton, Robert, 42, 47, 49, 57, 66, 75, 85, 86, 88, 91, 116, 117, 150, 163, 168, 170, 184, 188, 191, 216, 217, 265, 267, 287, 288, 299, 313, 328, 340, 341, 342, 346, 349, 356, 358, 362, 370, 379, 383, 387.
Heaton, Robert, Junior, 291, 310, 408, 413.
Heats, Andrew, 246.
Hedley, Richard, 10.
Heesem, see Heesum.
Heesome, see Heesum.
Henbery, Joseph, 172, 246, 344.
Henbry, see Henbery.
Henry, Joseph, **134**.
Herrote, George, 10.
Hewett, John, 274.
Hewit, 178.
Hickman, Eliza, 75.
Hill, James, 94, 154, 194, 253.
Hill, John, 20.
Hill, Josias, 163, 168, 266, **415**.
Hinksonte, see Hinkstone.
Hinkstone, Abel, 102, 201, 396, 414.
Hodson, Thomas, 375.
Holden, Joseph, 130, 131, 138, 139, 140, 142, 145, 146, 149, 162, 175, 224, 227, 228, 229, 231, 232, 236, 242, 261, 270, 296, 298.
Holden's Case, 176.
Holgat, Robert, 47.
Hollinshead, John, 148.
Hollinshead, Joseph, 32, 33, 78, 94, 95, 194, 195, 235.
Holm, see Holme.
Holme, Thomas, 33, 47, 67, 68, 69, 70, 73.
Holmes, see Holme.
Holt, Martin, 22, 24.
Hoops, Daniel, 309.
Hoops, Joshua, 25, 29, 80, 123, 128, 130, 140, 147, 163, 171, 182, 205, 214, 222, 230, 233, 239, 240, 242, 245, 253, 268, 276, 295, 298, 299, 303, 306, 309, 313, 316, 327, 339, 340, 341, 349, 356, 358, 370, 371, 376, 377, 394, 397, 398, 415, 416.
Horner, John, 50, 287, 309, 378, 383, 387, 389.
Hoste, William, 278.
Hough, Francis, 29, 30, 49, 57, 71, 90, 91, 191.
Hough, John, 58, 93, 193, 205, 238, 269, 280, 283, 299, 303, 358, 371, 375, 376.
Hough, Richard, 41, 47, 88, 100, 123, 157, 168, 171, 188, 199, 210, 222, 255, 265, 267, 268, 285, 286, 288, 291, 293, 295, 297, 300, 301, 302, 304, 309, 310, 313, 316, 323, 325, 330, 338, **342**, **345**, 348, 352, 358, 366, 368, 370, 372, 373, 378, 380, 381, 385, 397, 414, 415.
Hough, Samuel, 33, 94, 95, 194, 195, 307, 322, 339, 357, 396.
Houghton, John, 276.
Houghtons, 180.
Houle, Job, 103, 107, 177, 179, 202, 203, 205, 274, 378.
Howard, William, 299.
Howel, Philip, 350.
Hudelston, see Hudlestone.
Hudleston, see Hudlestone.

INDEX OF PERSONS

Hudlestone, Henry, 102, 161, 163, 201, 214, 215, 217, 238, 259, 278, 279, 299, 313, 321, 328, 356, 371, 375, 377, 393, 394, 403, 413.
Hudlestone, Valentine, 324.
Hudson, Thomas, 151, 164, 250, 262, 309, 310, 322, 325, 334, 344, 373, 375, 415.
Huff, Joan, 83, 84, 91, 95, 191, 195.
Huff, Micheal, 42, 44, 45, 47, 57.
Hughes, William, 305.
Hull, Jo:, 79.
Hunlock, Edward, 127, 135, 154, 238, 246, 252, 253, 347, 351, 373, 374, 390, 399, 400.
Hunloke, see Hunlock.
Huntley, William, 384, 388, 389, 400.
Hutchins, Thomas, 111, 209, 220.
Hutchinson, George, 154, 155, 252, 253.
Hycock, William, 20, 25.

J—Claws, 177.
Jackson, Epharm, 36.
Jacob, James, 350.
James II, King, 55, 66, 78, 81, 83, 86, 90, 92, 93, 101, 280.
Janney, Abel, 287, 310, 394, 398.
Jamey, Jacob, 76, 77, 171, 267, 281, 353, 358, 360.
Jamey, Joseph, 399, 401.
Janney, Thomas, 9, 11, 12, 15, 23, 25, 31, 40, 46, 48, 49, 56, 66, 71, 81, 123, 126, 129, 130, 132, 133, 138, 139, 140, 157, 159, 161, 171, 198, 222, 228, 230, 237, 241, 242, 243, 255, 259, 268, 291, 357, 358, 360, 394, 397, 398.
Janney, Thomas, Junior, 304.
Janney, Thomas, Senior, 94, 99, 96.
Jeffs, Mary, 187.
Jeffs, Robert, 96, 196.
Jenings, Peter, 125, 126, 236, 238.
Jenings, Samuel, 181, 367.
Jenks, Andrew, 115.
Jennings, see Jenings.
Jenner, Thomas, 296.
Jerrome, Samuel, 316, 317, 319, 320, 321, 345.
John, 181.
Johnson, see Jonson.
Jolly, James, 401, 402.

Jones, Benjamin, 88, 109, 127, 188, 189, 207, 239.
Jones, Daniel, 66, 346.
Jones, Francis, 286.
Jones, Griffith, 33, 82.
Jones, John, 93, 132, 138, 139, 142, 145, 176, 224, 227, 228, 231, 394.
Jones, Joseph, 394.
Jonson, 158.
Jonson, Brighta, 166, 181, 182, 263, 296.
Jonson, Claws, 10, 20, 112, 166, 210, 263, 270, 277, 298, 299, 313, 330.
Jonson, Derrick, 128, 129, 182, 240, 277.
Jonson, Elizabeth, 181, 182, 296.
Jonson, John, 157, 256, 299.
Jonson, Katherine, 296.
Joseph, 409.
Jonson als Clawson, Derrick, 165, 166, 181, 263.
Jonson, Derrick's Case, 175.

Kan, Matts [Matthias Keen], 296.
Kelly, Paterick, 100, 198.
Kenerley, William, 309.
King, the, 185, 190, 192, 193, 200, 203, 284, 286, 288, 289, 295, 302, 308.
King James II, 280.
King, Thomas, 147, 148, 233, 234, 235.
King, William, 304.
King and Queen, 111, 123, 126, 138, 152, 157, 161, 162, 163, 166, 173, 180, 209, 222, 227, 237, 244, 251, 255, 259, 260, 261, 264, 271, 273, 275, 276, 277, 278, 279, 280, 281, 283.
Kirkbride, Joseph, 82, 91, 158, 168, 182, 191, 245, 255, 257, 265, 268, 276, 291, 295, 301, 304, 306, 311, 315, 325, 328, 340, 341, 352, 356, 362, 364, 369, 370, 375, 381, 383, 387, 389, 398.
Kirkbridge, see Kirkbride.
Kirkham, James, 345.
Kirl, see Kirle.
Kirle, see Cearll.
Kirle, Joseph, 326.
Kirle, Julian, 379.
Kirle, Thomas, 112, 134, 211, 246,

INDEX OF PERSONS

303, 339, 341, 342, 343, 344, 349, 356, 394, 397.
Knight, Joseph, 53, 55, 150, 249.
Knight, Katherin, 21.
Knight, Thomas, 325, 358.

L, Wm., 184.
Lacy, Thomas, 178, 179, 275, 277, 280.
Lambert, Thomas, 97, 197, 365.
Lancaster, Edward, 99, 198.
Lane, Edward, 166, 181, 203, 298, 299.
Langhorn, Grace, 109, 175, 207, 318, 355, 398.
Langhorn, Jeremiah, 299, 307, 318, 328, 339, 342, 349, 358, 371, 375, 377, 397, 398.
Langhorn, Thomas, 75, 78.
Large, Joseph, 292, 293, 377.
Lavally, Lewis, 279.
Lawrence, William, 309, 415.
Leacy, see Lacy.
Lee, John, 126, 127, 143, 225, 230, 237, 238, 244.
Lee, Martha, 143, 225.
Lee, Rachel, 143, 225.
Lees, John, 132, 133.
Lilly, David, 82.
Linck, Denis, 163, 261.
Linstone, Denis, 159, 160, 258.
Litgraine, Roger, 172.
Lloyd, David, 78, 90, 190, 361.
Lloyd, Thomas, 33, 73.
Looker, Wm., 67, 84.
Lovet, Ed:, 20, 41.
Lovet, Edmund, 32, 76, 77, 168, 169, 171, 233, 245, 265, 266, 267, 269, 289, 291, 304, 312, 313, 316, 323, 324, 328, 344, 353, 358, 359, 401.
Loyke, Hance, 296.
Lucas, Edward, 158, 169, 173, 174, 256, 266, 271, 289, 291, 337, 340, 341, 353, 358, 359, 370, 397.
Lucas, Elizabeth, 38, 337.
Lucas, Giles, 337, 349, 376.
Lucas, Robert, 3, 10, 34, 40, 41, 63, 329, 337.
Lucas, Widow, 268, 303, 306.
Luff, Edward, 97, 197.
Luinn, Joseph, 20.
Lundy, Richard, 25, 37, 67, 68, 72,

82, 86, 88, 90, 98, 112, 174, 186, 188, 190, 197, 210, 214, 215, 217, 238, 272.
Lyon, Jane, 16.

Man, Abraham, 25.
Man, Elizabeth, 25.
Manarte, Ellenor, 220.
Marg, see Margerum.
Margorm, see Margerum.
Margerum, Henry, 20, 22, 25, 41, 42, 79, 80, 86, 88, 97, 98, 116, 148, 186, 188, 197, 211, 216, 233, 235, 238, 255, 256, 279, 281, 289, 291, 295, 299, 307, 316, 336, 353, 358, 359, 363, 370.
Marjerum, see Margerum.
Marjoron, see Margerum.
Markham, Captain, 118, 218.
Markham, William, 213, 218, 289, 318.
March, see Marsh.
Marle, Thomas, 93.
Marsh, Hugh, 103, 105, 132, 134, 136, 139, 146, 147, 163, 168, 179, 202, 227, 228, 229, 232, 234, 244, 245, 247, 255, 266, 275.
Marsh, Robert, 24, 132, 134, 136, 147, 163, 179, 234, 244, 245, 247.
Marsh, Samuel, 179.
Marshall, James, 98.
Martin, George, 66.
Martin, John, 95, 195.
Masley, Moses, 204, 332.
Mathews, Thomas, 22, 24.
Matthews, Margret, 299.
Mayos, Edward, 326, 355.
Merriot, see Merriott.
Merriott, Isaac, 316, 317, 320, 368.
Milcome, Ann, 7, 18, 19, 21.
Milcome, Widow, 11.
Miles, Abigaile, 360.
Millar, see Miller.
Millard, Thomas, 82, 92, 93, 97, 98, 99, 100, 103, 104, 193, 197, 199, 202.
Millenor, see Milner.
Miller, Joseph, 80, 93, 100, 280.
Miller, Mathew, 141, 143, 224, 231.
Mills, James, 346.
Milner, Joseph, 11, 12, 20, 36, 58, 79, 80, 91, 121, 132, 133, 168, 171, 182, 186, 191, 193, 199, 205, 210,

INDEX OF PERSONS

221, 233, 238, 244, 265, 267, 276, 278, 279, 285, 301, 310, 312, 313, 323, 328, 334, 340, 341, 353, 356, 358, 359.
Milner, Rachel, 58, 59.
Milner, Ralph, 53, 55, 58, 59, 70.
Milnor, see Milner.
Moon, see Moone.
Moone, James, 76, 77, 86, 88, 94, 98, 158, 186, 188, 194, 197, 210, 256, 272, 287, 289, 291, 313, 316, 339, 358, 359.
Moone, James, Junior, 157, 194, 255, 307, 308, 401.
Moone, James, Senior, 157, 255, 279, 307.
Moone, Joan, 287.
Moore, Edmund, 107, 205.
Moore, Nicholas, 27, 28, 45, 46.
More, see Moore.
Morgan, Anthony, 168, 266, 415.
Morow, Peter, 279.
Morris, Israel, 346.
Morris, John, 372.
Morton, William, 30, 79.
Murfen, see Murfey.
Murfey, Rodger, 279, 280.
Murfeyn, see Murfey.
Murfyn, John, 280.
Musgrave, Thomas, 311, 324.
Myers, Will, 404.

Naylor, John, 88, 92, 127, 128, 188, 205, 239, 240, 296, 394, 403, 413.
Negro (George), 107, 201, 202.
Negro Will, 399.
Neild, John, 11, 12, 132, 244, 296, 299, 342.
Newell, Stephen, 102, 104, 107, 176, 177, 201, 202, 203, 205, 238, 273, 283, 305, 306, 307, 308, 313, 322, 327, 344.
Newell, Elizabeth, 307.
Nicholls, see Nichols.
Nichols, Elias, 59, 87, 186, 329, 366, 367, 380, 381, 382, 383, 386.
Nichols, John, 59, 75, 172, 173, 187, 270, 329, 366, 367, 380, 381, 382, 383, 386.
Nichols, William, 166, 167, 264 265.
Noble, 363.
Noble, Richard, 15, 25, 61, 106, 204, 318, 323, 331, 332, 333, 341, 349, 379, 384.
Norris, Isaac, 319, 320, 366, 381, 383, 385, 386, 388.
Nowel, see Newell.

Oldale, Samuel, 326, 345, 347, 351, 358, 361, 363, 364, 377, 382, 388, 389, 393, 416.
Oldfeild, John, 91, 92, 192, 193.
Oldfield, see Oldfeild.
Oldham, Jonathan, 378, 382.
Otter, John, 9, 10, 15, 19, 23, 24, 31, 40, 46, 49, 66, 73, 112, 151, 153, 210, 250, 257, 304.
Otter, Justice, 10, 24.
Overton, Hannah, 80.
Overton, Samuel, 7, 8, 26, 27, 28, 29, 47, 58, 76, 77, 162, 260.
Owen, John, 87, 186.
Oxley, Ann, 84, 183.

Page, Isaac, 178, 275.
Palmer, John, 42, 79, 80, 93, 182, 193, 205, 210, 230, 276, 280, 283, 289, 291, 295, 313, 316, 339, 342, 358, 384, 397, 398.
Pamar, see Palmer.
Parker, Lawrence, 150, 249.
Parker, Philip, 107, 205.
Parsely, see Purslone.
Partington, Isaoc, 57.
Paul, Joseph, 326.
Pawlin, Henry, 71, 72, 79, 80, 169, 184, 238, 266, 312, 391, 397.
Paxson, Henry, 25, 49, 70, 71, 72, 75, 86, 93, 105, 106, 109, 114, 182, 186, 193, 204, 207, 230, 239, 245, 276, 278, 280, 338, 340, 358, 360.
Paxson, James, 20, 67, 68, 86, 88, 98, 158, 165, 168, 182, 186, 188, 197, 204, 205, 214, 238, 245, 253, 255, 256, 265, 276, 278, 280, 295, 306, 346, 352, 363, 393,
Paxson, William, 20, 43, 47, 58, 85, 152, 184, 214, 215, 217, 233, 239, 245, 253, 255, 272, 278, 295, 298, 306, 318, 346, 349, 358, 371, 373, 375, 376, 377, 393, 416.
Paxston, see Paxson.
Paxton, see Paxson.
Pearce, Richard, 399.

Pearson, Edward, 269, 289, 291.
Pearson, Enoch, 377.
Pearson, Lawrence, 377.
Peart, Mary, 350.
Peart, Thomas, 350.
Peas, William, 71, 72.
Pegg, Elizabeth, 164, 262.
Peirce, Thomas, 131, 133, 135, 136, 152, 272.
Pellexon, Jacob, 25.
Pemberton, Phenihas, 414, 415.
Pemberton, Phineas, 297, 300, 301, 302, 304, 305, 307, 309, 311, 313, 314, 315, 316, 318, 323, 324, 325, 326, 328, 330, 331, 333, 337, 345, 349, 355, 358, 366, 370, 373, 378, 379, 380, 382, 391, 397, 398.
Pemberton, Phinehas, 9, 10, 11, 15, 19, 23, 25, 32, 34, 37, 41, 42, 45, 47, 50, 56, 59, 66, 71, 73, 74, 75, 78, 81, 83, 86, 88, 90, 92, 93, 101, 105, 111, 121, 123, 126, 128, 130, 133, 138, 140, 152, 157, 159, 160, 161, 162, 163, 167, 171, 172, 173, 174, 176, 178, 181, 182, 185, 189, 190, 192, 193, 200, 203, 209, 218, 221, 222, 227, 230, 237, 240, 241, 242, 243, 244, 245, 246, 247, 251, 255, 259, 260, 261, 262, 264, 268, 270, 271, 274, 286, 287, 288, 290, 291, 292, 293, 295.
Penn, William, 9, 15, 19, 23, 31, 46, 56, 66, 71, 74, 78, 81, 83, 86, 90, 92, 93, 101, 105, 110, 111, 120, 123, 126, 133, 138, 154, 157, 161, 163, 166, 173, 176, 180, 182, 185, 190, 192, 193, 200, 203, 209, 213, 220, 227, 237, 245, 251, 255, 259, 260, 261, 264, 271, 273, 284, 286, 288, 289, 295, 297, 302, 304, 308, 315, 316, 323, 329, 338, 345, 348, 358, 369, 384, 390, 397, 401, 413, 414.
Penquoit, John, 84, 98, 179, 180, 183, 197, 233, 277, 397.
Philips, George, 159, 160, 161, 162, 163, 169, 257, 258, 259, 261, 266.
Philips, Thomas, 36.
Pickring, Charles, 34, 35, 36, 41, 48, 66, 101, 103, 200, 201.
Pickring, William, 84, 183.
Pidcock, John, 55, 57, 58, 68, 112, 133, 135, 136, 143, 144, 147, 148, 149, 152, 187, 191, 203, 225, 233, 234, 235, 236, 237, 243, 244, 246, 247, 279, 281, 299, 347, 351, 371, 372, 373, 377, 393, 399.
Plumley, James, 350, 360, 372, 399, 403, 413.
Plumley, John, 354, 360. ,
Plumley, William, 71, 72, 105, 179, 204.
Pointer, Henry, 41, 75, 76, 89, 91, 122, 138, 190, 191, 210, 221, 227, 233, 245, 253, 278, 279, 283, 394.
Pointr, see Pointer.
Pomferet, Walter, 4, 5, 6, 11, 16, 21, 183, 324, 350, 353, 358, 359, 390, 400.
Powel, David, 33, 43, 324, 325, 327, 331, 338, 344.
Pownal, Ellenor, 29, 30, 49.
Pownal, Ruben, 149, 158, 169, 171, 236, 256, 266, 267, 279, 283, 285, 289, 291, 310, 316, 349, 371, 376, 377.
Pownd, John, 279, 280.
Poyntar, see Pointer.
Poynter, see Pointer.
Preistcorin, Thomas, 109, 207.
Presmall, Robert, 71.
Prothera, Evan, 168, 266.
Prudence the negro, 177.
Purley, see Purslone.
Pursley, see Purslone.
Purslone, John, 19, 25, 58, 75, 82, 112, 115, 118, 147, 163, 165, 181, 210, 213, 215, 218, 233, 278, 280.
Pursly, see Purslone.
Pursone, see Purslone.

Queen Mary, 110.

Radclif, Mary, 140, 230.
Rakestraw, William, 286, 290, 293, 297, 308.
Rambo, Peter, 177, 270.
Randel, Nicholas, 188.
Randle, Nicholas, 117, 212, 217.
Randol, George, 355, 356, 362.
Randol, Nicholas, 350, 394.
Randolph, see Randulph.
Randulph, Nicholas, 88, 183, 188, 278.
Rawle, Francis, 396.
Read, Anne, 323.

Read, Charles, 323.
Reale, William, 102, 201.
Redman, John, 86, 186.
Revel, 129, 136, 241.
Revel, Thomas, 97, 105, 108, 110, 111, 118, 119, 122, 132, 133, 136, 151, 153, 154, 157, 200, 204, 207, 208, 209, 213, 219, 220, 243, 245, 253, 351.
Revell, see Revel.
Revell case, 175.
Richards, 172.
Richards, John, 180.
Richards, Philip, 130, 131, 139, 140, 142, 149, 162, 176, 224, 229, 242, 260.
Richards, Philip's case, 236.
Richardson, John, 132, 276, 394.
Richardson, Joyce, 394.
Richardson, Samuel, 415.
Ridgway, Elizabeth, 38, 75.
Ridgway, Richard, 20, 42, 50, 57, 59, 67, 68, 75, 76, 79, 80, 82, 88, 90, 93, 96, 102, 105, 107, 147, 164, 188, 191, 193, 196, 201, 204, 205, 210, 234, 263, 399.
Robeson, Andrew, 66.
Robinson, Paterick, 139, 142, 224, 227, 228, 229.
Rogers, Thomas, 94, 99, 194, 198, 255, 283, 306, 334.
Rogrs, see Rogers.
Roles, Mary, 178, 179, 275, 277, 280.
Roles, William, 144, 226.
Rose, 147.
Rose, Pilocarpus, 135, 143, 149, 225, 233, 234, 236, 247.
Rose, Samuel, 114.
Rosell, see Rossill.
Rossill, Francis, 47, 79, 80, 86, 93, 98, 103, 112, 119, 141, 143, 151, 152, 153, 154, 174, 182, 186, 191, 193, 197, 210, 219, 224, 231, 250, 252, 276, 278, 280, 283, 293, 338.
Rouse case, 184.
Rouse case agt Biles, 84.
Rouse, Simon, 67, 69, 70, 85, 184.
Rowland, John, 25, 33, 59, 75, 76, 100, 106, 130, 141, 158, 163, 168, 199, 204, 205, 230, 242, 245, 257, 262, 265, 268, 272, 283, 291, 304, 313, 318, 319, 324, 327, 331, 339, 348, 352, 363, 370, 391.
Rowland, Priscilla, 324.
Rowland, Thomas, 20, 33, 76, 77, 94, 98, 103, 121, 124, 194, 197, 202, 221, 223.
Rumford, John, 415.
Rush, Francis, 409.
Rush, John, 91, 92, 192.

Salter, Hannah, 33, 73.
Sands, Stephen, 67, 68, 98, 197, 306, 374, 376, 391.
Sanford, William, 14, 15, 32.
Saterthwait, Joseph, 376.
Scafe, see Scaife.
Scaife, Jonathan, 25, 32, 42, 75, 163, 182, 230, 238, 253, 269, 276, 280, 283, 285, 289, 291, 295, 298, 299, 301, 303, 308, 309, 310, 312, 316, 323, 324, 344, 345, 346, 348, 358, 370, 375, 391, 393, 415.
Sraife, Mary, 285, 289, 292.
Scarborough, John, 339, 340, 341, 364, 365, 373, 377, 379, 382, 388, 389, 391, 392, 393, 394, 400, 415.
Scarborough, John (of London), 394.
Scot, John, 391.
Scot, Roger, 91, 191.
Scot, Thomas, 141, 231.
Searle, Francis, 233, 234, 325, 328, 357, 396.
Searle, Francis's Wife, 147.
Searle, Joan, 148, 233.
Shackhars, see Stackhouse.
Shallow, Gabriel, 88, 188.
Shaw, John, 318, 326, 353, 358, 359, 379, 390, 392.
Shippen, Edwaid, 351.
Shippey, J., 122.
Shippey, James, 116.
Shippey, John, 111, 115, 144, 145, 146, 209, 215, 216, 220, 225, 232.
Siddall, Henry, 106, 107, 204, 205, 206.
Siddall, John, 291, 297, 312, 394, 396, 397, 398, 400.
Sidwell, Ralph, 8, 9, 10, 251.
Skeane, Mary, 83, 84, 183.
Smalwood, 184.
Smalwood, Joseph, 306, 346, 350, 362, 365, 379, 382, 388, 389, 391.

Smalwood, Randulph, 57, 58, 59, 70, 84.
Smith, Charles, 416.
Smith, Daniel, 346.
Smith, Edward, 7, 10, 315.
Smith, John, 68, 92, 131, 135, 136, 173, 193, 238, 243, 246, 289, 291, 306, 310, 311, 314, 318, 333, 339, 370, 397.
Smith, Samuel, 7, 377, 391.
Smith, William, 82, 280, 295, 318, 326, 328, 345, 349, 370, 372, 397.
Snowdon, Christopher, 156, 158, 255, 257, 347, 351, 357, 361, 363, 377, 382, 388, 389, 393.
Snowdon, John, 284, 285, 295, 306, 316, 366, 376, 377, 391, 394.
Spencer's Children, 73.
Spencer, James, 79.
Stacey, Mahlon, 86, 186, 329, 364, 367, 380, 383, 386, 388.
Stackhous, see Stackhouse.
Stackhouse, John, 290, 316, 353, 358, 360.
Stackhouse, Thomas, 25, 41, 59, 67, 68, 79, 91, 163, 165, 176, 186, 191, 214, 215, 217, 253, 255, 279, 280, 316, 340, 341, 342, 358, 397, 398.
Stackhouse, Thomas, Junior, 50, 79, 80, 86, 88, 161, 173, 186, 188, 238, 259, 277, 289, 295, 296, 325, 391, 397, 398.
Stackhouse, Thomas, Senior, 20, 47, 57, 75, 86, 88, 169, 181, 188, 206, 233, 238, 245, 266, 280, 397.
Stakehouse, see Stackhouse.
Stacy, Robert, 400.
Staniland, Mary, 86, 186.
Stanton, Edward, 50, 68.
Stanton, Edward, Junior, 67.
Stedon, John, 141, 143, 231.
Stetton, see Stotton.
Steward, Joseph, 134, 156, 157, 246, 254, 255.
Stewards, see Steward.
Stolon, John, 127.
Stone, George, 398.
Stork, John, 356.
Stotton, John, 224, 238, 393.
Surket, John, 328, 349, 358, 370, 396, 403, 413.

Sutton, James, 83, 132, 134, 206, 246, 303, 358, 396, 414.
Swafer, James, 93, 193.
Swift, Francis, 87, 187.
Swift, John, 19, 41, 76, 86, 87, 88, 92, 93, 103, 105, 106, 107, 108, 109, 116, 117, 118, 122, 125, 138, 140, 142, 145, 176, 182, 186, 187, 188, 193, 202, 204, 205, 206, 207, 208, 211, 212, 213, 217, 224, 226, 227, 229, 233, 245, 253, 276, 278, 279, 280, 282, 283, 284, 286, 287, 291, 293, 300, 302, 304, 313, 316, 320, 321, 323, 325, 345, 348, 350, 370, 372, 378, 383, 387, 391, 394, 395, 397, 401, 402, 414.
Swift, John's wife, 188.
Swift's Case, 188, 223.

Talman, John, 309.
Tatham, John, 125, 127, 131, 133, 134, 135, 136, 137, 150, 151, 155, 156, 157, 158, 159, 160, 237, 238, 242, 245, 246, 247, 248, 249, 250, 253, 254, 255, 257, 258, 350, 402, 408, 409, 410, 413, 414.
Tayler, see Taylor.
Taylor, 188.
Taylor, Christopher, 331.
Taylor, Israel, 41, 49, 56, 57, 67, 68, 69, 70, 71, 73, 83, 87, 88, 90, 91, 105, 108, 109, 110, 111, 115, 116, 118, 119, 122, 123, 124, 127, 128, 129, 130, 132, 133, 136, 141, 143, 144, 145, 146, 153, 163, 175, 178, 179, 182, 185, 187, 189, 191, 207, 208, 209, 211, 215, 216, 219, 220, 222, 223, 231, 232, 233, 240, 241, 243, 245, 247, 249, 251, 275, 280, 291, 314, 379.
Taylor, John, 184, 193.
Taylor, Joseph, 339, 379.
Taylor, William, 214, 215, 217, 245, 272, 277, 278, 299, 335.
Taylor's Case, 175.
Taylor's wife, 127, 128.
Tellner, Jacob, 25, 90, 190.
Terry, Jasper, 377.
Terry, Thomas, 98, 197, 286, 377.
Terrey, see Terry.
Test, John, 126, 160, 167, 175, 236, 238, 264.
Thakorf, see Stackhouse.

Thatcher, 175, 241, 276.
Thatcher, Amos, 172, 270.
Thatcher, Bartholomew, 128, 172, 239, 240, 270, 279, 356, 369, 383, 387, 389.
Thatcher, Joseph, 172, 270, 307, 356.
Thatcher, Richard, 49, 67, 68, 74, 75, 76, 82, 83, 85, 102, 107, 122, 127, 128, 129, 130, 134, 172, 173, 175, 177, 179, 180, 185, 201, 207, 208, 211, 218, 219, 239, 240, 249, 251, 270, 271, 273, 274, 275, 276, 282, 297, 306, 307, 329, 331, 335, 336, 337, 340, 344, 346, 349, 355, 361, 373, 384, 388, 389, 390, 394, 400.
Thatcher, Richard, Junior, 100, 101, 105, 108, 110, 115, 118, 119, 120, 123, 198, 199, 207, 213, 215, 216, 218, 219, 220.
Thatcher, Richard, Senior, 109, 207.
Thatcher's declaration, 84.
Thather, see Thatcher.
Thathar, see Thatcher.
Thacher, see Thatcher.
Thomas, 177.
Thomas, Charles, 21, 114, 115, 119, 120, 212, 215, 220, 221.
Thomas, William, 134, 222.
Thompkins, Anthony, 66, 82.
Thorn, Joseph, 309.
Thorn, Samuel, 309.
Tomkins, see Thompkins.
Tomlinson, John, 404.
Town, John, 88, 98, 188, 197, 209, 238, 296, 311, 322, 327, 331, 334, 372.
Towne, see Town.
Trevithan, see Trevithan.
Trevithan, Joseph, 138, 145, 146, 147, 149, 227, 231, 232, 233, 235, 236.
Trivithan, see Trevithan.
Turner, Robert, 112, 210.
Taunclifte, see Tunneclift.
Tunneclift, Francis, 289, 291, 307, 334, 365, 400.
Tunneclift, Thomas, 47, 57, 58, 76, 77, 80, 84, 116, 123, 126, 127, 134, 205, 211, 216, 222, 230, 237, 238, 246, 280, 281, 390, 393.

Twineing, Stephen, 288, 339, 358, 370, 397, 399.

Vandegreift, Frederick, 330, 373.
Vandegreift, Johannes, 330.
Vandegreift, Leonard, 330, 373.
Vandegreift, Nicholas, 327, 328, 357.
van Sand, Cornelius, 398.
van Sand, Garret, 398.
Venables, 346.
Venables, Elizabeth, 203.
Venables Estate, 61.
Venables, William, 61, 63, 64.
Verrier, James, 371, 372, 374, 378.
Virkirk, Barndt, 330, 340, 341, 373.
Vose, Samuel, 212, 214.

Waddy, Henry, 68.
Walen, see Waln.
Walker, Francis, 10, 20.
Walley, Shadrach, 47, 49, 75, 93, 124, 193, 230, 223, 238, 255, 278, 316, 397.
Wally, see Walley.
Walmsley, Henry, 73, 327.
Walmsley, Thomas, 73, 396.
Waln, Nicholas, 31, 41, 47, 48, 49, 62, 66, 73, 74, 75, 78, 81, 82, 83, 86, 90, 93, 101, 103, 105, 110, 111, 121, 123, 126, 129, 130, 133, 138, 139, 152, 162, 163, 167, 170, 171, 174, 176, 178, 182, 185, 190, 193, 200, 202, 203, 209, 221, 222, 227, 228, 237, 241, 242, 245, 251, 260, 264, 267, 268, 269, 271, 272, 282, 290, 293, 346, 372.
Walne, see Waln.
Walter, Richard, 333.
Walters, Jonathan, 230.
Walton, Nathaniel, 340, 341.
Ward, Ralph, 296.
Warwin, 345.
Warwin, Henry, 344, 346, 347, 355, 358, 361.
Watson, John, 415.
Watson, Joseph, 244.
Webb, Elizabeth, 318.
Webb, Robert, 318.
Webstar, see Webster.
Webster, John, 149, 236, 279, 304, 305.

INDEX OF PERSONS

Webster, Peter, 325, 357, 362, 363, 379, 394, 397.
Weire, John, 325.
Wells, Edmund, 384, 385.
West, Nathaniel, 11, 16.
Wharley, Abraham, 56, 66, 71, 73, 74, 75, 78, 79, 81, 83, 84, 86, 88, 90, 93, 185, 189, 190, 193, 256.
Whearley, see Wharley.
Wheeler, Gilbert, 4, 11, 16, 18, 19, 21, 22, 23, 24, 25, 27, 28, 33, 37, 39, 40, 45, 46, 55, 56, 57, 58, 60, 68, 69, 70, 76, 77, 78, 84, 89, 95, 96, 100, 112, 116, 126, 129, 130, 131, 135, 141, 144, 148, 150, 154, 155, 156, 157, 158, 165, 167, 168, 169, 170, 189, 195, 196, 199, 209, 210, 216, 225, 230, 234, 235, 237, 241, 243, 247, 249, 252, 253, 254, 255, 257, 264, 265, 267, 277, 278, 279, 280, 281, 282, 283, 284, 285, 290, 291, 293, 297, 298, 299, 303, 307, 308, 321, 322, 327, 329, 334, 335, 338, 365, 379.
Wheeler, Martha, 18, 19, 21, 38, 77.
Wherley, see Wharley.
White, 271, 341, 363.
White, Benjamin, 371, 372.
White, Elizabeth, 295, 301, 302, 305, 307, 318, 333, 349, 353, 371, 372.
White, Francis, 180, 275, 276, 277, 316, 322, 327, 333, 347, 353, 356, 357, 359, 370, 372, 384, 385, 391, 403, 413.
White, John, 32, 75, 79, 80, 106, 147, 160, 168, 204, 230, 233, 250, 255, 258, 265, 279, 280, 310, 316, 349, 370, 371, 372.
White, John Pinck, 278.
White, Joseph, 279, 370, 372.
White, Peter, 278, 290, 295, 296, 299, 301, 302, 305, 306, 307, 318, 319, 323, 331, 333, 349, 353, 370, 371, 372, 379, 384.
White, William, 370, 372.
Whitpaine, John, 166, 167, 175, 264, 265.
Whitpaine, Zachariah, 131, 150, 243.
Whoops, see Hoops.
Whoops, Joshua, 283.
Wildman, Martin, 340.

Willard, George, 290, 318, 326, 379.
William, King, 110.
William & Mary, 152, 161, 166, 209, 251, 259, 261, 264, 273.
Williams, Duncan, 162, 261, 296, 326.
Williams, Dunk, 315, 328.
Williams, Hannah, 162.
Williams, Hugh, 87, 186.
Williams, Nicholas, 362, 363, 375, 376.
Williams, Thomas, 82, 91, 191, 278, 288.
Williams, William, 162, 261.
Willits, Hannah, 305.
Willits, Richard, 305.
Willsford, see Wilsford.
Willson, see Wilson.
Wilsford, John, 293.
Wilsford, Joseph, 102, 201.
Wilsford, Rebecca, 331
Wilson, Elizabeth, 57.
Wilson, Richard, 90, 93, 108, 149, 158, 169, 190, 193, 206, 236, 256, 266, 281, 295, 306, 344, 377, 403, 413.
Wilson, Stephen, 280, 316, 334, 399.
Wilton, Samuel, 79.
Wms., see Williams.
Wood, James 326,
Wood, John, 40, 47, 59, 87, 93, 121, 134, 140, 144, 145, 147, 148, 193, 205, 214, 215, 217, 226, 229, 234, 239, 246, 268.
Woods, Joseph, 57, 86, 87, 95, 148, 186, 187, 195, 234, 277, 278, 279, 280, 281, 282, 283, 284, 286, 287, 291, 295, 306, 335, 339, 340, 341, 348, 350.
Wood, Mary, 87, 187.
Wood, Sarah, 87, 187.
Wood, Thomas, 79, 80, 191.
Woolf, Thomas, 20, 41, 47, 76, 77.
Woolly, see Walley.
Worral, Peter, 98, 101, 106, 108, 169, 194, 197, 200, 204, 206, 230, 266, 272, 289, 291, 292, 293, 299, 300, 302, 309, 310, 316, 349, 358, 365, 390, 393, 394, 396, 397, 398, 400.
Worrall, see Worral.
Worrilow, Elizabeth, 285.

Worrilow, John, 123, 222, 284, 285.
Worrilow, Walter, 123, 222, 284.
Wright, John, 30, 31, 39, 76.
Wright, Thomas, 16, 17.

Yardley, Enoch, 171, 267, 283, 285, 291, 293, 300, 302, 310, 313, 339, 358, 371, 375, 377, 389, 403, 413.
Yardley, Thomas, 310, 357.
Yardley, William, 9, 15, 19, 23, 31, 36, 40, 42, 46, 48, 49, 56, 57, 62, 64, 65, 66, 71, 74, 75, 78, 80, 81, 83, 86, 90, 92, 93, 100, 111, 121, 123, 124, 125, 126, 129, 130, 131, 132, 133, 134, 138, 140, 142, 143, 149, 150, 157, 159, 161, 162, 173, 185, 190, 192, 193, 199, 209, 221, 222, 223, 224, 225, 226, 227, 230, 236, 237, 241, 243, 244, 245, 247, 249, 251, 255, 259, 260.
Yates, James, 178, 272, 274, 307, 328, 340, 341, 357, 396.

GENERAL INDEX

Only one reference in kind is given for a page.

Action, *ejectione fermae* 43, 167, 264, 367, 369, 681; for cutting and carrying away grass 79; for damages 290; of covenant 16, 57, 396; of *detinue* 290; **of replevin for oxen** 52; of trover and conversion 8; continued 155, 159, 164, 192, 253, 256, 279, 297, 327, 338, 346, 360, 361, 363, 377, 382, 383, 385, 387, 388, 389, 390, 393, 400; deferred 21, 101, 257, 340, 351; referred to another court 157, 256,

Actions, entered 3, 4, 5, 6, 7, 8, 10, 11, 12, 13, 14, 16, 17, 18, 22, 23, 26, 27, 28, 29, 34, 35, 37, 39, 43, 45, 51, 52, 53, 67, 68, 70, 74, 82, 83, 84, 86, 90, 96, 97, 105, 108, 110, 111, 112, 115, 119, 125, 126, 129, 131, 132, 133, 136, 138, 139, 140, 142, 143, 144, 145, 147, 150, 152, 155, 156, 159, 160, 161, 165, 166, 167, 172, 173, 224, 225, 226, 243, 244, 249, 250, 251, 254, 259, 264, 271, 316, 318, 319, 322, 324, 325, 329, 338, 341, 344, 347, 348, 358, 363, 364, 365, 366, 367, 368, 369, 378, 383, 384, 389, 390 396; for assault and trespass 70, 105, 108, 143, 160, 243, 258, 259, 324, 325, 342, 343, 347, 351, 352, 353, 358, 361; for debt 3, 4, 5, 6, 7, 11, 13, 22, 26, 27, 28, 29, 30, 34, 39, 51, 53, 55, 56, 57, 67, 79, 90, 96, 97, 129, 138, 139, 140, 142, 145, 153, 197, 224, 227, 228, 229, 232, 234, 237, 241, 242, 243, 249, 252, 270, 279, 317, 348, 350, 378, 387, 390, 392, 395; suspended 134, 160, 245, 255, 262, 306; withdrawn 24, 28, 29, 31, 34, 40, 46, 82, 83, 84, 105, 112, 150, 151, 156, 157, 158, 167, 173, 178, 203, 204, 209, 222, 233, 238, 243, 249, 250, 258, 259, 263, 264, 274, 286, 322, 334, 358, 366, 367, 368, 382, 389.

Abuse, 182; of bench 80; of the jury 110, 208; to a Justice 83.
Abusing, 57; his father 211.
Account, of lands and males to be returned 222, 223; of lands surveyed and seated to be brought in 124, 223.
Accounting ordered 61, 64.
Accounts, deferred 300; exhibited 10, 62, 175, 176, 235, 405, 406, 407, 408, 409, 410, 411, 412, 413; to be brought in 59, 65, 287, 298; to be examined 59, 83; for wolf heads 313.
Adjournment of court during elections 41, 73.
Age of a boy adjudged by the Court 325, 399.
Agreement for service 280.
Appeals, to Provincial Circular Court granted 100, 169, 199, 246, 266, 280, 344, 413; refused 174, 272.
Appraisement 152, 163, 261, 348.
Appraisers appointed 85, 158, 184, 257, 323.
Arbitration 48, 49, 82, 104, 335, 352.
Arrest, granted 4, 5, 6, 145, 150, 173, 226, 227, 251, 271, 316, 319, 322, 329, 342, 345, 347, 365, 366, 367, 368, 369, 384, 390; made 184.
A Roman T to be worn 401, 402.
Assault, 58, 134, 356; and abuse 137; and abusing Justices 248; and attempt to rob 199; and bat-

433

tery 37, 297, 306, 330; threatened 75.
Assessors appointed 124, 312, 344.
Assistance ordered 288, 293, 337.
Attachment granted 4, 5, 6, 22, 31, 133, 142, 144, 224, 226, 243, 244, 323, 324, 364, 365, 366, 368, 378, 383, 384, 389, 390.
Attestation 260.
Advisers appointed 301.
Bail ordered 270.
Banishment from the Province 220.
Beating and abusing, his grandchild 362; his wife 346, 362; and wounding 371.
Bill of sale delivered in court 33.
Bonds, accepted 73; forfeited 81; given 20, 40, 48, 60, 80, 92, 116, 138, 154, 203, 248, 274, 275, 378; required 216, 228, 275, 277.
Bound to good behavior 20.
Breaking the peace 306, 326.
Bridge, necessity for a 306, 362, 416; to be repaired 110, 256; between Bucks and Philadelphia Counties in need of repairs 314; and road want repairs 321.
Carrying away a log 298.
Case referred to the bench 246, 427.
Certificate of being alive signed 287, 306.
Coming into court drunk 111, 210.
Commitment, 33, 100, 101, 102, 103, 110, 111, 135, 138, 162, 179, 187, 198, 201, 202, 208, 210, 227, 261, 276, 306, 330, 346, 374, 376; for murder 165; on suspicion of felony 274.
Complaint, 3, 5, 6, 7, 8, 12, 13, 14, 17, 18, 22, 23, 27, 35, 36, 37, 39, 44, 45, 49, 51, 124, 134, 162, 164, 184, 196, 210, 223, 261, 262, 278, 291, 292, 293, 312, 319, 320, 337, 340, 356, 361, 373, 391, 394, 395, 402; about wolves' heads 112; further 274.
Constables, appointed 25, 34, 59, 91, 101, 106, 112, 147, 159, 169, 191, 200, 204, 210, 233, 266, 278, 303, 327, 357, 362, 396; attested 10, 397; excused on account of age 361; presentments 42; continued 159, 257.
Contempt of court 208.
Conveyance 57, 334.
Coroner, to be appointed 124, 223; his commission read 309; fees ordered paid 392; return of deaths 91, 127, 164, 165, 166, 191, 222, 238, 263, 312, 391.
County Clerk, to retain money in his custody 160, 161; discharged therefrom 259.
County records to be brought in 287.
County Treasurer's reports to be examined 59.
Cow sold at an outcry 339.
Cruelty to a horse 377.
Cursing 76, 81, 204, 340.
Debt, acknowledged 380, 385, 386, 398; denied 403.
Debtor to the County 313.
Declarations read 3, 7, 331, 334, 342, 350, 352, 381.
Deeds acknowledged and delivered in court 25, 33, 41, 47, 49, 50, 57, 59, 60, 63, 66, 68, 71, 73, 74, 75, 76, 81, 82, 83, 84, 85, 86, 88, 89, 90, 91, 92, 93, 94, 97, 99, 102, 103, 105, 106, 108, 110, 112, 116, 119, 123, 128, 140, 141, 148, 157, 163, 164, 168, 170, 174, 177, 178, 179, 183, 184, 186, 188, 190, 191, 193, 194, 197, 198, 201, 204, 206, 208, 210, 216, 219, 230, 231, 235, 240, 255, 262, 265, 267, 273, 279, 280, 281, 287, 288, 290, 291, 292, 299, 301, 302, 304, 305, 309, 310, 311, 312, 318, 323, 324, 325, 326, 329, 330, 331, 333, 336, 337, 339, 340, 345, 346, 349, 350, 352, 355, 356, 370, 371, 372, 373, 374, 375, 378, 379, 387, 393, 394, 398, 399, 415.
Deed of mortgage, delivered and acknowledged 9, 135, 168, 204, 266, 314, 333; refused 246; satisfied 386.
Deed of sale and mortgage 66, 202, 292.
Deed, in trust 222; of partition 295, 296; sheriff's 296.

GENERAL INDEX 435

Defamation, 57, 148, 187, 233; and scandalizing 58.
Discharge produced 247.
Discharged by the Court 11, 24, 32, 33, 67, 68, 91, 100, 102, 103, 108, 123, 129, 144, 158, 177, 179, 180, 182, 191, 192, 198, 201, 202, 206, 222, 235, 236, 241, 257, 273, 277, 278, 283, 336, 341, 355, 357, 370, 386, 393, 395.
Disclaim of attachment 286.
Ear mark, necessity for an 356.
Estreats 90, 91, 112, 116, 190, 192, 204, 208, 211, 220, 295.
Examination, 183, 231, 359; about a horse 145.
Execution, craved 374; granted 37, 81, 125, 129, 145, 152, 184, 187, 231, 236, 237, 242, 260, 287, 338, 339, 341, 356, 363, 384; ordered 122, 136, 153, 220, 374; returned 149, 297.
Extortion in ferriage 141, 230.
Evidence 86, 87, 88, 98, 107, 109, 113, 114, 115, 116, 117, 118, 119, 122, 127, 128, 146, 147, 169, 180, 188, 213, 233, 234, 239, 240, 246, 253, 276, 353, 354, 355, 372.
Fornication and bastardy 21, 178, 180, 183, 275, 277, 285, 289, 290.
Fine remitted 58.
Fined by the Court, 58, 59, 67, 68, 101, 112, 199, 204, 211, 285, 292, 295, 297, 319, 327, 330, 346, 359, 374, 377, 391; for absence 68; for abuse 80; for being a common swearer 78; for threatened assault 77; for contempt 77; for oaths and curses 76; for rude behavior 21; for scolding 77; for selling rum to the Indians 33; for slander and abuse 72.
Grand Jury, attested 57, 75, 93, 126 141, 157, 193, 206, 209, 230, 238, 255, 278, 280, 283, 295, 306, 313, 316, 325, 339, 349, 358, 370, 397, 401, 414; complaint 355.
Grand Jury presentments, 19, 20, 76, 84, 94, 95, 96, 109, 113, 114, 115, 158, 181, 185, 187, 194, 196, 207, 208, 211, 214, 216, 230, 232, 238, 240, 242, 256, 280, 285, 287, 298, 299, 306, 314, 321, 326, 327, 328, 340, 341, 356, 362, 371, 375, 376, 401, 414, 416; for murder 181; attested 276; no presentments 278; return Ignoramus 109.
Guardian appointed 16.
Highway in an intolerable condition 362.
Housebreaking 113, 211.
Illegal proceedings of a jury 359.
Indentures drawn and sealed 62.
Judgment, acknowledged 282; approved 240; confirmed 329, 382.
Judgment given, by the Court 10, 47, 58, 69, 70, 72, 77, 78, 80, 82, 85, 86, 87, 88, 96, 99, 102, 109, 110, 115, 119, 120, 122, 128, 136, 139, 140, 141, 146, 148, 149, 153, 154, 155, 157, 160, 174, 185, 186, 187, 188, 198, 201 207, 208, 219, 220, 227, 228, 229, 231, 232, 235 240, 241, 247, 248, 251, 252, 256, 258, 272, 286, 290, 292, 293, 300, 306, 307, 320, 325, 333, 335, 341, 350, 360, 361, 374, 376, 377, 380, 381, 382, 385, 386, 387, 392, 395, 399, 401; by default 41, 130, 148, 196, 234.
Judgment requested 379.
Jurors fined for non-attendance 391.
Jury submits to the Court 359.
Justices commissions read 75, 93, 101, 181, 193, 200, 345.
Justices to meet 292, 294, 299.
Keeping ordinary without a license 415.
Killing a colt 106.
Land to be laid out for a County Prison 11.
Laws of the last Assembly read 93, 193, 385.
Letters of attorney, acknowledged 84, 85, 184, 185, 373; allowed 344; certified 379; proven 394; signed and sealed 9.
Letters read 168, 404.
Levying of fines and forfeitures 90, 190.
License to keep an ordinary 326, 329.
List of fines and forfeitures sent to the Governor's Secretary 85.

436　　　　　　　　　GENERAL INDEX

Maintenance, of way 306; of wife 340.
Men named to view fences 42.
Message from the Assembly 123, 222.
Money taken from a negro secured 107.
Necessity for a court house near the middle of the County 415; for a ferry 321; for an Ear Mark 356; for a house of entertainment 362.
New table to be made 278.
No court held 92, 111, 203, 222, 236, 249, 284.
Non-suit 76, 91, 103, 151, 155, 191, 201, 253, 256, 286, 289, 390, 392, 400.
Notice not to pay quit rents 112, 210.
Official, deficiency 401; neglect 362.
Orders by the Court, 10, 20, 25, 62, 97, 104, 112, 160, 163, 164, 202, 205, 206, 208, 210, 223, 228, 266, 278, 287, 288, 292, 293, 298, 299, 300 301, 308, 311, 312, 319, 328, 345, 352, 363, 370, 374; payment for orphans 15.
Orphans placed 62, 64, 65.
Overseers of the Highways, appointed 25, 91, 109, 149, 158, 169, 191, 207, 236, 256, 266, 278, 303, 304, 327, 356, 396; continued 81; to summon the inhabitants 370.
Patents 56, 97, 197.
Payment time extended 11.
Payment ordered for attendance in Council and Assembly 314, 315.
Payment ordered for disbursements in building the court house 314.
Payment, ordered by a Justice of the Peace 366; for services of a negro 379.
Payment promised 320.
Peacemakers appointed 25, 59.
Petition for a town to be laid out 321.
Petition, read 345; concerning a boy 60; rejected 334; for relief 299, 308; for restoration of goods 312; for a road deferred 315.
Petit Jury, attested 57, 58, 67, 68, 76, 77, 79, 80, 86, 88, 197, 214, 215, 218, 219, 233, 235, 245, 253, 265, 279, 289, 291, 299, 340, 341, 342, 371, 375, 377, 400, 403, 413; not agreed 108; returned 108, 216.
Petit Jury returned by the Sheriff 31, 98, 168, 186, 187, 188, 205, 207, 232, 234, 239, 245, 246, 247, 253, 265, 272, 289, 291, 299, 307, 340, 341, 342, 353, 371, 375, 377, 400, 403.
Presentment from Philadelphia County 24.
Private session of court 42, 281.
Proclamations from the Governor read, against vice 153, 252; about the Scoth 385; for apprehending pirates, privateers and sea rovers 345.
Promise of repairs 370.
Rails ordered for the Court House 277.
Receipt produced 404.
Recognizances, 104, 105, 123, 148, 170, 177, 188, 235, 251, 267, 297, 307, 308, 313, 336, 337, 344, 350, 358, 359, 362, 363, 377, 413; continued 152; forfeited 91, 192, 220, 280, 306.
Recommendation to keep an ordinary 388.
Reconveyance 334.
Refusal to pay fees 218.
Register to be appointed 223.
Release, delivered 73, 82; from fine 289.
Release from imprisonment ordered 70.
Repairs to Court House ordered 337.
Replevin granted 344, 347.
Requests, for an attorney 231; an audit of accounts 351; for examination of a witness to a will 205; for deferment of trial 200; for pay for Council and Assemblymen 121; for a Register of Wills 108, 206; for payment for services 221; for respite of

GENERAL INDEX 437

action 238. trial 127, 131; for sale of land 294, 296; for suspension of judgment 122, trial 164; for termination of bond 288.
Restoration of goods ordered 312.
Roads, necessity for 96, 109, 196, 256, 298, 328, 356, 362, 376, 401, 414, 416; to be laid out 10, 41, 49, 100, 170, 198, 267, 281, 293, 299, 328, 363, 394; returns on 285, 379, 397, 398; fenced up 24, 32; laid out 302, 303; not laid out well 41; neglect of 298; petitions for 124, 223, 315, 379; payment for laying out 382; view of ordered 49; to be repaired 78, 110, 185, 208, 256.
Robbing of a colt 113.
Runaways 401; searched 159, 257.
Satisfaction acknowledged 61, 128, 149, 199, 220, 236, 240, 308, 308,
Search ordered by the Court 165.
Security, entered 333; ordered for orphan's estate 42.
Selling, beer by unlawful measure 362; without a license 211; his wife 336; liquors illegally 116, 211, 216; rum to the Indians 32, 33, 37, 60, 77, without a license 321; a servant 273.
Servitude, 161, 169; ordered 11, 16, 235, 258; extended by the Court 401, 402; petition concerning 266.
Setting fire to the tail of a horse 377.
Sheriff fined 360.
Sheriff's returns 3, 4, 6, 7, 9, 17, 21, 23, 26, 28, 29, 30, 35, 38, 40, 45, 46, 51, 53, 55, 92, 125, 126, 128, 130, 131, 132, 133, 142, 143, 144, 145, 150, 152, 162, 167, 172, 173, 184, 192, 196, 223, 224, 225, 226, 236, 237, 240, 241, 243, 244, 249, 250, 251, 254, 270, 271, 316, 319, 322, 323, 324, 329, 338, 339, 342, 345, 347, 348, 349, 365, 367, 369, 383, 384, 390.
Sheriff's sale ordered 16.
Slander 18, 150.
Sold at an outcry 339.
Speaking an untruth 319.

Special court granted 275.
Stealing, a mare 113, 116, 179; a mare and colt 275; a colt 283; clothing 195; half a hide of leather 113, 212, 215; a heifer 239; a hog 213, 218, 219; the Governor's mare 118, 122, 212, 216, 218; turkeys etc. 194.
Stopping passage by the river side 256.
Striking a blow 356.
Subpoenas 26, 30.
Summonses granted 8, 9, 12, 13, 15, 17, 19, 23, 26, 27, 28, 29, 30, 35, 36, 38, 39, 40, 45, 51, 53, 55, 63, 126, 131, 132, 143, 144, 145, 152, 155, 156, 160, 161, 167, 172, 173, 177, 225, 226, 236, 237, 243, 244, 249, 250, 254, 255, 258, 259, 271, 322, 338, 347, 348, 358, 364, 367, 369, 384, 387, 390.
Supposed murder 263.
Surveys and returns to be perfected 69.
Suspects examined 166.
Swearing, 20, 21, 24, 75, 116, 216, 327, 346; and cursing 340.
Taking, forcibly a colt 213, 218; goods from a chest 306, from a house by felonious entry 375; horses 361, 401, 416; a sow 341.
Tax, arrears to be collected 89, 97, 292, 321; book to be brought into Court 300; collectors accountable to the Court 269, accounts 88, 189, 300, 329, 355, ordered to pay money 69, 308, 312, appointed 121, 221, 301, 319; collection ordered 130, 190, 196; necessity for 113, 114, 214, 298, 327, 356; ordered to be raised 121, 159, 171, 211, 221, 257, 269, 281, 282.
Telling a lie in Court 207.
To be whipt 21, 59, 120, 160, 180, 198, 219, 220, 221, 258, 279, 401, 402.
To wear a Roman T 401, 402.
Townships, the County to be divided into 130, 137, 171; necessity to divide the county into 211, 240; division into ordered 242, 248; division made 268.
Unlawful, cattle 3; swine 256.

Verdict 307.
Warrant, granted 340, 366, 367, 368; for a negro 177.
Weights and Measures 131, 240, 242, 285.
Whipping, see to be whipt.
Will, to be kept by the Clerk of Court 128, 240; to be sent to the Governor 331; and inventory read 332.
Witnesses, 134, 186, 188, 194, 195, 197, 198, 205, 212, 213, 214, 215, 217, 218, 219, 227, 232, 239, 335, 344, 354; to a will 107.
Writ for a jury 8, 9, 17, 27, 28, 30.